THE AUTHOR
the U.S. Na
World War and then served for three years as a translator
and interpreter. After the war, he pursued his studies in Japanese literature at Columbia University, where he received a
Ph.D. in 1949. He then became a Lecturer in Japanese at
Cambridge University, and in 1953 returned to Japan to
study at Kyoto University. He is currently Professor of Japanese at Columbia.

Professor Keene's original scholarship and excellent translations have established him as a leading authority in the field
of Japanese studies. Among his many outstanding publications are *Japanese Literature: An Introduction for Western Readers*,
Anthology of Japanese Literature, *Living Japan*, *The Japanese
Discovery of Europe*, *Bunraku: The Art of the Japanese Pupp
Theatre* and *Nō: The Classical Theatre of Japan*. In 1974 h
received the Order of the Rising Sun, and in 1978 he wa
awarded the degree of Doctor of Letters at Cambridg
University.

Donald Keene

Appreciations of Japanese Culture

DONALD KEENE

KODANSHA INTERNATIONAL
Tokyo • New York • London

Originally published by Kodansha International Ltd. as
Landscapes and Portraits.

Distributed in the United States by Kodansha America, Inc.,
114 Fifth Avenue, New York, N.Y. 10011, and in the United
Kingdom and continental Europe by Kodansha Europe Ltd.,
Gillingham House, 38-44 Gillingham Street, London SW1V
1HU. Published by Kodansha International Ltd., 17-14
Otowa 1-chome, Bunkyo-ku, Tokyo 112, and Kodansha
America, Inc. Copyright in Japan 1971 by Kodansha Inter-
national Ltd. All rights reserved. Printed in Japan.

LCC 80-85387
ISBN 4-7700-0956-9

First edition, 1971
First paperback edition, 1981
91 92 93 10 9 8 7 6 5 4

This book is dedicated to
ALICE AND OTIS CARY
with thanks for Kyoto

CONTENTS

ILLUSTRATIONS

Following page 240

Acknowledgements

Philosophy East and West for 'Japanese Aesthetics' (July, 1969).

La Literature Japonesa Entre Oriente y Occidente for "Feminine Sensibility in the Heian Era" (1967) and "Individuality and Pattern in Japanese Culture" (1967).

Drama Survey for "Realism and Unreality in Japanese Drama" (1964).

Asia Major for "Bashō's Journey of 1684" (1959).

Transactions of the Asiatic Society of Japan for "Bashō's Journey to Sarashina" (1957).

The Center for Japanese Studies of the University of Michigan for "Modern Japanese Poetry", a 1963 lecture delivered at the same University; copyright © 1964 by the same Center. Reprinted by permission.

Chūōkōron for "Shiki and Takuboku" (1967), "Tanizaki Junichirō" (1967) and "Dazai Osamu" (1964); "Dazai Osamu" appeared later in English in *East-West Review* (1965).

Archives of Asian Art for "The Portrait of Ikkyū" (1966–67).

Columbia Forum for "Fujimoto Kizan and *The Great Mirror of Love*" (1969).

New Japan for "Hanako" (1962).

Journal of Asian Studies for "Japanese Writers and the Great East Asia War" (1964).

Harper & Row Publishers, Inc. for "Translation" from *Writers Roundtable*, ed. Helen Hull and Michael Drury (1959).

Walker & Company for "Arthur Waley" from *Madly Singing in the Mountains*, ed. Ivan Morris (1970).

Otto Harrassowitz for "Matsunaga Teitoku" from the festschrift honoring Professor Horst Hammitzsch in which it first appeared.

The New York Times Company for "Confessions of a Specialist"; copyright © 1968 by the same company. Reprinted by permission.

"The Sino-Japanese War of 1894–95 and Japanese Culture": from Donald Keene, "The Sino-Japanese War and Its Cultural Effects in Japan," in *Tradition and Modernization in Japanese Culture*, ed. D. H. Shively. To be published by Princeton University Press, 1971. Reprinted by permission.

I. SOME JAPANESE LANDSCAPES

Japanese Aesthetics

ALMOST ANY general statement made about Japanese aesthetics can easily be disputed and even disproved by citing well-known contrary examples. *Shibui*, the one term of Japanese aesthetics that seems to have found its way into the English language, evokes the understatement and refinement typical of much Japanese artistic expression; but how should this ideal be reconciled with the flamboyance of a performance of Kabuki or with the garish, polychromed temples at Nikkō, long considered by the Japanese themselves as a summit of beauty? It goes without saying that Japanese taste did not stay frozen throughout the centuries, nor were aesthetic preferences unaffected by social class and education, and in making general remarks about Japanese aesthetics these cautions must be remembered. Nevertheless, for all the exceptions that might be adduced, I believe it is possible to say of certain aesthetic ideals that they are characteristically and distinctively Japanese.

A few generalizations probably can be made without fear of contradiction. First of all, one might mention the importance of aesthetic considerations even in seemingly irrelevant areas of Japanese life. Despite the modernization and the internationalization of standards today, the visitor to Japan never fails to notice the flowers, real or artificial, clustered in a little holder near the bus driver's head; or the flowers gracefully bending down from a wall-bracket over the toilet; or the artistically brushed signboard in the railway station which proves to mean "Left Luggage Room"; or, for that matter, the maddening artistry with which a parcel is likely to be wrapped in a department store when one is in a hurry. These sights surprise the visitor, who marvels that aestheticism should be so pervasive, but he might equally wonder, of course, why buses, toilets and left luggage rooms in his own country are not considered the appropriate places for floral or calligraphic embellishment. Or, to take the most famous instance of all, the exquisite appearance of Japanese food, despite its often pallid taste, has been praised by every foreign visitor;

indeed, a meal served in the private room of a fine restaurant, where every detail from the color of the cushions on the *tatami* and the flower in the alcove to the last little sauce dish has been artistically planned, tends to make the occasion an aesthetic, rather than a gustatory experience. One has only to know how a first-rate Chinese dinner would be served in Djakarta today or in Shanghai in bygone years to become aware of the special place of aestheticism in Japanese life, as contrasted with other countries of Asia.

These examples may seem facetious, but however trivial they should suggest how important is the role played in daily Japanese life today of aesthetic preferences that go back very far in Japanese history. Descriptions in the works of fiction of a thousand years ago, as well as the diaries and essays, plainly indicate how absorbed the Japanese were with considerations of beauty. The European knight wore his lady's glove in his helmet, but it would not have occurred to him to examine the glove first to make sure it met his aesthetic standards and confirmed his judgment that his lady was worth dying for; he was quite content to think that the glove had once graced her hand, and an overly fastidious examination of the material, color, pattern and so on would not have endeared him to the lady. The Japanese courtier of the eleventh century, on the other hand, was adamant in his insistence on aesthetic accomplishments in any woman he might offer his love. A note from her in somewhat less than flawless calligraphy, or a disillusioning glimpse of her sleeve that suggested the lady lacked a perfect sensitivity to color harmonies, might easily have dampened his ardor.

The elevation of aestheticism to something close to a religion was achieved at the Japanese court in the tenth century. It naturally involved an insistence on elegance of manners and an attention to protocol that may remind us of Versailles. But at the Japanese court, unlike Versailles, it was not only the *petit marquis*, the fop, who composed verses to his lady, but everyone, from the Emperor down. Letters normally took the form of poems, exquisitely penned on paper of an exactly appropriate texture and in ink of the correct degree of blackness; folded with dexterity, and attached to a spray of seasonal flowers, they were entrusted to a page attired in a manner worthy of his master's dignity.

Aestheticism spread from the court to the provinces, and from the upper classes to the commoners. The cult of cherry blossoms, which apparently originated at the court in Kyoto, today is universal: radio announcements inform the breathless public at which sites the blossoms are eight-tenths opened and at which only seven-tenths, and eager busloads of factory workers head for the suitable spots. Not all Japanese homes are aesthetically pleasing, of course, but whenever financially possible it is attempted to create at least in one corner something suggesting the simplicity and elegance of the traditional aesthetics.

Japanese aesthetics can be approached not only through the relatively scant writings of the old literature specifically devoted to the subject, but through the evidence in works of literature or criticism, in objects of art, and even in the manner of life of the Japanese as a whole, so pervasive has aestheticism been. A number of headings under which Japanese aesthetics might be discussed come to mind: suggestion, irregularity, simplicity, and perishability. These related concepts point to the most typical forms of Japanese aesthetic expression, though, as I have indicated, exaggeration, uniformity, profusion and durability are by no means absent.

SUGGESTION

The poet and critic Fujiwara no Kintō (966–1041), dividing poetry into nine categories of excellence, described the highest category thus: "The language is magical and conveys more meanings than the words themselves express." To illustrate this criterion he offered the following poem:

honobono to	Dimly, dimly
Akashi no ura no	The day breaks at Akashi Bay;
asagiri ni	And in the morning mist
shimagakureyuku	My heart follows a vanishing ship
fune wo shi zo omou	As it goes behind an island.

Part of the beauty of this poem lies in the use of language and even the sounds (for example, the *o* sounds of the first line echoed at the end), but its chief claim to distinction in the eyes of Fujiwara no Kintō was its power of suggesting unspoken implications. The poem would be less if more specific: if, for example, it made clear that the poet's sweetheart was aboard the disappearing ship or that the poet himself for some reason wished he were aboard. The ambiguity, a well-known feature of the Japanese language, which commonly omits the subjects of sentences, is exploited in this poem so as to expand the thirty-one syllables of the *tanka* to suggest an atmosphere and an emotional state nowhere specifically stated. A sense of mystery is intensified by the mist obscuring the dawn seascape as the ship disappears. What did this sight mean to the poet?

Clearly he did not remain impassive, a mere observer. But if the instant when the ship disappeared he felt a stab of parting, he does not choose to explain why.

The reliance of this poem on suggestion, if not a uniquely Japanese phenomenon, is certainly unlike the common European forms of literary expression. Ambiguity was not highly esteemed by, say, Renaissance writers on poetics, who associated it with the humor of the pun.[1] However rich in ambiguity the sonnets of Shakespeare may actually be, some statement of truth or experience is invariably made. But what is the statement in this Japanese poem? Surely it is not the simple recording of a casual event of an autumn morning; the sight unquestionably had meaning for the poet, and he assumes it will have meaning for the reader too, but he does not define its nature.

The element of suggestion in the poem is the source of its beauty, yet when compared to later Japanese poetry its level of suggestion may seem shallow. By the end of the twelfth century the ideal known as *yūgen* (or, mystery and depth) was developed by Fujiwara Shunzei (1114–1204). *Yūgen* as an aesthetic principle has been defined by Brower and Miner in *Japanese Court Poetry* as "The mid-classical ideal of tonal complexity conveyed by the overtones ... of poems typically in the mode of descriptive symbolism."[2] This ideal may recall Poe's "suggestive indefiniteness of vague and therefore of spiritual effect." The vagueness admired by Poe was easily achieved by Japanese poets, thanks to the Japanese language. The lack of distinctions between singular and plural or between definite and indefinite contributes to the ambiguity, at least to the Western reader who is accustomed to such distinctions. For a Japanese poet precision in language would limit the range of suggestion, as we can easily see from a famous *haiku* by Bashō (1644–94):

kareeda ni	On the withered bough
karasu no tomarikeri	A crow has alighted:
aki no kure	Nightfall in autumn.

This English translation represents a possible interpretation of the Japanese words, but the arbitrary nature of its choices of singular and plural is apparent from an eighteenth century painting illustrating this *haiku* that depicts no less than eight crows alighted on a number of withered branches. This equally possible interpretation of the poem presents a landscape less lonely than that of a single crow on a single withered branch, an interpretation of the poem found in other illustrative paintings, but may convey an even more brooding intensity. Again, the last line of the *haiku*,

aki no kure, can also be interpreted as meaning "the nightfall of autumn"—
that is, the end of autumn. If we were to insist on determining which
meaning the poet intended, whether the nightfall of a particular autumn
day or the end of the autumnal season, the answer might well be that *both*
were intended. If Bashō's phrase were interpreted as meaning nightfall,
regardless of whether it were early or late in autumn, it might suggest
that the crow (or crows) was alighting on a withered branch in a tree
otherwise filled with bright leaves, producing a disharmonious impression;
but if the scene intended had been an unspecified time of day towards the
end of autumn, it might mean that the crow was alighting in the full
glare of noon, an equally inappropriate possibility. Many meanings and
implications may be extracted from the seventeen syllables of this *haiku*,
thanks to the ambiguity of the language, but Bashō's ultimate meaning
may still elude us: what he intended the two elements of the *haiku* to
say about each other, and how far beyond the words themselves the suggestions reach.

The *haiku* on the alighting crow exemplifies a related aspect of Japanese
aesthetics, the preference for monochromes to bright colors. It is true that
magnificent examples of Japanese art—the celebrated *Tale of Genji*
scroll among them—are brilliantly colored, but I believe that most Japanese critics would agree that the prevailing preference in Japanese aesthetics
has been for the monochrome. The black crow alighting on a withered
branch at a time of day and season when all color has vanished suggests
the lonely beauty admired by countless Japanese poets, or the severity of
Japanese gardens consisting of stones and sand, or the unpainted interiors
and exteriors of a Japanese house. The use of color can be brilliant, but it
inevitably limits the suggestive range: when a flower is painted red, it
can be no other color, but the black outline of a flower on white paper
will let us imagine whatever color we choose.

These words may suggest the aesthetics of Zen Buddhism. Indeed,
much of what is considered most typical in Japanese aesthetics stems from
Zen. Or, it might be more accurate to say, it coincides with Zen. The
simplicity of a Shinto shrine building, the bare lines of its architecture and
grounds, was an expression of an indigenous preference which coincided
with Zen ideals, and made the Japanese receptive to the more sophisticated
aesthetics of the continental religion. The Japanese were equally receptive
to the aesthetics of the Chinese artists and poets of the Sung Dynasty
who also favored monochromes. But the principle of suggestion as an
aesthetic technique need not have been learned from abroad.

Suggestion as an artistic technique is given one of its most perfect

forms of expression in the Nō theatre. The undecorated stage, the absence
of props other than bare outlines, the disregard for all considerations of
time and space in the drama, the use of a language that is usually obscure
and of abstract gestures that are scarcely related to the words, all make it
evident that this theatre, unlike representational examples elsewhere (or
Kabuki in Japan), was meant to be the outward, beautiful form suggestive
of remoter truths or experiences, the nature of which will differ from
person to person. The large role played by suggestion, as contrasted with
the explicit descriptions of people and situations we more normally
encounter in the theatre, gives the Nō an absolute character. It baffles or
bores many Japanese, but it moves others in ways that more conventional,
dated varieties of drama cannot, and the same holds true of Western spectators. The groans, the harsh music that precedes the entrance of the actors,
may irritate a contemporary spectator, but they may also make him sense
in a way impossible with words alone the distance separating the world of
the dead from the world of the living, the terrible attachment to this
world that causes ghosts to return again to suffer the past, or the pain of
being born.

No can profoundly move even Western spectators totally unfamiliar
with Japanese culture, but it can equally repel others who are committed
to a representational variety of theatre. Performances staged in Europe
and America have been criticized as having insignificant plots and
inadequate characterization. After a performance in New York a member
of the Actors' Studio complained that the character Tsunemasa did
nothing to convince the audience he was indeed a great musician. Such
objections, which would be scornfully rejected by admirers of Nō,
cannot be attributed merely to the hostility of people ignorant of tradition. Suggestion as an aesthetic method is always open to the charge of
deception—of being no more than the Emperor's new clothes. The monk
Shōtetsu, writing in the fifteenth century, recognized that the mysterious
powers of suggestion designated by the term *yūgen* could not be appreciated by most men:

"*Yūgen* can be apprehended by the mind, but it cannot be expressed in
words. Its quality may be suggested by the sight of a thin cloud veiling
the moon or by autumn mist swathing the scarlet leaves on a mountainside. If one is asked where in these sights lies the *yūgen*, one cannot say,
and it is not surprising that a man who fails to understand this truth is
likely to prefer the sight of a perfectly clear, cloudless sky. It is quite
impossible to explain wherein lies the interest or the remarkable nature
of *yūgen*."[3]

Perhaps this is what Fujiwara no Teika (1162–1241) had in mind when he wrote this famous poem:

miwataseba	In this wide landscape
hana mo momiji mo	I see no cherry blossoms
nakarikeri	And no crimson leaves—
ura no tomaya no	Evening in autumn over
aki no yūgure	A straw-thatched hut by the bay.

Teika looks out on a landscape that lacks the conventionally admired sights of Japanese poetry, but he discovers that it is precisely the austerity of the monochrome landscape that stirs in him an awareness of a deeper beauty. If someone were to deny the existence of this beauty and say that all the poet saw was a wretched fisherman's hut and the rest was an illusion, Teika could not defend himself. Suggestion depends on a willingness to admit that meanings exist beyond what can be seen or described. In the theatre the Nō actors risk failure if the audience refuses to make this concession, but for the Japanese poet or connoisseur of art the pleasures of suggestion could become an end in themselves, to the exclusion of considerations of convincing representation. We can infer this from a famous passage found in *Essays in Idleness* by Kenkō (1283–1350):

> Are we to look at cherry blossoms only in full bloom, the moon only when it is cloudless? To long for the moon while looking on the rain, to lower the blinds and be unaware of the passing of the spring—these are even more deeply moving. Branches about to blossom or gardens strewn with faded flowers are worthier of our admiration.[4]

A more common Western conception is that of the climax, the terrible moment when Laocoön and his sons are caught in the serpent's embrace, or the ecstatic moment when the soprano hits high C; but for Kenkō the climax was less interesting than the beginnings and ends, for it left nothing to be imagined. The full moon or the cherry blossoms at their peak do not suggest the crescent or the buds, though the crescent and buds (or the waning moon and the strewn flowers) do suggest the full moon and full flowering. Perfection, like some inviolable sphere, repels the imagination, allowing it no room to penetrate. Bashō's only poem about Mount Fuji describes a day when fog prevented him from seeing the peak. Beginnings that suggest what is to come, or ends that suggest what has been, allow the imagination room to expand beyond the literal facts to the limits of the capacities of the reader of a poem, the spectator at a Nō play, or the connoisseur of a monochrome painting. Beginnings and ends are also of special interest with respect to the development of the form itself: primitive painting or the moderns are more apt to excite people today than the works of Raphael or of Andrea del Sarto, the perfect painter. Here, as so often, a curious coincidence brings traditional Japanese tastes into congruence with those of the contemporary West.

IRREGULARITY

The emphasis on beginnings and ends implied a rejection of regularity as well as of perfection. We know from the earliest literary and artistic remains that the Japanese have generally avoided symmetry and regularity, perhaps finding them constricting and obstructive to the powers of suggestion. Symmetry in Japanese literature and art, whether in the use of parallel prose or architectural constructions arranged along a central axis, almost invariably reflect Chinese or other continental influence. In the *Fudoki*, gazetteers compiled by imperial order early in the eighth century, we find such passages as: "In spring the cherry trees along the shore are a thousand shades of color; in autumn the leaves on the banks are tinted a hundred hues. The warbler's song is heard in the fields, and cranes are seen dancing on the strand. Village boys and fisher girls throng the shore; merchants and farmers pole their boats to and fro." The relentless insistence on parallel expression, so natural to the Chinese, was normally antithetical to the Japanese, despite occasional experimentations. This passage represented an ill-digested emulation of Chinese writing that contrasts with the almost invariable preference for irregularity, and even for prime numbers: for example, the thirty-one syllables of the *tanka*, the classic verse form, are arranged in lines of 5, 7, 5, 7 and 7 syllables. Nothing could be farther removed from the couplets and quatrains that make up normal poetic usage in so many countries. Even when the Japanese intended to take over bodily a Chinese artistic conception, such as the architectural plan of a monastery, they seem to have felt uncomfortable with the stark symmetry prescribed, and before long broke the monotony by moving some buildings to the other side of the central axis. Soper contrasted the regularity of Chinese temple architecture with its subsequent development in Japan: "What remained from the first generation was a sensible irregularity of plan. . . . At the Shingon Kongōbuji on Kōyasan, the central cleared area is a fairly spacious and level one that might have permitted at least a minimal Chinese scheme. Instead, as if by deliberate rejection, the main elements, though they face south, are on independent axes."[5]

Kenkō suggested why the Japanese were so fond of irregularity: "In everything, no matter what it may be, uniformity is undesirable. Leaving something incomplete makes it interesting, and gives one the feeling that there is room for growth." Or again, "People often say that a set of books looks ugly if all volumes are not in the same format, but I was impressed to hear the Abbot Kōyū say, 'It is typical of the unintelligent man to insist on assembling complete sets of everything. Imperfect sets are better.'"[6] Undoubtedly librarians in Kenkō's day were less enthusiastic than he about the desirability of incomplete sets, but as anyone knows who has ever confronted the grim volumes of a complete set of the Harvard Classics, they do not invite browsing.

A partiality for irregularity reveals itself also in the ceramics preferred by the Japanese. If you are a guest at a tea ceremony and are offered your choice of bowl—a lovely celadon piece, or a fine porcelain with delicate patterns, or a bumpy, misshapen pot rather suggesting an old shoe—it is easy to prove your appreciation of Japanese aesthetics by unhesitatingly selecting the old shoe. A perfectly formed round bowl is boring to the Japanese, for it lacks any trace of the individuality of the potter.

In calligraphy too, copybook perfection is ridiculed or condescendingly dismissed as something best left to the Chinese; Japanese preference tends to favor the lop-sided, exaggeratedly individual characters written by a *haiku* or tea ceremony master. In gardens too, the geometrically executed formations of the Alhambra or Versailles would seem to the Japanese less a place to repose the eyes and heart than a rigid mathematical demonstration. The Chinese garden, more natural than the European formal garden, inspired the romanticism of design so dear to the eighteenth-century English landscape architects. But the Japanese went far beyond the Chinese in the irregularity and even eccentricity of their gardens. Derek Clifford in *A History of Garden Design* expressed his disapproval of Japanese gardens, contrasting them with the more agreeable Chinese; according to Clifford, "the Chinese stopped short at the extreme lengths of development to which the Japanese went."[7] Clifford seems never to have actually seen a Japanese garden, but he found the famous stone and sand garden of the Ryōanji, the subject of an admiring essay by Sacheverell Sitwell, to be offensive and even dangerous: "It is the logical conclusion of the refinement of the senses, the precipitous world of the abstract painter, a world in which the stains on the cover of a book can absorb one more utterly than the ceiling of the Sistine chapel; it is the narrow knife edge of art, overthrowing and discarding all that man has ever been and achieved in favour of some mystic contemplative ecstasy, a sort of suspended explosion of the mind, the dissolution of identity. You really cannot go much further than this unless you sit on a cushion like Oscar Wilde and contemplate the symmetry of an orange."[8]

The symmetry of an orange was hardly calculated to absorb the attention of the architects of this exceedingly asymmetrical garden. The marvellous irregularity of the disposition of the stones eludes the analysis of the most sensitive observer. Far from being the artless "stains on the cover of a book," the Ryōanji garden is the product of a philosophical system— that of Zen Buddhism—as serious as that which inspired the ceiling of the Sistine Chapel. And, it might be argued, even a European might derive greater pleasure from daily contemplation of the fifteen stones of the Ryōanji garden than of the Sistine Chapel, without "overthrowing and discarding all that man has ever been and achieved." The Sistine Chapel is magnificent, but it asks our admiration rather than our participation; the stones of the Ryōanji, irregular in shape and position, by allowing us to participate in the creation of the garden may move us even more. But that may be, again, because our own age is closer in artistic expression to that of the Ryōanji than to that of Michelangelo.

SIMPLICITY

The use of the most economical means to obtain the desired effect, the product of Zen philosophy, is another characteristic of the garden of the Ryōanji. The same philosophy affected the creation of many other gardens—the waterless river that swirls through the landscape of the Tenryūji garden, foaming over artfully placed rocks, or the waterless cascade that tumbles through green moss at the Saihōji. But the preference for simplicity in gardens is not restricted to those of Zen temples. The use of a single natural rock for the bridge over a tiny pond or for a water basin suggests the love of the texture of the stone untampered with by human skill. Even the disdain for flowers as a distracting and disruptive element in a garden suggests an insistence on the bare bones of the abstract garden, which has no need for the superficial charm of an herbaceous border or a flower bed that is "a riot of color." Simplicity and the natural qualities of the materials employed may have been first emphasized by the Zen teachers, but they are now common ideals of the Japanese people. Soper has pointed out: "A feature of Zen buildings which their origin makes curious is their frequently complete lack of painted decoration, interiors and exteriors alike being left in natural wood. Such austerity

JAPANESE AESTHETICS   21

is certainly non-Chinese, and must mark a deliberate choice on the part of early Japanese Zen masters . . . in compliance with the spirit of simplicity inherent in Zen teachings."[9] Early Buddhist temples in Japan had been painted on the outside, generally a dull red (as we may see today at the Byōdōin), but from the thirteenth century onwards most temples, regardless of their sect, tended to be built of unpainted wood. The same held true of palaces and private houses.

Kenkō's expression of his own preference for simplicity in the decoration of a house came to be shared by most Japanese: "A house which multitudes of workmen have polished with every care, where strange and rare Chinese and Japanese furnishings are displayed, and even the grasses and trees of the garden have been trained unnaturally, is ugly to look at and most depressing."[10] It is easier for us to assent to this opinion than it would have been for Western writers fifty years ago. Few writers on Japanese aesthetics today would describe the Ginkakuji (Silver Pavilion) in Sansom's words as "an insignificant structure which belies its name . . . simple to the verge of insipidity."[11] The Ginkakuji does not strike me as an insignificant structure; I certainly prefer it to the elaborate mausolea of the Tokugawa at Nikkō, and I believe most other students of Japan would share my views. But traditionally in the West the house which "multitudes of workmen have polished with every care" has been considered the most desirable, as we know from old photographs showing the profusion of treasures with which the drawing rooms of the rich were commonly adorned. Gardens where even the trees and grasses have been trained unnaturally still attract visitors to the great houses of Europe.

Probably the most extreme expression of the Japanese love for unobtrusive elegance is the tea ceremony. The ideal sought by the great teamaster Sen no Rikyū (1521-91) was *sabi*, a word related to *sabi* "rust" or *sabireru* "to become desolate." This may seem to be a curious aesthetic ideal, but it arose as a reaction to the parvenu extravagance of Rikyū's master, the dictator Hideyoshi, who had built a solid gold portable teahouse he doted on so much he took it with him everywhere on his travels. Rikyū's *sabi* was not the enforced simplicity of the man who could not afford better, but a refusal of easily obtainable luxury, a preference for a rusty-looking kettle to one of gold or gleaming newness, a preference for a tiny undecorated hut to the splendors of a palace. This was not the same as Marie Antoinette playing at shepherdess; in fact, it represented a return to the normal Japanese fondness for simplicity and was in no sense an affectation. *Sabi* was accepted because it accorded with deep-seated aesthetic beliefs. The tea ceremony today is sometimes attacked as being a perversion of the ideals it once embodied, but the expense of a great deal of money to achieve a look of bare simplicity is entirely in keeping with Japanese tradition.

The tea ceremony developed as an art concealing art, an extravagance masked in the garb of noble poverty. The Portuguese missionary João Rodrigues (1561–1634) left behind an appreciative description of a tea ceremony he had attended, but he could not restrain his astonishment over the lengths to which the Japanese carried their passion for unobtrusive luxury: "Because they greatly value and enjoy this kind of gathering to drink tea, they spend large sums of money in building such a house, rough though it may be, and in purchasing the things needed for drinking the kind of tea which is offered in these meetings. Thus there are utensils, albeit of earthenware, which come to be worth ten, twenty or thirty thousand *cruzados* or even more—a thing which will appear as madness and barbarity to other nations that know of it."[12]

Madness perhaps, but surely not barbarity! Everything about the tea ceremony was controlled by the most highly developed aesthetic sensibilities. The avoidance of conspicuous wealth was reinforced by an avoidance of color in the hut, of perfume in the flowers displayed, and of taste in the food offered. The interior of the hut, though it embraces many textures of wood and matting, tends to be almost exclusively in shades of brown, with perhaps a pale dot of color in the alcove. There may be incense burnt, generally of an astringent nature, but the typical scents of Western flowers—rose, carnation or lilac—would be unthinkable. This preference for understatement may stem from the "climate" of Japan. A Japanese teacher once suggested to me that the colors preferred in Japanese art owed their muted hues to the natural colors of seashells. Whether this is strictly true or not, it is certainly easy to distinguish Japanese prints before and after the introduction of Western dyes. But after a brief period of fascination with the screaming purples, crimsons and emeralds of the new, exotic colors, the Japanese returned to the seashells. It is true that the Japanese landscape offers few bright floral colors, and the native flowers have virtually no smell. The aesthetic choices made in the tea hut may owe as much to nature as to deliberate policy.

Japanese food too, and not only that served in the tea ceremony, lacks the intensity of taste found elsewhere. Just as the faint perfume of the plum blossoms is preferred to the heavy odor of the lily, the barely perceptible differences in flavor between different varieties of raw fish are prized extravagantly. The Zen monastery vegetarian cuisine, though the subject of much self-adulation, offers a meagre range of tastes, and the fineness of a man's palate can be tested by his ability to distinguish virtually tasteless dishes of the same species. The virtuosity is impressive, but it would be hard to convince a Chinese or a European that a lump of cold bean curd dotted with a dash of soy sauce is indeed superior to the supposedly cloying flavors of *haute cuisine*. The early European visitors to Japan, though they praised almost everything else, had nothing good to say about Japanese food. Bernardo de Avila Girón wrote, "I will not praise Japanese food for it is not good, albeit it is pleasing to the eye, but instead I will describe the clean and peculiar way in which it is served."[13] The absence of meat, in conformance with the Buddhist proscription, undoubtedly limited the appeal of Japanese cuisine to the Portuguese and Spanish visitors, but the characteristic preference for simplicity and naturalness—the undisguised flavors of vegetables and fish—was essentially aesthetic.

The insistence on simplicity and naturalness placed a premium on the connoisseur's appreciation of quality. An unpainted wooden column shows the natural quality of the tree from which it was formed just as an uncooked piece of fish reveals its freshness more than one surrounded by sauce. In the Nō theatre too the lack of the usual distractions in a performance—sets, lighting and the rest—focuses all attention on the actor, and demands a connoisseur to appreciate the slight differences in gesture or voice that distinguish a great actor from a merely competent one. Within the limited ranges permitted in their traditional arts the Japanese prized shadings. Seldom did the painter, poet or Nō actor take the risks involved in bold statement, as opposed to controlled simplicity; for this reason there is almost nothing of bad taste in traditional Japan. Simplicity is safer than profusion as an aesthetic guide, but if the outsider fails to develop the virtuoso sensibilities of the Japanese he may find that he craves something beyond understatement—whether the brilliance of a chandelier, the depth of taste of a great wine, or the overpowering sound of the Miserere in *Il Trovatore*. The Japanese by choosing suggestion and simplicity forfeited a part of the possible artistic effects, but when they succeeded they created works of art of a beauty unaffected by the shifting tides of taste.

PERISHABILITY

Beyond the preference for simplicity and the natural qualities of things lies what is perhaps the most distinctively Japanese aesthetic ideal, perishability. The desire in the West has generally been to achieve artistic immortality, and this has led men to erect monuments in deathless marble. The realization that even such monuments crumble and disappear has brought tears to the eyes of the poets. The Japanese have built for impermanence, though paradoxically some of the oldest buildings in the world exist in Japan. The Japanese belief that perishability is a necessary element in beauty does not of course mean that they have been insensitive to the poignance of the passage of time. Far from it. Whatever the subject matter of the old poems, the underlying meaning was often an expression of grief over the fragility of beauty and love. Yet the Japanese were keenly aware that without this mortality there could be no beauty. Kenkō wrote, "If man were never to fade away like the dews of Adashino, never to vanish like the smoke over Toribeyama, but lingered on forever in the world, how things would lose their power to move us! The most precious thing in life is its uncertainty."[14] The frailty of human existence, a common theme in literature throughout the world, has rarely been recognized as the necessary condition of beauty. The Japanese not only knew this, but expressed their preference for varieties of beauty which most conspicuously betrayed their impermanence. Their favorite flower is of course the cherry blossom, precisely because the period of blossoming is so poignantly brief and the danger that the flowers may scatter even before one has properly seen them is so terribly great. Yet for the day or two of pleasure of the blossoming the Japanese dote on a fruit tree that bears no fruit, but instead attracts a disagreeable quantity of insects. Plum blossoms look much the same and are graced with a scent so faint that even a teamaster could not object, but they are less highly prized because they linger so long on the boughs. The samurai was traditionally compared to the cherry blossoms, and his ideal was to drop dramatically, at the height of his strength and beauty, rather than to become an old soldier gradually fading away.

The visible presence of perishability in the cracked tea bowl carefully mended in gold has been appreciated not because it makes the object an indisputable antique, but because without the possibility of aging with time and usage there could be no real beauty. Kenkō quoted with approval the poet Ton'a who said, "It is only after the silk wrapper has frayed at top and bottom, and the mother-of-pearl has fallen from the roller, that a scroll looks beautiful."[15] This delight in shabbiness may suggest the Arabic conception of *barak*, the magical quality an object acquires through long use and care. It is obviously at variance not only with the common Western craving for objects in mint condition, but with the desire to annihilate time by restoring a painting so perfectly that people will exclaim, "It could have been painted yesterday!" An object of gleaming stainless steel that never aged would surely have been repugnant to the Japanese of the past whose love of old things implied the accretions of time.

The traditional Japanese aesthetics cannot be summed up in a few pages, but even without verbalizing what they were it is easy to sense them at work in the objects created and in the objects for which we will look in vain. The virtuoso connoisseur seems now to have shifted his talents to distinguishing between brands of beer or tobacco, and the perfectionist workman may be replaced by a machine, but it seems safe to say that the aesthetic ideals which have formed Japanese taste over the centuries will find their outlet in media yet undiscovered and maintain their distinctive existence.

NOTES

1. See for example the views of Giangiorgio Trissino in Allan H. Gilbert, *Literary Criticism: Plato to Dryden*, pp. 228–31.
2. Robert H. Brower and Earl Miner, *Japanese Court Poetry*, p. 514.
3. Quoted in Tsunoda, de Bary and Keene, *Sources of Japanese Tradition*, p. 285.
4. Kenkō, *Essays in Idleness*, translated by Keene, p. 115.
5. Paine and Soper, *The Art and Architecture of Japan*, pp. 210–11.
6. Kenkō, p. 70.
7. Clifford, p. 116.
8. Clifford, p. 122.
9. Alexander C. Soper, *The Evolution of Architecture in Japan*, p. 246.
10. Kenkō, p. 10.
11. G. B. Sansom, *Japan, a Short Cultural History*, p. 401.
12. Quoted in Michael Cooper, *They Came to Japan*, p. 265.
13. Cooper, p. 194.
14. Kenkō, p. 7. Adashino was a graveyard, and Toribeyama the site of a crematorium.
15. Kenkō, p. 70.

Feminine Sensibility in the Heian Era

ONE OF THE most striking features of Japanese literature is that so many masterpieces were written by women. This is not true, however, of all periods. Although women poets and novelists were prominent between the eighth and twelfth centuries, hardly a woman writer of distinction appeared between the thirteenth and nineteenth centuries, and in modern Japanese literature the role of the woman writer has been relatively modest. Obviously, the varying position of women at different epochs of Japanese history accounts in large part for the extent of their participation in literary activity. During the long medieval period, when women were badly educated and kept in a position of subservience to men, they had little opportunity to display literary talent. In contrast, the position of women at the Heian court in the tenth and eleventh centuries was perhaps the highest of any period in Japanese history, at least until recent days. Of course, only a few thousand people enjoyed the particular kind of freedom that prevailed at the court. Elsewhere in the country the people lived under conditions of extreme duress. But these few thousand people created a body of writing that is considered today to be the finest flowering of Japanese literature, and the chief works were written by women.

In this essay I shall consider both the reasons why women played so conspicuous a part in Heian literature and the peculiar significance for Japanese literature in general of the triumph of feminine sensibility.

If we examine the *Manyōshū*, the oldest anthology of Japanese poetry, compiled in the middle of the eighth century, we find poems by women even among the earliest works included. One by the Empress Kōgyoku, who died in 661, indicates how far back the tradition of women writing artistic poetry goes. Other examples are found from every period covered by the anthology. Many poems were exchanged with men, as part of a real or pretended courtship; this was to become an important function of Japanese poetry in later times. In the *Manyōshū* we find already a characteristically feminine poetry that later became the dominant tone of Japanese poetry as a whole, but the *Manyōshū* is prevailingly masculine in its tone. The most masculine of the poems are the *chōka*, or long poems, written by such men as Kakinomoto no Hitomaro and Yamanoe no Okura. Their poems are often public: that is, they describe not the poet's private emotions but the splendor of a new palace, the grief of the nation over the death of a princess or perhaps the misery of poverty or the uncertainty of life. The greater amplitude of the *chōka*, which might be in as many as fifty or a hundred lines, as contrasted with the five lines of the *tanka*, which became the classic verse form, permitted the poets to treat themes of greater intellectual complexity than was possible in the *tanka*. Women rarely wrote *chōka*, either at this time or later, and those they wrote are identical in tone with their *tanka*, taking no advantage of the greater scope. On the other hand, their *tanka* differ not only from the *chōka* written by the male poets of the *Manyōshū*, but also from their poems in the same form. To make this more concrete, let me give the example of *tanka* by Lady Kasa and her lover Ōtomo Yakamochi, two *Manyōshū* poets. Here is a poem Lady Kasa sent to Yakamochi:

> In the loneliness of my heart
> I feel as if I should perish
> Like the pale dewdrop
> Upon the grass of my garden
> In the gathering shades of twilight.[1]

The images found in this poem occur in much later Japanese poetry, and all are feminine. The woman is alone, waiting in vain for her lover to come. In her grief she imagines she will fade away like the dew. The lover's negligence does not arouse her anger, nor is she torn by violent jealousy or apprehension. Instead, she yields despondently to her fate. And the time of day is twilight, not the glare of noon nor the blackness of the night, but the hour of melancholy and bittersweet pain rather than of tragedy. In contrast, here is a poem by Yakamochi, possibly addressed to Lady Kasa:

> Over the river ferry of Saho,
> Where the sanderlings cry—
> When can I come to you,
> Crossing on horseback
> The crystal-clear shallows ?[2]

This obviously is an entirely masculine poem in both its tone and imagery. But even in a sadder poem by Yakamochi, suggesting an unhappy love affair, the masculinity is apparent:

> Rather than that I should thus pine for you,
> Would I had been transmuted
> Into a tree or a stone,
> Nevermore to feel the pangs of love.[3]

The disappointed lover, unlike his mistress, has no desire to fade away like the dew. Instead, he would prefer to become an object insensitive to the pangs of love.

This difference between masculine and feminine expression is obvious, and parallels may of course be found in many other literatures. What makes it of special relevance to Japanese literature is that the masculine tone of the *Manyōshū* was to yield in future centuries to a feminine sensibility even on the part of male poets. In other words, the poetry in the *Manyōshū* written by women was to set the tone for later compositions both by men and women.

It is hard to say why this should have been true, but probably it was related to the functions of poetry in Japan. Already in the time when the *Manyōshū* was compiled men at the court were composing chiefly poems in the Chinese language. The court, in the attempt to emulate the great continental civilization, had taken over bodily the framework of Chinese government and laws, imported Chinese architecture and sculpture, and adopted Chinese dress. All these importations were presently modified to suit the different Japanese temperament, but their origins were unmistakably Chinese. The Japanese court also felt the need of proving to the Chinese that their country was civilized. Earlier, the Japanese had compiled in 720 an official history of the country, the *Nihon Shoki*, written in Chinese after a Chinese model, and they probably felt the need of showing off a literature in Chinese as well. Chinese had the dignity enjoyed by Latin in medieval Europe, and writing in the vernacular was considered to be undignified if not vulgar. Promotion at court was granted to noblemen who could produce poems in Chinese, but not in Japanese. Furthermore, in keeping with Chinese views, literature came to mean poetry and learned essays, and did not include fiction or works of a frivolous nature. The members of the court, who had ample leisure for such pursuits, devoted themselves increasingly to writing poetry and essays in Chinese.

Chinese, however, was a foreign language, and the Japanese could not acquire it easily. Most of them achieved in their compositions no more than grammatical accuracy, though even this was sometimes beyond their capacities. Their poems in Chinese were rather like the Latin poems composed by schoolboys today; though they are incapable of expressing themselves freely in Latin they can get good marks by patching together phrases from Latin writers and observing the rules of metrics. Composition in Chinese not only involved using a language totally dissimilar to Japanese both in structure and sounds, but also the characteristic imagery of the language. The poets of the *Manyōshū* had used such familiar Japanese imagery as the swaying seaweeds in the ocean, the great ship one can trust in, the clarity of the mountain stream, but these are not typical of Chinese poetry. Instead, the Japanese poets writing in Chinese were forced to describe mountains in China they had never seen, compare sad or felicitous occurences in their own lives to ancient Chinese examples, or to sing the praises of flowers or trees merely because their names fitted easily into Chinese metrics. As may easily be imagined, most of this poetry is exceedingly poor.

Women, however, were not expected to learn Chinese. For one thing, they did not serve as officials, and had no need therefore of proving their ability at Chinese. Chinese, in any case, was considered to be unladylike, rather as the study of surgery or hydraulic engineering would be in our day. The women of the court in fact sometimes learned Chinese, but it was considered to be in bad taste if they revealed this. They therefore continued to write poetry in Japanese, usually in the *tanka* form. By the ninth century the invention and widespread adoption of the Japanese syllabary, the *kana*, made it far easier to write Japanese poetry than with the Chinese characters used by the *Manyōshū* poets. The *kana* naturally came to be associated with women's writings since men were expected to write in Chinese. However, men still composed Japanese poetry when addressing themselves to women, as a part of courtship. Had it not been for this circumstance the writing of Japanese might have been discontinued altogether, or relegated to a minor place. In Korea and Viet Nam, two other countries that had fallen into the orbit of Chinese culture and adopted the Chinese writing, literature in the vernacular was almost swamped by the superior prestige of Chinese.

The first statement of the ideals of Japanese poetry was given by a man, Ki no Tsurayuki, in the preface to the collection *Kokinshū*, completed in 905. It enumerated the circumstances under which men composed poetry: "When they looked at the scattered cherry blossoms of a spring morning; when they listened on an autumn evening to the falling of the leaves; when they sighed over the snow and waves reflected with each passing year by their looking-glasses; when they were startled into thoughts on the brevity of their lives by seeing the dew on the grass or the foam on the water; or when, yesterday all proud and splendid, they have fallen from fortune into loneliness; or when, having been dearly loved, they are neglected."

These occasions are all melancholy, in the vein of Lady Kasa's poetry. The list suggests that poets were not likely to be moved to write poetry by joy or cheerful sentiments, and that powerful tragedies, such as the death of a wife or child, the destruction of one's city by a disaster, or the horrors of war were not proper themes for Japanese poetry. These limitations would not have been admitted by the *Manyōshū* poets, who wrote in exhilaration or admiration and sometimes with a sharp awareness of tragedy. Of course, the shortness of the *tanka* did not permit the poet to treat adequately an intellectual subject or, for that matter, emotions harsher than melancholy. But the list of circumstances when men are moved to poetry also indicates that a feminine sensibility had become dominant by the time of the *Kokinshū*, in the early tenth century. If we analyze this list, the items reduce themselves to regret over the passage of time, especially to the decline of beauty, in itself a feminine preoccupation.

By far the most common subjects of Japanese poetry are the cherry blossoms and the reddening maple leaves of autumn. If one were obliged to read through the twenty-one imperial anthologies between the tenth and fifteenth centuries, one would certainly end by being thoroughly bored with both cherry blossoms and maple leaves. Both were used to suggest the passing of time, being symbols for the end of spring or the end of autumn. Although the cherry blossom is now established as the national flower of Japan, it does not figure importantly in the *Manyōshū*, where the most often mentioned blossoms are the plum. Plum blossoms seem to have been displaced because of an aesthetic consideration: they linger on the boughs for weeks, unlike the cherry blossoms that fall dramatically after two or three days. The perishability of beauty never failed to excite the tears of the beholders; perishability, as we have seen, came to be a necessary condition of beauty. The innumerable poems on the cherry blossoms are therefore rarely concerned with their appearance but instead with their significance as symbols for the perishing beauty of the beholders. The ladies of the Heian court, grieving over their loneliness or over being abandoned by their lovers, turned to writing poetry for consolation, and did not hesitate to use familiar, even hackneyed imagery to suggest their emotions. They infused this poetry with an intense sense of melancholy, as in a great poem by Ono no Komachi, a ninth-century poetess:

> The flowers withered,
> Their color faded away,
> While meaninglessly
> I spent my days in the world
> And the long rains were falling.

The best poetry of the Heian period, whether written by men or women, tends to be in this vein, though of course more masculine poetry existed. Not only did men abandon the public themes of the *Manyōshū* poetry or Yakamochi's powerful statements in favor of suggestion, but sometimes they even wrote in the guise of women, describing their anguish over a faithless lover. Women, as far as I know, never wrote in the guise of men.

The first important sustained work of Japanese prose by a known author is the *Tosa Diary*, written in 936 by Ki no Tsurayuki, the compiler of the anthology *Kokinshū*. It begins, "Diaries are things written by men, I am told. Nevertheless, I am writing one to see what a woman can do." The author, a man, pretends to be a woman so that he may write this diary in Japanese, instead of Chinese, as would be customary in a man. Why did Tsurayuki wish to write in Japanese? Probably he felt that the highly personal nature of the contents could not be expressed in the formal Chinese the court scholars learned. Such personal writing, in any case, belonged to the domain of women. No earlier diaries by women survive, if any were written, but the introspective nature of the *Tosa Diary*, which describes, under the surface account of a sea journey, the grief of a man whose daughter has recently died, made it imperative to use Japanese.

Nevertheless, most literary men of the Heian period avoided using the Japanese language or creating anything resembling fiction. This meant that the literature of the supreme period of Japanese civilization was left by default to the women, who were at liberty both to write in Japanese and to express themselves in the genre of fiction.

The first major literary work of the Heian period is the *Kagerō Nikki*, translated by Edward Seidensticker into English as *The Gossamer Years*, an autobiography-diary covering the period 954 to 974. There can hardly be a more intensely feminine piece of writing. It is concerned almost exclusively with the personal feelings of the author. Not one word is devoted to the social or political life of the time, though the author was the wife of the prime minister, and not one trace of objectivity may be found in the author's descriptions of her activities. So intent is she on describing her woes that she gives no thought to possible reactions to her attitudes. She writes with a candor no man could approximate. We are stunned to read such a paragraph as:

> It began to appear that the lady in the alley [her husband's mistress] had fallen from favor since the birth of her child. I had prayed, at the height of my unhappiness, that she would live to know what I was then suffering, and it seemed that my prayers were being answered. She was alone, and now her child was dead, the child that had been the cause of that unseemly racket. The lady was of frightfully bad birth—the unrecog-

nized child of a rather odd prince, it was said. For a moment she was able
to use a noble gentleman who was unaware of her shortcomings, and
now she was abandoned. The pain must be even sharper than mine had
been. I was satisfied.[4]

The author states at the beginning of *Kagerō Nikki* that she decided
to write her diary because she felt dissatisfied with the fabrications of
the old romances. She tells us that she will be honest, and indeed, such
undiluted honesty, when she gloats over a rival's downfall or rejoices
over the death of her baby, would be hard to encounter elsewhere in
literature. Certainly it does not make us feel affectionately towards the
woman, but, on the other hand, we feel no barrier whatsoever between
us and this tenth-century court lady. We may not approve of her, but we
understand her perfectly. Because she confines herself to describing her
emotions, always with the same naked honesty, and does not describe
ephemeral events or intellectual speculations, her diary, like most other
products of the Heian feminine sensibility, has a modernity that astonishes
us today.

Kagerō Nikki is devoted mainly to the description of a woman unhap-
pily married to a man who betrays her for many other women. Although
of high birth herself, she is not the first wife of the prime minister but the
second, and has therefore little hope of drawing her husband back once
his affections begin to wander. We sympathize with her when she discovers he has taken up with another woman, but gradually her feelings
become obsessive, and she is in the end incapable of responding when her
husband attempts to make amends. She even seems to take a perverse
delight in destroying what is left of his affection, and she almost pleasur-
ably records his coldness or his infidelities. When, after her husband has
neglected her for some time, he finally pays her a visit, she pours out all
her resentment. She records, "It may not have been entirely gracious of
me, but I behaved like a stone for the rest of the night, and he left early
in the morning without a word."

The author almost always feels sorry for herself. Again and again we
find such sentences as, "The loneliness, the pain, the sorrow I felt as we
set off down the river can surely have had few parallels." Her absorption
with herself makes her indifferent to other people's suffering: "There
was a dead body lying in the river bottom as we passed, but I was quite
beyond being frightened by that sort of thing."[5] In the *Manyōshū* there
is a repertory of poems written by men on seeing dead bodies lying by the
road or on the shore, in which the poet wonders who the man was and
sympathizes with his family waiting for someone destined never to return.

But the author of *Kagerō Nikki* has no compassion to spare.

The manner in which I have described the author may make her sound unattractive, but this perhaps is a hypocritical male judgment. The male poet on seeing a dead body felt he must respond to it in the appropriate manner, whether or not it actually aroused his deep emotions, and he attempted therefore to imagine the sufferings of others. For the poetess, however, a dead body and falling cherry blossoms had the same meaning: they tell her of her own mortality, her own loss of beauty. If the essential meaning is the same, it is clearly more elegant to speak of cherry blossoms than of corpses; hence, the development of a strict poetic diction in the Heian period. But if the author of the *Kagerō Nikki* does not react in the approved, hypocritical manner to news of her rival's unhappiness or to the death of someone she hates, there can be no doubting the genuineness of her feelings. She is bored, she has nothing to do but brood over her misfortunes, she feels that no one can be as unfortunate as herself, but she is a woman of extraordinary sensitivity, and she captures her feelings with such precision that we, reading her diary a thousand years after it was written, and living in a civilization that has nothing to do with hers, feel she is one of us. She is as much to be pitied and despised and loved as we are.

This diary, more than the various fairy tales and adventure stories of the tenth century, is the ancestor of *The Tale of Genji* by Lady Murasaki, the supreme masterpiece of Japanese literature. The earlier stories sometimes have charm, but we cannot believe in their characters any more than we can in the characters of the Greek romances with their incessant and tedious adventures. We believe in the characters of *The Tale of Genji* as we believe in the author of *Kagerō Nikki*. That no doubt is why it has often been referred to as the oldest novel in the world. It is also a modern novel in that it is introspective. The characters are not simply good or bad, young or old, but complex people torn by doubts and uncertainties. Grief arises not because of the machinations of villains or the spite of malevolent demons but as a necessary part of the human condition.

Lady Murasaki describes in her novel a supremely accomplished man. Prince Genji is peerlessly handsome, endowed with every artistic talent, intelligent and witty, an incomparable lover; but, above all, he is sensitive. He is a hero quite dissimilar to those found in normal Western novels or even in Japanese novels written by men. Not one word is said about Genji as a statesman, though we are told he occupies high office; not one word suggests he was accomplished at arms or possessed physical strength. He is not required to avenge his father's death, protect his country, rescue distressed damsels or, for that matter, to govern his country for the benefit of the people. The novel hardly contains any action in the normal sense, though it runs to over twelve hundred pages in English translation. Yet it is always absorbing, whether read in the manner of a conventional novel, or as the creation of a world. It describes a court that could never have existed, not because it is haunted by monsters or under some magic spell, but because it is totally lacking in ugliness. The world is incredibly beautiful. The nobles of the Heian court, having no need to occupy themselves with warfare or administration or economic planning, devoted themselves entirely to the cult of beauty. In most societies where men have possessed unlimited wealth and unlimited leisure they have turned naturally to depravity, like the Roman emperors, but in the world of Lady Murasaki's novel the creation of beauty in every aspect of life was the chief concern. Infinite care was given to the palaces and gardens, to costuming and furnishings; but above all, the center of the courtiers' lives was love.

Courtship was extremely elaborate. The court ladies were almost always hidden, seated behind screens from which they could see out but which rendered them invisible, even to their lovers. A young man, hearing rumors about a beautiful woman, might pay a visit. Of course he could not hope to see her or even to hear her voice, but she might condescend to exchange poems with him. He would eagerly scan her answer, judging by the calligraphy, the ink, the paper, even by the way the paper was folded (as well as by the contents of the poem) whether or not he should pursue the affair. Or perhaps he might catch a glimpse of the long, trailing sleeves of her elaborate, twelve-fold robes, and decide from the exquisite harmonies of the colors of the different layers, revealed at the opening of her sleeve, that this indeed was a woman worth courting. Even when he had made his way behind her screen and into her chamber he might never enjoy a proper look at her. Not only was she enveloped in a tent-like set of robes, but she lived in the dark, hidden from the light of day, and her lover was obliged by custom and the fear of rumors to leave before the dawn. Even after a nobleman had married a woman he often did not live with her, and his visits at night hardly differed from those of a secret lover.

The world that appears in *The Tale of Genji* is so compelling that we have no choice but to believe in it. Yet we know from other evidence that the courtiers of the day were not all flawlessly behaved. There was violence, drunkenness, cruelty, all the familiar elements of our world. The fact that we do not miss these ugly elements is a tribute to the triumph of Lady Murasaki's feminine sensibility. Genji is the lover every woman dreams of. In the course of the novel he has a great many love affairs, but he is quite the opposite of Don Juan, at least as we see him in Mozart's opera. Don Juan is summed up by Leporello's catalogue. We are told how many women he has conquered in France, Turkey, Italy and Spain, that some are tall and some short, some blond and some dark, but nothing suggests that all these women mean anything more to Don Juan than numbers. The more women the better, and once a woman's name has been entered in Leporello's catalogue Don Juan wants to get rid of her as quickly as possible. If, like Dona Elvira, she insists on pursuing Don Juan even after he has lost interest in her, he humiliates her by having Leporello make love to her. Despite the number of Genji's affairs, however, he never forgets or abandons a woman. Moreover, he acts differently towards each, responding to her temperament. He is the great noble when he makes love to Lady Rokujō, the demon lover when with Yūgao, tender and unassertive with the timid Lady of Akashi, fatherly to Tamakazura. He needs each woman for precisely this reason: if, having found his ideal in Murasaki, who becomes his wife, he had forsaken all other women, or had, on the other hand, merely conquered women instead of giving himself to them, his greatest artistic accomplishment, his skill at love-making, would have been wasted. This would have choked him artistically and it would also have deprived many women of their greatest happiness, for they were content even with the smallest part of Genji's affection. Genji never abandons a mistress merely because she had become old. Even when he makes a serious mistake and courts a woman who, when at last he sees her, proves to be comically ugly, he does not run from the scene like Don Juan, but looks after her as tenderly as if he truly loved her.

When we read this novel it never occurs to us to doubt that Genji could be so considerate, so sensitive, yet surely no such man has ever existed. His is a perfection we can believe in, an ideal that becomes a reality. This is not only a tribute to the novelistic skill of Lady Murasaki but to her femininity. No male author could have created such a character. The one thing Murasaki could not do with Genji was to allow him to grow old. The last glimpse she gives of him, as a man in his forties, is of a man handsomer than ever before.

The next chapter, which occurs about two-thirds of the way through the novel, opens with the words, "Genji was dead." I can think of no other novel in which the principal character dies at that point in the work, but Murasaki, by a stroke of genius, realized that to give full dimension to Prince Genji she must move from the world of his perfection to one more recognizably like our own. The last third of the novel deals mainly with two princes, Niou and Kaoru. Both are handsome and accomplished, but they are only fragmentations of Genji. Niou has Genji's ardor, his success with women, but he is insensitive and even at times cruel. Kaoru has Genji's sensitivity, but it is overdeveloped and renders him neurotic and incapable of action. The world, though still beautiful, is tinged by failure. It is a world where people love but misunderstand, where Niou conquers women he does not love and Kaoru is so paralyzed by his love for a woman that he cannot conquer her.

In the novels and diaries that followed *The Tale of Genji*, most of them by women, Kaoru rather than Genji is evoked. Genji, the ever-triumphant, flawless lover proved inimitable. Perhaps, as the Heian court itself lost its brilliance, it became harder for women to hope for a Genji. Instead we have many touching, sometimes heartbreaking accounts of frustrated love. The author of the *Sarashina Diary*, writing not long after the composition of *The Tale of Genji* in the early eleventh century, describes how she grew up in the provinces, far away from the capital. She heard about *The Tale of Genji*, apparently from people who recited chapters from memory, and prayed devoutly she might go to the capital where she would be able to read the whole work. In 1020, when she was twelve, her prayers were granted when her father took her to the court. She tells us that she was still ugly and immature, but she hoped that one day she would develop into a beautiful woman like Yūgao whom Genji had loved, or Ukifune, loved by Kaoru. She imagined herself especially as Ukifune, living in some lonely mountain retreat. She wrote, "Even if he came but once a year I would be content." But even that much happiness was denied her. Perhaps she never became a beauty; in any event, she was neglected. No Genji ever took pity on her and courted her. She spent her time alone, with nothing better to do than to immerse herself in *The Tale of Genji* and other old romances, finding in them a refuge from her life.

One night, at a religious ceremony, a certain gentleman addressed her. She writes, "He spoke gently and quietly. There was nothing about him to be regretted. . . . He said nothing rude or amorous like other men, but talked delicately of the sad, sweet things of the world, and many a phrase of his enticed me by its strange power into the conversation." The two talked of the beauty of the different seasons, and the man described a visit on a wintry night to the Great Shrine of Ise. He ended with, "Hereafter every dark night with gentle rain like tonight will touch my heart; I feel this has not been inferior to the snowy night at the palace of the Ise vestal." He left with these words. Not until the following year did the author of the diary have another glimpse of the man. He approached and assured her he had never forgotten the night of softly falling rain, but before they could converse people interrupted them.

She writes, "In the next year one tranquil evening I heard he had come into the princess's palace, so I crept out of my chamber with my companion. But there were many people waiting within and without the palace, and I turned back. He must have been of the same mind. He had come because it was so still a night, and he returned because it was noisy." She concludes the section, "There is nothing more to tell. His personality was excellent and he was not an ordinary man, but time passed, and neither called to the other."[6]

This is a far cry from *The Tale of Genji* where even an ugly princess can hope for a visit from the peerless Genji. But the *Sarashina Diary*, though a miniature work in a minor key, is curiously affecting.

In many other later works of the Heian period the failure of love is chronicled. The most unusual example is the story of *The Lady Who Loved Insects*, the twelfth-century account of a young woman who refuses to obey the social conventions. She deliberately allows her eyebrows to grow instead of plucking them, does not blacken her teeth in the manner expected of a court lady, and instead of admiring cherry blossoms and maple leaves, spends her time collecting disagreeable insects like caterpillars. She dislikes anything smacking of artifice, and asserts that her only interest is to "inquire into everything that exists and find out how it began." A certain captain, hearing of this curious young lady, goes to her house and peeps in on her. Intrigued, he sends in a poem, to which she can barely be persuaded to vouchsafe a reply. The captain apparently has had enough of this fantastic creature by this time, for he writes another poem, "In all the world, I fear, no man exists so delicate that to the hairtips of a caterpillar's brow he could attune his life."[7]

The comic resolution is unusual, but we are left with a pang of disappointment that the captain could not recognize the merits of this unconventional but somehow attractive girl. The failure of love becomes a conspicuous feature of the novels written by women; in those by men a happy ending is generally achieved, however unnaturally. For all its exaggeration, *The Lady Who Loved Insects* is entirely believable. The heroine with her alarmingly white teeth lives only for a moment, but she lives. In the works of fiction written by men of the time it is impossible to believe in the characters even for a moment. Such works as *Utsubo Monogatari* or *Ochikubo Monogatari*, presumably by men, are totally lacking in the introspection of the works by women authors, and tend to be crude and fantastic. The diaries by men are unrelievedly boring, consisting mainly of careful notations on meteorological phenomena and lists of ceremonies and promotions.

It is not hard to imagine why this was the case. The members of the Japanese court, despite the way they are portrayed in *The Tale of Genji*, were much occupied with official business. Love-making was undoubtedly of great importance to them, as to anyone else, but it was only a part of their lives, whereas it was everything to the court ladies. The women, as we know from their diaries, were bored and rarely left their quarters save for an occasional visit to a temple. Yet, unlike the ladies of a Turkish harem, they were well educated and their status was high. They were by no means mere playthings or the passive victims of the men's appetites. They spent their time reading, composing poetry and, above all, waiting for something to happen. They brooded over their lives, they worried about other people's feelings and motives, they imagined men who would be more considerate than the ones that actually visited them. Fiction was for them an extension of their lives, and not an excursion into fantasy, as it was for the men.

Not all the women writers were given to melancholy. The finest example of humorous writing in Japanese, perhaps the only truly witty book in the language, is the *Pillow Book* by Sei Shōnagon, who wrote in the late tenth century. Sei Shōnagon served the Empress Sadako, a learned and accomplished woman who gathered around her a salon of amusing court ladies. For this small and special group of women there were more pleasant occupations than waiting for evening and the chance some man would visit them. Their privileged position enabled them to deal with men on equal terms. Sei Shōnagon especially delighted in discomfiting men with a well-placed witticism or with a display of her erudition. George Meredith in his *Essay on Comedy* put forward the proposition that only in a society where men and women met on equal footing was wit possible, though lower forms of humor always exist. Perhaps this was the one time that wit in Meredith's sense was possible in Japan. Be that as it may, the *Pillow Book* is unique in Japanese literature in its sharp observations, its brilliantly evoked vignettes of the court society, its apt generalizations on human nature. Its prevailingly cheerful tone distinguishes it from other writings by women of this period, but it shares with them a contemporary quality that comes from direct description of human experiences.

The appearance of this extraordinary group of women writers was to mold the shape of Japanese literature for centuries to come. The shadow of *The Tale of Genji*, the last third especially, lay over the novels composed for the next six hundred years. Imitations, variations and distortions of its plot recurred in works written by men and women alike. The diary too, thanks to the Heian court ladies, developed in Japan into an important literary genre, rather than being considered as in the West a marginal form of literature. Again, whether the writer was a man or a woman, the style and manner of composition was tinged by the femininity of the Heian period. For centuries the court writers produced imitations of Heian literature, clinging to a language that had become archaic or obsolete. This kind of feminine sensibility was more likely to produce works that are still readable today than the masculine stories of a moralistic or didactic nature. The melancholy of a rainy evening, the preciousness of a beauty soon faded, the unspoken overtones of a casual remark, and all the rest of the characteristic features of the writings inspired by feminine sensibility in the Heian period, became the heritage not only of the handful of nobles at the court but of the entire Japanese people.

NOTES

1. Translation from *Manyōshū*, edited by Nihon Gakujutsu Shinkōkai (Columbia University Press, 1965), p. 106
2. *Ibid.*, p. 134
3. *Ibid.*, p. 134
4. *The Gossamer Years*, translated by Edward G. Seidensticker.
5. *Ibid.*, p. 88
6. Translation by Doi and Omori, in Keene, *Anthology of Japanese Literature*, p. 161
7. Translation by Arthur Waley, in Keene, *Anthology of Japanese Literature*, p. 176

Individuality and Pattern in Japanese Literature

FROM THE end of the fifteenth century to the end of the sixteenth century Japan was torn by incessant warfare. The fighting sometimes involved large armies pitted against each other in major battles, but more often it consisted of minor skirmishes between small bands of men. The age was characterized by writers of the time as being one of *gekokujō*—of men underneath overthrowing those above. In the process of all this fighting the traditional, aristocratic Japanese culture was nearly destroyed. Almost every building of consequence within the city of Kyoto, the capital, was burned between 1477 and 1479. This represented a staggering blow to Japanese culture, for it had been concentrated in this one city, the seat of the court since the end of the eighth century. Not only were buildings and works of art destroyed, but libraries of irreplaceable manuscripts were pillaged and their contents wantonly scattered. The Japanese had been familiar with the art of printing since the eighth century, but only used it for Buddhist texts; the rest of Japanese literature existed only in manuscript. Inevitably, many books disappeared forever as the result of the warfare, and with them, much of the traditional culture.

Not all the effects of the wars were undesirable. Many educated men, fleeing the capital, settled down in the provinces, and literature for the first time came to be written in remote parts of the country. These men, nobles and priests for the most part, served also as tutors for the semi-literate military lords who had come into power, and eventually founded schools where they imparted the rudiments of the traditional culture to the sons and vassals of these lords. In contrast, moreover, to the older society in which birth had counted for everything, a freer atmosphere now reigned. Farmers, despairing of peacefully tilling the soil, sometimes became soldiers and made their fortunes, and the merchants discovered ways of taking advantage of the chaotic conditions. This was an age of unusual mobility, especially in contrast to the stable society that was to emerge in the seventeenth century. Throughout the sixteenth century men who knew nothing about their own ancestors emerged into prominence by virtue of their physical strength or intelligence.

In the same period the age-old isolation of Japan was interrupted by the appearance of Europeans. In 1542 some Portuguese seafarers reached the southernmost Japanese islands, and in the following years Portuguese and Spanish soldiers and priests became increasingly prominent in Japan. Firearms, introduced by the Portuguese, enabled some military leaders to win battles against adversaries armed only with swords and arrows. Other warlords entrenched themselves in stone fortresses built on European models. Japan attracted attention in Europe, for the first time in history. The letters sent back to Europe by the missionaries indicate how greatly Japan had impressed them. One Spanish priest wrote, "The Japanese are better disposed to embrace our holy Faith than any other people in the world. They are as prudent as could be desired and are governed by reason as much as, or even more than, Spaniards; they are more inquisitive than any other people I have met. No men in the world would more like to hear sermons on how to serve their Creator and save their souls."[1]

European influence extended not only to religious doctrines but to the arts. Japanese converts painted familiar Christian subjects in the idiom of sixteenth-century Iberian artists. Many European luxury articles, such as glass and velvet, were imported and Japanese learned how to manufacture them. One missionary even wrote that the bread sold in Edo was the most delicious in the world, testimony to how rapidly the Japanese mastered European techniques. In the domain of literature, however, the influence was less strong. The missionaries and converts translated various theological tracts and even a few secular works like Aesop's Fables, but it was far more difficult for Japanese to read books written in foreign languages than to copy paintings or learn to make European cakes. The missionaries, moreover, were not interested in transmitting to the Japanese the plays of Shakespeare or *Don Quixote*. If the period of contact with Europe had been longer Japanese literature would certainly have been affected. Indeed, a reasonable prediction made about 1580 would have indicated that with the breakdown of the old order and the successful introduction of European culture, Japan would take its place as a member of a Europe-centered world civilization, however distant and distinct. The same might be said of Japan today, of course.

But with the unification of the country in the late seventeenth century the rulers of Japan turned against the missionaries. They feared that religious indoctrination might be the prelude to colonization, as had occurred in the Philippines, or that the Japanese generals who had been converted to Christianity might betray their country in favor of their faith. Increasingly severe decrees were issued that limited and finally prohibited Christianity altogether. By 1640 the country was closed to the outside world. No Europeans, with the exception of a handful of Dutch merchants, might visit Japan, and no Japanese could go abroad. Every effort was made to suppress all traces of foreign influence. People who owned Christian books or paintings concealed or destroyed them.

The rulers of Japan during the renaissance of the seventeenth century were shoguns, or generalissimos, of the Tokugawa family. The founder of the line, Tokugawa Ieyasu, won a decisive victory at the Battle of Sekigahara in 1600, and in 1615 wiped out the remaining opposition to his regime, ushering in an era of peace that lasted over 250 years. He and his successors, determined that their rule be perpetuated for ages to come, were obsessed with the importance of maintaining order. For this reason they had prohibited and persecuted Christianity, as being subversive to the secular order, and instead encouraged Confucian studies that insisted on each man knowing his place in society. The texts of Confucianism acquired overwhelming prestige, and their prescriptions were obeyed with almost fanatical literalness. The period of civil warfare had brought great hardships, but the division of authority had permitted some opportunity for the assertion of independent beliefs. That is why the missionaries were able in the course of a few years to convert thousands of Japanese of all classes. But the Tokugawa rulers decided that all must conform to one approved philosophy. The Confucian scholars drew up elaborate codes of propriety intended to regulate the whole of society. Loyalty, filial piety, the sense of duty and the other Confucian virtues became absolute requirements. Instead of becoming a state on European lines, as might have been predicted, Japan in the seventeenth century turned into a rigidly feudal state. The country, enjoying peace after the wars, was prosperous and well ordered, but individualism in a Western sense was not tolerated.

The government was adamant in its insistence on the maintenance of order, but it recognized tacitly that however strictly it might attempt to control men's actions, irrational and violent emotions were part of human nature. At the beginning of the seventeenth century the Tokugawa rulers were troubled especially by the problem of what to do with the many bloodthirsty soldiers who in times of peace had lost their occupation. There was always a danger that these men, adept at the use of weapons, might act lawlessly or even incite revolts. The rulers frequently issued injunctions, urging on these soldiers the importance of literary pursuits, by which they meant, of course, the writings of the Chinese philosophers, and not frivolous novels. But it was understood that the rough veterans of the civil wars would not all become Confucian scholars.

The government therefore permitted the establishment of licensed quarters where they could dissipate their energies in sexual pleasures, feasting and watching entertainments. It is paradoxical that the rigorously moral Tokugawa government should have condoned immorality, but no doubt it considered immorality less dangerous than disorder.

During the seventeenth century licensed quarters sprang up in all the cities. The women inside were hierarchically graded in rank, from great courtesans down to lowly prostitutes, with someone for every taste. As Japanese society as a whole became increasingly rigid and constricting, the licensed quarters became indispensable outlets for pent-up frustrations. The proper relations between husbands and wives, for example, had been meticulously prescribed by the Confucian philosophers in terms of duties and obligations, but no importance was given to affection. Indeed, any display of love for his wife or children would have seemed indecorous and ridiculous in a husband. It might even lead to his neglecting the path of duty to his superiors. The wife, for her part, was required to obey her husband unquestioningly in every particular. This may seem to contemporary males to have been an ideal arrangement, but the mute, utterly submissive wife must have been an exceedingly boring partner. The husband, when he needed diversion, could escape from the Confucian paradise at home by going to the licensed quarters. No matter what liaisons he might form with the courtesans, his wife was never allowed to show any jealousy, not even if he ransomed a courtesan and established her under the same roof with his wife. The husband, on the other hand, had no need to worry that his wife might take up with another man while he was disporting himself in the gay quarters: the penalty for adultery on a wife's part was swiftly administered death. The greatest consoling pleasure given the wife, it would seem, was becoming a mother-in-law and having a daughter-in-law to torment.

The gay quarters were not merely houses of prostitution, but developed into the chief artistic centers of the country, displacing the palaces of Kyoto. The Kabuki theatre, for example, had its origins in this milieu, and for years after its inception in the early seventeenth century served mainly as singing and dancing advertisements for the products displayed, the actresses themselves. The *ukiyo-e*, the woodblock prints, also originated in the quarters and many of the finest examples depict courtesans. The music of the time is typified by the samisen, an instrument imported in the sixteenth century that came to be popular especially among the courtesans. Outside the licensed quarters men moved with decorum and gravity in strict observance of their place in society, but inside, any man who had the money to pay for a courtesan could buy her favors. This was the only democracy tolerated in seventeenth-century Japan.

During the Tokugawa era Japanese society was divided by government decree into four classes: samurai, farmers, artisans and merchants. Attempts were made to keep these classes entirely distinct, but in the course of the seventeenth century rich merchants began to marry their daughters to samurai, farmers moved into the cities to become artisans, and so on. The government had originally encouraged the samurai to indulge in luxuries, both in order to soften their warlike tempers and to drain their finances (and thus their power to create trouble). Before long, however, the samurai were in debt to the merchants because of their extravagances, and the government had to protect the hapless samurai. The financial strength of the merchants enabled them to create in the gay quarters havens where they needed fear no domination from the samurai and where they could enjoy for themselves the privileges that formerly belonged to the aristocracy. The courtesans took names derived from *The Tale of Genji* in order to give the merchants the illusion that they, like Prince Genji of long ago, had the most elegant princesses of the land at their disposal.

It took a long time, however, before a new *Tale of Genji* was to appear. The literary works of the first three-quarters of the seventeenth century were either archaistic in manner, continuing the desiccated traditions of earlier ages, or else trivial collections of jokes and anecdotes. Both varieties were known as *kana* books because they were written mainly in *kana*, the Japanese syllabary, and therefore easy to read. Though occasionally of some interest, even today, they do not form part of the seventeenth-century renaissance of Japanese literature.

The first major work of the renaissance was *The Life of an Amorous Man* by Ihara Saikaku, published in 1682. It is worthy of note that this book was printed, showing that even popular writings had by now acquired the dignity formerly reserved for sacred texts. These books were not cheap, judged in terms of the prices of other commodities, but they were widely read and brought Saikaku fame. He had previously been known as a poet, specializing in the rapid composition of impromptu linked verse. On one occasion he is reported to have composed by himself twenty thousand verses in a single day, a record that was never again approached. These verses have not survived, but it is to be doubted that they possessed much literary merit. Nevertheless they afforded proof of his fertility of invention and the quickness of his wit.

The Life of an Amorous Man was the first novel of significance to have appeared for almost five hundred years. In between there had been numerous works of historical fiction, as well as folk and fairy tales, but few novels signed by their authors. This work may be considered in some sense to be the *Tale of Genji* of Saikaku's time. It is in fifty-four episodes, corresponding to the fifty-four chapters of *The Tale of Genji*, and is devoted to describing the love life of the hero. But at this point resemblances cease. Prince Genji was the incarnation of sensitivity and gentility, but Yonosuke, the hero of Saikaku's novel, is a type more familiar in the Occident, the man of enormous sexual prowess who manages to conquer hundreds of women without showing a flicker of sensibility. Yonosuke's career begins precociously when, as a boy of seven, he uses a telescope, an exotic European invention, to peep on a maidservant in her bath. Intrigued by what he sees, he makes advances to her, despite his tender age. The novel painstakingly follows Yonosuke's subsequent adventures. At nineteen he is disinherited by his father for being a libertine, and for the next fifteen years he wanders all over Japan, sampling every variety of amorous pleasure. At thirty-four he inherits his father's fortune, and this enables him to become a great patron of the gay quarters. At the end of the book he is about to set sail, at the age of sixty, for an island populated exclusively by women. His ship is called the S.S. *Lust*, and it is loaded with aphrodisiacs.

The barest outline of the novel suffices to show how vastly it differs in spirit from *The Tale of Genji* with its poetically evoked romances. Of course, Lady Murasaki, the author of *The Tale of Genji*, was a woman, and Saikaku a man, accounting for some of the discrepancy. But the difference is mainly in the times. The old aristocratic culture had vanished and so had the medieval nostalgia for bygone glories. Instead, Saikaku presents the picture of a self-confident world that is brash and rather vulgar. His novels have been called *ukiyo* books. This word had meant in medieval times something like "the sad world," but a pun on the word gave it in Saikaku's time a new meaning, "the floating world." For Saikaku, as for his hero Yonosuke (whose name is a shortened form of Ukiyo-nosuke), t e world was a place of uncertain ups and downs like the waves of the sea. But unlike the people of the past who had lamented this, Saikaku and his hero exult in change. Anything not in the latest fashion was discarded. Yonosuke's lightning shifts of affection from one hardly remembered woman to the next typify this craving for novelty.

The floating world did not designate Japanese society as a whole but specifically the gay quarters. Outside the gates of this special domain, a deadly orthodoxy ruled, leaving no possibility for fantasy or caprices of spirit. Any merchant who ostentatiously displayed his wealth risked being imprisoned by the government and having his fortune confiscated, as a violation of the behavior appropriate to his station in life. Again and again decrees were issued to curb the extravagance of the merchants, forbidding them to wear silk or regulating the sizes of their houses. A considerable part of the wealth of the merchants accordingly found its way into the gay quarters.

When we examine today the *ukiyo-e* prints that depict the floating world so brilliantly, we may marvel so much at the skill of their use of line and color that we do not immediately notice how two-dimensional they are. No attempt is made to achieve perspective, even in the old Japanese manner. Moreover, we eventually notice that even though the poses and costumes differ greatly, the faces of the women painted by any one artist tend to be exactly the same. In extreme cases, such as the prints of Haru-nobu and Utamaro, it is often almost impossible to distinguish even between the young men and the young women. The prints lack depth and individuality. This does not prevent them from being indisputable masterpieces.

The same holds true of Saikaku's writings. His first novel is by no means his best, but its lively descriptions captivate the reader. In vain would one look for the depth of portrayal found in *The Tale of Genji*. The characters are drawn not in the round but as flat, colorful surfaces. Above all, they lack the contradictions and ambiguities that constitute the truly human part of any human being. We cannot believe in Saikaku's characters as real people if only because they are so consistent. The women who wrote diaries in the Heian period sometimes shock us by sudden revelations of spite or cruelty, but it is at precisely such moments that we recognize them as fellow human beings. The characters in Saikaku's novels are too stylized to be believed in. Yet this does not impair their charm. Indeed, this was the effect that Saikaku aimed at. In reading his novels we obtain the impression that he looked at human society through the wrong end of a telescope. By reducing his figures to the size of fleas—enchanting little fleas—and robbing them of their third dimension, he made it possible to laugh at the human comedy even when the events described are tragic. The laughter is by no means derisory. It is full of affection for these curious creatures who love, fight and strut about with such airs of importance, even though they are no bigger than fleas.

Saikaku's masterpiece is the collection of short novels called *Five Amorous Women*, written in 1686. His five heroines are women of the merchant class driven by love to risk death. One of them, Osan, the wife of a prosperous merchant, unintentionally sleeps with a clerk who works in her husband's shop. Knowing that the penalty for adultery is death, regardless of the circumstances, she decides to run off with the clerk and make the best of the situation. Their flight takes them over difficult roads, and Osan is exhausted by the unaccustomed hardships. Saikaku tells us, "Her pulse beat more and more faintly; any minute might be her last." Her lover has no medicine to offer her, but on a sudden impulse he bends and whispers into her ear, "Just a little farther on we shall come to the village of some people I know. There we can forget all our misery, indulge our hearts' desire with pillows side by side, and talk again of love!" When she hears this Osan feels better immediately, and says, "How good that sounds! Oh, you are worth paying with one's life for!" Saikaku comments, "A pitiful woman indeed, whom lust alone could arouse!"[2]

At the end of this story Osan and her lover are executed for their crime of adultery. Saikaku's final words are: "Their story spread every-where, and today the name of Osan still brings to mind her beautiful figure clothed in the pale-blue slip which she wore to her execution."[3] The story should move us by the death of a beautiful young woman. But the effect is actually to make us smile with affection, rather than grieve over her fate. Osan, by Saikaku's intent, is so far removed from us that at the conclusion she is a charming spot of pale-blue color rather than a real woman facing death. Saikaku does not permit us to imagine what anguish she may have experienced in her last hours or even to sympathize with her. He has frequently been called a realist and his descriptions of daily life sometimes have the vividness of photographs, but the distance he maintains from his characters and the two-dimensional quality he gives them made it possible for him to present tragedy most unrealistically, in comic terms.

The two-dimensional nature of Saikaku's characters is typical of most Japanese literature of the seventeenth and eighteenth centuries. The Japanese renaissance in the arts, after the long arid period of the sixteenth century, was in this sense strikingly dissimilar to the renaissance in Europe. If Christianity had not been wiped out by the Tokugawa government, a three-dimensional humanism might have been part of the Japanese renaissance too, but the Confucian philosophers allowed no place for the vagaries of the individual. Personal preferences were denied in favor of conformity to prescribed ideals. Naturally, the government permitted nothing in the nature of satire or protest against the policies of the régime. The result of the rigid application of Confucian morality to all aspects of life, with the notable exception of male sexual activities, was not to arouse sharp opposition, but to produce a society that neither understood nor desired the three-dimensionalism of the individual. The creation of the individual, the adding of an extra dimension of depth, was to become a main concern of Japanese writers in the twentieth century.

To speak of two-dimensional literature and art may sound pejorative. In fact, I have the highest admiration for the writings of Saikaku and the masterpieces of *ukiyo-e*. If I had to choose between Saikaku and Tolstoi or, for that matter, between Saikaku and *The Tale of Genji*, I would reject Saikaku, but fortunately there is no need to make such a choice. It may be, too, that the choice would not be the same for everyone. The many nineteenth-century European painters who were inspired by the Japanese prints found something in them that was more stimulating than the masterpieces of Rembrandt or Velazquez. For that matter, the *nouveau roman* is certainly closer to Saikaku than to Tolstoi. The lack of individuality in works of the Japanese renaissance can be as much a virtue as a defect.

Saikaku's novels typify the restlessness of his age, whether they deal with the amours of a courtesan or a businessman's desperate pursuit of wealth. Intensely absorbed by this world, he never tired of watching men at their various, frantic activities. Saikaku had no interest in religious or contemplative matters, and rarely even suggests that his characters ever had more than one idea in their heads. For that matter, he was indifferent to the beauties of nature and seemed happiest in the city. The floating world was his chosen medium.

It is hard to realize that Saikaku was almost an exact contemporary of the poet Matsuo Bashō, who seems his diametric opposite in almost every respect. Bashō also lived in the city, but almost as a hermit, at times barring his gate to strangers for months at a time. His travels, unlike Saikaku's, were intended to renew his poetry by bringing him into contact with the sources of inspiration of the poets of the past. He wrote comparatively little, sometimes spending years polishing a few dozen pages or even abandoning poetry altogether. The world of the gay quarters was of no interest to him, and passing vogues concerned him less than the eternal verities in art. Yet, no less than Saikaku, he rejected the heavy burden of the past. He chose to write not in the *tanka*, the classic verse form, but in the *haiku*, a short, popular form that had previously been used mainly as a vehicle for ephemeral flashes of wit. He insisted that poetry must at once embody change and permanence, by which he meant that it must be new and not merely derivative from the past, but that it must also possess unchanging truth.

Bashō's poetry is obviously more introspective than Saikaku's writings, but, judged by Western standards, it is strangely impersonal. Even his diaries, written in a mixture of prose and poetry, contain hardly an intimation of individual feelings. In his most famous work, *The Narrow Road of Oku*, he figures in the role of an itinerant poet, with little to suggest he differs from other poets who might have made the journey. Rousseau began his *Confessions* with the declaration that although he might not be better than other men he was at least different. Bashō might have said that although he was no different from other men, his poetry was superior. But the poetry, though it bears the unmistakeable marks of his craftsmanship and profound sense of association with what he describes, is rarely about himself. Not only does it lack the personal tone we would expect in a romantic poet, but tends to be about experiences not even dependent on the presence of man.

Occasionally Basho expresses personal emotions in his diaries, but these are the emotions appropriate to him as a poet, not expressions of individuality. A surprising discovery concerning *The Narrow Road of Oku* was made when the diary of Bashō's companion was first published in 1943. There are numerous discrepancies between the two accounts. The most revealing, perhaps, is when the two men visit a town called Ishinomaki. Bashō wrote, "We lost our way, and finally took entirely the wrong road, to emerge at a harbor called Ishinomaki. . . . Hundreds of merchant ships were gathered in the bay. In the town the houses fought for space, and smoke rose continuously from the salt-kilns. I thought to myself, 'I never intended to come anywhere like this. . . .' We looked for lodgings but were refused by everyone. Finally, we found a miserable little hut where we passed the night." The companion's diary, on the other hand, states that they went by invitation to Ishinomaki, and were hospitably received at the home of a prominent businessman. It is clear that he is telling the truth. Why then should Basho have lied? The reason is not difficult to guess. Bashō felt that his role as a poet demanded that he not visit a bustling, commercial city. Poets were supposed to commune with nature, not visit the steel works of Pittsburgh. It was incongruous, too, that an unassuming poet should be lavishly received by a merchant. Bashō therefore altered the facts to maintain his role. He preferred being a type to being an individual.

The theatre during the seventeenth-century renaissance was also dedicated to the depiction of types rather than individuals. This was true even of Chikamatsu Monzaemon, perhaps the greatest of all Japanese dramatists. Chikamatsu wrote chiefly for the puppet theatre, which became, as the result of his successes, the leading Japanese dramatic art for over a century. The puppets provided Chikamatsu with certain advantages. Unlike temperamental actors, they performed his plays exactly as written. But the puppets had severe limitations. It was possible for the playwright to create a good or a bad young man and have the characters distinguished by an appropriate puppet head, but greater subtlety of delineation was difficult, and once a character was determined as good or bad he had to remain the same throughout the performance. If *Hamlet* were performed by puppets the hero might be given the head of a good man of thirty, but the unvarying expression on the puppet's face would accord poorly, say, with the scene where Hamlet rages in Gertrude's bedroom. And should Macbeth be presented with the head of a good middle-aged man or a bad middle-aged man? Comparison with European drama suggests that puppets could be used effectively only in a theatre of types, not to represent human beings of the complexity of a Hamlet or a Macbeth.

Nevertheless, Chikamatsu, almost alone of the writers of the seventeenth and eighteenth centuries, attempted to create characters with a third dimension. In his early work, *Kagekiyo Victorious*, written in 1686, the same year as Saikaku's *Five Amorous Women*, he created one character reminiscent of the Greek theatre. Akoya, the mistress of the general Kagekiyo, learns he has abandoned her for another woman. Giving way to her wounded pride and rage, she reveals to Kagekiyo's enemy where he is hiding. Kagekiyo is captured, and now Akoya is overcome with remorse. She goes to plead with him, begging his forgiveness. She takes with her the two sons she has borne him, to strengthen her pleas. But Kagekiyo refuses to listen. In despair, she draws to her the two children and kills them before their father's eyes. This Medea-like role is beyond the capacities of a puppet. The shifting emotions are too vivid for their stylization. In contrast to the other characters in the play, which are utterly unbelievable, she alone bursts into life. By so doing, she wrecks the play. It is as if one figure in an *ukiyo-e* print were drawn by Rembrandt. No matter how brilliantly executed, it would destroy the harmony of the rest.

In several later plays Chikamatsu experimented with ambiguous characters who could not readily be labelled as good or bad. In each instance this resulted in failure with the audiences, as we know from later adaptions of the play, which invariably eliminate all ambiguities. The audiences seem to have been puzzled and even resentful of characters who could not clearly be identified as being heroes or villains. But of course that would be precisely the appeal of a character like Macbeth.

Chikamatsu's greatest success was with *The Battles of Coxinga*, a puppet play in five acts first staged in 1715. The plot is hopelessly unconvincing by any standards of realism. Scenes of wild fantasy and prodigious feats of strength mingle with down-to-earth domestic scenes or the tragic grief of a woman torn between father and husband. The play's success was due especially to Chikamatsu's masterful exploitation of the puppets, his ability to convert their limitations into assets. A puppet's face cannot change its expression, but its body can perform actions beyond human strength. The characters are two-dimensional, lacking in shading or subtlety, but they fascinate us by their ever-changing pattern of actions.

Of greater literary value are Chikamatsu's domestic tragedies. They tell of the suicides of unimportant, inconspicuous members of society, unable to oppose in any other way the merciless restrictions imposed on them. Chikamatsu was perhaps the first playwright anywhere in the world to have chosen shop assistants for the heroes of his plays, and prostitutes for his heroines. He derived his plots from current gossip and scandals, but by the magic of his language he transmuted the rather shabby stories of the deaths of humble little people into the stuff of tragedy. But if we search for individuality in these different pairs of lovers we shall be disappointed. Chikamatsu's genius enabled him to make believable people out of types, but they remain types, and any attempt to discover another dimension in their portrayals can only destroy them.

The Japanese renaissance of the seventeenth century produced the first popular literature. For centuries the bulk of literary works had consisted of imitations of court novels and poetry. The new writing, which described the commoners and the world in which they lived, was intended primarily for their pleasure, but it is marked too by the Confucian philosophy that prevailed, both in the advocacy of its doctrines and, contrarily, by the search for pleasure in the only place free from Confucianism, the gay quarters. The literature is peculiarly Japanese, and virtually untouched by foreign influence. The Japanese have often been accused of being imitative, but the novels, poetry and drama produced at this time are uniquely their own. Depending on personal preference, we may find this writing more or less attractive than the more individual writing of the Heian period. It represents another aspect of Japanese genius, and we should be grateful for both.

NOTES

1. Cosme de Torre, quoted in Cooper, *They Came to Japan*, p. 40.
2. Translated by W. T. de Bary in *Five Women who Loved Love*, p. 143.
3. *Ibid.*, p. 156.

Realism and Unreality in Japanese Drama

I think it unlikely that anyone attending the traditional Japanese theatre for the first time would be struck by its realism. Whatever variety he chose—the solemn, hieratical spectacle of Nō, the flamboyant brilliance of Kabuki, or the uncanny man-made life of the *jōruri* puppets—he would surely receive the impression of a theatre which had deliberately turned its back on literal expression. Western critics and theatrical producers who have praised the traditional Japanese theatre invariably contrast the drab realism of the contemporary Western theatre with the fantasy and excitement of a Japanese production. The never-interrupted flow of pictorial compositions on the Kabuki stage, the breathtaking power of the Kabuki actor when he crosses his eyes at the climax of a grotesque pose, the stylization in the use of body and voice in the Nō theatre have been singled out for special praise as examples of non-realism. For the Japanese playwrights, however, even as far back as the Nō dramas of the fourteenth century, realism was no less important than the stylization or fantasy which so captivates the Western visitor to the Japanese theatre. In the Kabuki theatre of the eighteenth century, especially, the balance between these two aspects of stage presentation was carefully considered in order to please audiences which insisted on verisimilitude, however achieved.

The term "realism" obviously admits of many interpretations. A typical definition is that found in Cassell's *Encyclopaedia of Literature:* "Realism in literature is an attitude which purports to depict life and to reproduce nature, in all its aspects, as faithfully as possible. It rejects the idealizing of reality in favour of beauty together with stylization in expression and the treatment of transcendental and supernatural subject-matter." To a Japanese dramatist of the eighteenth century the two statements of this definition would probably have seemed contradictory. His intention was certainly to depict life and reproduce nature, but he would have felt that idealization and stylization were essential to this end, and transcendental and supernatural subject-matter could by no means be excluded.

Kabuki, especially in the mid-nineteenth century, was a highly realistic art by almost any standards. The most popular dramatist, Kawatake Mokuami, wrote mainly about the denizens of the underworld, and

his vividly drawn swindlers, prositisutes and cutthroats expressed themselves in a racy colloquial filled with allusions to current happenings,
even when the play, for reasons of censorship, was ostensibly set in the
distant past. No European dramatist of the same period surpasses Mokuami in his ability to create, intermittently at least, the impression of a
seedy slice of life. Yet the total effect is very different from, say, an O'Neill
play set in the same milieu. Mokuami included with the realistic dialogue
poetic passages chanted and sung by a narrator, not a character in the play,
as well as scenes calling for the actors to add non-verbal delineations to
their parts, sometimes by striking poses intended to epitomize internal
conflicts. Such non-realistic elements were expected by Mokuami's
audiences; despite their pleasure in realistic dialogue and plots, they
demanded that an actor really act, which meant for them that the actor
must use non-realistic methods in projecting the internal qualities of the
character he is portraying. When plays acted with Western realism were
first presented to the Japanese public in the 1880's, the spectators, accustomed to Mokuami's methods, were bored by the static, unmod-
ulated performances. The two varieties of realism were mutually
unintelligible.

One obstacle to Western understanding of the place of realism in the
traditional Japanese theatre has been the equation, often made, between
the drama in Japan and the West. Because, for example, the great period
of the Nō plays corresponds roughly to that of the European miracle and
mystery plays, some scholars have made comparisons, attempting to find
parallel developments. One authority claimed that, as a result of the decline
of interest in religious themes, the Nō dramas, like the medieval plays of
England, "gave way before the demand for a play in the sense of play,
not playing at religion but real life." Perhaps this actually occurred in
England, but no simple shift from religion to real life took place in the
Japanese theatre. Real life is depicted in some of the earliest Nō plays as
well as in works of the fifteenth and sixteenth centuries. The jōruri (or
puppet theatre), on the other hand, from its inception in the seventeenth
century depended on religious themes, and never in its long history
freed itself completely from the supernatural.

The fourteenth-century Nō play The Priest Jinen by Kannami, to
cite one example, is far more realistic than the average Kabuki or jōruri
play of four centuries later. The plot involves a girl who has sold herself
to a white slaver in order to raise money to offer a mass for her dead
parents. The priest Jinen, discovering what has happened, follows the girl,
hoping to rescue her. He reaches the shore of Lake Biwa just as a boat,

with the girl and the two slavers aboard, is about to push off. The girl, tied and gagged, lies in the bottom of the boat. The two men at first abuse Jinen for his interference, but when he threatens them they finally agree to surrender the girl. They insist in return that Jinen perform the songs and dances with which the play concludes. The story of *The Priest Jinen* is simple but dramatically effective; despite the presence of a priest, there is little suggestion of the unreal or miraculous.

Kannami's son and successor Zeami (1363–1443) is celebrated for his plays embodying the mysterious, elusive beauty associated with the concept of *yūgen*. Needless to say, these plays bear not the remotest resemblance to the European mysteries, despite the similarity in period; far from being the primitive forerunners of more advanced types of drama, they include some of the supreme creations for the Japanese stage. Western appreciation of the Nō did not come easily. W. G. Aston, the author of the only history in English of Japanese literature, had a particularly poor opinion of the art. He wrote, "The Nō are not classical poems. They are too deficient in lucidity, method, coherence, and good taste to deserve this description . . . As dramas the Nō have little value. There is no action to speak of, and dramatic propriety and effect are hardly thought of." Lord Redesdale, going one step further, pronounced the Nō to be "wholly unintelligible."

We have happily left behind the ignorance of these nineteenth-century scholars, not only because of superior knowledge, but because twentieth-century theatre, for reasons of its own, has come to prefer ambiguity and a relative lack of plot to the carefully contrived, realistic dramas which for so long passed in Europe as the standard for all theatres. But if we think of the Nō plays as being modern (in any sense except that they appeal to people today) we shall be guilty of as great a misunderstanding as Aston and his generation. The symbolist or non-realistic aspects of Nō were not, as in twentieth-century drama, a reaction to excessive realism; no conflict between realism and non-realism was sensed. Zeami created not only poetic works about ghosts and the spirits of flowers, but also realistic dramas lacking any suggestion of the supernatural and possessing little symbolic intent. Recent scholarship, which has drastically reduced the estimated number of authentic works by Zeami from 129 to a mere twenty-one, has left in this number some works of uncompromising, even banal realism like *Shunnei*, a long, repetitive tale about two self-sacrificing brothers. The Nō dramatists of the period following Zeami often included more dramatic action in their plays, but this action might be either realistic or non-realistic, and did not indicate a preference for real life, as opposed to religion. Plays of the category called *genzaimono*, of a realistic nature, were among the plays most often presented, and were considered an important element in the programs performed on a single day.

With the emergence at the end of the sixteenth century of Kabuki and *jōruri*, dramatic entertainments catering to a mass audience, rather than to the small, aristocratic audience that normally witnessed Nō, the Nō dramas tended increasingly to become ceremonial performances not requiring dramatic conviction or action. Sixteenth-century records indicate that it took less than half the time to perform a given Nō play than it does today, a clear indication of how markedly the stately, solemn character came to be emphasized in later times. Zeami, in the fifteenth century, seems to have had realistic performances in mind, even of his ghostly plays. He devoted great attention to the importance of training actors in the three principal roles—the woman, the warrior and the old man. It was not enough for an actor to suggest these characters by beautiful, stylized gestures; he had to represent them convincingly. Such was the meaning of Zeami's word *monomane*, or "imitation of things." The Nō masks, so greatly admired by Yeats as artistic substitutes for the commonplace reality of an actor's face, may actually have been intended to promote realism, rather than stylized beauty. Obviously the mask of a young woman would make an actor more believable in that part than if he played with unadorned face. Zeami stated in his writings that when an actor took the part of a man of his own age, he need not wear a mask; in other words, if the audience could believe that the actor was the person he was portraying, there was no need to improve his face with art. The actors, it is true, always wore masks when taking the part of ghosts, but this may have been because people in the fifteenth century had very definite ideas of what ghosts looked like.

It is not my intention to insist on the paradox that Nō was a realistic theatre. Clearly it was not; compared to other stage entertainments, whether in Japan or the West, Nō was unusually stylized and poetic. I should like, however, to underline the fact that realism and stylization were both present in Nō, as in all later types of Japanese theatre. Zeami wrote plays of both varieties—symbolic and realistic—not because of any change over the years in his outlook, nor because of changing demands on the part of his audience, but because both aspects of his art seemed essential. In a famous passage Zeami described how an actor should perform a demon's dance; even while the actor's feet are pounding the stage in frenzied, realistic movements, the upper part of his body should remain calm. This combination of violence and tranquillity, like the combination of realism and stylization, was to mark Kabuki and *jōruri* throughout their history. An emphasis on one usually was accompanied by an almost equal emphasis on its opposite, rather than any diminution. The harmony of these opposites lies close to the genius of the Japanese theatre.

Contrary again to the impression created by parallels with medieval European drama, Nō did not disappear with the rise of newer, more popular stage entertainments. It is true that relatively few new plays were written for the Nō theatre during the Tokugawa period (1600–1868), but it was actively supported by the shogunate and the daimyos. Like opera today in the West, it survived on a repertory which had almost ceased to grow. The history of Nō during this period would have been quite otherwise if Kabuki and *jōruri* had not made their appearance. Certain curious, even revolutionary developments had occurred in Nō in the middle of the sixteenth century. Letters from Catholic missionaries dating from the 1560's describe Japanese plays treating Biblical subjects— Adam and Eve, Noah's Ark, the Judgment of Solomon, the Birth of Christ, the Last Judgment, etc.—apparently in the form of Nō, the roles being assigned to *shite* (protagonist), *waki* (deuteragonist), *tsure* (companions) and chorus, in the usual manner. Unfortunately, none of the texts has survived, but the stories themselves are so unlike the normal plots of Nō plays that we must suppose that the conventions were strained if not entirely altered.

Another variety of newly written Nō plays was presented in 1594 during a performance staged by command of Toyotomi Hideyoshi at Osaka Castle. One play described Hideyoshi's visit in the previous year to see the cherry blossoms at Yoshino; another was devoted to his subsequent visit to Mount Kōya. In both plays the *shite* was none other than Hideyoshi himself. Zeami's plays were invariably set in the past of a century or more before, possibly to avoid any contamination from excessive this-worldliness, but these new Nō plays treated realistically events of the preceding year. Once the traditional materials and treatment had been enriched by foreign and contemporary stories, it should have been an easy step to develop an entirely new variety of Nō, recognizable as belonging to the Nō traditions, but possessing broader expressive possibilities and appeal. This never happened, probably because the establishment of the Tokugawa shogunate, a far more conservative and inflexible government than Hideyoshi's, caused the Nō to freeze into a kind of ritual drama without possibility of free development.

The Tokugawa shogunate had for its guiding philosophy the orthodox neo-Confucian teachings introduced to Japan in the sixteenth century. The court philosophers were for the most part men of narrow and unaccommodating views. For them all literature was suspect; the composition of poetry in Chinese, more as an exercise in classical Chinese composition than as an expression of feelings, represented the only grudging concession to what they considered to be a frivolous waste of time. They did not especially approve of Nō—on occasion they rebuked samurai who displayed an excessive interest in the art—but they came tacitly to recognize Nō as the official "music" of the shogunate. Since ancient times rites and music had been considered an essential part of good Confucian government, and Nō, originally patronized by the Muromachi shogunate, was the logical choice for the state music. The elevation of Nō to official ceremonial was to preserve it almost unaltered for 250 years, but by the same token Nō narrowly escaped destruction after 1868, when the shogunate, to which it had been so closely attached, was overthrown.

During the Tokugawa period occasional public performances of Nō were permitted, especially the "subscription Nō," benefit performances for an actor before his retirement. The rise of Kabuki and *jōruri*, however, deprived Nō of its popularity with the common people, and the development into a theatre of general appeal, seemingly foreshadowed by the Christian and contemporary works of the sixteenth century, never materialized. Nō was, however, to exert considerable influence on Kabuki, especially in the eighteenth and nineteenth centuries.

The earliest performances known as *kabuki* apparently took place in Kyoto in 1603, when a priestess from the Izumo Shrine named Okuni led a troupe of dancers in a variety program. Similar performances under other names had existed for many years previous. Our knowledge of the long process leading up to the early Kabuki has greatly increased in recent years, thanks especially to folkloristic studies. Scholars have discovered in remote villages survivals of almost every element traceable in Kabuki. The dances and songs were ultimately of religious origins, not usually the formal Shinto or Buddhist worship, but the popular observances of the late middle ages. Often these origins are now completely forgotten. To cite a single instance: Kabuki plays are today performed at what is considered to be the appropriate season of year for them. If one asks a Japanese friend why, for example, ghost plays are invariably performed in summer, he will probably reply that the audience wishes in summer to be agreeably chilled by the frightening spectacle—in other words, that ghost plays are a form of primitive air-conditioning. Folklorists, however, have established that Japanese ghosts were traditionally believed to walk abroad in summer, and ghost plays are therefore performed in that season. Innumerable other elements in Kabuki reveal traces of all but forgotten beliefs.

The puppet theatre came into prominence at almost the identical time as Kabuki. The first recorded performances took place about 1610, but the characteristic combination of a narration, acted by puppets and accompanied by the music of the samisen, apparently is some decades older. The puppets may be traced back to those used in performances at temples and shrines during the eleventh century, and the recitation of a dramatic tale to musical accompaniment was a familiar practice in medieval Japan. The puppet theatre, like Kabuki, was born in the capital, but it remained a popular, rather than aristocratic theatre. Kabuki and *jōruri* were rivals throughout the Tokugawa period for public favor. Until about 1683 Kabuki was the stronger, but *jōruri* then, for almost a century, became the more vital theatre, only to be replaced once more by Kabuki. Though both theatres eventually developed repertoires of almost the same plays, the two theatres are basically dissimilar; Kabuki is above all a theatre of virtuoso actors, but *jōruri* is a spoken and acted literary form.

The early history of Kabuki, from Okuni's day to the middle of the seventeenth century, suggested little of the magnificence which the art was to attain. Okuni herself performed in a reasonably dignified manner and was even invited to entertain at court, but her successors turned Kabuki into a kind of singing commercial, the products offered being the actresses themselves. The government finally stepped in, banning women from the Kabuki stage in 1629. It should not be supposed that prudery swayed the government in making this decision. The Confucian philosophers, needless to say, disapproved of Kabuki, but it was literally beneath their contempt, and it never occurred to them to suggest improvements. For them the theatre scarcely differed from brothels; Kabuki theatres, indeed, were closely associated with the licensed quarters throughout the Tokugawa period and, if anything, actors ranked below prostitutes in the social scale. However, the Confucian philosophers recognized that these disgraceful appurtenances of society had their uses.

The government authorized the establishment of licensed quarters and with them the theatres. But if the government tolerated such un-Confucian amusements, it would not countenance disorder. The immediate occasion for the prohibition of women's Kabuki in Kyoto (in 1629), for example, was a quarrel which broke out at the theatre, resulting in many deaths and injuries. When women could no longer appear on any

Japanese stage, their place was taken by handsome young men called *wakashū*. Command performances of *wakashū* Kabuki were given before the shogun Iemitsu in 1651, an indication of the popularity it had attained, but in the following year *wakashū* Kabuki in turn was prohibited, apparently because of quarrels among samurai over the favors of the young actors. In 1656 an argument between an actor and a customer in a box led to the closing for thirteen years of all theatres in Koyto. The chief artistic result of the government's concern over the maintenance of public order in the theatres was that from 1653 on all parts in Kabuki were taken by grown men, whose heads were shaven to diminish their physical charms. This more or less accidental development was to prove the most important shaping factor of Kabuki as an art, for with the disappearance of seductive women or young men from the stage, Kabuki was forced to turn to drama in order to attract audiences. The *onnagata*, or actor who plays female roles, a necessary product of the banning of women from the stage, contributed more than any other factor to the characteristic combination of real and unreal in Kabuki.

The government, as part of its watchfulness over possible causes of unrest, exercised censorship over the stage throughout the Tokugawa period. Events possessing even the faintest political implications could not be represented on the stage unless, following a practice known also in the West since Juvenal's day, they were transposed to some bygone era and thereby rendered innocuous. The authorities did not, however, object to the depiction of purely emotional matters. Recent love suicides, for example, were frequently treated on the stage until it seemed that these plays were promoting a dangerous craze; at this point the government intervened. Kabuki thus, both by heritage from Okuni's dances and because of restrictions on other themes, acquired a strong erotic flavor. The ability of actors, even late in life, to suggest the seductive beauty of a young girl accounted for the success of many plays; not surprisingly, the arts of theatrical costuming and makeup developed to a degree unknown in less stylized theatres. Much of what seems most typical of Kabuki today results from efforts to make *onnagata* believable—more realistic, if one will—in their roles.

During the first half of the seventeenth century—roughly, until the appearance of the *onnagata*, the puppet theatre, though less popular, was a more serious form of drama than Kabuki. The seriousness was, however, only relative: judged either by the standards of Nō or of the later *jōruri*, the plays were exceedingly primitive. The plots were usually Buddhistic or fantastic in nature, relying heavily for effect on the capacity of puppets to leap through the air and perform other feats impossible for actors. The puppets were operated from underneath, each by one man who held the puppet over his head and manipulated it with internal armatures. Both the operator and the chanter (who recited the lines for the puppets) were concealed from the audience by screens; it was attempted, as in our marionette theatre, to produce the illusion that the puppets were moving and speaking of their own accord, without human aid. The operators were able to achieve realistic effects, as we know from contemporary accounts. A 1647 visitor to the puppet theatre recorded in his diary, "They seemed to be alive!" Such realism, combined with the fundamental unrealism of wooden puppets, achieved the typical Japanese blend of opposites.

In time, as the plots grew more realistic, the chanters took their places at the side of the stage in full public view, thereby destroying the illusion that the puppets themselves were speaking, but preserving the balance between real and unreal. In 1703, when *Love Suicides at Sonezaki*, an unprecedentedly realistic play, was presented, the screen hiding the puppet operators was replaced by a gauzy material which permitted the spectators to watch the men moving the puppets. Soon afterwards the screens were removed altogether, and the operators have performed ever since in full view of the audience. No explanation has ever been offered as to why the chanters and operators were brought before the audience at this time, except to suggest that the public preferred this innovation. I wonder if the reason was not that the increased realism in the plots of the plays required a compensating unreality in the presentation.

It is sometimes difficult, however, to determine whether a given innovation was intended to promote or reduce realism. The adoption of the three-man puppet in 1734 was probably conceived of as a further advance in the direction of realism. Three men operating a single puppet made it possible, for example, to simulate agitated breathing, to move the fingers and even the eyebrows freely, and to achieve a fluidity of gesture beyond the capacities of a one-man puppet or marionette. But the three-man puppet entailed the conspicuous presence of operators hovering over the peculiarly proportioned wooden figures. No one who has not actually witnessed a performance of *jōruri* can imagine from photographs that it would be possible to forget the three operators, especially the chief operator, watching impassively in his formal costume the gestures of the puppets. Yet the audience is carried from the world of human beings— the operators—to the world of the puppets, and if occasionally its eyes return to the faces of the operators, it is for the additional pleasure of seeing these men, at once masters and slaves of the puppets. This shift from world to world enhances the *jōruri;* one is tempted even to measure its artistic importance in terms of the degrees of unreality it can make the audience accept in the interest of a greater reality.

Kabuki, being a theatre of actors rather than puppets, was from the start more realistic than *jōruri*, but the plots and stage techniques were highly artificial, and the appearance of male actors in the female roles especially produced an unreal effect. The presence of the *onnagata*, at first considered a handicap, came in time to be central to Kabuki. Audiences continued to admire men, even sixty or seventy years old, in the parts of young women. One still hears today of famous *onnagata* who are ravishingly beautiful in the roles of twenty-year-old girls. Photographs do not always confirm such impressions; they negatively suggest instead that the magic of an actor's stage presence is enough to create an illusion of youthful feminine beauty. At this point we reach the paradox, frequently expressed, that a skilful imitator of women actually comes closer to the feminine ideal than a real woman. Yoshizawa Ayame (1653–1729), a celebrated *onnagata*, is reputed to have said, "If an actress were to appear on the stage she could not express ideal feminine beauty, for she would rely only on the exploitation of her physical characteristics, and therefore not express the synthetic ideal. The ideal woman can be expressed only by an actor." In other words, an actress might, in a strict sense, be more realistic than a man in female parts, but she could not communicate the essential qualities of womanhood as skilfully as a man who has studied from childhood precisely how a woman behaves. When a great *onnagata* performs, he displays an almost eerie awareness of each gesture; nothing is accidental.

Within this larger paradox we find yet another paradox. Assuming that it were necessary for actors to create convincing representations of women, it would seem logical that the persons who train the company select effeminate, or at any rate feminine-looking young men as the future *onnagata*, and then give them instruction in falsetto voice production and other elements necessary in achieving realistic portrayals of women. Careful training should make it possible to produce actors virtually indistinguishable from real women in their parts; female impersonators in the West and the actors of female parts in the Chinese opera certainly attain this proficiency. But, as anyone who has seen a Kabuki performance knows, the great *onnagata* are not likely to be mistaken for real women. The two finest *onnagata* of today are not only extraordinarily ugly as women, but their voices bring to mind less the languishing maidens the actors are depicting than the raucous cries of peacocks. Only an inferior *onnagata* would attempt to convince the audience that he is actually a woman. The ideal of the *onnagata* being an abstraction of womanhood, rather than any particular woman, the superior *onnagata* quite naturally follows the acting traditions of *onnagata* of the past, rather than imitates the behavior of women he might observe. This rejection of reality in favor of an unearthly, stylized beauty can dazzle audiences into believing that an old man with a heavily powdered face is a miracle of feminine loveliness.

The great *onnagata* of the past presumably followed the same practices, but stylization, the main artistic *raison d'être* of the *onnagata*, seems seldom to have been consciously considered. If we judge their performances by surviving descriptions, the *onnagata* of the Tokugawa period attempted to resemble women as closely as possible. Yoshizawa Ayame wrote, "An *onnagata* should act like an *onnagata* even in the dressing-room. When he eats his meals he should turn away from other people." Or, "Unless an actor lives like a woman even in daily life, he will probably never be considered a successful *onnagata*." It was the custom until recently for *onnagata* to wear women's clothes even away from the theatre, and an *onnagata*, if walking together with his stage "husband," would follow one step behind, like a dutiful wife. If he had a real wife and children of his own, he never mentioned them publicly. In the early nineteenth century an *onnagata* was arrested for attempting to bathe in the women's section of a public bathhouse. Yet, despite such extreme measures, undertaken in order to make the portrayal of women completely realistic, the art of the *onnagata* lay elsewhere.

The habitual wearing of women's clothes made it possible for an *onnagata* to act un-selfconsciously when he wore them onstage, and this was important: Yoshizawa Ayame stated that the instant when an *onnagata* became aware in his performance that he was making a typically feminine gesture, he ceased to be a woman and reverted to being a man. Daily habit thus made such externals as the proper way of wearing a woman's kimono an automatic part of an actor's performance, but when it came to representing women's actions in moments of great emotional intensity, the *onnagata* had few models in real life and had to turn to the art of his predecessors. In the Tokugawa period, at least according to surviving evidence, women rarely gave vent to their emotions. Chikamatsu stated, "In recent plays the female characters often say things which real women could not say. Such utterances fall under the heading of art: only because the characters say what could never come from a real woman's lips are their true emotions disclosed. If in such instances the author

were to make his characters conform to the ways of real women and keep
their feelings hidden, such realism, far from being admired, would destroy
the interest of the work." In order to reach the emotional depths which
a woman might actually be experiencing beneath the calm surface, the
playwright had to depart from the literal truth. Similarly, the Kabuki
actors, though trained with infinite care to play the parts of women
authoritatively, in critical moments acted with stylization as *onnagata* and
not as real women.

Chikamatsu's remarks referred specifically to the *jōruri*, but parallel
views may be found in Kabuki criticism. When someone asked Yoshizawa Ayame's advice on performing techniques, he replied, "Kabuki is
not merely a matter of reason. A performance which is half truth and half
kabuki is probably best." Chikamatsu himself gave the most famous
definition of the part of realism in the Japanese theatre. "Someone told me,
'Audiences nowadays will not accept plays unless they are realistic and well
reasoned out. The old plots are full of things which people will no longer
tolerate. That is why Kabuki actors are considered skilful to the degree
that their acting resembles reality. The first consideration is to have the
retainer in the play resemble a real retainer, and to have the daimyo look
like a real daimyo. People will not stand for the childish nonsense they
took in the past.' I answered, 'What you say seems plausible, but your
theory does not take into account the true methods of art. Art is something
which lies in the slender margin between the real and the unreal. Of
course it seems desirable, in view of the current taste for realism, to
have the retainer in the play copy the gestures and speech of a real retainer,
but should a real retainer rouge and powder his face like an actor? Or,
would the audiences like it if an actor, on the grounds that real retainers
pay no attention to their faces, were to perform on the stage unshaven
or with a bald head? The theatre is unreal, and yet not unreal, real and yet
not real. Entertainment lies between the two.' "

This statement deserves its fame as the classic expression of the artistic
aims of the Japanese theatre, the puppet theatre especially. In practice,
however, Chikamatsu was not always equal to his own prescription.
The history plays (*jidaimono*) which make up the bulk of his works are
filled with the wildest, most improbable nonsense. Chikamatsu stated his
view of the place of unreality in the theatre: "If, when one paints an image
or carves it of wood there are, in the name of artistic license, some stylized
parts in a work otherwise resembling the real form, this is, after all, what
people love in art. The same is true of literary composition. While bearing resemblance to the original, it should have stylization. This makes it

art and delights men's minds." But battles triumphantly waged by a single unarmed man against a whole army, paintings that come to life and leap at critical moments from the wall, and heroes who soar over the treetops when cornered by their foes cannot be explained merely in terms of stylization, nor does enough reality accompany this unreality to bring it safely within the slender margin of credibility.

Despite his clearly expressed views, Chikamatsu in his history plays often seemed less interested in achieving a delicate balance between the real and unreal than in exploiting the basic unreality of the puppets in order to create effects impossible in a more realistic theatre. The first act of *The Battles of Coxinga*, for example, contains at least two scenes which would be unendurable if presented realistically on any stage except that of the puppet theatre. In the first, the villainous Ri Tōten gouges out his eye and offers it on a ceremonial baton to the Tartars as a mark of fealty; in the second, Go Sankei performs a Caesarian operation on the dead empress, and safely delivers her child. Such overpoweringly dramatic scenes would, of course, be inconceivable in Nō. If presented in Kabuki it would be necessary to mitigate the brutal reality by painting the villain's face with grotesque makeup, and by having him perform his actions with elaborate, highly stylized gestures. Horror scenes in Kabuki tend to be funny; wild mayhem, with arms and legs lopped off in a lively ballet, generally makes the audience roar delightedly. Japanese commentators have noted that villains in Kabuki are more bearable than those in *jōruri* because their disagreeable qualities are tempered by artificiality and puppet-like behavior. The behavior of *jōruri* villains, however, is no more puppet-like than that of the heroes, and the most horrible actions appear just as realistic as the most innocent ones. The *jōruri* audience is thus shocked rather than amused when Ri Tōten gouges out his eye, but at the moment that this experience threatens to become painful, the basic unreality of the puppets reassures the spectators. A realistic portrayal by actors would lack this reassuring unreality and would probably suggest Grand Guignol rather than tragedy. Chikamatsu in his history plays emphasized unreality, apparently in order to please audiences seeking a kind of excitement not found in Kabuki.

Chikamatsu's domestic tragedies (*sewamono*) more closely approached his expressed ideals, and their literary quality played an important part in the rivalry between *jōruri* and Kabuki. The two theatres had, until Chikamatsu's day, remained distinct. Chikamatsu himself had written Kabuki plays early in his career, but eventually decided to devote himself entirely to *jōruri*. One reason often given by Japanese scholars for this decision was

Chikamatsu's dissatisfaction with the liberties actors took with his texts. Kabuki plays were normally no more than vehicles intended to permit the actors to display their virtuoso talents, and had little or no literary merit. An author, having a particular actor in mind, might establish a scene but not write any dialogue, leaving the actor free to improvise. It is easy to understand why Chikamatsu, who prided himself on his texts, should have been irritated by the cavalier treatment frequently accorded by actors to his carefully composed dialogue. Shifting from Kabuki to *jōruri* involved more for Chikamatsu, however, than finding another set of performers for his plays. Unlike a Kabuki play, which might consist entirely of dialogue (like a European play), a work for the *jōruri* theatre had to make allowances for the limited expressive power of the puppets. Not only was it necessary to introduce the action by long descriptive passages, but the speeches were usually followed by such phrases as, "thus he spoke in anger," as if to clarify the puppet's mood. Unlike Kabuki again, nothing was left to improvisation. The texts became of paramount importance; even today, before a chanter begins a performance he reverently lifts the text to his forehead.

One man normally narrated for all the puppets in a given scene. The *jōruri* texts by Chikamatsu were therefore not divided into parts; the chanter indicated who was supposed to be speaking by varying his voice, depending on whether he took the part of a man, woman or child. Dramatic declamation rose into melody in passages of description in which a narrator set the scene verbally for the puppets. The vagueness as to speaker (or lack of speaker) was no obstacle in the puppet theatre, though it would create problems in a more realistic theatre.

Writing for the puppets, though more agreeable in some respects, presented difficulties for Chikamatsu. The use of one, unchanging puppet head through the entire performance meant that the personages must also remain the same; developments in character could not be revealed in the puppet's face. A few plays by Chikamatsu apparently failed because he attempted to depict complex, ambiguous characters, possible in a theatre of actors but not in one of puppets, where types and not individuals can best be represented. On the whole, however, Chikamatsu demonstrated a mastery of the requirements of the puppet theatre. The difficult style of his poetic passages may not have been fully intelligible to his audiences, but their literary brilliance gave the chanter opportunities to intoxicate the audience with streams of beautiful phrases. Though Kabuki had at first shown little interest in literary texts, the actors eventually humbled themselves before Chikamatsu's greatness when, early in the eighteenth century, it became apparent that the superiority of his plays had caused the *jōruri* to outstrip Kabuki in public favor.

With Chikamatsu the popular theatre acquired for the first time a recognized author after decades of hacks who had contented themselves with turning out vehicles for the Kabuki actors. Chikamatsu's plays seldom reach the poetic summits of the finest Nō dramas, but such scenes as the last journey of the suicidally intent lovers have remarkable beauty. We can easily imagine why Chikamatsu's audiences, composed mainly of poorly educated townsmen, should have delighted in the spectacle of his history plays, with their rapid alternations of fantasy and down-to-earth realism. These plays, abounding in bombastic declamation and opportunities for prolonged sobbing or hysterical laughter, also displayed to best advantage the virtuoso talents of the chanters. Yet, another paradox of the Japanese theatre, the audiences responded with almost equal enthusiasm to Chikamatsu's domestic tragedies, though they are almost static in performance and afford the chanters few occasions for histrionics. The Osaka townsmen enjoyed seeing on the puppet stage not only the ranting, leaping heroes, but ordinary merchants like themselves, torn between the conflicting claims of love and family obligations.

Most of Chikamatsu's domestic tragedies were based on actual events known to the spectators. The dialogue is generally realistic, and the sense of actuality is heightened by mention of well-known places and people. Little seems to be left of the unreality which had been the hallmark of Kabuki and the early *jōruri*, but the domestic tragedies contain Chikamatsu's most poetic writing, which transmutes the sordid details of the scandal sheets into literature. The merchants and prostitutes who actually committed suicide were assuredly not surrounded by the magical atmosphere in which Chikamatsu envelopes his characters, but by revealing to us with his poetry the hidden nobility of his humble figures, he lifted their excessively realistic tales into the slender margin between the real and the unreal.

An intense rivalry existed between *jōruri* and Kabuki in Chikamatsu's day. He described the difficulties which the puppet theatre had to overcome: "*Jōruri* differs from other forms of writing in that (since it is composed especially for puppets) the words must all be living and full of action. *Jōruri* is performed in theatres which operate in close competition with those of Kabuki, which is the art of living actors, and the author must therefore be at particular pains to impart a variety of emotions to lifeless wooden puppets, and attempt in this way to capture the interest of the audience." Unless the audience could suspend its initial disbelief in the activities of wooden creatures, it would prefer the immediate impact of Kabuki actors. At the time the Edo Kabuki, inspired by the first Danjūrō (1660–1704), was famous for its *aragoto*, or "rough business," a style of performance which emphasized the strength and ferocity of the actors. The Osaka Kabuki preferred works of a more romantic nature. But audiences began to tire of both varieties and turned instead to the puppet theatre. In 1715 a new era opened in the relations between Kabuki and *jōruri* with the production of Chikamatsu's immensely successful *The Battles of Coxinga;* so great was the popularity of the play that it was adapted in 1716 for the Kabuki stage in Kyoto and in the following year for both Osaka and Edo Kabuki theatres. This marked the first time that a work embodying the superior literary qualities of *jōruri* was pe ɔrmed by Kabuki actors. In Edo the second Danjūrō (1688–1758), a master of the powerful *aragoto* style, was so impressed by Chikamatsu's plays that he gladly performed in 1719 and 1720 as the weakling hero in *Love Suicide at Sonezaki* and *Love Suicides at Amijima.* The borrowing of *jōruri* plays for the Kabuki stage became a regular practice from this time on. Most of the present mainstays of the Kabuki theatre—*Chūshingura, Moritsuna's Camp, Kumagai's Camp,* etc.—were written for puppets and may be distinguished even today from plays of Kabuki origins by the presence of a chanter at one side of the stage, who sings the descriptive passages that are actually unnecessary in a theatre of actors.

Kabuki actors, when performing plays originally written for *jōruri,* sometimes imitate the jerky movements of puppets in order to associate their manner of acting with the older tradition. Unless the spectator realizes that such is the actor's intent, he will be disconcerted when, for example, during the climactic recitation in *Kumagai's Camp* the actor suddenly begins to gesture and declaim in a startlingly unrealistic manner, suggesting a man of wood rather than of flesh. This extreme example of the celebrated Kabuki stylization indicates the manner in which Kabuki enriches itself by adopting not only the *jōruri* texts but the special atmosphere of unreality surrounding the not-quite-human movements of the puppets. It might be supposed that when Kabuki actors originally performed a work like *Love Suicides at Sonezaki* they would have chosen to emphasize the warmth and tenderness that actors can communicate, in contrast to the stiff, formalized movements of the puppets, but the actors were well aware that the text would not bear overly realistic treatment. Stripped of its poetic, unreal atmosphere, *Love Suicides at Sonezaki* is little more than an anecdote. A clerk working for a merchant of soy sauce is tricked out of his money by an unscrupulous friend. Faced with losing his sweetheart, a prostitute, to some customer with more money, the clerk commits suicide with the girl. The characters possess little depth, and there is only one moment of genuine dramatic intensity, when Tokubei, the clerk, hiding under the porch, takes his sweetheart's foot and passes it across his throat as a sign that he wishes to commit suicide. The first act consists largely of a long, virtually stationary monologue; the last act is a ballet-like sequence with little dialogue or incident until the last few moments. *Love Suicides at Sonezaki* could not hold an audience's attention if performed realistically, but Chikamatsu never intended a realistic presentation. The long monologue of the first act is given variety by the contrasting styles of musical accompaniment, and punctuated by the stark, stylized gestures of the puppets. The lovers' journey (*michiyuki*) of the last act is a texture of declamation, recitative and song, which not only creates an atmosphere of pathos, but lends the characters, a sales clerk and a prostitute, the dignity they need if their deaths are to be tragic and not merely painful. A realistic presentation would be unthinkable. The Kabuki actors, aware of this, were—and still are—at pains to preserve the special atmosphere of the puppet theatre, though it means sacrificing their advantage in portraying Chikamatsu's realistic characters.

Jōruri maintained its popularity well into the eighteenth century, even after Chikamatsu's death in 1725, thanks to a series of gifted playwrights. New techniques in puppetry also helped to maintain public favor. But Kabuki, displaced from its position of pre-eminence by Chikamatsu, began to reassert its old supremacy. The new Kabuki plays of the eighteenth century were mainly dances like *Dōjōji*, derived from the Nō play of the same name, but the staples of the repertory were the Kabuki adaptations of *jōruri* successes. The renewed popularity of Kabuki caused the *jōruri* artists in self-defense to imitate Kabuki techniques, though influences had previously gone the other way. Bold dramatic effects and colorful scenes were prized more, even in *jōruri*, than the restrained action of the domestic tragedies. The *hanamichi* (the passageway from the back of the theatre through the audience to the stage), a characteristic feature of the Kabuki theatre, came to be used in *jōruri* too, though it was hardly flattering to the puppets, which require some distance between themselves and the audience. *Jōruri* resorted increasingly to *karakuri*, or stage machinery, in the attempt to outdo Kabuki in spectacular effects, but the more determinedly *jōruri* emulated Kabuki, the more it weakened its own appeal.

The general shift of Japanese culture from the Kansai (Kyoto-Osaka) region to Edo during the late eighteenth century also adversely affected

jōruri, turning it into a provincial entertainment. The important dramatists of the nineteenth century all wrote for Kabuki, not *jōruri*. In the last
fifty years *jōruri* has gradually lost its popularity even in Osaka, and is
today preserved as highly subsidized, little-patronized regional art.
Kabuki itself is in danger of suffering the same fate before long, though at
present it attracts many tourists who visit Tokyo from the Japanese
hinterland or abroad.

The failure of Kabuki and *jōruri* to attract new audiences may be
attributed to many causes. Chief of them, probably, is the popularity
of such mass entertainments as the films and television. The steady loss
of proficiency in the classical language on the part of successive generations of Japanese students has also made the old plays harder to understand.
Increased costs of admission have kept away many working-class people
who formerly supported the Kabuki. But even if none of these causes
existed, Kabuki and *jōruri* might still have lost their popularity because
their excessive fidelity to a vanished age has made them dated in the eyes
of contemporary audiences. The domestic plays belonged to a particular
age and society; with the enormous changes in Japanese life during the
past half-century, it has become increasingly hard for Japanese to sympathize with the problems presented in these plays. The morality of the
Tokugawa theatre is today often stigmatized as "feudal," and the Confucian ideals which inspired Chikamatsu and his successors have lost their
unquestioned authority.

The domestic tragedies of Chikamatsu provide us with probably
our best picture of Tokugawa life. They depict Japan in the Genroku
era far more realistically than Shakespeare's plays depict England in
Elizabethan times. They describe not only the emotional conflicts of
the characters but their economic and social circumstances, often in
surprising detail. Taken as a whole, they are truly a mirror of their time,
despite Chikamatsu's occasional falsification in the name of art. But their
very accuracy has brought them unpopularity today. They so faithfully
describe their time that we are repeatedly made aware of the alien nature
of the unspoken assumptions. If we do not feel that suicide is a man's
most obvious course when he is confronted with a difficult problem, or
that a husband is obliged to slash down a wife who has unintentionally
committed adultery, we may be repelled by many actions in Chikamatsu's
plays. Or, if we do not assume that appearances are no less important than
reality, we may be exasperated rather than moved by the final scene of
Love Suicides at Amijima, where the suicidal lovers seem more concerned
about what people will think when their bodies are discovered than about

the consequences of their act. Chikamatsu recognized the necessity of tempering with stylization the dialogue and actions of his characters in the interests of achieving greater realism, as he conceived it, but he does not appear to have considered a stylization in the details of the domestic tragedies which might have permitted them to survive intact even after the events that inspired them had been forgotten. The world of the Nō is surely much remoter than that of the *jōruri*, but it figures so slightly in the plays that it does not interfere with the spectator's enjoyment. If Chikamatsu's plays had been less realistic in their detailed depiction of their time they might have been better able to stand separation from it. As it was, his plays had to be revised constantly in later years in order to render them acceptable to audiences with a different outlook.

After the Meiji Restoration of 1868 reformers attempted to improve Kabuki and *jōruri* by making them more accurate and realistic. The necessary balance between unreal and real seems to have been forgotten: fantasy was curbed; the makeup of actors became more naturalistic; real names for historical figures were substituted for the pseudonyms employed by dramatists to avoid the Tokugawa censorship; and literal accuracy took precedence over purely artistic considerations. When Kikugorō V staged the dance-play *Modori Bridge*, he sent a man to Kyoto to determine the exact number of boards in the actual bridge. The passion of this age of enlightenment for realism was so great that it was even proposed that actresses replace *onnagata* in the female parts. Soon, however, it became apparent that all these desperate stabs at realism brought the audiences no closer to reality. Indeed, fussy attention to such small details as authentic period hair-styling exposed the artificiality of the stories more than a stylized presentation, just as extreme precision in one corner of an otherwise impressionistic painting would create a jarring disharmony.

The great plays of the Japanese theatre have always combined realism and unreality in intimate conjunction. It may be that the Japanese have permanently lost their taste for this unique variety of theatre; certainly their films, for all their excellence, show few of the old traditions. I think it more likely, however, that the combination of the seeming opposites which has proved so congenial to Japanese audiences over the centuries will again exert its appeal, and add to the generous contribution Japan has already made to the theatre of the world.

II. THE WORLD OF HAIKAI POETRY

Matsunaga Teitoku
and the Beginning of *Haikai* Poetry

IT WOULD be impossible to write a history of *haikai*[1] poetry without mention of Matsunaga Teitoku (1571–1653).[2] Most accounts, however, content themselves with a brief description of Teitoku and his school, and with a few generalizations about their contributions to the art that would be perfected by the great Bashō. Little is said about Teitoku's own poetry or prose, and it is seldom quoted. Of the thousands of verses he wrote in his lifetime, hardly a dozen are included in the standard collections.[3] His treatment in Western-language books has been equally unkind. A typical judgment is the inaccurate appraisal found in *Haiku and Haikai*: "At the beginning of the Edo period Matsunaga Teitoku attempted to classicize *haikai* and return to *renga*, but only achieved an unsatisfactory compromise."[4]

It is unquestionably as a historical figure that Teitoku merits our study today, when his writings have largely lost their appeal. Few people now can appreciate *haikai* poetry that is so dependent on poetic conceits and plays on words, and that provides us with so few flashes of insight or emotion. Teitoku was famed also in his day for his *waka* (the classic verse form in thirty-one syllables) and his *renga* (linked-verse), but they are depressingly bland and lacking in character. His prose writings, with the exception of the autobiographical *Taionki* ("A Record of Favors Received"), can give little pleasure. But Teitoku for half a century was the leading literary figure in Japan, and he commands attention not only because of developments in poetry he initiated but because he was the pivotal figure of the Japanese literary world during an extraordinary era.

Teitoku was born in the age of Oda Nobunaga. He served while a young man as a scribe to Toyotomi Hideyoshi,[5] studied with nobles of the emperor's court and with daimyos, and was the intimate friend of Hayashi Razan, the Confucian adviser to Tokugawa Ieyasu. He knew Christian converts,[6] had one brother who was exiled for violent Nichiren

Buddhism, and another who engaged in trade with the Portuguese and died in the "South Seas."[7] He himself rose to be the first important man of letters of the Tokugawa era. Though a conservative, he became the acclaimed leader of the newest and most controversial movements in poetry; though he bitterly regretted his birth did not permit him to share fully in the court traditions he passionately admired, he devoted himself to the education of classes lower than his own, and has been acclaimed in our day as a *philosophe*, a man of the Enlightenment.[8]

Little in Teitoku's background presaged a career as a *philosophe*. He was born in Kyoto, the second son of Matsunaga Eishu (1538?–1600?), a professional *renga* poet.[9] Teitoku's family was distinguished. His paternal grandfather, the daimyo of Takatsuki (an important castle town between Kyoto and Osaka), had a family that could be traced back to the twelfth century, when his ancestors fought on the side of Minamoto Yoritomo. His paternal grandmother came from a branch of the Fujiwara family that claimed descent from the great poet Teika, but had thrown in its lot with the military aristocracy. In 1541, when Eishu was only three, his father was killed in battle, and two years later his mother also died. The boy was sent at six to Tōfuku-ji, a centre of Zen studies in Kyoto, and received his education from the monks. Eishu was, however, converted to Nichiren Buddhism, and his children were brought up in this militant faith. Eishu returned to the laity before he was twenty, and applied himself to the study of *renga*. Soon he was making his living as a teacher and "corrector" of poetry. His excellent education and his family connections enabled him to associate on familiar terms with the important poets of the day, including the daimyo Hosokawa Yūsai (1534–1610). Thanks to his father's acquaintances Teitoku was to receive instruction as a child from the best scholars.

Eishu never rose above the second rank of *renga* poets. He was by no means so highly esteemed as Satomura Jōha (1544–1602), a man of plebeian origins and appearance. Teitoku gave a vivid description of Jōha: "His face was large and without eyebrows. His eyes were sharply outlined, and his large, prominent nose had dark spots here and there. His ear lobes were thick. He had a loud voice with a fierce ring, so that even when he made a joke he sounded as if he were angry."[10] Eishu and Jōha had a serious falling-out, probably in 1582 (when Teitoku was eleven). Eishu felt he had been insulted because he was asked to participate in a *renga* session after a man he considered his inferior. Jōha attempted to mollify him, but Eishu, conscious of his dignity as the son of a daimyo, never permitted the dispute to be healed.[11] Eishu with this proud gesture cut himself off from the main stream of *renga* composition, to the harm of his career as a poet and his finances. He may have been obliged to become a merchant in order to make a living,[12] though probably he received support from his rich relations. Virtually our only subsequent information about Eishu's career as a poet dates from 1596, when he and Jōha took part in a one-thousand-link *renga* session held by command of Hideyoshi. Nothing suggests a reconciliation; no doubt the leading *renga* poets had assembled in response to an order they could not disobey.

Teitoku wrote relatively little about his father in his autobiography. One passage, however, stands out. In 1573, when Teitoku was two years old, fighting broke out in Kyoto between the supporters of Oda Nobunaga and those of the shogun, Ashikaga Yoshiaki. The inhabitants fled the capital, seeking refuge in the countryside. Eishu, his wife, and their four children (the oldest five years old), headed north. Teitoku wrote, "The worst point was when we came to a mountain torrent where waves boiled furiously over the rocks. Wading across was out of the question, and there was only a narrow log bridge. My father, taking one small child under his right arm, and leading my sister (who was only five) with his left hand, slowly moved sideways over the log. My mother stood on the near shore, one baby on her back and the other in her arms, watching him. I remember her telling me how, when my father reached the middle of the bridge, his face looked paler than the waters below."[13]

This early experience may explain Teitoku's conspicuously timid and conservative disposition. Though he could claim a samurai ancestry going back four hundred years, he recalled with horror the warfare he had witnessed as a child, and rejoiced in the peace and stability of the Tokugawa régime. He declared that the debt he owed the shoguns for their well-ordered rule was "higher than the mountains and deeper than the sea."[14]

When Teitoku was six he and a brother, two years older than himself, both expressed the wish to become Buddhist priests. Eishu was unwilling for both sons to become priests, but told them to draw lots. The elder brother won and soon afterwards entered a monastery of the Nichiren sect, where he served under the celebrated Nichiō (1565–1630), an exponent of the extremist doctrine of *fuju fuse* ("receive not, give not").[15] Teitoku's brother accompanied Nichiō into exile and died on the island of Tsushima. Teitoku himself remained a devout believer throughout his life.[16]

Eishu recognized Teitoku's precocious gifts as a poet and sent him to study *waka* with the courtier Kujō Tanemichi (1507–94), revered as the repository of the authentic poetic traditions. Tanemichi must also have been impressed by the boy prodigy. Not only did he instruct Teitoku in the art of poetry, but transmitted to the eleven-year-old the secret traditions of *Genji Monogatari*. If we had no firm evidence it would be difficult to believe that Tanemichi had entrusted a child with such jealously guarded secrets, but fortunately we have not only Teitoku's own testimony[17] but the manuscript of the *renga* sequence in one hundred links composed on March 11, 1582, to celebrate Teitoku's induction into the mysteries. The sequence begins:

hana ni nao michiwake soen yukue ka na	Still shall I offer guidance among the blossoms: the path lies beyond. *Kujō Tanemichi*
haru wa kasumi ni hikarenuru sode	In the spring how one's sleeves are tugged ahead by the mists. *Matsunaga Teitoku*
taka tobō susono no kigisu nakisutete	The hawk soars above mountain fields where the pheasant leaves its song behind. *Hosokawa Yūsai*[18]

These verses are by no means memorable as poetry, but they convey gracefully the teacher's delight in his promising student, the pupil's gratitude for the guidance he has received, and the distinguished visitor's admiration not only for the youth ("the hawk") but for his father, "pheasant" having been a familiar image for a devoted parent.[19] The gathering was attended by members of the military aristocracy, including Ōmura Yūko, the companion and chronicler of Hideyoshi; presumably they were drawn both by Eishu's illustrious family and by curiosity about the boy genius. Jōha was not present, suggesting that the rift between him and Eishu had already occurred.

Teitoku was profoundly grateful for the instruction Tanemichi gave him. He recalled in his autobiography, "When I went to study under him he was already eighty years old, but not in the least senile."[20] Tanemichi's scholarship was traditional: he devoted great attention to explanations of unusual words and pronunciations, relishing the unpredictable, highly irregular readings. But he genuinely loved *Genji Monogatari*, as we know from Teitoku: "After his meals he would always spend hours leaning over his desk reading *Genji*. He often said, 'Nothing gives me as much pleasure as this novel. I have been reading it for over sixty years, but I never tire of it. When I am reading this book I feel as if I were living in the reign of the Engi emperor.' "[21] Like the medieval commentators, Tanemichi searched for Buddhist meanings behind *Genji Monogatari*, finding in the novel the embodiment of the doctrine of Concentration and Insight (*shikan*). His scholarship belonged to an earlier age.

Tanemichi believed he was the guardian of the orthodox traditions of the court, and displayed his contempt for any departures from them. Teitoku recorded, "When I read *Genji Monogatari* aloud to Lord Kujō I thought I was pronouncing the words correctly, but he laughed at me, and said everything I uttered had a provincial ring. He added, 'It's not your fault. Ever since Lord Nobunaga came here from Owari everyone here in the capital, noble and commoner alike, has tended to change considerably in his speech habits.' "[22] Tanemichi's insistence on the standard court speech, especially proper intonation, impressed Teitoku so much that he later induced a disciple to compile the pioneer study of this subject.[23]

By the standards of the time Teitoku was fortunate to have studied under Tanemichi, but the content of the instruction would be of little interest today. A knowledge of the peculiar readings in *Genji Monogatari* is no longer believed to constitute a profound understanding of the work, and the mind boggles at the thought of the boy Teitoku spending months memorizing the secret traditions of how to pronounce the names of the successive emperors and the reign-names (*nengō*). Yet Teitoku, at least until late in life, never questioned that this was what scholarship meant. Nor had he any doubts about the value of the kind of *waka* in which Tanemichi guided him, the lifeless, formalistic poetry of the Nijō school.[24] He accepted Tanemichi's teachings as the sole legitimate tradition in poetry. But Teitoku was aware, even as a boy, that he could never be recognized as a master of *waka*, no matter how skillful he became. This art was considered to be the privilege of the nobility, and a samurai of modest means could not hope to acquire the aura that birth alone conferred. This tendency became more pronounced after the establishment of the Tokugawa régime. The court nobles in Kyoto, shorn of every other form of authority, were officially ensconced as the guardians of the *waka*.[25]

One means the nobles employed to enforce their monopoly of *waka* was their control of the transmission of the secret traditions of the *Kokinshū*, known as the *Kokin Denju*. The origins of these traditions are obscure, but they acquired their great authority with Sōgi (1421–1502), the supreme *renga* poet, though he, paradoxically, was of humble origins. The climax to the steady exaltation of *Kokin Denju* occurred in 1600 when Hosokawa Yūsai presented a new compilation of the three existing traditions to the Emperor Go-Yōzei, thereby lending the prestige of the imperial family to the almost stupefyingly inconsequential bits of lore that made up the work.[26] Teitoku undoubtedly would have given anything to be inducted into these secret traditions, but the closest he came was when, some years earlier, he was shown the covers of the volumes. He recorded, "On the twenty-fourth of November, 1593, I went with my father to call on Hosokawa Yūsai. He took us to the back room of his house where he opened a box and showed us the contents, saying, 'These are all the secret books of the Tradition. Look at them!' There were four books of different sizes with the words 'transmitted texts' on the covers."[27] Teitoku felt especially chagrined because he knew that in an earlier day, before *Kokin Denju* became the exclusive privilege of the nobility, he might have received instruction. He knew moreover that without this instruction he could never gain recognition as a fully qualified practitioner of the art of *waka*.

It may have been for this reason that Teitoku's father sent him at the age of eleven or twelve to study *renga* with Jōha, despite the bad relations prevailing between the two men. Jōha gladly accepted the boy, even though he apparently could not pay the usual fees. Teitoku recalled in his autobiography, "People are wrong to accuse Jōha of having been miserly. If he had been miserly, why should he have invited a poor boy like myself to his house and treated me with such kindness?"[28] Eishu's decision to have his son study with Jōha may have reflected not only his awareness that Jōha was a superior *renga* poet but also his desire for Teitoku to associate with the nobles who frequented Jōha's house, craving his instruction.[29] In any case, Teitoku showed such great aptitude for *renga* that he was allowed when he was barely eighteen to participate in sessions with the acknowledged masters.[30]

Tanemichi disapproved of this activity. Teitoku related, "Once I asked His Excellency the best way for me to learn to compose *waka*. He answered, 'The first thing you should do is give up *renga*. It belongs to the same art of poetry, but it is a hindrance to the beginner. *Renga* gives greatest emphasis to capping what is said in the previous verse. This means that poets at times must resort to inelegant words. Once they have become accustomed to seeing and hearing these words, they cease to think of them as being coarse and use them in their *waka*. This seriously impedes their progress. In writing *waka* the proper choice of words is essential.'"[31]

Renga had originally been a much freer verse form than *waka*, which was indissolubly bound by old traditions, but the court poets, seeing the literary possibilities of the form, had created an aristocratic variety of *renga*. Under the influence of such courtiers as Nijō Yoshimoto (1320–88) *renga* had been provided with "codes" laying down the authorized manner of conducting sessions and determining such technical matters as the number of successive links in which a particular season should be mentioned. Even with such codes *renga* was more flexible that *waka*, though the differences in themes and language had tended to disappear. These differences nevertheless seemed of immense importance to a conservative poet like Tanemichi, who was convinced that any departures from the strict limits of the vocabulary of *Kokinshū*, a collection seven hundred years old, were intolerable. Teitoku probably shared these views. Although in later years he acknowledged his indebtedness to the many (over fifty) *waka* poets under whom he studied, however briefly, he seemed somewhat embarrassed about his long association with Jōha. Once Tanemichi criticized Jōha, saying he was "clever at *renga* but has never attained an understanding of the old poetry." Teitoku, though only a boy, thought this criticism was justified.[32] Far from attempting to "return to *renga*," as has frequently been claimed, Teitoku undoubtedly felt that art was beneath him. He took greatest pride in his *waka*.

Close to three thousand *waka* by Teitoku have been preserved, most of them in the posthumous collection *Shōyū Gusō*.[33] Although these poems were written over a period of sixty years, in the absence of prefatory notes it would be impossible to assign them to particular periods in his life or to detect stylistic development. Some were written before he was twenty, but the impetuosity of youth did not occasion any challenge of the established conventions; he used precisely the same vocabulary and allusions as the countless other poets of the Nijō school. Teitoku's biographer, Odaka Toshio, who otherwise displayed the greatest enthusiasm for Teitoku's writings, said of the *waka* that they were all "mediocre and platitudinous, utterly monotonous."[34] Teitoku would not have been upset by this judgment of an outsider. He once sarcastically expressed his doubts that amateurs could appreciate his *waka*: "I find it absolutely intolerable that ordinary people should praise or condemn *waka*, saying so-and-so is skillful or so-and-so is inept. Everybody seems to say whatever he pleases, giving free rein to his prejudices. I do not mean to imply that there is no such thing as good or bad in *waka*. The way to distinguish the two is described in detail in the teachings of the masters, but although these teachings enable one to tell the difference between an extremely good poem and an extremely bad one, it is not easy to recognize a middling poem as such. It goes without saying that amateurs who have not had the benefit of such guidance can have no notion of the matter whatsoever. They seem to judge whether a poem is good or bad entirely by the name of the poet. If I affixed my name to a poem by Lord Teika they would be sure to denounce it. If, on the other hand, I affixed Lord Teika's name to a poem, even by myself, they would certainly praise it."[35]

Teitoku believed that only the expert, the man absolutely familiar with the traditions of *waka*, can judge the value of a poem; and that the poem itself merited praise not by its unique expression of emotions or unusual phrasing, but by its exact conformance to tradition and total avoidance of the innumerable "faults" defined by the compilers of the Japanese poetic canons. The restrictions imposed on his range of expression by the Nijō school assuredly did not frustrate Teitoku. He had no burning emotions that demanded voice in his *waka*. Composing poetry required no justification, and he was satisfied with the praise of his peers. In any case, his placid disposition did not dispose him to choose the course of controversy in poetry or in life.

After the death of Tanemichi in 1594 Teitoku continued his studies of *waka* under Hosokawa Yūsai. Teitoku's admiration for this teacher was unbounded. Unlike most daimyos (whose boorish ways Teitoku denounced at length), Yūsai "did not despise ordinary people," but showed the utmost consideration for his talented pupil. Yūsai, moreover, "from his youthful days was familiar not only with the martial arts but with *waka*, *renga*, football, cookery, and even drum playing, and devoted himself to each art until he mastered it so thoroughly there was none in which he did not excel."[36]

Yūsai's virtuosity excited Teitoku's admiration, but he revered Yūsai above all for his unique knowledge of *Kokin Denju*. In 1600, for example, Prince Tomohito requested permission of Tokugawa Ieyasu to study *Kokin Denju* with Yūsai; so momentous an event as the transmission of these teachings requiring authorization from the highest quarters. Later that year, as the Battle of Sekigahara was looming, Yūsai was besieged for two months in Tanabe Castle by a vastly superior force under the command of Ishida Mitsunari. Some of Yūsai's disciples at the emperor's court, fearful that if Yūsai died in the siege "the profound inner truths of the Way of the Japanese Gods, the secrets of the Art of Poetry, would disappear forever and the teachings of the Land of the Gods come to naught," arranged for the siege to be lifted.[37] It is small wonder that Teitoku should have worshipped a man whose knowledge of *Kokin Denju* was considered to be more precious than victory in a siege! He recorded Yūsai's casual remarks and pleasantries as if they were pronouncements, and repeatedly expressed his profound gratitude for Yūsai's instruction. No doubt it flattered the young man to associate intimately with a celebrated daimyo, and he gladly humored the old man's taste for idle chatter.

In 1603 Teitoku made an important friend twelve years younger than himself, Hayashi Razan (1583–1657). Razan, who had been studying the Ch'eng-Chu texts of Confucianism for several years at Kenninji, a Zen monastery in Kyoto, decided to offer public lectures on their interpretations for the benefit of friends, mainly young Confucian scholars and physicians. They in turn requested Teitoku to lecture on the fourteenth century work *Tsurezuregusa* ("Essays in Idleness").[38] Teitoku was reluctant to take the unprecedented step of lecturing publicly on teaching he had received privately. Only after Razan's father and uncle had joined in the persuasion, urging Teitoku to make the venture of giving public lectures respectable by participating himself, did he finally consent.[39] As so often in his life, Teitoku's initial negative reaction, the product of his naturally conservative and cautious attitudes, was shaken in the end by other people's enthusiasm. The man who so enjoyed hobnobbing with the nobility found himself in the role of a bringer of enlightenment to the general public. Odaka Toshio remarked that "unlike Hayashi Razan who captured the spirit of the new age, Teitoku was overcome by it."[40] Teitoku was to find his most lasting fame as the guiding spirit of the new popular culture, though it would have mortified him had anyone predicted it.

Teitoku delivered lectures "to the crowd" on two works, *Tsurezuregusa* and the famous collection of poetry *Hyakunin Isshu*. He himself had only recently heard lectures on the former from Nakanoin Michikatsu (1558–1610), a courtier and expert on classical literature, and on the latter from Hosokawa Yūsai. Both works, though they were to be of enormous importance in the education of all classes during the Tokugawa period, had up to this time been relatively obscure.[41]

Teitoku's commentary on *Tsurezuregusa*, called *Nagusamigusa*, seems also to have been prepared largely at this time, though it was not published until 1652. It ranks among the best commentaries of the Tokugawa period, not because it explains words in the traditional manner, but because Teitoku reveals an excellent understanding of the work in his essays appended to each episode. As for *Hyakunin Isshu*, it had formerly been taught with the usual secrecy by such men as Nakanoin Michikatsu, and even emperors had written commentaries, but its extraordinary popularity with the general public, retained to this day, can be traced to Teitoku's lectures.[42] It is perhaps no accident that Teitoku chose for his lectures the two literary works that were to exercise the greatest influence on popular culture for several hundred years.

Another major development at this time dramatically changed the nature of instruction in the classics. The art of printing was introduced to Japan from Korea after the campaign of 1593, and beginning in 1599 a series of printed editions of the classics, some associated with political figures like Tokugawa Ieyasu or Toyotomi Hideyoshi, and some with artists like Hon'ami Kōetsu, made the classics (which hitherto had circulated in the form of expensive manuscripts) available to everyone. Printing, of course, had been known in Japan much earlier. Indeed, the oldest surviving examples of printing from blocks are from eighth-century Japan. But until this period printing had been reserved for Buddhist works, perhaps because the expense of carving the blocks had been begrudged for literary texts, perhaps because the artistic appearance of a book—the calligraphy and illustrations especially—had seemed an integral part of any work. The reintroduction of printing was probably accompanied by new opinions on what deserved to be printed. Within twenty or thirty years the classics and even distinctly non-classical literary works were being printed and published for the general public. Teitoku, by allowing himself to be persuaded to offer lectures to the public, had unwittingly placed himself in the vanguard of the new movement in education and popular culture.

The nobles' reactions to Teitoku's lectures were predictable. Nakanoin Michikatsu, his teacher of *Tsurezuregusa*, was furious that Teitoku should have revealed secret traditions to the "vulgar public." He rebuked Teitoku for having violated the Confucian dictum, "To tell on the road what one has heard on the way is to cast away virtue."[43] Teitoku, far from resenting this criticism, felt deeply ashamed of himself. He wrote about Michikatsu, "If he had been a base person (*hisen*) like myself, he would have called me to him and struck me, but being a member of the upper classes, he did not even reveal his anger on his face when he saw me."[44] Despite this embarrassment, however, the course of Teitoku's future activities as a bringer of the "enlightenment" had been set.

The impulse for his public lectures, as we have seen, came from a Confucianist, Hayashi Razan. Confucian studies had been pursued in Japan since the Heian period, but contrary to their original intent, they were transmitted mainly as secret traditions, the property of the Kiyohara and Nakahara families. The heads of these families jealously preserved their secrets, in some cases passing them on only to their eldest sons, just as the secrets of Japanese poetry or the arts were transmitted. Free inquiry into the interpretation or even the Japanese pronunciations of the texts was prohibited. Even the Zen Buddhist priests who had imported from China works of Sung Confucian scholarship showed no desire to break away from the esoteric mode of teaching the Confucian doctrines.[45] The first departure occurred in 1599 when Fujiwara Seika (1561–1619, an uncle of Teitoku) had at the request of Akamatsu Hiromichi punctuated some of the Chinese classics for Japanese reading. This unsensational event is considered to mark the emergence of the new spirit of Tokugawa Confucian scholarship and the end of medieval secrecy.[46] Razan, quite independently of Seika, had been studying the commentaries by Chu Hsi and others, borrowing books wherever he could find them, and passing on his knowledge in private lectures, beginning in 1600.[47] (He would not meet Seika until 1604.) It was by a stroke of irony that Razan, whose enthusiasm so contrasted with the caution of Teitoku, became in later years the pillar of orthodoxy, even as Teitoku moved steadily in the direction of becoming the central figure in the new, unorthodox culture. Perhaps it was under Razan's influence that Teitoku came to reject the secret traditions to which he had so long aspired. He wrote in his autobiography, "The Japanese from the distant past have had a narrow outlook, and when they have learned something that was not generally known, they have kept it a secret and refused to divulge it to other people. As a result, a great deal of information concerning the art of poetry has been lost, because it was kept hidden. I have examined the books of medicine imported here from China in recent years and discovered they conceal nothing about the preparation of even the most secret medicines. This, I thought, is what one might expect of the country where the Sage was born."[48]

Razan's rise to fame started in 1605, when he appeared for the first time before Tokugawa Ieyasu. The young scholar brilliantly answered Ieyasu's questions, laying the groundwork for his appointment in 1607 as Confucian adviser to the shogunate. Razan moved to Edo, the shogun's capital, and established his school Shōheikō there. His branch of Confucian philosophy, emphasizing rationalism and human loyalties in place of the abstract doctrines of Buddhism, fitted well with the Tokugawa plans of establishing an orderly society, and was soon accepted by the state as an official philosophy.[49]

Perhaps it was again under Razan's influence that Teitoku also founded a school, prior to 1619. His school was situated in his house in Kyoto, and was apparently quite distinct from the instruction he gave in *waka, renga*

and *haikai*. The pupils were children ranging in age from four to eleven,
most of them from the samurai class. The celebrated philosopher Arai
Hakuseki provides us with a second-hand description of the school:
"My teacher [Kinoshita Jun'an] once told me, 'When I was a boy we had
nobody to teach us punctuation and reading of the classics until Teitoku
established his school. He taught calligraphy and *sodoku*. Itō Jinsai, Hayashi's sons and myself all studied with him.' "[50] On "graduation" from Teitoku's elementary school, some pupils studied Confucianism with his
son, Matsunaga Sekigo (1592–1657), a highly respected scholar, and others
studied poetry with Teitoku himself. A textbook called *Teitoku Bunshū*,
compiled by Teitoku about 1628, was apparently intended for use in his
school.[51] The book, of the genre known as *ōraimono*, consists of 174 brief
letters on various subjects, supposedly sent by real or imaginary persons,
dated and arranged through the course of a year. The pupils imitated the
calligraphy of the text, which was written in both the running hand and
the cursive, and learned incidentally how to compose letters in the episto-
lary style. The subjects included Japanese poetry, the tea ceremony,
medicine, food, divination, and so on. *Teitoku Bunshū* is of special interest
today for its glimpses into the daily life of the time, whether the description of a festival or of opening a cask of foreign wine obtained from Naga-
saki. *Teitoku Bunshū* is probably the best *ōraimono* of the early Tokugawa
period. Certainly it contrasted favorably with older textbooks like *Teikin
Ōrai*, still widely used at the time though by now almost incomprehensible
to school children.[52] Teitoku's school lasted until 1635, and the one
founded by his son survived through ten generations of Matsunagas until
1889.[53]

Teitoku seems to have earned a comfortable living between his teaching
and his guidance of aspiring poets. Gradually the latter occupation came
to absorb most of his time, though he retained to the end of his life an
interest in education of the young.[54] Teitoku still considered his primary
work to be composing and correcting Nijō-style *waka*, though for years
he had also been composing comic poetry, both the comic *waka* (known
as *kyōka*) and the comic *renga* (known as *haikai*). *Kyōka* had first attracted
attention as a poetic form in 1595 with the publication of a collection edited
by Yūchōrō, a priest of the Kenninji, and continued to be a popular, if
minor genre, throughout the Tokugawa period. *Haikai*, a far more important medium, had been developed in the sixteenth century out of the court
style of *renga* by such men as Yamazaki Sōkan (1465?–1553?) and Arakida
Moritake (1473–1549), a learned Shinto priest from Ise.[55] Teitoku's
facility with language enabled him to excel at both. He related how when

he visited Yūsai the old man would amuse himself by composing twenty or thirty *haikai* verses for Teitoku to cap.[56] In time he came to be considered the outstanding poet of both *kyōka* and *haikai*.

Teitoku was hardly proud of this reputation, and treated his own compositions with scant respect. He published altogether only one hundred of his *kyōka* (in 1636), never considering these "wild verses" to be more than a pastime. Teitoku's *kyōka*, lacking the sharpness or bite of true wit, consist mainly of ponderous plays on words or frivolous references to the classics. His *kyōka* on the *aoi*, or "hollyhock", is typical:

fukabuka to	The dew that has formed
aoi no ue ni	thickly, ever so thickly
oku tsuyu ya	on the hollyhocks
miyasundokoro no	must surely be the tears
namida naruran	of Lady Rokujō.[57]

The reference to the *Aoi* chapter of *Genji Monogatari* is adroit, but scarcely funny. A slightly more interesting *kyōka* runs:

urameshi ya	"Beware my wrath!"
omoi wa oni to	But even if my love turns
narinu to mo	into a demon,
sasuga ni kimi wo	I'm sure I'll never manage
kui wa korosazu	to bite you to death![58]

Teitoku's heavy-handed drollery did not suit the genius of *kyōka*, even when he ventured on an unconventional theme. His attitude remained equally unbending and conservative when he composed *haikai*. Teitoku, it should be remembered, never thought of his *haikai* as being *haiku* in the modern sense—independent verses, complete in themselves, that demand a poet's full attention. On the contrary, he excelled especially at demonstrating his virtuosity by composing dozens of *tsukeku* ("added verses") to the same *hokku* ("opening verse"). Teitoku's codes of *haikai* composition, which established him as the leader in this art, were concerned almost exclusively with the conduct of a session of comic linked-verse.

Haikai might have remained for Teitoku no more than impromptu witticisms unworthy of being recorded had his disciples not been more aggressive than himself. Two of them, Matsue Shigeyori (1602–80) and Nonoguchi Ryūho (1595–1669), asked Teitoku's permission to publish a collection of *hokku* and *tsukeku*. He refused, insisting that the word "collection" (*shū*) could not properly be used for so lowly a form of

poetry as *haikai*.[59] The two men persisted, and eventually obtained
Teitoku's consent to compile a "child" anthology to Sōkan's *Inu Tsukuba
Shū* ("Mongrel *Renga* Collection"); its name, appropriately, was *Enoko
Shū* ("Puppy Collection"). The two men at first collaborated on the project, gathering notable examples of *haikai* from all over Japan, especially
from Ise, where Moritake's traditions still lingered on. During the
process of compilation, which lasted from 1631 to 1633, Shigeyori and
Ryūho quarrelled, and Shigeyori alone published *Enoko Shū*, apparently
at his own expense. The collection included over fifteen hundred *hokku*
and one thousand *tsukeku* by 178 poets.[60] Teitoku refused to associate
himself with the collection, even though he was the most prominent con-
tributor. Shigeyori's postface spoke merely of showing the work to
"a certain old gentleman," as if embarrassed to mention Teitoku by
name.[61] The collection proved of major importance in the history of *haikai*.
It encouraged poets everywhere, and attracted such favorable attention
that Teitoku reconsidered his negative stand. Despite his wishes, he had
become enthroned as the chief figure in the world of *haikai*.

The characteristic features of the *haikai* poetry included in *Enoko
Shū* may be illustrated by a few examples written by Teitoku.

kasumi sae   Even the mist
madara ni tatsu ya   rises in spots
tora no toshi   this Year of the Tiger.[62]

The poetic convention of mist rising at the beginning of the year is
given a new twist by suggesting that because this is the Year of the Tiger
the mist is spotted. (The Japanese of Teitoku's time supposed that the
leopard was the female of the tiger!)

neburasete   Let him lick them—
yashinaitate yo   that's the way to bring him up:
hana no ame   the flower sweets.[63]

This cryptic verse, presented to a man who had just had a child, depends
for its effect on puns and allusions. It is typical of Teitoku at his best
and worst. *Ame* means both "sweets" and "rain." *Hana no ame* is "rain
on the flowers," recalling the line in the Nō play *Yuya* that calls rain
the "parent" of the flowers; it also refers to the "rain of flowers" that fell
when Shakyamuni Buddha was born. The verse is deliberately ambiguous,
but the expanded meaning is something like: "Raise your child by giving

him sweets to lick, as the rain raises the flowers, your child born as Shakya-muni was, amidst a rain of flowers."

shioruru wa	Do they droop because
nanika anzu no	of some grief? The apricot
hana no iro	blossoms' color.

The key word is *anzu*, meaning "apricot" and also "to grieve," and used here in both senses as a *kakekotoba* ("pivot word"). *Hana no iro* ("color of the blossoms") is probably an allusion to the famous poem by Ono no Komachi, "The color of the flowers faded, while meaninglessly I spent my days in the world and the long rains were falling."[64] The poem thus combines a pun and a classical allusion.

minahito no	Is it the reason
hiru ne no tane ya	why everyone is napping—
aki no tsuki	the autumn moon.[65]

People have been up until late the night before admiring the moon, and that is why everybody is sleepy today.

Each of the above four examples suggests a facet of Teitoku's *haikai*. The poems are all humorous, but the nature of the humor differs conspicuously. The first example employs a poetic conceit: even the mist is spotted in the Year of the Tiger. Teitoku composed similar verses on the Year of the Dragon and the Year of the Ox.

The humor in the second example depends on a *haigon*, or comic word. Here it is *neburasete* ("let him lick"). So earthy a word could not have appeared in the traditional poetry, but in Teitoku's *haikai* the presence of a *haigon* became the touchstone of whether or not a verse was truly *haikai*. Poets were not merely allowed to use non-traditional vocabulary but absolutely required to do so. The same verse also alludes to *Yuya* and to Buddhist legends, typically for Teitoku and his school who, though they insisted on the importance of comic words, were determined not to lapse like Yamazaki Sōkan into vulgarity. Allusions to literature of the past imparted some elegance to an otherwise frivolous verse. Teitoku was so sure that even the humor of *haikai* must accord with the dignity of the new age that he declared, "*Haikai* is a form of *waka*; one must not write anything at variance with morality."[66] This comment clearly does not mean that Teitoku advocated a form of *haikai* similar to *waka* (as some scholars have stated), but that *haikai*, being a part of the legacy of Japanese poetry bequeathed by the gods, should not stoop to

vulgarities that might offend them. Teitoku's attitude threatened to emas-
culate *haikai*, as *renga* had long since been emasculated, by depriving it
of its vigor and making it almost identical with the older poetry in tone,
but his insistence on specifically comic words saved *haikai* from that fate.

The third example from *Enoko Shū* contains a variety of *haigon* that
is neither comic nor mundane: it is the word *anzu*, derived from the
Chinese. Only words of pure Yamato origin were permitted in the *waka*
or the court *renga*, and the use of a Chinese-derived word, as well as the
somewhat humorous pun, established this verse as being *haikai*.

Finally, in the fourth example we have a verse that is humorous in
conception rather than in language. The autumn moon had been used
countless times in Japanese poetry for its beauty and as a symbol of
enlightenment, but poets had not given much thought to the consequences
of staying up all night gazing at the moon. The mention of napping the
next day gives the poem its *haikai* quality.

It need hardly be said that these verses, among Teitoku's best, in no
way compare to the superb creations of Bashō or Buson. We sense
nothing resembling a world reduced to a microcosm, the poet's profound
experiences given in their barest, most evocative essentials. These verses
are moreover totally lacking in poetic tension. They generally have a *kireji*
("cutting word") dividing the elements, like the *ya* in the first example,
but no attempt is made to suggest that two worlds, one eternal and the
other momentary, are at once separated and held in equilibrium by the
kireji. Such ideals were quite foreign to Teitoku. Even when he grudgingly came to admit that writing *haikai* could be more than a game,
and even after he had been acclaimed to his discomfort the guiding spirit
of the *haikai* movement, he never conceived that *haikai* poetry could be
the vehicle for a man's deepest emotions.

Teitoku's *waka* expressed more serious feelings, but even they contain
little that is personal. The fact is, for Teitoku and most of his contemporaries, the expression of individual emotions was not a function of poetry.
Teitoku defined the value of poetry in quite other terms: "Every day of
a man's life is tormented by a trillion deluded thoughts, all stemming
from greed, wrath and folly, the three poisons. . . . In Japan the gods,
initiating the art of poetry written in thirty-one syllables, created the
tradition of our country. This, we are told, was because they knew
that while a man is beguiling himself by writing poetry he does not allow
the three poisons to rise within him. Should we not be most grateful for
this art?"[67] Teitoku recounted how the *waka* had gradually been displaced in popularity by *renga*, only for *renga* composition to prove even

more difficult; few people now aspired to write poetry in that form. "Then, just when sensitive people were lamenting this situation, thinking it must have arisen because people's hearts had become shallow, *haikai* quite unexpectedly gained popularity in recent days. It would seem that young and old, both in the capital and the countryside, are finding solace in this art.... *Haikai* is a form of *waka*. It should not be despised as a vulgar pastime. In these Latter Days of the Buddhist Law its virtue (*toku*) is broader even than that of the *waka*."[68]

Teitoku believed that Japanese poetry, first created by the gods, had changed in form with the times from *waka* to *renga* to *haikai*. The last, he felt, was most suited to his own age. Teitoku elsewhere expressed his conviction that unless the times are propitious, a work of literature cannot be appreciated. He wrote, "Nothing is admired until its time has come. *Genji Monogatari*, though written at the beginning of the Kankō era [1004–11], was buried for a hundred years and first was recognized as a treasure of the nation about the Kōwa era [1099–1103]. *Tsurezuregusa* was hardly known to anyone until the Tenshō era [1573–91], but since Keichō [1596–1614] has come to be widely admired."[69] Teitoku felt that in the orderly but superficial world of his day *haikai* was more effective than *waka* in turning a man to cultural pursuits and thereby ridding him of the "three poisons." Literature was a diversion that kept a man out of worse mischief.

Teitoku's school was to publish over 260 collections of *haikai* before it finally petered out in the nineteenth century. The first two collections, *Enoko Shū* and *Haikai Hokku Chō* edited by Nonoguchi Ryūho, were welcomed by much the same readers as the early fiction (*kana zōshi*).[70] Their popularity must have surprised Teitoku and induced him to reconsider his aversion to publishing *haikai* collections. In 1638, five years after the appearance of the first two collections, Teitoku authorized his disciple Yamamoto Saimu to publish *Taka Tsukuba*. The postface indicates how greatly Teitoku's attitude had changed: far from being reluctant to publish, he now begrudged wasting any time arranging the contributions properly. He mentioned also how many *haikai* had been "difficult to reject," though at one time it would have seemed strange to preserve any.[71] Teitoku attempted to bolster the authority of *haikai* by revealing what great men had indulged in the art; the fifth volume of *Taka Tsukuba* includes verses by Hideyoshi, Yūsai, Sen no Rikyū and other giants of the late sixteenth century.[72] Only now, after the success of two unauthorized collections, had Teitoku decided to give *haikai* the dignity of a past.

Teitoku's *haikai*, unlike his *waka*, acquired depth with time, though their interest lies primarily in the increasing awareness they display of the legitimacy of *haikai* as a poetic form. It has often been asserted that Teitoku considered *haikai* to be merely a kind of stepping-stone to the composition of *renga* and eventually *waka*, but his writings do not substantiate this claim.[73] Originally Teitoku had dismissed *haikai* as a mere diversion. He moved then to tolerating it as a poetic form written in a lighter mood than *renga* but with its own qualities. Finally, he defended *haikai* as a medium with entirely distinct aims and rules.

The most important statement of his final position is found in the collection *Tensuishō*, edited after 1644 from Teitoku's manuscript by his disciple Kaedei Ryōtoku (1589–1679). *Tensuishō* seems to have been one of the most widely read books of *haikai* composition although it was never printed. Perhaps it was as a concession to the deep-rooted medieval tradition of esoteric transmission of knowledge that the book circulated only in manuscript among members of Teitoku's school. Or perhaps the secrecy was dictated by Teitoku's dependence on fees from his *haikai* pupils, who insisted on being privy to secrets not known to outsiders. In any case, there were so many pupils of Teitoku that *Tensuishō*, even in manuscript form, sufficed to establish his authority as the master of *haikai* theory.

In this work Teitoku insisted especially on the integrity of *haikai* as a poetic form: "Some people believe that there is *haikai* present even in *waka* and that, in general, the proper way to write in this form is to imitate *renga*, merely adding a slightly comic flavor. But this is a most foolish and shallow criterion. The poetry written by men who have won fame because of their excellence—Sōkan, the priest Genri, Moritake from Ise—shares nothing in common with *renga*, nor has it the qualities of *waka*. These masters apparently considered that the words rejected by *waka* and *renga* were appropriate for their purposes, and created a new art, the comic linked-verse."[74] By "words rejected by *waka* and *renga*" Teitoku meant, of course, the *haigon*. He believed that the use of these words taken from daily life made *haikai* poetry at once simpler and closer to the lives of ordinary men than the older forms. People who felt that poetry must be elegant should devote themselves to *waka* and *renga*; they had no need of the humble *haikai*.[75]

At the same time that Teitoku defended the unpretentiousness of *haikai* he tried to establish the form as a serious art. The way he found most natural to achieve this end was to draw up a code of composition, similar to the old codes for *waka* and *renga*. As *haikai* gained in popularity Teitoku had repeatedly been urged to prepare a code, but he yielded now, only after many refusals. His first attempt was highly informal, consisting of the ten injunctions in the form of *waka* appended to the collection *Aburakasu* published in 1643. The general sense of Teitoku's prescriptions is that *haikai*, although an informal variety of *renga*, is subject to its own principles of composition. His emphasis was not on literary excellence but on the technical procedure of a sequence of comic linked-verse. Here is one example:

oni onna	"Devil," "woman,"
tora ōkami no	"tiger," or "wolf" may appear
senku mono	in a thousand verses
omote ni mo suredo	even on the front page, but
ichiza ichiku zo	only once in a session.[76]

Words considered too "frightening" for *renga* were permitted even on the front page of the transcript of a thousand-link *haikai* sequence, but could be used only once. This typical piece of advice could hardly have provided more than marginal assistance to a would-be *haikai* poet.

Teitoku was stimulated into preparing more detailed rules by the appearance in 1636 of the code compiled by his former disciple Ryūho. Teitoku and Yamamoto Saimu prepared the volume *Kururu* in response to many requests for guidance from poets who flocked to Teitoku's house "like children begging their father for something."[77] The book appeared only in 1651; until then it circulated privately among Teitoku's pupils. *Kururu* consists of specific advice on the use of words, as in this example:

> *Inazuma* [lightning]. Not necessary to avoid mentioning 'moon' or 'sun' afterwards. The sounds *tsuru* should not occur for two verses. Autumn.[78]

The principle of *sarikirau*, words that must be omitted or avoided after certain other words, was inherited by Teitoku from *renga*. After the word for "lightning," however, there was no need to avoid the words for "moon" or "sun." On the other hand, a poet who used the sounds *tsuru* in his link to a verse containing "lightning" revealed his incompetence, regardless of what *tsuru* might mean in context. The word "lightning" is further assigned to a season, autumn, though it occurs at other times, probably because of the importance of seasonal words in *renga*.

This typical selection from a *haikai* code indicates how much less Teitoku and his school were concerned about the content of their poetry than its technical correctness. All the same, the care Teitoku devoted to elaborating such codes enabled *haikai* to take a great step forward. If Teitoku had not established *haikai* as a legitimate occupation for a poet, Bashō and the other masters might never have chosen this form. Under Teitoku's leadership, as Howard Hibbett has said, *haikai* became a "well-regulated, demanding, and eminently respectable art."[79]

Teitoku's final efforts as a codifier of *haikai* resulted in the publication (in 1651) of the immensely long and detailed *Gosan*, a compendium of the usage and overtones of words likely to appear in *haikai*. *Gosan* did not represent any great advance on *Kururu*, but it gave the final stamp of authority to the medium and made Teitoku's views available to everyone interested. His school came to enjoy popularity even in remote parts of the country, as we may gather from a passage from *The Narrow Road of Oku*. When Bashō visited the poets at Ōishida in northern Japan, he discovered that the "seeds of the old *haikai* had been scattered here, and the poets fondly recalled the unforgotten days of their flowering."[80]

Teitoku's greatest contribution to Japanese literature, then, was to elevate *haikai* to the position of a recognized poetic form. Yamazaki Sōkan and his followers had created in *Inu Tsukuba Shū* a work of crude exuberance, but their traditions were ephemeral. Most poets of the early seventeenth century supposed that *haikai*, as opposed to *waka* or *renga*, was a mere "spewing forth of whatever came to one's lips."[81] Teitoku, though he agreed at first with this opinion, came bit by bit to recognize the legitimate functions of *haikai*. His insistence on *haigon* not only enriched the vocabulary of poetry but opened up large areas of experience that could not be described except with such words. *Haikai* was especially popular with the merchant class, which, though it retained a lingering admiration for the cherry blossoms and maple leaves of the old poetry, welcomed a variety of poetry that could describe their pleasures in an age of peace and prosperity. Teitoku's codes have sometimes been decried for their inhibiting effect on the liveliness of *haikai*, but without his formal guidance *haikai* poetry might have remained forever on the level of the limerick.

The *haikai* verses Teitoku wrote towards the end of his long career go beyond his customary plays on words, and sometimes he disregarded his own dicta on the importance of *haigon*. Even this more mature poetry is not of much interest today, but it suggested the direction *haikai* would ultimately take in later generations. Teitoku failed as a poet. His verses are today seldom read, and most people hardly know his name. But his place in literary history is assured, as the reluctant innovator who founded the most popular form of Japanese poetry.

NOTES

1. The word *haikai*, written with various characters, was used as early as *Kokinshū* for comic poetry. In this essay it designates *haikai no renga*, or comic linked-verse. For a discussion of this form, see Howard S. Hibbett, "The Japanese Comic Linked-Verse Tradition," in *Harvard Journal of Asiatic Studies*, Vol. 23, 1960–61.

2. As a boy Teitoku was known as Katsuguma. The characters for that name in Sino-Japanese pronunciation yielded another name, Shōyū. The name Teitoku was first employed about 1605. In his old age Teitoku called himself Chōzumaru, a boyish name probably assumed after his sixty-first birthday.

   It will be evident from my footnotes how heavily I am indebted to two works by the late Professor Odaka Toshio: *Matsunaga Teitoku no Kenkyū* (1953) and its continuation *Zokuhen* (1956). (The former will be referred to as MTK, the latter as Z.)

3. Commented selections of Teitoku's poetry may be found in *Haiku Kōza*, Vol. IV, pp. 39–51 (edited by Odaka Toshio); Abe Kimio and Asō Isoji, *Kinsei Haiku Haibun Shū*, pp. 36–38; and Ebara Taizō, *Haiku Hyōshaku*, I, pp. 17–21.

4. Nippon Gakujutsu Shinkōkai, *Haiku and Haikai*, p. x. Harold G. Henderson, *An Introduction to Haiku*, p. 11, quotes what is possibly Teitoku's least typical and least attractive verse. Although R. H. Blyth in *A History of Haiku*, I, p. 67, terms Teitoku the most remarkable *haiku* poet before Bashō he concludes his discussion (p. 77): "This verse is one of the most painfully labored of the Teimon school, which one is somewhat glad to take leave of." More favorable appraisals of Teitoku may be found in the Hibbett article mentioned in footnote 1 and in Tsunoda, *Sources of Japanese Tradition*, pp. 454–5.

5. See Teitoku's remark in *Taka Tsukuba* (in *Teimon Haikai Shū*, I, a volume of *Haisho Taikei*), p. 250.

6. This fact was established by Shimmura Izuru in "Hayashi Dōshun oyobi Matsunaga Teitoku to Yasokaisha Fukan Habian," included in *Shimmura Izuru Senshū*, I. See also Hori Isao, *Hayashi Razan*, p. 103.

7. The elder brother, Nichiyō, died in exile on Tsushima. (See MTK, p. 161). The younger brother, Nichijū, probably died abroad in 1594. (MTK, p. 92.)

8. See Odaka Toshio, *Kinsei Shoki Bundan no Kenkyū*, p. 154.

9. A biographical sketch of Eishu is given in MTK, pp. 8–31.

10. *Taionki* (henceforth abbreviated TOK), edited by Odaka Toshio, in *Nihon Koten Bungaku Taikei*, Vol. 95, p. 67.

11. TOK, p. 66. MTK, p. 29.

12. Odaka suggests from the location of Eishu's house that he may have sold clothing, the district having contained many clothing shops. (MTK, p. 18.)

13. TOK, p. 93.

14. TOK, p. 89.

15. This doctrine held that it was wrong for believers in Nichiren Buddhism to conduct transactions with non-believers. See Tsunoda, *op. cit.*, p. 222.

16. Teitoku's defense of Buddhism against the attacks of Hayashi Razan is described in Odaka, *Kinsei Shoki*, pp. 191–203.

17. TOK, p. 45.

18. MTK, p. 47.

19. Compare the *haiku* by Bashō: *Chichi haha no/shikiri ni koishi/kiji no koe.*

20. TOK, p. 41.

21. TOK, p. 44.

22. MTK, p. 65.

23. This was *Katakoto* by Yasuhara Teishitsu (1610–1673), written in 1650.

24. See Ogata Isao, "Teimon Danrin Hairon," in *Haiku Kōza*, V, p. 30.

25. Z, pp. 19–20.

26. Z, p. 55.

27. *Teitoku Ō no Ki* in *Zoku Gunsho Ruijū*, kan 959 (p. 4 in 1927 edition).

28. TOK, p. 67.

29. See Morozumi Sōichi, "Satomura Jōha Shōden," in *Renga Haikai Kenkyū*, 24, p. 5.

30. MTK, pp. 72–3.

31. TOK, p. 43.

32. TOK, p. 43.

33. MTK, p. 347.

34. MTK, p. 81.

35. TOK, pp. 75–6.

36. TOK, p. 48.

37. MTK, pp. 108–9.

38. MTK, p. 124.

39. Hori, *Hayashi Razan*, pp. 50–1.

40. Z, p. 36.

41. The first commentary on *Tsurezuregusa*, *Jumyōin Shō*, by the physician Hata Sōha (1550?–1607), appeared in 1604. It was followed by *Tsurezuregusa Nozuchi* by Hayashi Razan, published in 1621. Razan's work antedates Teitoku's but Teitoku apparently was Razan's teacher. See "Tsurezuregusa Kenkyūshi," by Shigematsu Nobuhiro, in *Kokugo to Kokubungaku*, VI, No. 6, June 1929, pp. 63–111.

42. Z, p. 25.

43. *Analects*, XVII, 14.

44. TOK, p. 60.

45. MTK, p. 130.

46. Ōe Fumiki, *Hompō Jugakushi Ronkō*, p. 89.

47. Hori, *Hayashi Razan*, p. 37.

48. MTK, p. 131.

49. See Tsunoda, *Sources of Japanese Tradition*, pp. 340–4, for a concise statement of Razan's philosophy.

50. MTK, p. 202. By *sodoku* was meant reading the Chinese classics in Japanese renderings, without necessarily attempting to understand what they said. See R. P. Dore, *Education in Tokugawa Japan*, pp. 127–36, for a description of *sodoku*.

51. The text is reprinted in *Kaihyō Sōsho*, IV, edited by Shimmura Izuru. The work is analyzed by Okada Mareo in "*Teitoku Bunshū* no Jidai ni tsuite," in *Geimon*, XXI, No. 6, June 1930, pp. 467–503.

52. See Dore, *op. cit.*, pp. 276–8.

53. Ōe, *op. cit.*, p. 149.

54. MTK, pp. 303–4.

55. For a general discussion of this early period, see the Hibbett article mentioned in footnote 1.

56. MTK, p. 153.

57. *Teitoku Hyakushu Kyōka*, p. 58. Reference is being made of course to the hostility between Lady Rokujō (*miyasundokoro*) and Aoi, Genji's wife.

58. *Ibid.*, p. 60. *Urameshi ya*, the opening line, was the standard greeting of tortured spirits who return to earth.

59. Nakamura Shunjō, "Teimon Haikai Shi," in *Haiku Kōza*, I, p. 26.

60. MTK, p. 235.

61. Z, p. 138.

62. Abe and Asō, *Kinsei Haiku Haibun Shū*, p. 36.

63. *Ibid.*, p. 37.
64. *Ibid.*, p. 37. The poem by Komachi is *Kokinshū*, 113.
65. *Ibid.*, p. 37.
66. Z, p. 193.
67. Z, p. 141.
68. Z, p. 140.
69. Shigematsu, "Tsurezuregusa Kenkyūshi," p. 65.
70. Nakamura, "Teimon Haikai Shi," p. 29.
71. *Teimon Haikai Shū*, I, p. 274.
72. *Ibid.*, pp. 249–50. See also Nakamura, p. 31.
73. Ogata (p. 30) repeats this view, but it is specifically denied by Odaka (Z, p. 145) and Nakamura (p. 43.)
74. Z, p. 144.
75. Z, p. 144.
76. *Teimon Haikai Shū*, I, p. 102. See also MTK, p. 253. Although first published in 1643, these *waka* seem to have been written in 1635.
77. Z, p. 168.
78. Z, p. 171.
79. Hibbett, p. 86.
80. Sugiura Shōichirō, *Bashō Bunshū*, p. 87. "Old *haikai*" is somewhat ambiguous, but Teitoku's school best answered that description.
81. MTK, p. 255. The remark was made by Karasumaru Mitsuhiro (1579–1638), a *waka* poet.

Bashō's Journey of 1684

IN THE eighth month of 1684 the celebrated *haikai* poet Matsuo Bashō (1644–94) set out from Edo on a journey to his birthplace in Iga Province, some hundreds of miles away. He would not return until the fourth month of the following year. His journey took him considerably beyond Iga, to Mount Yoshino, Nara, and Kyoto, and finally back along the Kiso Road to Edo. Much of the way was on foot over mountainous roads, an arduous undertaking for a man in good health, but almost unthinkable for the sickly and prematurely aged Bashō.

The occasion for this journey was ostensibly the death of Bashō's mother in Iga during the sixth month of 1683. Bashō could not have reached Iga in time for the funeral, but had he been moved solely by filial piety, he surely could have attended the anniversary services in the sixth month. His slowness in departing suggests that other considerations —especially those of his art—took precedence over filial sentiments. But once Bashō had made up his mind to undertake the journey, he was not to be swayed. In the opening verse of his *Journey of the Year 1684*[1] he says that he is prepared even for death on the way. Perhaps he exaggerated somewhat the dangers of travel along roads that in his day had become well-known thoroughfares with comfortable inns and places of amusement along the way, but Bashō, seeing himself in the traditional role of the poet-wayfarer, threw himself into the part. This was not a pose but an effort to savor to the utmost the essence of travel: not a pleasant room and a good dinner at a wayside inn but the uncertainty, fatigue and even danger that being alone and far from home had always involved.

Bashō felt that the time had come to create a new style of *haikai*, and that the most effective preparation was to leave Edo and travel through the countryside for inspiration. His decision to leave in 1684 may also have been influenced by the accident that it was the first year of a new cycle of sixty, an auspicious time for making changes.

In 1684 Bashō was still groping towards what would be his distinctive style of *haikai*. He had shown his dissatisfaction with the superficial humor of the Danrin School, but such Danrin mannerisms as a prominent use of Chinese vocabulary and allusions persist in the *Journey*, if not as markedly as in poems composed a short time earlier. In the *Journey* Bashō was at pains to "naturalize" poetic ideas derived from Chinese literature: one verse was twice recast with this intent.[2] Bashō did not renounce the practice of alluding to earlier Chinese and Japanese writings, but he was no longer content with verses that appealed mainly to members of a coterie.

The opening verse *nozarashi wo/kokoro ni kaze no/shimu mi kana* ("At the thought my body may lie exposed in a field, how the wind cuts into my flesh") gave rise to the alternate title *Nozarashi Kikō*, literally "Exposed in a Field Travel Account." The date of composition of the diary is nowhere indicated, but most probably Bashō wrote it between the middle of 1685 and the eighth moon of 1687. Several contemporary manuscripts are extant, one supposedly in Bashō's own hand.[3] The first printed edition is contained in *Hakusenshū*, compiled in 1698 by Itō Fūkoku (d. 1701).

The *Journey* is important not only because of its place in Bashō's career, but because of the development it marks in a characteristic Japanese literary form, the travel-diary. This was the first of his five works in this genre, culminating in the celebrated *Oku no Hosomichi* ("The Narrow Road of Oku"). Earlier examples of the travel-diary (such as *Tōkan Kikō*, written in 1242), usually consisted of prosaic descriptions of a journey interspersed with almost unrelated poems. Bashō once criticized such works: "Of course, anyone can keep a diary with such entries as 'On this day it rained ... in the afternoon it cleared ... at that place is a pine ... at this place flows a river called Such-and-such'; but unless sights are truly remarkable, they shouldn't be mentioned at all."[4] In Bashō's travel-diaries, beginning with the *Journey*, the prose is almost as concise and evocative as the poetry, and the transitions between the two are more smoothly made than in the older diaries. Bashō was eventually able in *Oku no Hosomichi* to fuse the two elements perfectly. Even in this less successful work, the verses are sometimes so closely related to the prose that they are impossible to understand without the accompanying descriptions. For example, the verse "Taken in my hand it would melt, my tears are so warm—this autumnal frost" was composed as Bashō took in his hand a lock of his dead mother's hair. One can, of course, find a surface meaning even in this verse, but its full effect is apparent only if one knows that Bashō was using the word "frost" to describe his mother's white hair.

The historical importance of the *Journey* can hardly be exaggerated, but as literature it does not compare with some of Bashō's later works in the same form. Despite his intention of breaking away from the old conventions and using fresh language to describe the sights before him, allusions to Chinese and Japanese literature are tediously in evidence. Bashō undoubtedly found such allusions a convenient way of enriching his private observations with those of the poets of the past, but readers today are likely to find that recondite allusions weaken the impact of Bashō's perceptions.

Bashō clearly considered the verses composed on the journey far more important than the prose. This explains why the last third of the *Journey* consists almost entirely of *haikai*, with hardly more than a line of accompanying description. The new style of travel-diary, so auspiciously begun, breaks down, though some of the poems are beautiful enough to make us forgive this lapse. Other *haikai* are little more than greetings to Bashō's various hosts—appropriate salutations to inscribe in guest books, but not necessarily worthy of preservation.

Perhaps the most important *haikai* composed on the journey was *michinobe no/mukuge wa uma ni/kuwarekeri* ("The rose of Sharon by the side of the road was eaten by my horse"). This verse unfortunately loses everything in translation.[5] The reader must visualize the scene, perhaps in terms of Bashō's two prefatory notes "On horseback" and "Before my eyes." Bashō is riding along, not paying much attention to the road, when his horse suddenly lowers its head and devours a white flower. Only then does Bashō become aware of the flower, its whiteness, and its brief moment of glory. Some Japanese commentators have claimed that Bashō intended to impart a moral lesson with the verse: the flower was eaten because it chose to blossom conspicuously by the road instead of in humble safety within a field. But this lesson would hardly make the verse memorable; it is striking because of Bashō's evocation of his sudden awareness of beauty in the moment of its destruction. Such flashes of understanding were the object of his travels; in this verse Bashō gave expression to real experience, rather than to intellectualized emotions. This development in his art was so important that many critics have declared that the poetry composed during this journey marked the true beginnings of Bashō's *haikai* style.

TRANSLATION

When I set out on my journey of a thousand leagues, I packed no provisions for the road.[6] I clung to the staff of that pilgrim of old who, it is said, 'entered the realm of no-mind under the moon after midnight.'[7]

When I set out from my tumbledown cottage on the river[8] in the eighth month of the Year of the Rat, 1684, the voice of the wind sounded strangely cold.

> nozarashi wo
> kokoro ni kaze no
> shimu mi kana

> Bones exposed in a field—
> At the thought, how the wind
> Bites into my flesh!

> aki tō tose
> kaette Edo wo
> sasu kokyō

> Autumn—this makes ten years;
> Now I really mean Edo
> When I speak of 'home.'[9]

Rain fell the day I crossed the barrier,[10] and the mountains were all hidden in cloud.

> kirishigure
> Fuji wo minu hi zo
> omoshiroki

> Fog filtering down—
>   A day you don't see Fuji
> Is most intriguing.[11]

A man named Chiri[12] was my helper and companion on this journey, and showered me with every kindness. He is a person who might well be described as 'completely understanding in his associations and faithful to his friends.'[13]

> Fukagawa ya
> bashō wo Fuji ni
> azukeyuku

> Goodbye, Fukagawa!
> The banana tree I leave,
> Fuji, to your care.[14]
>   Chiri

As we walked along the Fuji River, we noticed an abandoned child, perhaps three years old, weeping pitifully. I wondered if its parents, buffeted by the swift currents of this river and unable to withstand the rough waves of the floating world, had abandoned him here, thinking his life would last only so long as the dew. Would the tender clover blossoms scatter tonight in the autumn wind beneath the plant, or would they wither tomorrow? With these thoughts I took some food from my sleeve and threw it to the child as we passed.

> saru wo kiku hito
> sutego ni aki no
> kaze ika ni

> Poets have grieved to hear
> Monkeys—what of a child forsaken
> In the autumn wind?[15]

How did this come about? Were you hated by your father, neglected by your mother? No, it is not that your father hates you or your mother has turned her back. This is all the doing of Heaven, and you can only lament your unhappy fate.

It rained the day we crossed the Ōi River.

aki no hi no ame	The rain of an autumn day—
Edo ni yubi oran	In Edo they must be counting their fingers;
Ōigawa	We are at Ōi River.[16]

On horseback:

michinobe no	The rose of Sharon
mukuge wa uma ni	By the side of the road—
kuwarekeri	Devoured by my horse.

A waning moon hung pale in the sky, but it was very dark on the path at the base of the mountain. I let my whip dangle over the horse, and rode several leagues before cock-crow. The 'lingering dream' of Tu Mu's *Early Departure* was suddenly shattered when I arrived at Sayo no Naka-yama.

uma ni nete	I dozed on my horse;
zammu tsuki tōshi	Lingering dreams, the moon far off,
cha no keburi	And smoke from breakfast tea.[17]

I called on Matsubaya Fūbaku who lives in Ise, and rested my legs at his house for ten days or so. I wear no sword at my side, but carry an alms wallet around my neck and a rosary of eighteen beads in my hand.[18] I look like one of the laity, but my head is shaven. Here they consider everyone with a shaven head to belong to the tribe of priests, and they would not allow me to enter the Shrine. That evening I visited the Outer Shrine. The shadows were deepening under the First Torii, and sacred lanterns flickered here and there. From the holy peak came a wind fragrant with pines, penetrating my flesh and stirring profound emotions.

misoka tsuki nashi	The last of the month, no moon;
chitose no sugi wo	A storm holds in its embrace
daku arashi	The thousand-year cedar.

A stream flows through Saigyō Valley. I watched women washing potatoes:

imo arau onna	Potato-washing women—
Saigyō naraba	If I were only Saigyō
uta yoman	I'd write an uta.[19]

On the way back that day we stopped at a teahouse where a woman named Butterfly asked me to write a *haikai* on her name. She offered me a piece of white silk, on which I wrote:

ran no ka ya	A fragrance of orchids—
chō no tsubasa ni	Incense burnt into the wings
takimono su	Of a butterfly.[20]

On visiting a hermit's thatched cottage:

tsuta uete	Ivy planted here,
take shigo hon no	And four or five bamboo stalks
arashi kana	Rattle in the wind.

At the beginning of the ninth month I returned to my old home. The day-lilies in my mother's room had been withered by the frost, and there was no trace of them now.[21] Everything had changed from what it used to be. My brother's hair was white at the temples and his brows were wrinkled. 'We are still alive,' was all he said. Then, without a word, he opened his relic bag. He said, 'Pay your respects to Mother's white hairs! This is Urashima's magic box—see how your brows have greyed!'[22] For a while I wept.

te ni toraba kien	Taken in my hand it would melt,
namida zo atsuki	The tears are so warm—
aki no shimo	This autumnal frost.

Pursuing our journey into the province of Yamato, we arrived at a place called Takenouchi in Katsuragi County. This is Chiri's native town, and we rested ourselves for a few days.

At a house deep in the bamboo forest:

wata yumi ya	Cotton-whipping bows—
biwa ni nagusamu	We enjoy the sound of lutes
take no oku	Deep in the bamboos.[23]

We visited the Taima Temple on Futami Mountain. The pine in the garden looked at least a thousand years old, and was big enough 'to hide an ox.'[24] Though this tree is inanimate, its connections with the Buddha have kept it from harm by a woodsman's axe. How fortunate, and how inspiring!

sō asagao	Priests and morning glory,
iku shinikaeru	How often dead and reborn!
nori no matsu	The pine of the Law.[25]

I trudged alone far into Yoshino. The mountains truly stretch on and on, and white clouds lie piled on the peaks. A smoky rain buried the valleys, here and there interrupted by the huts of the mountain folk, very small. To the west, the sound of a tree being felled; to the east, the echo. The voices of the bells of many temples found a response deep in my heart. Many of the men who from ancient times have come to these mountains to forget the world have obtained a refuge in the poetry of China and Japan. Indeed, would it not be appropriate to call this mountain Lu Shan, like the one in China?[26] I passed the night in a small temple.

kinuta uchite	Strike your fulling-block
ware ni kikase yo ya	And let me hear it, won't you?
bō ga tsuma	Wife of the temple.[27]

The remains of Saigyō's thatched hut are reached by pushing some two hundred yards to the right, beyond the inner shrine, over what is scarcely a woodsman's trail. A steep valley lying in between produces a most powerful impression. The 'clear spring dripping through the rocks'[28] does not appear to have changed since Saigyō's time, and its water still falls drip-drop.

tsuyu toku toku	The dew falls drip-drop:
kokoromi ni ukiyo	Would I could dip myself here
susugabaya	And rinse away the world.

If Po I had lived in Japan he surely would have rinsed his mouth in this spring, and had Hsü Yu learned of it, this is undoubtedly where he would have washed his ears.[29]

By the time I had climbed the mountain and descended its slopes, the autumn sun was already slanting, and leaving unvisited many famous sites, I went directly to worship at the Emperor Godaigo's tomb.[30]

gobyō toshi hete　　　　　The royal tomb has aged—
shinobu wa nani wo　　　　Grass of longing, tell me, what
shinobugusa　　　　　　　Are you longing for?[31]

From Yamato I went through Yamashiro and then to Mino over the Ōmi Road. Beyond Imasu is Yamaka, the site of Tokiwa's old grave.[32] Ise no Moritake[33] once wrote of 'an autumn wind resembling Lord Yoshitomo,' and I had wondered where the resemblance lay. Now I wrote:

Yoshitomo no　　　　　　Yoshitomo's heart
kokoro ni nitari　　　　　Is what it most resembles—
aki no kaze　　　　　　　This autumnal wind.

At Fuwa:[34]

aki kaze ya　　　　　　　A cold autumn wind
yabu mo hatake mo　　　　Over bamboo groves and fields:
Fuwa no seki　　　　　　This was Fuwa Barrier.

I went on to Ōgaki where I stayed at Bokuin's house.[35] When I set out from Musashi Plain it was with the thought I might leave my bones in some lonely field.

shini mo senu　　　　　　I haven't died, after all,
tabine no hate yo　　　　And this is where my travels led—
aki no kure　　　　　　　The end of autumn.[36]

At the Hontō Temple in Kuwana:

fuyu botan　　　　　　　Winter peonies—
chidori yo yuki no　　　　Sanderlings, you should be called
hototogisu　　　　　　　Cuckoos of the snow![37]

Weary of sleeping every night in strange lodgings, I got up from bed while it was still dark and went out onto the beach.

akebono ya　　　　　　　At break of day
shirauo shiroki　　　　　The white-bait are
koto issun　　　　　　　A single inch of white.[38]

I worshipped at Atsuta. The shrine grounds were terribly ravaged. The earthen wall had tumbled down and was hidden now in clumps of weeds.

At one place ropes had been stretched to show where a small shrine had stood, at another a stone marker told the name of the god once worshipped here. The shrine, buried as it was under a rank growth of mugwort and longing-grass, was actually more affecting than in its full splendor.

shinobu sae	Even the longing-grass
karete mochi kau	Has withered; I buy stale cakes
yadori kana	At a roadside booth.[39]

On the way to Nagoya I wrote these poems:

Kyōku	*A Comic Verse:*
kogarashi no	In this wintry wind
mi wa Chikusai ni	I must look exactly like
nitaru kana	Chikusai, don't I ?[40]

kusa makura	Sleeping on a journey—
inu mo shigururu ka	Is some dog being rained on too?
yoru no koe	The voices of night.

On walking to see a famous snow-view:

ichibito yo	Men of the city!
kono kasa urō	I'll sell you this wicker hat,
yuki no kasa	A snow umbrella.[41]

On seeing a traveller:

uma wo sae	This snowy morning
nagamuru yuki no	I stare even at a horse,
ashita kana	Much less a man.[42]

After spending a day on the coast:

umi kurete	The sea darkens—
kamo no koe	The cries of the wild ducks
honoka ni shiroshi	Are faintly white.[43]

As the days went by in travel, untying my straw sandals at this place and laying down my walking stick at that, the year drew to a close.

toshi kurenu	The year has ended.
kasa kite waraji	Still I wear a wicker hat
hakinagara	And sandals of straw.

I murmured these words again and again. I spent the New Year in a mountain hut.

ta ga muko zo	Whose son-in-law is that,
shida ni mochi ou	Bringing rice-cakes and fern-fronds,
ushi no toshi	This Year of the Ox ?[44]

On the road to Nara:

haru nare ya	The spring has come!
na mo naki yama no	Over nameless mountains
asagasumi	The morning mist.[45]

While in retreat at the Hall of the Second Moon:[46]

mizutori ya	The water-dipping rite—
kōri no sō no	The clatter of the pattens
kutsu no oto	Of the frozen priests.[47]

I went to Kyoto and visited Mitsui Shūfū's house in the mountains at Narutaki.

A Plum Grove

mume shiroshi	How white the plum flowers!
kinō ya tsuru wo	Was it yesterday your cranes
nusumareshi	Were stolen from you ?[48]

kashi no ki no	See how the oak tree
hana ni kamawanu	Stands there, indifferent
sugata kana	To all those blossoms![49]

On meeting Ninku Shōnin at the Western Cliff Temple in Fushimi:

wa ga kinu ni	Sprinkle my cloak
Fushimi no momo no	With drops of dew from Fushimi,
shizuku se yo	Blossoming peach.[50]

Crossing the mountains on the road that goes to Ōtsu:

yamaji kite	Going a mountain road
nani yara yukashi	Something or other drew me:
sumiregusa	The wild violets.

A view of the lake:

Karasaki no	Pine of Karasaki
matsu wa hana yori	Mistier even
oboro ni te	Than cherry blossoms.[51]

Sitting down at an inn for lunch:

tsutsuji ikete	Azaleas in a pot—
sono kage ni hidara	In their shadow a woman
saku onna	Slicing salted cod.

Poem written on an excursion:

nabatake ni	In the fields of rape,
hanamigao naru	With faces like blossom-viewers,
suzume kana	Look at those sparrows!

At Minakuchi I met an old friend I had not seen for twenty years:[52]

inochi futatsu	In our two separate lives
naka ni ikitaru	It has lived all this time:
sakura kana	The cherry has blossomed.[53]

A priest from the Isle of Hiru in Izu Province, a man who, like myself, has been travelling since last autumn, asked on learning my name if he might accompany me on my journey. He followed as far as Owari Province.

iza tomo ni	Come on! We'll nibble
homugi kurawan	On ears of wheat together,
kusa makura	A poor man's journey.[54]

This priest informed me that the Abbot Daiten of the Enkaku Temple had passed away at the beginning of the first moon. I couldn't believe the news—it seemed like a bad dream. I at once wrote Kikaku:[55]

ume koite	Longing for plum blossoms
u no hana ogamu	I bow before verbena—
namida kana	Behold my tears![56]

Sent to Tokoku:[57]

shirakeshi ni	In the white poppy
hane mogu chō no	A butterfly tears off his wings:
katami kana	A keepsake of himself.

I stayed for a second time with Tōyō.[58] When about to return to Edo I wrote:

botan shibe	Grief over parting:
fukaku wakeizuru	From the peony heart the bee
hachi no nagori kana	Struggles to the surface.

I stopped at a hut in the mountains of Kai.

yuku koma no	The horse I rode on
mugi ni nagusamu	Is solaced with oats, and I
yadori kana	With lodgings tonight![59]

At the end of the fourth moon I returned to my hut. When I had rested from the fatigue of the journey I wrote:

natsugoromo	My summer garments—
imada shirami wo	I still haven't quite finished
toritsukusazu	Picking out the lice.

NOTES

1. *Kasshi ginkō* 甲子吟行 means literally, "a poetry-making journey of the *kasshi* year." *Kasshi* corresponds to the first year of the Jōkyō era, or 1684. The journey extended into 1685.
2. See below, note 17.
3. The text was reproduced in 1932 by Meiji Shoin. It is noteworthy in that it contains two or three word descriptions of illustrations which are now lost.
4. From *Oi no Kobumi*. See Sugiura Shōichirō et al, *Bashō Bunshū* (in Nihon Koten Bungaku Taikei series), p. 53.
5. I am not implying that *all* Japanese poetry loses everything in translation.
6. An allusion to Chuang Tzu: "If you are going a thousand li, you must start getting the provisions together three months in advance." (Burton Watson, *The Complete Works of Chuang Tzu*, p. 30).
7. An illuminating discussion of the meaning for Bashō of the lines by the Chinese Zen monk Kuang-wen (1189–1263) is found in Akabane Manabu, "Nozarashi Kikō to Gōko Fūgetsu Shū," in *Renga Haikai Kenkyū*, 9, pp. 29–40. The passage tells us that Bashō, like the Zen monk of the past, is about to journey into a realm untouched by mundane human concerns.
8. Bashō's hut at Fukagawa on the Sumida River had been rebuilt the previous year after a fire.
9. Various commentators have pointed out that "autumn" (*aki*) often merely means "time,"

but I have kept the original word since the season is in fact autumn. Bashō had lived twelve, not ten, years in Edo.

10. The Barrier of Hakone, where travellers were examined.

11. Matsukura Ranran (1647–93) once stated, "My master in all his lifetime never wrote a poem about Fuji or Yoshino." (Fujii Otoo, *Fūzoku Monzen Tsūshaku*, p. 205.) The present verse is about Fuji, but Ranran's statement was essentially true: Bashō wrote about *not* seeing Fuji.

12. Naemura Chiri (1647–1716).

13. Apparently a quote from Chuang Tzu. See Watson, p. 84.

14. Bashō's hut in Fukagawa had a banana tree (*bashō*) in the garden from which he derived his name as a *haikai* poet.

15. T'ang and later Chinese poets frequently expressed grief over hearing the doleful cries of monkeys, and the theme passed over into Japanese poetry. Bashō's seeming callousness in passing by the abandoned child has been much debated; perhaps the simplest explanation is that a waif by the roadside was a far more common sight in Bashō's day than in our own.

16. That is, friends in Edo, counting the days on their fingers, try to guess how far Bashō has gone. He and his companion have reached the Ōi River, one of the most dangerous places on the road.

17. This verse was extensively rewritten by Bashō. His pupil Hattori Tohō (1657–1730) described the process in *Akazōshi* (c. 1710): "At first the poem ran *Bajō nemuran to shite/ zammu zangetsu/cha no keburi.* He changed the opening line to *Uma ni nete.* Later Bashō decided that the poem had too jingling a rhythm, and changed it to read *tsuki tōshi cha no keburi.*" (Nose Asaji, *Sanzōshi Hyōshaku*, p. 132.) The first two lines of the *haikai* are derived directly from lines by Tu Mu, and even the final line, "tea smoke," is found in another well-known poem. Bashō was interested in the perfection of the Japanese wording, and he was not ashamed to have borrowed his images.

18. Rosaries normally had 108 beads, but Bashō's abbreviated version had only one-sixth that number.

19. The verse, like a number of others in this work, does not have the proper number of syllables, an indication that Bashō was still under Danrin influence. It is hard, in any case, to imagine Saigyō writing an *uta* about women washing potatoes.

20. The butterfly that alights on an orchid is permeated with its scent, just as silk was by the perfumes burnt into it.

21. Some commentators take the whole sentence as meaning simply: "My mother was dead and nothing remained of her." There is an allusion to the *Shih Ching*. See Yokozawa Saburō, *Bashō Kōza*, VIII, p. 71.

22. Urashima Tarō received a jewelled casket similar to Pandora's; when he opened it he suddenly aged many years.

23. The bow was used for whipping impurities out of raw cotton. Its sound was compared to that of the *biwa*.

24. Another allusion to Chuang Tzu: "He saw a serrate oak standing by the village shrine. It was broad enough to shelter several thousand oxen." (Watson, p. 63.)

25. The priests and the morning glories come and go, but the tree remains.

26. A mountain in Kiangsi famous for its scenery, and the retreat of many priests and poets.

27. The sound of the fulling-block was a hackneyed winter image. Bashō wants his stay to be typical, so he asks the wife to strike the block. The priests of some of the Yoshino temples married, and their wives helped them to run the temples as inns.

28. Allusion to a famous poem attributed to Saigyō.

29. These two well-known figures of ancient China were frequently evoked as men of incorruptible purity, who rinsed their mouth and ears to free them from taint after being offered the throne.

30. The Emperor Godaigo died in Yoshino in 1339.

31. *Shinobu*, the hare's-foot fern, is the homonym of a word meaning "to recall the past."

32. Tokiwa was the mistress of Minamoto no Yoritomo (1123–60). Yoshitomo is generally thought of as having been an extremely cruel man, but Bashō seems to have considered him to be a tragic, lonely figure.

33. Arakida Moritake (1473–1549), a Shinto priest of the Ise Shrine, was often styled an "ancestor" of *haikai* poetry.

34. The Barrier of Fuwa was one of the three famous barriers of ancient Japan. It was abandoned by the end of the Heian period, and poets generally wrote of its desolation.

35. Tani Bokuin (1646–1725).

36. Bashō seems to have felt that the most difficult part of the journey was over. There is a markedly more cheerful tone in the remainder of the *Journey* than in the earlier part. *Aki no kure* usually means "autumn nightfall" in *haikai* poetry, but probably means "late autumn" here.

37. Both the peony and the cuckoo are associated with summer; seeing a winter peony, Bashō likens the sanderling (a winter bird) to the cuckoo.

38. Bashō may have been influenced in writing this verse by a line of Tu Fu. See Katō Shūson, *Bashō Kōza*, I, Part II, p. 355.

39. Ebara Taizō and Yamazaki Kiyoshi, *Bashō Kushū*, p. 256, suggested that the cakes were stale, intensifying the loneliness of the poem.

40. Many, many pages have been devoted to the question whether or not the word *kyōku* is inside the poem or a title. I have followed the majority of commentators in making it into a title.
Chikusai, an impoverished quack doctor, was the hero of *Chikusai Monogatari* by Isoda Dōya (1585–1634), an inconsequential, frivolous example of *kana zōshi*.

41. I have followed Katō (p. 366) in giving two meanings for *kasa*, but the characters used for "wicker hat" and "umbrella" were interchangeable at the time. The meaning may therefore be: "Men of the city! I'll sell you my wicker hat, a snow-covered wicker hat."

42. I have added the last line to my translation, following the interpretation of the verse by Katō, pp. 367–9.

43. A poem famous for its use of equivalence of the senses. The form of the verse is irregular (5, 5 and 7 syllables), as if to emphasize the voices of the wild ducks. As the sea darkens the sound of the ducks crying is apprehended in terms of pale flashes of white against the blackness.

44. Rice-cakes (*mochi*) and fern-fronds (*shida*) are both associated with the New Year. The Year of the Ox was 1685.

45. Mountains celebrated in poetry were always worthy of being admired, but the spring mist gives charm even to nameless mountains.

46. Nigatsudō, a part of the Tōdaiji monastery in Nara. Every year from the first to the fourteenth day of the second month the Mizutori celebration is held. During one part of the rite, priests wearing wooden shoes race around the altar, making as loud a noise as possible.

47. The words *kōri no sō* are so unusual that editors have sometimes emended it to *komori no sō*, "priests in retreat." But the line probably refers to the coldness of the night, freezing the priests, like ice, into solemn attitudes.

48. An allusion to an anecdote about the Sung poet Lin Ho-ching (967–1028) who lived by a lake and "considered his plum trees his wife and his cranes his son." Bashō compliments his host by likening him to the Chinese.

49. It has been suggested that Bashō himself is the sombre oak tree, unaffected by the changes brought by the spring.

50. Fushimi (south of Kyoto) was noted for its peaches. The verse seems to indicate Bashō's desire to share in the virtue and wisdom of the holy man Ninku (1606?–86).

51. This verse has also occasioned much controversy. The ending *ni te* seems too inconclusive for a *hokku*, though it was commonly used for the third verse in a linked-verse series. The verse also lacks a *kireji*. Pupils of Bashō advanced subtle reasons for these departures from established usage, but Bashō himself denied that anything more was involved than a simple perception. The verse is apparently derived from one by the Emperor Gotoba: *Karasaki no/matsu no midori mo/oboro ni te/hana yori tsuzuku/haru no akebono.*

52. Hattori Tohō, like Bashō a native of Iga. Tohō was 28 in 1685, the year of the meeting, and only nine when Bashō left Iga, but Bashō apparently remembered him.

53. Meaning that, though the two men have changed, the cherry tree continues to blossom as in the past.

54. I have supplied "poor man's" because that is what nibbling on ears of wheat implies.

55. Takarai (or Enomoto) Kikaku (1661–1707). The letter may be found in Nunami Keion, *Kikaku Zenshū*, p. 61.

56. Plum blossoms are associated with the first month, when Daiten died. They are also associated with scholars. The verbena (*unohana*) blossoms in the fourth month, when Bashō wrote the letter.

57. Tsuboi Tokoku (1660?–90), a pupil of whom Bashō was especially fond.

58. Hayashi Tōyō (1650?–1712).

59. Probably a greeting to someone who was thoughtful not only to Bashō but his horse.

Bashō's Journey to Sarashina

THE YEAR before Bashō wrote his most famous travel diary, *The Narrow Road of Oku* (*Oku no Hosomichi*), describing his journey to the north of Japan in 1689, he visited Sarashina (in the present Nagano Prefecture) and left behind a short account of his travels. It is in prose with a number of verses appended. The *Sarashina Kikō* ("Sarashina Travel Record"), the shortest of his works in this form, has been the least discussed. The reason for this neglect is obvious: it lacks the sustained beauty of the longer accounts, and the *haiku* it contains are not of the first quality. However, it is of interest not only as any work by the greatest poet of the Tokugawa period automatically must be, but because it helps illuminate in a delightful manner an important period in Bashō's development.

I. THE JOURNEY

In the spring of 1688, Bashō, only lately returned from the long journey described in *Oi no Kobumi*, first began to think of taking the Kiso Road to Sarashina.[1] He had his heart set on seeing the harvest moon—the "famous" moon of the eighth month—and his anticipation was the keener because rain had spoiled his moon-viewing at Kashima the previous year. There are many spots in Japan celebrated for their moon-viewing, but in Bashō's day the moon at Sarashina was the most renowned. Many poets from the time of Ki no Tsurayuki in the tenth century had sung its beauty, a beauty tinged with the melancholy overtones of the legend of Obasute Mountain. In the summer of 1688, while Bashō was staying at Ōtsu (near Kyoto), he was impatiently waiting for the Sarashina autumn moon, as a *haiku* he wrote attests. It bears the prefatory note, "Thinking of journeying along the Kiso Road, I went while staying at Ōtsu to see the fireflies at Seta." The *haiku* ran:

kono hotaru	These fireflies
tagoto no tsuki ni	To the moonlight in each field
kurabemin	I shall compare.[2]

Bashō does not directly mention Sarashina, but the words *tagoto no tsuki*, "the moonlight in each field," were used as an epithet for the moon seen reflected in the innumerable rice paddies flanking the hills at Sarashina.

Bashō went from Ōtsu to Gifu, where he watched the famous cormorant fishing. From Gifu he continued his journey to Nagoya, and spent most of the seventh month there. Early in the eighth month[3] Bashō departed Nagoya for Sarashina, again stopping at Gifu. He was accompanied by his disciple Ochi Etsujin, with whom he had journeyed to Yoshino earlier in the year, and by the servant whom another Nagoya disciple, Yamamoto Kakei, sent along to help Bashō on the way.[4] Bashō planned to arrive in Sarashina by the fourteenth of the month at the latest, in order to be able to enjoy the full moon on the fifteenth. From Sarashina he planned to return to his home in Edo after over a year's absence. Etsujin and the servant accompanied him all the way.

Bashō wrote four farewell verses for his friends in Gifu. This was the second time in the course of a few months that he had parted from them.

> okuraretsu
> okuritsu hate wa
> Kiso no aki
>
> So often seen off,
> Or seeing you off, journey's end—
> Autumn in Kiso.[5]

This poem suggests the loneliness of autumn in Kiso awaiting Bashō after leaving his friends in Gifu a final time. A second poem composed on the same occasion ran:

> kusa iro iro
> ono ono hana no
> tegara ka na
>
> Many kinds of plants,
> And each one triumphant in
> Its special blossoms.[6]

This poem was probably intended as a salutation to a group of poets; Bashō is saying that each excels at his particular style of writing.

Two other verses were composed on this occasion by Bashō "after being seen off to the outskirts of the town by the others and drinking three cups of parting."[7] They were:

> asagao wa
> sakamori shiranu
> sakari kana
>
> The morning glories,
> Knowing nothing of drinking-bouts,
> Are in full splendor.[8]

Perhaps Bashō, noticing the morning glories as he set out early on the morning of his journey, was contrasting their freshness with the drinking-bout of the night before and its aftereffects; or perhaps he meant to say that these flowers, unlike cherry blossoms or chrysanthemums, had attained their full bloom without attracting the attention of saké-drinking celebrants. This, again, seems to have been an impromptu verse. The last of the four parting verses at Gifu was:

> hyoro hyoro to   Trembling and swaying,
> kokete tsuyukeshi   And bent down with dewiness,
> ominaeshi   The lady-flowers.[9]

This verse apparently refers to flowers Bashō saw nearby, laden with morning dew, but *hyoro hyoro to*, an onomatopoetic expression used of trembling things, may also have been intended to suggest the shaking legs of those who had been imbibing farewell drinks.

Bashō's account of the journey to Sarashina along the Kiso Road is cursory, with hardly a place-name to help us identify his course. It may be imagined that he travelled with great speed to reach Sarashina from Gifu, mainly on foot, in three days. Bashō wrote, "The road was long, and the days left before the full moon were few, so I had to set out by night and not sleep till evening, grass for my pillow."[10] We may also indirectly infer his haste from the fact this journey failed to produce any of the usual exchanges of linked verse with local poets on the way. Perhaps the haste was responsible also for Bashō's complete confusion of the order of the sights he passed on his journey.

The diary proper concludes with an account of staying at an inn where the chatter of a tiresome old monk prevented Bashō from writing any poetry. The appended poems mention some additional sights of the journey including (in one version) the Zenkōji in the city of Nagano, presumably the farthest point he reached. A poem about Mount Asama has led critics to suppose that Bashō returned to Edo by way of Karuizawa and Usui Pass, a well-known route that passed by Asama.

In addition to *Sarashina Kikō*, Bashō wrote a shorter prose piece called *Sarashina Obasute Tsuki no Ben* (On the Moon at Obasute in Sarashina). A section of this work was inserted into the text of *Sarashina Kikō* by the poet-priest Chōmu in his edition of 1776, and it has been retained by many modern editors, anxious to expand a rather slight work.

Bashō was back in Edo by the early part of the ninth month. On the tenth of that month, the day after the chrysanthemum festival, he visited his disciple Yamaguchi Sodō, and composed a verse comparing the moon of the night of the sixteenth (the night after the full moon) to chrysanthemums on the day after the festival.[11] On the thirteenth of the same month Bashō was invited to a party, where he wrote:

Kiso no yase mo	Still not recovered
mada naoranu ni	From my thinness of Kiso,
nochi no tsuki.	The late moon-viewing.[12]

As early as the reign of the Emperor Uda (889–98) it had become customary to admire the moon on the night of the thirteenth of the ninth month, and Bashō alludes to this practice. He followed his poem with a brief prose statement that began with the words: "It is now the thirteenth night of the ninth month, and still the remembrance of the mid-autumn moon at the village of Sarashina, high above Obasute Mountain, where it is hard to be consoled, does not leave my eyes in all its pathos."[13]

From that winter came a poem prefaced by the statement: "Written the winter he spent in the Bashō-an, thin and worn from his autumn in Kiso."

itsutsu mutsu	Five or six of them
cha no ko ni narabu	Lined up before the tea cakes
irori kana	Around the hearth fire.[14]

On New Year's Day of 1689 Bashō's verse recalled his journey to Sarashina:

ganjitsu wa	First day of the year!
tagoto no hi koso	It is the sunlight on each field
koishikere	That stirs my longing.[15]

Here, in place of *tagoto no tsuki*, the moon reflected in the Sarashina rice paddies, Bashō imagines the first sun of the new year glinting in the same fields.[16]

Another verse, possibly written on the journey but not included in any text of *Sarashina Kikō*, bears the prefatory note, "On travelling the road to Shinano."

yuki chiru ya	Snow is flaking down—
hoya no susuki no	By the hut for storing grain
karinokoshi	The last of the sheaves.[17]

Still other echoes of the Sarashina journey may be found in a letter written in the first or second month of 1689, quoted below, and in such verses as those addressed to Bashō's disciple Morikawa Kyoriku (1656– 1715). Kyoriku, a samurai, was about to travel the Kiso Road in 1693, and Bashō urged him to try, in his heart at least, to savor the hardships of that remote region, rather than journey in state.

shii no hana no	Let your heart at least
kokoro ni mo niyo	Be like the *shii* flowers,
Kiso no tabi	On your Kiso journey.[18]

The *shii* (pasania) flower was a small, inconspicuous blossom, suggestive of Bashō's own retiring nature.

ukibito no	From a wayfarer
tabi ni mo narae	Learn what it means to travel—
Kiso no hae	The flies of Kiso.[19]

That is, Kyoriku should imagine what it is like to stay in the kind of fly-infested inn that Bashō normally frequented.

The impressions aroused by the journey to Sarashina were, however, dimmed by the longer and more memorable travels in the north of Japan, recorded in *Oku no Hosomichi*, and few other references are found in his later writings.

2. THE TEXT

It is not surprising, in view of the general lack of interest in *Sarashina Kikō*, that no text was established as the definitive one. So great was Chōmu's fame as an editor that most books continued to reproduce without question his 1776 text though, as I have mentioned, it was suspect. Chōmu's fondness as an illustrator for the sight of the moon shining over Obasute Mountain apparently even led him to prefer the short "On the Moon at Obasute in Sarashina" to the diary itself, and that was presumably why he used it to augment the text.[20]

Three texts survive of the diary. The first, the Okimori text first published in 1967,[21] is a manuscript in Bashō's own hand. Clearly, it is a rough draft: a dozen or so passages in the prose have been crossed out or altered, and three of the appended *haiku* are given in more than one version. The text is of unique importance because of the glimpse it provides of Bashō at work as an artist.

The second text was published in 1709 as an appendix to Bashō's other travel account *Oi no Kobumi*, and edited by his pupil Kawai Otokuni. The prose is almost identical with the Okimori text, as corrected, but there is one additional *haiku*, the verse written in Gifu about seeing off friends. The Otokuni text is generally accepted as Bashō's final version.

The third text is included in *Kiso no Tani* (The Valley of Kiso), a volume compiled in 1704 by Bashō's neighbor Taisui. The prose part of the text is very similar to the Okimori manuscript, but there are about twenty variants, including a major one. Only six *haiku* are appended, in contrast to the twelve of the Okimori manuscript. Two of the *haiku*, not found in either of the other texts, refer to events after Bashō's return from Sarashina, one on his thinness after the journey, and the other about the New Year sunlight in the fields. This text was apparently in the possession of Bashō's close disciple Sugiyama Sampū, and was reprinted by a descendant of Sampū in 1799; it is therefore often referred to as the Sampū text.

Japanese scholars, insofar as they have chosen among these texts, have invariably preferred the Otokuni text, and it appears in all the standard editions. Nevertheless, I believe that the Sampū text should be considered the final form of the diary and not a preliminary draft, as so often stated.[22] It should not be forgotten, however, that the *haikai* writings are cursed by copyists' errors, occasioned in large part by the exceedingly difficult handwriting preferred by the *haikai* masters in their manuscripts, and these sometimes make textual criticism exceedingly difficult. The inescapably subjective nature of any attempt to decide which of two alternate versions of *haikai* prose or poetry is literarily superior also makes any conclusion at best tentative. Nevertheless, the evidence available to me strongly suggests that the hitherto neglected Sampū text should be taken as Bashō's definitive version.

The normal means to which Japanese editors have recourse in determining the superior of two *haikai* texts is to compare the verses. When the same poem appears in two different forms, one clearly better than the other, it is assumed that it must be later. In the case of the Otokuni and Sampū texts, however, this is not possible, for the poems are either the same or else completely different. We may note, however, that two of the Otokuni verses were written in Gifu, before the journey began, one on the lady-flowers, and the other on being seen off. The Sampū text contains neither of these poems but, as mentioned above, has two written after Bashō's return to Edo. In other words, if, as generally assumed, Bashō wrote the three texts in the order Sampū-Okimori-Otokuni, in moving from the Sampū text to the Okimori manuscript he added one poem written before he started on his journey and eight others written during the journey, but deleted the two poems composed most recently, after his return. This is possible, of course, but it seems more likely that Bashō moved from the Okimori manuscript, with the various revisions indicating Bashō's dissatisfaction with his verses, to the fair copy in the Otokuni text, and then to the Sampū text with its briefer selection of verses, representing Bashō's final thoughts.

As far as the prose is concerned, most of the variants are minor, consisting of different ways of writing the same words (whether using characters only, *kana* only, or a mixture of the two). The Otokuni text agrees almost in every respect with the Okimori manuscript and may be considered a fair copy and nothing more.[23] The Sampū text, on the other hand, has at least one important variant. After the words, "We had not a moment free of anxiety," it adds, "I got off the horse and put the servant on instead." Bashō apparently forgot this important detail in his first version of the account, and that is why we have him at one moment riding on the horse and then, without explanation, walking behind it. The *haikai* style of prose often omits unimportant details in the attempt to suggest more than is specifically stated, but this detail is necessary.[24] The other changes in the prose do not necessarily indicate Bashō's final choices, but since the Sampū text generally incorporates the corrections made in the Okimori manuscript, it is hard to imagine that it could have preceded it. If we agree with the majority of Japanese scholars that the Sampū text was a first draft, it would mean, for example, that when Bashō wrote the Okimori manuscript he omitted some of the sights (the hanging bridge, the Rocks of Awakening) mentioned in the earlier version, then restored them in marginal corrections. This is hard to imagine.

In addition to internal evidence, a few other facts help to establish the order of the texts. A letter Bashō wrote early in 1689 relates: "In the autumn of last year I travelled with a poet named Etsujin along the Kiso Road. When we passed by the hanging bridge where our lives were in peril, when I felt the impossibility of consolation at Obasute, when I heard the sounds of the fulling-blocks and scarecrow clappers and of men chasing away the deer, all sights filled with a poetic melancholy, I could not but think of you. When the New Year dawned, my mind was still occupied by thoughts of travel." Bashō followed these words with the verse "First day of the year." Bashō described the sights of the journey in much the same manner as in *Sarashina Kikō*, suggesting that the text was still fresh in his mind.

A postscript to the Sampū text (in *Kiso no Tani*) notes, moreover: "The Master returned to his cottage after seeing the Sarashina moon and travelling along the Kiso Road in the first year of Genroku (1688). Unable to describe all that weighed on his heart, he wrote down his remembrances as they came to him, then discarded what he had written. His words have remained in my library, and I here publish them." It is not entirely clear who wrote the note and whose library is referred to, but most probably it is Sampū writing of his own library.[25] It would have been natural for Sampū to have been given the final manuscript when Bashō moved into Sampū's house in the third month of 1689, just prior to setting out for the north. It is unlikely that Bashō wrote *Sarashina Kikō* much after the second or third month of 1689, for his mind was soon to be absorbed by his later journey.

We may conjecture then that the first draft (the Okimori manuscript) of *Sarashina Kikō* was written towards the end of 1688, after Bashō returned to Edo.[26] The Sampū text, with its New Year poem, must have been composed in 1689.

One reason sometimes given for preferring the Otokuni text to the Sampū text is that it contains more *haiku*. This very fact, however, suggests it was not the final form, for Bashō's practice was to reduce and eliminate rather than to augment. Only about half the *haiku* composed on the *Oku no Hosomichi* journey are preserved in the final version. Besides, the "First day of the year" poem is possibly the best of those arising from the journey; it is hard to believe Bashō suppressed it in favor of some of the less interesting poems found in the Otokuni text.

3. THE JOURNEY TO SARASHINA
(translation of the Sampū text)

The insistent autumn moon kept stirring in my heart a longing to see the moon at Obasute Mountain in the village of Sarashina. My friend Etsujin also urged me to share with him the pleasures of travel. The Kiso Road leads through remote mountains where the roads are steep, and Kakei, fearing that the journey might prove too much for us, sent a servant along. These companions were determined to help me in any way they could, but having had no experience of travel, as it would seem, they were both quite helpless. Everything went topsy-turvy and was utterly disorganized, but it all made for a delightful journey.

At a certain place we met a priest of about sixty years, a man with nothing of interest or humor about him. He was trudging along in grim silence, his body bent by the weight on his back. He was panting heavily, and his feet advanced in mincing little steps. My companions, moved to pity, bundled the things we were shouldering together with the priest's burden, piled them on a horse, and set me on top of the lot.

High mountains and curiously formed peaks hung in layers above our heads. In the valley a great river flowed; below us dropped an abyss that seemed a thousand fathoms deep. There was not a bare foot of level ground, and it was most alarming to be in the saddle. One terrifying and dreadful moment succeeded another, until finally I got off the horse and put the servant on instead.

We passed the hanging bridge over the gorge, the Rocks of Awakening and various other places.[27] Next came the Monkey's Racecourse and Tachi Pass, as we followed what they call the "Forty-eight Turnings." The road twisted and turned so often that I felt as though we were winding our way up into the clouds. Even the two of us on foot felt so dizzy and frightened that our legs trembled under us, but the servant was calmly dozing on the back of the horse, absolutely untouched by fear. Very often he almost fell off, sending a chill of fear through me as I looked up at him from behind. The turbulent world must appear even so to the mind of Buddha, and when we reflect that change in its inexorable swiftness visits all men, we can see why "the whirlpool of Awa is free of wind and waves."[28]

At night we found lodgings. I took out my brush and lay on the floor with my eyes shut underneath the lamp. I beat my head and moaned as I tried to get down on paper the sights of the day which I had thought of turning into verse, as well as various *hokku* on which I had not quite finished working. While I was so engaged the old priest, imagining that I was depressed by the journey or worried about something, attempted to comfort me. He told me all about the holy places he had visited as a pilgrim when he was young, and recounted the innumerable wonders of Amida. Then followed story on story about things which he considered to be remarkable. The result was that my poetic impulse was blocked, and it was quite impossible for me to compose a single verse.

The moonlight, from which I was distracted by his chatter, was streaming in from among the trees through a hole in the wall, and from here and there came the sound of scarecrow clappers and the voices of deer-hunters. Autumn could not have been more melancholy.

"Well," I cried, "let's have something to drink at this feast of moonlight!" Wine-cups were produced, about twice the circumference of

normal ones and of a coarse lacquer flecked with gold leaf. A Kyoto
gentleman would have found such a cup in deplorable taste and refused
even to touch it, but I felt surprisingly elated, as though I held a cup of
chalcedony or of finest jade,[29] no doubt because it suited the place.

ano naka ni[30]	Inside your surface
makie kakitashi	I'd like to sprinkle gold leaf—
yado no tsuki	Moon at the inn!

(Two different meanings have been suggested: the moon is too perfect
and Bashō perversely wishes to flaw it; or that Bashō, amused by the
unusually large wine-cup, suggests that the moon would make an even
bigger cup if coated with gold leaf. The verse lacks great depth, but was
presumably retained by Bashō because it follows so closely on the preceding prose.)

BRIDGE OVER THE GORGE

kakehashi ya	Bridge over the gorge:
inochi wo karamu	Clinging for their very lives,
tsuta katsura	The ivy and vines.

(The bridge is so unsafe that even the ivy and vines twined round it
must cling for their lives. Imagine how terrifying it must be for anyone
to cross!)

kiri harete	The mist having cleared
kakehashi wa me mo	On the bridge over the gorge
fusagarezu	You dare not shut your eyes.
	Etsujin

(When the mist clears the enormous depth of the gorge is plainly seen,
making the hanging bridge all the more frightening.)

SARASHINA

izayoi mo	The moon of the sixteenth
mada Sarashina no	And still in Sarashina
kōri kana	County, it would seem!

(Bashō spent three nights moon-viewing at Sarashina, unable to tear
himself away.)

ON THE NIGHT OF THE THIRTEENTH, AFTER RETURNING TO MY HUT

Kiso no yase	Still not recovered
mada naoranu ni	From my thinness of Kiso,
nochi no tsuki	The late moon-viewing.

WELCOMING THE NEW YEAR: ON NEW YEAR'S DAY

ganjitsu wa	First day of the year!
tagoto no hi koso	It is the sunlight on each field
koishikere	That stirs my longing.

At this point the Sampū text concludes, but the Okimori manuscript includes the following additional poems.

kakehashi ya	Bridge over the gorge!
mazu omoiizu	The first thing it brings to mind:
koma mukae	How they met the colts.

(The verse describes an ancient practice of presenting horses to the court from all parts of Japan. By the end of the Kamakura period this was restricted to horses from Shinano. An envoy from the court went to Shinano on the sixteenth day of the eighth month, just when Bashō was there, to "meet" the presentation horses. Bashō perhaps imagines a frightened colt being led over the rickety bridge.)

Sarashina ya	Sarashina!
miyosa no tsukimi	Three nights of moon-viewing
kumo mo nashi	Without a cloud.

Etsujin

OBASUTE MOUNTAIN

omokage ya	I can see her face—
oba hitori naku	The old woman, weeping alone,
tsuki no tomo	The moon her companion.

(Two different interpretations have been given: the first, that the old woman has the moon as her only companion while she weeps alone; the second, that Bashō makes his image of the old woman weeping alone his "companion" as he gazes at the moon over Obasute Mountain.[31] This verse is also found in *On the Moon at Obasute in Sarashina*.)

hyoro hyoro to	Trembling and swaying,
nao tsuyukeshi ya	And dewier than ever,
ominaeshi	The lady-flowers.

(The Okimori manuscript shows how Bashō changed the verse from its original form, written when leaving Gifu, into this more effective version.)

yo ni orishi	I would present it
hito ni torasen	To a man still in this world—
Kiso no tochi	A Kiso chestnut.

(This verse is crossed out in the Okimori manuscript and replaced by the following.)

Kiso no tochi	A Kiso chestnut—
ukiyo no hito no	A suitable present for
miyage kana	A man of the world.

(The chestnuts of Kiso were considered to be a very humble variety, unlikely to be eaten by a man in society who had his pick of the best chestnuts. Bashō, or perhaps Etsujin, gave one of these chestnuts to Kakei as a souvenir. Kakei later wrote, "I received a chestnut as a souvenir from someone who had returned from moon-viewing in Kiso, and thinking I would keep it until the end of the year as a decoration, I wrote, 'End of the year/And one lonely chestnut,/Rolling, rolling.' "[32])

mi ni shimite	Radishes so sharp
daikon karashi	They send a shudder through me—
aki no kaze	O autumnal wind.

(Bashō here, as in other poems, equates the senses. The sharp taste of the radishes corresponds to the feel of the autumn wind. Perhaps also the "whiteness" of the autumn wind is brought to mind by the white radish.)

ZENKŌJI

tsuki kage ya	The light of the moon!
shimon shishū mo	Four the gates and four the sects,
tada hitotsu	And yet only one.

(The Zenkōji is a great temple in the city of Nagano, today shared by Tendai and Jōdo Buddhists. The exact meaning of the second line of the verse has been much debated, but it would seem that the light of the moon, a common image for Buddhist knowledge, shines impartially on all the different varieties of the religion practiced at the Zenkōji)

aki kaze ya	O autumn wind!
ishi fukiorosu	Blowing down the stones
Asama-yama	On Mount Asama.

(This verse is crossed out.)

fuku oroshi	The blowing down-wind:
Asama wa ishi no	At Asama a storm gale
nowaki kana	Of stones!

(This verse has a correction in the first line to *fukiotosu*, but the whole verse was subsequently crossed out.)

fukiotosu	Stones blown down—
ishi wo Asama no	This is the autumn storm
nowaki kana	Of Asama.

(This verse is corrected to read:

fukitobasu	Sending stones flying—
ishi wa Asama no	This is the autumn storm
nowaki kana	Of Asama.)[33]

4. ON THE MOON AT OBASUTE IN SARASHINA (translation)

I have at times been tempted on hearing of Shirara and Fukiage,[34] and this year I kept thinking how I should like to see the moon at Obasute. I departed from the province of Mino on the eleventh day of the eighth month. The road was long and the days left before the full moon were few, so I had to set out by night and not sleep till evening, grass for my pillow. My plans did not go amiss: I arrived in the village of Sarashina on the night of the full moon. The mountain stretches in a southwesterly direction, about one *ri* south of the village of Yawata. It is not exceptionally tall, and has not even curiously formed boulders. But the mountain's appearance is filled with deep melancholy. I could understand why they said it is "hard to be consoled"[35] here. I felt vaguely depressed and, even as I wondered why anyone should have abandoned an old woman, my tears began to fall.

omokage ya[36]	I can see her face—
oba hitori naku	The old woman, weeping alone,
tsuki no tomo	The moon her companion.

izayoi mo	The moon of the sixteenth
mada Sarashina no	And still in Sarashina
kōri kana	County, it would seem!

5. THE IMPORTANCE OF SARASHINA KIKŌ

Apart from the intrinsic literary worth of *Sarashina Kikō*, it is of great
interest because of what it reveals of Bashō's personality and methods
of composing poetry. The popular image of Bashō, fostered during the
centuries since his death, is of a poet-saint, and it is not entirely mistaken. Although his age was celebrated for its ostentatious brilliance,
Bashō led a life of simplicity and sobriety. He seems to have indulged in
worldly pleasures as a young man, and some scholars in recent years have
attempted to prove he had a mistress,[37] but Bashō's way of life certainly
had little to do with the Genroku ideals. It is nevertheless rather misleading if one thinks of him entirely in terms of humility and benevolence.
Bashō was the leading poet of his day, and he could on occasion be sharp
in his criticisms even of his own disciples.[38] He moreover took a certain
amount of deference for granted. In this diary, for example, when Bashō
and his companions overtake the monk, it is not the panting old man but
the still vigorous Bashō who gets on the horse. He does not even suggest
he should walk; evidently Bashō considered that his place was on the
horse. His attitude towards the monk is also revealing. He finds the old
man a bore and a nuisance, without a single redeeming feature. I think
we would agree with Bashō, but believers in the poet-saint have been
shocked by his attitude.[39]

Sarashina Kikō also gives an amusing picture of Bashō at work as a
poet, the only one I know. Persons unacquainted with the techniques of
composing *haiku* sometimes imagine that the *haiku* poet can effortlessly
dash off an exquisite little verse whenever the occasion requires. That
sometimes happened: Bashō wrote many impromptu *haiku*, some of
them excellent. For the most part, however, Bashō's best poems were the
result of many revisions and reworkings of the kind found in the Okimori
manuscript.

The final *haiku*, as we have seen, is given in four different stages of
composition. The first mentions merely the autumn wind (*aki no kaze*),

but in subsequent versions Bashō changed this to *nowaki*, the equinoctial storm wind that is characteristic of Mount Asama. In order to suggest the force of this wind Bashō at first had it blow stones down Mount Asama, but in the final version he has the wind send the stones flying through the air, an effective exaggeration. The grammar of the succeeding verses becomes increasingly complex, as Bashō attempted to put more and more meaning into his lines, until the final version defies normal parsing and can be understood only intuitively. Even the final version of this *haiku* is surely not wholly successful; it was not included in any other collection of Bashō's poetry. But we can only be impressed by the care Bashō gave to capturing in the seventeen syllables of a *haiku* the tremendous spectacle of an autumn storm over Asama.

Painstaking revision, perhaps accompanied as in *Sarashina Kikō* by Bashō's groans and moans, lay behind his finest *haiku*. The impromptu poems sometimes have a winning freshness, but they are not the *haiku* that made Bashō immortal. They satisfied certain social requirements—a greeting to Bashō's host, a reply to a local poet's effort, the graceful compliance with a plea to write something in a guest book—but the facility with which Bashō (and countless *haiku* poets since) turned out such verses is no indication of the labor involved in creating a masterpiece.

Another popular misconception is that Bashō was a "poet of nature." It is evident from *Sarashina Kikō*, where he devotes a bare line or two to nature, that he was far more interested in the people he encountered on his journeys. In his letter about the Kiso Road he mentioned the things that lingered in his memory some months after his return: "the hanging bridge where our lives were in peril ... the impossibility of consolation at Obasute ... the sounds of the fulling-blocks and of men chasing away the deer." The melancholy of Obasute—the story of the abandoned old woman—and the desolate sound of the fulling-blocks were conventionally recognized poetic images that Bashō probably would not have noticed if he had not already known about them. We cannot but be surprised that Bashō showed no greater interest in the wildly picturesque landscape of the Valley of Kiso.

Bashō travelled widely in Japan, but wrote surprisingly few poems about the most famous sights of his journeys. Usually he described them in prose, if at all. When he reached Matsushima on his *Oku no Hosomichi* journey he was unable to compose a single poem, but included one by his companion Sora. His most famous poem about Mount Fuji, as we have seen, describes a day when the mountain is invisible. It was almost as if he were paralyzed before sights that overwhelmed him. The poetic associations, rather than the sights themselves, meant most to him. If, for example, he visited a place famous for its wisteria at a time of year when the wisteria were not in bloom, he nevertheless wished to look at the leafy vines, for his imagination enabled him to visualize the purple waves of blossoms. If he came in mid-summer to a pass in the mountains famous in poetry for its snow, he could recapture its appearance in the snow from the whiteness of the summer flowers. Bashō tended to see landscapes through the poetry written about them.

The generalization holds true of *Sarashina Kikō*. When he reached Obasute Mountain its featurelessness seems to have disappointed him, but he managed all the same to detect an atmosphere of deep melancholy. The *haiku* he wrote on this occasion was literary, almost impersonal, and hardly required a visit to the site for inspiration. But Bashō was satisfied, for he had seen the most famous moon-view in Japan. Kinoshita Chō-shōshi (1569-1649), a *tanka* poet who influenced Bashō, had written, "Cherry blossoms should be admired at Yoshino, the moon at Sarashina, snow on the peak of Fuji."[40] The moon at Sarashina was so compelling a sight to Bashō and countless other poets not because of any unique, visible beauty—it hardly differed from the view at countless other spots in Japan—but because of its poetic associations, especially the legend of Obasute.

6. THE LEGEND OF OBASUTE

The earliest surviving account of the legend of Obasute is found in *Yamato Monogatari*, a poem-tale (*uta-monogatari*), written in the tenth century:

> Once there lived a man at Sarashina in the province of Shinano. He had lost his parents while still a boy, but his aunt stayed with him until he grew to manhood, caring for him no less than if he had been her own child. But when the man married, his wife had a heart of mischief, and constantly complained about the bent old woman. She insisted to her husband that his aunt was evil and wicked, and so poisoned his mind that he began to neglect her, though he had always treated her kindly before. The aunt was so very old she was bent quite double. The man's wife grew increasingly annoyed by the aunt, and it infuriated her that the old woman refused to die. Often she would say disagreeable things about her, time and time again returning to the subject with the recommendation, "Take her off and abandon her deep in the mountains somewhere." Finally, in desperation, the man agreed.

One night when the moon was very bright the man said, "Auntie, won't you come with me? There's to be a splendid ceremony at the temple, and I'll take you there." The aunt was delighted, and the man took her on his back. The man lived at the foot of a tall mountain, and he carried his aunt deep into the recesses of this mountain. When he finally reached a spot so remote it seemed improbable his aunt would ever be able to find her way back home, he left her there and ran off. The aunt cried after him, but the man rushed straight home without so much as turning back. There he sat for a while reflecting on what he had done. His wife's abuse had provoked him into committing this deed, but now he could not help but feel unhappy over the fate of someone who had reared him and tended him for long years, in no way different from a mother. He stared at the moon, incomparably bright as it rose over the crest of the mountain, and could not sleep a wink that night. In his grief he wrote the poem:

> Wa ga kokoro / nagusamekanetsu / Sarashina ya
> Obasuteyama ni / teru tsuki wo mite
> My heart cannot be consoled at Sarashina,
> Looking at the moon that shines on Obasute Mountain.

The man went back to his aunt and carried her home again. From that time on the mountain was called Obasute, and that is why it is said to be so hard to be consoled there.[41]

As in other instances in *Yamato Monogatari*, we may surmise that the poem existed first and the story was later invented to explain or amplify it. The poem in turn probably originated in the place-name itself; folk etymologies played an important part in early Japanese literature. The true derivation of the name Obasute has been much discussed.[42] One of the most widely accepted views is that it was originally Obatsuse, a name that still survives in the Sarashina region. A simple phonetic change and the name became Obasute, which could easily be interpreted as *oba*, "aunt," and *sute*, from *sutsu*, "to abandon." This etymology may have given rise to the legend preserved in *Yamato Monogatari*, which in turn was assimilated with a Buddhist story known in Japan from the sixth or seventh century.

This story, found originally in the *Samyukta-Ratna-Pitaka Sūtra* (The Sutra of the Collection of Varied Jewels), describes a certain country where it had become the custom to drive old people from their homes and abandon them to their deaths. A great minister of state, filial at heart, was reluctant to comply with the law of the country, and instead hid his father in a cellar. About this time a god appeared before the king of the country and showed him two snakes, saying, "If you can distinguish which of these snakes is the male and which the female, your country will be granted peace. But if you fail, you and your country will both be destroyed within seven days." The king, in great distress, took counsel with his ministers, but none could help him. The king ordered that a search be made throughout the length and breadth of the country for someone who could tell the snakes apart, and promised generous rewards.

The only person who could answer the riddle proved to be the father of the great minister. The god, still not satisfied, proposed still other riddles, and each time the old man knew the solution and informed his son. Finally the god was satisfied, and the king, overjoyed to be relieved of the menace hanging over him, offered to give the minister anything he desired. The minister, disclaiming all credit for answering the riddles, revealed he had broken the law of the land by harboring his old father. The king immediately rescinded the cruel law, made the minister's father his own teacher, and urged all men henceforth to practice filial piety.[43]

Versions of this story are found in the legend of the Aridōshi Shrine, in *The Pillow Book of Sei Shōnagon*,[44] and in other works, but the Japanese children's story about Obasute Mountain, still popular today, combines this Buddhist account with the legend of Obasute. It tells how a farmer once lived in Shinano with his aged mother. The lord of the province, hating old people, ordered that they should all be abandoned to their deaths. The man had no choice but to take his mother to a lonely mountainside one moonlit night and leave her there. But after he had returned home he remembered all the devotion and love his mother had showed him, and he could not bear to let her die that way. He stole out that night, brought his mother back, and hid her in a hole under the floor. Just at this time the lord of a neighboring province sent the lord of Shinano some riddles as a test of wits. No one could answer them except the old woman. When the lord of Shinano eventually learned who had provided him with the answers, he withdrew his terrible edict.

The legend of Obasute also provided Zeami with the subject of one of his masterpieces, *The Deserted Crone* (*Obasute*).[45] The play opens with a traveller from the capital arriving at Obasute Mountain to view the autumn moon. He encounters an old woman, who eventually confesses that she is the "deserted crone" for whom the mountain was named. During the interlude between the first and second parts of the play a villager appears and tells the traveller about the man who abandoned his aunt on the mountain, where she turned to stone. Later the man, as an act of contrition, became a Buddhist priest. In the second part of the play the old woman reappears as a ghost, and describes the beauty of the moon over Obasute Mountain that once brought her such pleasure, but now is remembered with the bitterness of the fate she experienced.

The Obasute legend has continued to inspire the writers of recent years. Inoue Yasushi, in *Obasute* (1956), imagined what it would be like if a law enjoining the abandonment of all old people were in effect, obliging him to abandon to her death his own mother. In the story Inoue speculates on why the legend of Obasute has retained its grip on the imagination of the Japanese. Another version of the story, *The Oak Mountain Song* (*Narayama-bushi Kō*, 1957) by Fukasawa Shichirō, treated the theme from the point of view of an old woman who insists on being abandoned, and suggests that this attitude is admirable.[46]

In poetry the tradition has stemmed mainly from the poem in *Yamato Monogatari*. Nishizawa Shigejirō, in his *Obasute-yama Shinkō*, gave thirty-two pages of poetry about the mountain, including *haiku*, *tanka*, and even poems in Chinese. The *tanka* poets included Ki no Tsurayuki, Ono no Komachi, Shunzei, Teika, Saigyō, Nōin, the Emperors Gosaga and Goto-ba and, in more recent times, Kamo no Mabuchi, Motoori Norinaga, Itō Jinsai and Sakuma Shōzan.

These poets, however, were not all celebrating the beauty of the same mountain. The name Obasute has remained unchanged since the *Yamato Monogatari*, but three different mountains have been identified with the name.[47] The Obasute Mountain that probably gave rise to the legend ceased at some time during the Heian period to be so identified. Instead, Kaburigiyama, a much taller mountain, became Obasute. From the tenth to fifteenth centuries many poets visited this mountain and sang its doleful charms. The custom of making pilgrimages to Obasute seems to have died out during the warfare of the sixteenth century, and when the *haiku* poets began it again they were guided to still another mountain, one formerly called Yawata.

When Bashō visited Obasute Mountain and was struck by its haunting melancholy, he was not looking at the same mountain described by Saigyō and the other great poets of the past. The modern Obasute is a much smaller mountain, and had not Bashō gazed at it across the poetry written about Obasute, he might never have even glanced at the third mountain to bear that name. Kaburigiyama is more impressive, as we can gather from this *tanka* by Sakuma Shōzan:

> *Wa ga kuni no | Kaburigi-yama ni | miru tsuki wa*
> *Karihoruniya no | akebono no sora*

The moon we see at Kaburigi Mountain in our country
Is the sky of a California dawn.[48]

Obasute Mountain was beginning to recapture some of its past glory in Bashō's day, but it was not until he visited it that it became a tourist attraction. Numerous *haiku* poets followed in Bashō's steps to luxuriate in the melancholy legend and the moonlight. It is a popular skiing resort today.

7. SARASHINA KIKŌ IN BASHŌ'S WORK

Sarashina Kikō is a minor work that describes only a few days in Bashō's life. Despite the gruelling nature of the journey and the sometimes unwelcome company, this was a happy time for him. The diary itself represented a further development in his prose style. Most important, perhaps, it may have been on this journey that Bashō first thought of taking the narrow road of Oku.

NOTES

1. See the letter to Sampū from Ise, written in the middle of the second month. The text is in the Nihon Koten Bungaku Taikei series edited by Sugiura Shōichirō and others, *Bashō Bunshū*, p. 358.

2. See the text in *Bashō Kushū* (Nihon Koten Bungaku Taikei series) edited by Ōtani Tokuzō and Nakamura Shunjō, p. 103.

3. On the eighth day, if we can believe the often inaccurate *Jirōbei Monogatari*; quoted by Hagiwara Ragetsu, *Bashō no Zembō* (rev. ed.), p. 357.

4. The servant was possibly the Gonshichi to whom Bashō later dedicated a poem. See Katō Shūson, *Bashō Kōza*, II, p. 70.

5. Ōtani and Nakamura, p. 191.

6. *Ibid.*, p. 182.

7. *Ōi Nikki* (in Haisho Taikei series), p. 31. *Sarashina Obasute no Ben* (see section 4) dates the departure from Gifu as the eleventh of the eighth month.

8. Ōtani and Nakamura, p. 178.

9. *Ibid.*, p. 179.

10. From *Sarashina Obasute no Ben*. See section 4.

11. See Ebara Taizō and Yamazaki Kiyoshi, *Bashō Bunshū* (in Nihon Koten Zensho series), p. 104.

12. Ōtani and Nakamura, p. 154.

13. First determined to be a work by Bashō by Ogino Kiyoshi in *Bashō Ronkō*, pp. 88–92. See also the texts in Imoto Nōichi and Hori Nobuo, *Bashō Shū* (in Koten Haibungaku Taikei series), pp. 520–21.

14. Ōtani and Nakamura, p. 221.

15. *Ibid.*, p. 20. The first line is given as *Ganjitsu ni* in some texts, but this seems a less preferable variant.

16. Although this poem seems peculiarly appropriate to conclude Bashō's recollections of his journey, it is not found in the most commonly given versions of *Sarashina Kikō*. See below.

17. Ōtani and Nakamura, p. 208. See also their note on p. 274.

18. *Ibid.*, p. 115. A later version of the same poem runs: *tabibito no/kokoro ni mo niyo/shii no hana.*

19. *Ibid.*, p. 104.

20. See his *Bashō-ō Ekotoba-den*, edited by Kōda Rohan, pp. 37, 42.

21. Published in facsimile by the owner, Okimori Naozaburō, with an explanatory pamphlet entitled (*Bashō-ō Shinseki*) "*Sarashina Kikō*" *Sōkō*. Even before the discovery of the manuscript it was known from the tracing made in the early nineteenth century, reproduced in the Kaizō Bunko edition of *Oku no Hosomichi*, edited by Hagiwara Ragetsu in 1929.

22. I believe that I was the first to make this suggestion, when the present article was originally published in 1957. The same conclusion was independently reached by Muramatsu Yūji in "Sarashina Kikō no Seiritsu" (in *Tōyō Daigaku Tanki Daigaku Kiyō*, I, 1970). Muramatsu, comparing each of the variations in the prose of the Sampū text with the Okimori manuscript, concluded that the revisions incorporated in the Sampū text suggest it is later. However, eminent scholars of Bashō, notably Imoto Nōichi, continue to believe that the Okimori manuscript is superior, and therefore later. New materials discovered by Professor Imoto and briefly reported in his article "Sarashina Kikō de Mondai Teiki" (in *Asahi Shimbun* for 7 August 1970) also confirm him in this belief, especially a version of *Sarashina Obasute Tsuki no Ben* which includes elements found in the *Sarashina Kikō*. Some scholars who share Professor Imoto's views have even proposed that *Sarashina Kikō* was not written until after Bashō's return from his *Oku no Hosomichi* journey. But as yet not enough has been published for an outside scholar to form any opinion of these newly discovered documents, and I have not seen fit to change my conclusions.

23. See Muramatsu, pp. 96–97.

24. So famous a *haiku* poet and interpreter of Bashō as Ogihara Seisensui was baffled by this ambiguity and decided, not being acquainted with the Sampū text, that there must have been *two* horses! (See *Tabibito Bashō*, 1932 edition, p. 278.)

25. Muramatsu, p. 89.

26. The text includes the poem on the Kiso chestnut presumably written after his return to Edo. See Ōtani and Nakamura, p. 189.

27. The bridge was between Kiso Fukushima and Agematsu. A modern bridge bears the same name, but the spot is different. The Rocks of Awakening (Nezame no Toko) is a place of marvellous scenic beauty, consisting of huge, curiously shaped boulders rising from the Kiso River. These rocks are said to be where Urashima Tarō awakened from his long sleep. Tachi Pass and the Monkey's Race Course (Sarugabamba) are farther on, on the way to Sarashina.

28. Refers to a popular Buddhist poem: "Compared to our journey through this world, the whirlpool of Awa is free of wind and waves."

29. The characters Bashō used for the material of the wine-cups are non-existent, and commentators have offered many theories as to what he intended.

30. The Okimori manuscript shows that Bashō made several changes in this verse. It seems to have begun as *tsuki no naka ni*, but this eventually became *ano naka ni*. However, the Sampū text has *ano tsuki ni*, which may be a copyist's error; if not, the first line should be interpreted as "Inside that moon."

31. For the former interpretation see Katō in the Sanseidō *Bashō Kōza*; for the latter see Imoto Nōichi in the Sōgensha *Bashō Kōza*, I, p. 225.

32. In *Arano* (part of *Bashō Shichibu Shū*), Iwanami Bunko edition, p. 78.

33. See below for an analysis of the different versions of this *haiku*.

34. Places famous for moon-viewing in Kii.

35. Allusion to *Kokinshū* poem 878 and to *Yamato Monogatari*.

36. Most texts of this work give *omokage wa* as the first line of the *haiku*, but it seems inferior to *omokage ya*.

37. That Bashō had a mistress was proved by Nomura Kazumi in *Bashō Denki no Shinkenkyū* (1950), among others; that Bashō had no mistress was proved by Okamura Kenzō in *Bashō to Jutei-ni* (1956).

38. Bashō's harsh criticisms of his disciple Kagami Shikō were published in extract by Professor Imoto in "Sarashina Kikō de Mondai Teiki."

39. Komiya Hōryū, a somewhat old-fashioned Bashō scholar, expressed his dismay (in *Bashō to Kikōbun*, p. 23) that Bashō could have treated another person as a nuisance, no matter how boring he might have been.

40. See Fujii Otoo (ed.), *Kyohaku Shū*, p. 13.

41. *Yamato Monogatari*, section 156 (in Nihon Koten Bungaku Taikei series).

42. See Nishizawa Shigejirō, *Obasute-yama Shinkō*, pp. 102–07.

43. From *Zōhōzō-kyō* (Taishō Tripitaka, IV, section 447, p. 203).

44. See the translation by Ivan Morris, I, pp. 203–05. See also Morris' notes in II, pp. 157–58.

45. Translation by Stanleigh H. Jones, Jr., included in Donald Keene (ed.), *Twenty Plays of the Nō Theatre*.

46. Translation by Donald Keene included in *The Old Woman, the Wife and the Archer*.

47. See Nishizawa, whose frontispiece consists of photographs of the three different mountains.

48. Nishizawa, p. 53.

III. THE CREATION OF
MODERN JAPANESE POETRY

Modern Japanese Poetry

MODERN JAPANESE poetry, like everything else modern in Japan, is generally traced back to the accession to undisputed authority of the Emperor Meiji in 1868. This political event did not immediately inspire floods of poetic composition; in fact, as far as I can determine, not a single poet sang the glories of the new reign, and no book of poetry of consequence was published for some years afterwards. But the new Emperor was to show himself conspicuously unlike many generations of his ancestors, rulers whose arrivals, activities and departures had been of little concern to poets. Though the Emperor's direct role in the movement of modernization was minor, he set the spirit of the new age in his oath taken in 1868, when he promised, among other things, to end old ignorance and to seek learning throughout the world. Poets were soon to call themselves proudly "Meiji men," meaning that they belonged to the new, enlightened generation.

Eighteen sixty-eight is of interest in the history of Japanese poetry for another reason. In that year two poets died whose works, though in the classical *tanka* form, suggest that they might ultimately have found a way out of the impasse in which Japanese poetry was trapped. The first, Ōkuma Kotomichi, sounded a new note in his book of poetic criticism *Hitorigochi* (1857): "The poets of the past are my teachers, but they are not myself. I am a son of my time and not of the past. Were I to follow blindly the poets of former times, I should forget my own humble identity. The poems I wrote might seem impressive, but their excellence would be entirely on the surface; they would be merchants in princes' raiment. My art would be pure deceit, like a performance of Kabuki." Despite his insistence that poetry reflect its time, however, Kotomichi's works are scarcely revolutionary: in diction and structure they are sometimes barely distinguishable from the poems in the *Kokinshū* written nine hundred years earlier. It would be hard to conceive of an English poet writing in 1850, with no intention of fraud, verses which might have antedated Chaucer, but in the Japan of the nineteenth century the language of the *tanka* was with few exceptions a thousand years old. Words of other than pure Japanese origin were not tolerated; it was as if the English poets of the eighteenth and nineteenth centuries had been obliged to confine themselves to words of Anglo-Saxon derivation, and Coleridge had therefore written "The Hoary Seafarer" instead of "The Ancient Mariner."

The subjects of poetry were also prescribed with minute exactness. There were, for example, twenty-five varieties of flowers which might properly be mentioned in a *tanka*: cherry blossoms, plum blossoms, wisteria, azalea, etc. Other flowers could be mentioned only at the risk of the poet being denounced as an eccentric or a revolutionary. The standard collections of poetry were known by heart, and the critical works of poetic dicta, most of them dating back to the thirteenth century, were not so much helpful guides as absolute prescriptions. The poet was encouraged to demonstrate originality of conception, while restricting himself to the language of the tenth-century collections, but what this meant in practice was merely minor variation. Perfection of classical diction, successful evocation of the poetry of the past, were the aims of centuries of poets. Of course an expert can trace currents even within this seemingly static poetic: the proportion of nouns might show a tendency to increase in certain periods, or there might be a greater use of metaphor in the love poems. But no self-respecting poet in 1850 would have said, "I enjoyed a quiet smoke," though people had been smoking for two hundred years. That is why Kotomichi's declaration seems so important for its day. Poets of the time reconciled their seemingly contradictory beliefs in the necessity for contemporary expression, and in the desirability of preserving the language and mood of the *Kokinshū* poetry, by writing chiefly about subjects which had not changed much in nine hundred years. "Fragrance alone, I thought, was in the wind, but since this morning the plum garden sends me blossoms too" is a poem which might have been written at any time over the centuries, and could still be composed today; indeed, such relatively static elements in Japanese life as the quiet appreciation of nature within one's own garden contributed to the preservation of the old poetic traditions.

The second of the poets who died in 1868, Tachibana Akemi, is a more striking figure. He was involved in the patriotic movements which resulted in the restoration of power to the Imperial Family, and his poetry reflects his activities far more vividly than Kotomichi's. He wrote, for

example, a series of fifty *tanka* on the theme "Solitary Pleasures" including: "It is a pleasure when, a most infrequent treat, we've fish for dinner,
and my children cry with joy, 'Yum-yum!' and gobble it down"; or,
"It is a pleasure when, in a book which by chance I am perusing, I come
on a character who is exactly like me;" or, "It is a pleasure when, in these
days of delight in all things foreign, I come across a man who does not
forget our Empire." These *tanka* have almost none of the traditional
virtues of the form: they lack elegance, tone, depth, melody and so on.
But in their different ways they point to possibilities of poetic expression
which had largely been ignored: the pleasures (or sorrows) of ordinary
life, the pleasures of the intellect, and the involvement of the poet in political activity. Tachibana Akemi's *tanka*, however, barely touched on these
larger issues. It remained the task of the specifically modern poets to
explore them.

Before 1868 Japanese poets who did not wish to write *tanka* had two
other recognized possibilities open to them. The first was the *haiku*,
a form which had originally allowed much greater freedom, especially
in the vocabulary, than the hidebound *tanka*, but which by this time was
even more saddled with hackneyed phraseology. Not one *haiku* poet
of distinction was writing in 1868. The most important poetry was probably not that in Japanese but in Chinese. There was a thousand-year-old
tradition of Japanese poets writing in Chinese, and probably the finest
of this poetry was composed in the early nineteenth century. Poets who
felt their thoughts too large to stuff into the thirty-one syllables of the
tanka or into the even more cramped seventeen syllables of the *haiku*
enjoyed the greater amplitude of the Chinese poem, which could run to
thirty or more lines. This meant, however, writing in a language as unlike
Japanese as Latin is unlike English. But just as English poets at times in
the past chose Latin, not only for commemorative addresses but for their
most personal poetry, so many Japanese found that certain things could
be said easier in Chinese. For them Chinese was not the language of China,
a foreign country, so much as a heritage from the Japanese past. Chinese
influence was present in almost every variety of Japanese literature prior
to 1868. It was only gradually superseded by influences from the West.

Modern Japanese literature was indeed to be distinguished most particularly by the presence of the West. Whether accepted or rejected, the
West could not be ignored. The first stage in adapting Western influence
was, inevitably, that of imitation. The Japanese have often been taxed
with an excessive proclivity towards imitation, but it is difficult to see
how they could have achieved the revolution in their literature without

translation and imitation. It is surprising in fact how much the poets managed to salvage of the old traditions even when translating. The Japanese preference for alternating lines in five and seven syllables, going back at least to the seventh century, continued to be observed by almost all poets for decades. Even when translating English poetry they adhered to this rhythm, as in the version of "Elegy in a Country Churchyard" done by Yatabe Ryōkichi (1852–99):

yamayama kasumi	The mountains are misty
iriai no	And, as the evening
kane wa naritsutsu	Bell sounds,
no no ushi wa	The oxen on the lea
shizuka ni ayumi	Slowly walk
kaeri yuku	Returning home.
tagaesu hito mo	The ploughman too
uchitsukare	Is weary and
yōyaku sarite	At last departs;
ware hitori	I alone
tasogaredoki ni	In the twilight hour
nokorikeri	Remain behind.

Sometimes the adaptations were even freer, using Japanese equivalents in the imagery or construction, as in this version of "The Last Rose of Summer":

niwa no chigusa	The thousand grasses in the garden
mushi no ne mo	And the cries of insects too
karete sabishiku	Have dried up
narinikeri	And turned forlorn.
aa shiragiku	Ah, the white chrysanthemum,
aa shiragiku	Ah, the white chrysanthemum,
hitori okurete	Alone, after the others,
sakinikeri	Has blossomed.

The rose, a flower without poetic significance for the Japanese, was here transformed into a chrysanthemum, and in place of Moore's "All her lovely companions/are faded and gone," a use of personification unfamiliar to the Japanese, we are told of the "thousand grasses" and "cries of insects" in the garden.

The first collection of modern poetry, *Selection of Poems in the New Style* (*Shintaishi-shō*), was published in 1882. It included fourteen translations of English and American poems, one French poem translated from an English version, and five original poems by the compilers. Among the

English poems were "The Charge of the Light Brigade," "Elegy in a Country Churchyard," the "To be or not to be" soliloquy, and two translations of Longfellow's "A Psalm of Life." The translators were scholars of English who happened to have become interested in poetry, and their versions, like the translations of professors elsewhere, had little poetic grace. The original poems are modelled on Western examples, sometimes with ludicrous results, as in Yatabe Ryōkichi's attempt at rhymed Japanese verse:

haru wa monogoto yorokobashi	In spring everything is full of charm,
fuku kaze totemo atatakashi	The blowing wind is really warm.
niwa no sakura ya momo no hana	Cherry and peach, blossoming bright,
yo ni utsukushiku miyuru kana	Make an unusually pretty sight.
nobe no hibari wa ito takaku	The lark of the moors, very high,
kumoi haruka ni maite naku	Sings as it soars far in the sky.

One compiler wrote disarmingly in the preface, "We are rather pleased with this selection of poems, but for all we know, the public may contemptuously dismiss it as an exceedingly strange and uncouth performance. Good and evil, however, are not eternal. Values change with the age and with what different generations believe. Even if our poems win no favor among people today, it may be that future generations of modern Japanese poets will attain the heights of Homer or Shakespeare. Some great poet, impressed by the new style of this collection, may contribute more talent and write poetry which will move men's hearts and make the very gods and demons weep."

As predicted, the collection was subjected to considerable abuse, part of it justified. We can only question the grasp of the principles of Western poetry revealed by Toyama Chuzan (1848–1900), the author of the poem entitled "On the Principles of Sociology," which begins with the lines, "The sun and moon in the heavens and even the barely visible stars all move because of a force called gravity." This was hardly an imitation of any English poem, but rather a combination of the new learning (especially the writings of Herbert Spencer) with the new poetic forms. One man wrote a full-length geography of the world entirely in the new verse! But *Selection of Poems in the New Style* was ridiculed less because of its poetical ineptitude than because the authors had deliberately mingled elegant and unrefined words including, for example, Chinese-derived expressions in Japanese contexts. Despite such criticisms, the collection exerted enormous influence, and the words "poems in the new style" (*shintaishi*) of the title came to be employed as the normal designation of the new poetry. Collections of this verse appeared in rapid succession during the following years.

The instant popularity of the new poetry was obviously not due to its exceptional beauty. It came rather as an explosive reaction to the overly familiar stereotypes of Japanese poetics. Tachibana Akemi in a satirical essay had derided the old poetry: "In early spring one writes of the morning sun gently shining and of the spreading mists; at the end of the year one speaks of the 'waves of years crawling shorewards' and of waiting for the spring. For flowers there is 'the blessing of rain' and for snow 'regret over leaving footprints.' Poetic language has come to mean such phrases and nothing else. A hundred out of a hundred poets, the year before last, last year, and this year too have merely strung together the same old phrases. How depressing!" Tachibana Akemi, not knowing about Western poetry, could offer no way out of the impasse except his homely little verses on daily life. With the new translations, however, it became apparent that poetry could have a much wider range than anyone had previously suspected.

First of all, poetry could be much longer and in many forms. Long poems had been popular in eighth-century Japan, and some new poets justified their long compositions in terms of Japanese tradition, but the inspiration for long poems, particularly on contemporary subjects, came directly from the West. Secondly, the subject matter was entirely new. The variety of topics treated by Western poets made some Japanese novices suppose, not surprisingly, that *any* subject, even the principles of sociology, might be celebrated in verse. The liberation from the old themes was sometimes excessive, and poets were eventually to discover that some hackneyed old topics still had validity, but it would never again be possible to limit Japanese poetry to the obviously "poetic." Finally, the language of Japanese poetry was enormously expanded, though not as much as the pioneers expected. Komuro Kutsuzan, the editor of one of the early collections, wrote, "Persons with unenlightened views, not realizing how the processes of civilization operate, assert that it is wrong to use in poetry any words except the old ones. This attitude in practice often leads to unfortunate results. For example, where once one spoke of a soldier carrying a bow and arrows, today he carries a Snyder, and there should therefore be no objection to writing of a soldier's Snyder. But when the critics insist that the poet must continue to refer to bows and arrows, does this not lead to an unfortunate result? They are mistaken because they do not realize that Snyder has already become a Japanese word." The argument is cogent, but unfortunately for Komuro Kutsuzan, the Snyder gun was not long afterwards replaced by a Japanese-made rifle, and the word Snyder, despite his predictions, never replaced bow and arrows.

Komuro Kutsuzan exemplified his theories of poetry with his "Ode to Liberty," translated in part by Sansom:

> O Liberty, Ah Liberty, Liberty O
> Liberty, we two are plighted until the world ends.
> And who shall part us? Yet in this world there are
> clouds that hide the moon and winds that destroy the
> blossoms. Man is not master of his fate.
>
>> It is a long tale to tell
>> But once upon a time
>> There were men who wished
>> To give the people Liberty
>> And set up a republican government.
>> To that end... [1]

The first volume of new verse by a single poet was the collection *The Twelve Stone Tablets* (*Jūni no ishizuka*) by Yuasa Hangetsu, published in 1885. It consists of a series of poems based on the Old Testament, cast into the traditional rhythms in five and seven syllables of the ancient Japanese poetry. The language is replete with the stylistic devices of the past, and the vocabulary rich in old-fashioned elegance, but the presence of the Land of Canaan and the Walls of Jericho remind us that the enlightenment has occurred. The strongest cultural influence of the early Meiji period was indeed the translation of the New Testament, completed in 1879. This period marked the high point of Christianity in Japan, as many people were converted to the religion of the West, the source of the new culture. Believers and non-believers read the Bible and sang hymns. The hymns especially proved important in the development of the new poetry.

The first critical study of the new poetry, published in 1893, began with the remarks, "People constantly tell me, 'I am living in Meiji Japan, and I use the language of Meiji Japan. Why should I study the dead writings of the past and waste my time over the old circumlocutions?'" Ōwada Tateki, the author of this study, though sympathetic with the point of view expressed, felt that much was still to be learned from the past. He favored the use of modern Japanese, but noted how difficult it was to set standards for the ordinary, contemporary language of the Meiji era. In 1893 there was no standard spoken Japanese. The tradition of writing the spoken language was so recent that people were not even sure how to record common colloquial expressions, nor which words were standard speech and which were dialect. Ōwada felt that a certain artificiality was therefore inevitable. Above all, he counselled, there should be "moderation" in expression—avoidance of bizarre phraseology merely to achieve novelty of effect. He declared, for example, that "direct imitations of such Western expressions as 'the moon dances' or 'the mountains clap their hands' are likely to surprise, but they are not pleasing."

On the whole, however, Ōwada was optimistic about the future of Japanese poetry. "A new atmosphere is about to flood into our literary world. Already it is seeking cracks through which to gain admittance. Breathe in! Breathe in! Japanese poetry has its strange, unique beauty, but we must not forget that foreign poetry has extraordinary virtues. It would be a mistake to abandon our own traditions and adopt theirs in entirety, but if we add theirs to our own we shall widen our literary horizons. The long poem is unquestionably the special glory of their literatures; we should therefore transplant it in our garden, tender it, water it, and make Eastern flowers blossom on this Western plant. The Japanese Po Chü-i has long since completed his labors and sleeps in the ground. When will the day come that a Japanese Milton will write *Paradise Lost* at the Ishiyama Temple?"

Japanese Miltons, even of the mute, inglorious kind, were never to abound, but the lyricism of the past, assuming the freer and more varied forms inspired by the West, was to produce before long a fair number of Japanese Wordsworths, Shelleys, and eventually Verlaines. The lyric in the strict sense was to remain the dominant form for thirty or more years; many of the best lyrics are widely known even to school children in the musical settings later given them. Because the Japanese language was unable, like English, to rely on rhyme or a pronounced rhythm to differentiate poetry from prose, a sustained poem was difficult to manage, and the greatest successes continued to be in shorter works even after the *tanka* had been rejected for its excessive brevity.

The first collection of modern poetry still widely read today appeared in 1897. The fifty-one poems in *Seedlings* (*Wakana-shū*) by Shimazaki Tōson (1872–1943) described the poet's youthful loves with an overt romanticism which captivated his readers. A few years later Tōson related what his feelings had been when he published this collection:

"A new era in poetry had at last arrived. It was like the coming of a beautiful dawn. Some poets shouted their words like the prophets of old, others cried their thoughts like the poets of the West; all seemed intoxicated with the light, their new voices, and a sense of fantasy. Youthful imagination awoke from an age-old sleep and clad itself in the language of the common people. Traditions took on fresh colors again. A brilliant light shone on the life and death ahead of them, and illuminated the grandeur and decline of the past. Most of that crowd of young poets were merely simple youths. Their art was immature and incomplete. But it was free of falsity or artifice. Their youthful lives flowed from their lips, and their tears of passion streaked their cheeks. Try to remember that their fresh, overflowing emotions made many young men all but forget food and sleep. And remember too that the pathos and anguish of recent times drove many young men mad. I too, forgetting my incompetence, joined my voice with those of the new poets."

Tōson published two more collections of poetry, in 1899 and 1901, before turning to the novel. His most famous poem, "By the Old Castle of Komoro," appeared in 1900. Its opening lines are known to most Japanese:

> By the old castle of Komoro
> In white clouds, a wanderer laments.
> The green chickweed has not sprouted,
> The grass has yet to lay its carpet;
> The silver coverlet on the hills around
> Melting in the sun, the light snow flows.

Tōson's indebtedness to the West included imitations of Shakespeare and of the "Ode to the West Wind." Other Japanese poets turned to Keats or to Browning. Susukida Kyūkin (1877–1945) wrote one poem beginning, "Oh to be in Yamato, now that October's there." After this comically obvious imitation, he continues quite respectably:

> I would follow a lane through the wood of Kaminabi, with its sparse-leaved trees,
> To Ikaruga, at dawn, the dew on my hair—when the tall grass
> Ripples across the wide field of Heguri like a golden sea,
> And the colour fades from the dusty paper-window, and the sun is faint—
> Between the wooden columns, insatiably, I peer at the golden letters of the precious age-old scriptures,
> At the ancient Korean lyre, the grey unglazed pottery and the gold and silver paintings on the wall.[2]

Without Browning the poet would probably not have conceived of this sentimental journey to Yamato, but once on his way he chooses images that are real and Japanese. In this respect the influence of English poetry on Japanese differed categorically from the centuries-old influence of Chinese poetry. Imitation of Browning enabled Susukida Kyūkin to evoke effectively a Japanese scene, but imitation of Chinese poetry had generally imposed the obligation of describing China as well, even on poets who had never seen China. In a real sense, then, imitation of European poetry led to a liberation of Japanese poetry, giving direction to thoughts which poets had long entertained but never known how to express. Fortunately for the Japanese, the European languages were so remote in idiom that no possibility of closely imitating them existed; imitations were thus usually of conception rather than of imagery. The poem on Yamato in October is otherwise indebted to Browning in the use of enjambement, not unknown in traditional Japanese poetry, but generally avoided, in keeping with the dictates of Chinese poetics.

The most powerful Western influence on Japanese poetry came in 1905 with the translations by Ueda Bin (1874-1916) of the French Parnassian and Symbolist poets. Ueda's explanations of the functions of Symbolist poetry, based on the theories of Vigié-Lecoq, were to exert an enormous influence on subsequent Japanese poetry. His translations introduced to Japanese the works of Baudelaire, Mallarmé and Verlaine, all of whom at once became favorite poets of the intellectuals. The popularity achieved by the French Symbolists in Japan is not entirely surprising, in view of the worldwide success of the movement, but that this poetry should have blotted out almost all other Western influences surely indicates some special affinity with the Japanese. In the introduction to his 1905 collection entitled *Sound of the Tide* (*Kaichō-on*), Ueda wrote, "The function of symbols consists in borrowing their help to create in the reader an emotional state similar to that in the poet's mind; they do not necessarily attempt to communicate the same conception to everyone. The reader who quietly savors the symbolist poetry may thus, in accordance with his own taste, sense an indescribable beauty which the poet himself has not explicitly stated. The explanation of a given poem may vary from person to person; the essential thing is that it arouse a similar emotional state."

Such views, as I have indicated, were borrowed from the West, but at the same time they represent quite accurately the special qualities of the traditional Japanese *tanka*. Since the ambiguities of the Japanese language are so extreme—in the *tanka*, for example, personal pronouns are rarely used, there is no distinction between singular and plural, often no distinction in tense, and the subject is usually unexpressed—it is natural for a given poem to produce different effects on different readers. The important thing, as in symbolist poetry, was the communication of the poet's mood, and here the shadings were extremely fine. The relatively straightforward poetic statements of Shimazaki Tōson, reflecting the nineteenth-century English traditions, were welcomed by the general public, but the poets responded more enthusiastically to the indirection shared alike by the symbolists and their own country's classical poetry. If they had been urged to look to the past, to avoid contamination by foreign ideas, these poets would have been outraged. They would have declared that such obscurantism was contrary to the spirit of the enlightened Meiji age. But when told that eminent foreign poets had preferred ambiguity to informative clarity, the Japanese responded with double enthusiasm. Foreign appreciation of other Japanese traditional arts was to provide the impetus for Japanese rediscovery. When the German architect Bruno Taut proclaimed the uniquely Japanese beauty of the Katsura Palace, the Japanese rapidly and instinctively echoed his excitement. A Japanese love of ambiguity and suggestion, going back a thousand years, underlay the triumph of the Symbolist school.

Ueda Bin's translations were acclaimed not only because they introduced celebrated European poets to Japan, but because they were exceptionally beautiful as Japanese. He maintained in general the traditional fives and sevens of Japanese poetry, sometimes combining them in novel ways, as in the lines of five, five, five and seven syllables he used in translating Mallarmé's "Soupir." The vocabulary was entirely traditional, even slightly archaic, using the most natural Japanese words (rather than exotic, literally translated phrases) to communicate with remarkable fidelity the mood of the original. Ueda was a polyglot, and his collection *Sound of the Tide* includes a section from d'Annunzio's "Francesca da Rimini," a sonnet by Rossetti, some German lyrics, and even poems from the Provençal, but it was his translations from the French which affected most markedly the dominant stream in modern Japanese poetry.

English and American poetry on the whole has not been of great influence in Japan, at least since the time of Ueda Bin. For many years Japanese poetry remained under the spell of the French Symbolists, and they were succeeded by the Dadaists, Surrealists and so on. English poetry belonging to the same schools was welcomed, and T. S. Eliot in particular worked his gloomy magic on the younger poets, even before the war created bombed-out wastelands for them to celebrate, but his absorption with tradition and religion escaped them. For the most part, English and American poetry excited relatively little interest, perhaps because translations from the French were literarily superior, perhaps because of the allure of Paris, which captivated the Japanese in the twenties and thirties no less than the Americans. By the 1880's English had become the second language of Japan, and every schoolboy, however unlikely ever to leave his farm or fishing village, was required to study English until he could plod through one of Lamb's *Tales from Shakespeare* or an O. Henry story. But English tended to be thought of as a practical language, the language of commerce and information, not of poetry. Translation from the English was therefore generally left to teachers of English grammar, and most Japanese poets, as if to distinguish themselves from schoolmasters, studied French, though a few preferred German or Russian. Ueda Bin's translations influenced a whole generation of Japanese poets.

The volume of translated poetry, *Corals* (*Sangoshū*), published by the great novelist and poet Nagai Kafū in 1913, was also from the French, and consisted chiefly of Baudelaire, Verlaine, Henri de Régnier, and the Contesse de Noailles. Kafū's translations are close to the original, sometimes in the classical tongue and sometimes, a great rarity in those days, in the colloquial. His translation of Verlaine's "Colloque Sentimental" was particularly successful.

> Dans le vieux parc solitaire et glacé,
> Deux formes a tout à l'heure passé.
>
> Samui samushii furuniwa ni
> Ima shi tōtta futatsu no katachi.

By choosing for "solitaire et glacé" two Japanese words, both beginning with the sound *samu*, Kafū intensified the weariness of the atmosphere. Later in the poem we find

> —Te souvient-il de notre extase ancienne?
> —Pourquoi voulez-vous donc qu'il m'en souvienne?
>
> —Omae wa tanoshii mukashi no koto wo oboete iru ka?
> —Naze oboete iro to ossharu no desu?

Here the distinction between the *tu* employed by the man to the woman and the *vous* used by her in reply is preserved in the Japanese, though not possible in English. The tone is colloquial yet poetic, and completely natural, replacing such un-Japanese conceptions as *extase ancienne* with the familiar *tanoshii mukashi no koto*, "happy bygone things."

It is striking that although Kafū spent four years in the United States as a young man, including one year at Kalamazoo College, he never felt impelled to translate English poetry. His subsequent residence in France was only one year, including a bare two months in Paris, but his passion for French poetry and all things French remained with him for the rest of his long life, and influenced many younger men.

The next important collection of translated poetry was again from the French. The translator, Horiguchi Daigaku (b. 1892), was to gain fame in his own right as a poet, but his translations of Samain, Jammes, Apollinaire, and Cocteau, published after his return to Japan from France in 1924, exerted an extraordinary influence on modern Japanese writing. Most leading critics of Japanese literature today wrote on French poetry before turning to the works of their compatriots, and many developments in the Japanese novel may also be traced in terms of the effects of translations of novels by Cocteau and his generation. France itself was the dream of most young poets, painters and intellectuals, a sentiment commemorated by Hagiwara Sakutarō, the finest modern poet, in verses beginning:

> I wish I could go to France,
> But France is too far away ...

The Japanese painters who studied in Paris (most leading contemporaries spent a few years there) all depicted the Riviera, Montmartre, and the other frequently represented scenes. The poets, on the other hand, were much freer in their borrowings. Horiguchi Daigaku, for example, rewrote a fable of La Fontaine in the style of Apollinaire, but managed to remain Japanese:

> *The Cicada*
> There was a cicada.
> He spent the whole summer singing.
> The winter came.
> What a fix, what a fix!
>   (Moral)
> It was worth it.

Much earlier, the poet Kitahara Hakushū (1885–1942) had exploited the possibilities of exoticism, but his exoticism was drawn from the Japanese past, and not a recent importation:

> I believe in the heretical teachings of a degenerate age, the witchcraft of the Christian God,

> The captains of the black ships, the marvellous land of the Red Hairs,
> The scarlet glass, the sharp-scented carnation,
> The calico, arrack, and *vinho tinto* of the Southern Barbarians,
> The blue-eyed Dominicans chanting the liturgy who tell me even in
>   dreams
> Of the God of the forbidden faith, or of the blood-stained Cross,
> The cunning device that makes a mustard seed big as an apple,
> The strange collapsible spyglass that looks even at Paradise.

Hakushū attempted in this poem to intoxicate the reader with bizarre words derived from the Portuguese or Dutch dating back to the sixteenth and seventeenth centuries, when Japan was first in contact with the West. Often the sound of the words, rather than their meanings, was uppermost; Hakushū delighted in the cadences of *deus, kapitan, araki, bateren, birōdo*, and his poetry was heavy with absinthe, the odor of chloroform, the sobbing of violins, the putrefying of marble, and the moans of sick children. His exoticism easily turned into a fin-de-siècle overripeness, but his symbolism was sometimes simple and effective:

> The acacia blossoms gold and red are falling,
> In the dusky autumn light they fall.
> My sorrow wears the thin flannel garb of one-sided love.
> When I walk the towpath along the water
> Your gentle sighs are falling,
> The acacia blossoms gold and red are falling.

In this poem, a lingering trace of his partiality for exoticism, Hakushū deliberately wrote of the acacia, a foreign tree, rather than the normal Japanese cherry blossoms, which to modern poets would be anathema. Hakushū's early fondness for the sound of foreign words, however, eventually led him to appreciate the peculiar capabilities of Japanese sounds. As so often in Japan, the young man's passion for the exotic developed later in life into a rediscovery of the traditionally Japanese. Hakushū published in 1923 one of his most celebrated poems, "Chinese Pines" (*Rakuyōshō*)[3], in which sound is at least as important as meaning:

karamatsu no hayashi wo sugite	Passing the forest of Chinese pines,
karamatsu wo shimijimi to miki	I stared profoundly at the Chinese pines.
karamatsu wa sabishikarikeri	How lonely were the Chinese pines.
tabi yuku wa sabishikarikeri.	How lonely it was to travel.

karamatsu no hayashi wo idete	Coming out of the forest of Chinese pines
karamatsu no hayashi ni irinu	I entered the forest of Chinese pines.
karamatsu no hayashi ni irite	Entering the forest of Chinese pines,
mata oku michi wa tsuzukeri	Again the road within continued.

The last of the eight stanzas runs:

yo no naka yo, aware narikeri	Oh world, how sad you are,
tsune nakedo ureshikarikeri	Inconstant, and yet joyous.
yama kawa ni yamagawa no oto	In the hills and rivers, the sound of the mountain streams
karamatsu ni karamatsu no kaze	In the Chinese pines the wind of the Chinese pines.

In the final stanza Hakushū not only demonstrates the special musical qualities of the Japanese language, but deliberately employs the most hackneyed of the old Buddhist images, the transience of worldly things. The slightly novel twist, the discovery of joy even in this impermanence, suggests the aged philosopher who, after his solitary walk in the forest of pines carpeted with fallen needles, finds a quiet happiness in his solitude. We may think this typically and pleasingly Oriental. Indeed, it is normal for Western critics to observe with satisfaction that the Japanese poet, after years of aping Western ways, has at last returned to the ancient traditions of his own country. We should not, however, forget that these sentiments were expressed by a man whose earlier poetry was chiefly influenced by French symbolism. Moreover, although the emotions are sincerely stated, the fact that Hakushū, writing in 1923, should have chosen the language of a thousand years before to describe the truth taught him by his walk through the forest, suggests how acutely aware he was of performing a Japanese action, doing what Japanese poets traditionally did. In his walk along the towpath amidst the falling acacia blossoms, Hakushū was the poet, the lover, not necessarily Japanese, but not un-Japanese. As he walked through the pine forest he saw himself as a Japanese, almost with the eyes of an outsider, and he relished the beauties of the Japanese language, almost with the ears of an outsider, as once he himself had delighted in the strange music of arrack, *vinho tinto* and velvet. Though he states, using the ancient classical language, that the world is *aware* (sad) and *tsune nakedo* (inconstant), he has not returned miraculously to the outlook of the ancient Japanese; he has discovered that their manner of expression suits him at this stage of his life, as French symbolism had suited him earlier. He himself remains that enigma, the Japanese in the twentieth century.

Hakushū's poem on the pine forest is cast in the traditional alternating lines of five and seven syllables, and is in classical language. This was a deliberate case of archaism, one might suppose, but the retention of these features of traditional Japanese poetry was general until the 1920's, and did not entirely disappear afterwards. The classical language had certain advantages over the modern tongue. Its greater variety of inflections enabled the poet, if he chose, to be more concise than modern language permits, or, on the other hand, to draw out a single word the full length of a line for special effect. For example, in Hakushū's poem "Chinese Pines" *sabishikarikeri*, meaning "it was lonely," is grammatically a single word in seven syllables; the modern word *sabishikatta* is not only two syllables shorter, but its double consonant destroys the prolonged, mournful tone desired.

Japanese poets found it hard to sense overtones in words without poetic ancestry. Writing modern Japanese was for them what writing poetry in Basic English or even in Esperanto would be for us. Even revolutionary poetry was cast in the classical grammar:

> We know what we are seeking,
> We know what the people want,
> And we know what we must do.
> We know more than the young men of Russia fifty years ago—
> Yet no one with clenched fist bangs on the table
> To proclaim V NAROD.[4]

The modern language was used most effectively when the poet's intent was to disillusion or to be unpoetic. A pioneer effort, published in 1909, was entitled "The Rubbish Heap," and graphically described the odors, maggots, rotting objects and so forth found in the garbage. The poem was a step in the right direction, but not one that all poets wished to take.

The first truly successful poet of the modern language was Hagiwara Sakutarō (1886–1942). He used it not to startle with unpleasant images or vulgar colloquialisms, but for its own music, unlike that of the classical language but no less capable of moving the reader. The dissatisfaction of earlier poets with the modern language had stemmed from their attempts to make it respond in the same manner as the classical language; Hagiwara abandoned that attempt and wrote a free, colloquial verse which, as he himself recognized, altered the course of Japanese poetry. His themes often skirt the neurotic, and his sensitivity is akin to morbidity, but a haunting beauty remains.

The Corpse of a Cat

The spongelike scenery
Is gently swollen with moisture.
No sign of man or beast in sight.
A water wheel is weeping.
From the blurred shadows of a willow
I see the gentle form of a woman waiting.
Wrapping her thin shawl around her,
Dragging her lovely, vaporous garments,
She wanders calmly, like a spirit.
Ah, Ura, lonely woman!
"You're always late, aren't you?"
We have no past, no future,
And have faded away from the things of reality.
Ura!
Here in this weird landscape.
Bury the corpse of the drowned cat!

With Hagiwara modern Japanese poetry attained its maturity. The subject of his poems was the Japanese artist in the twentieth century, attracted by the West, savoring its civilization, but living in the ghost-ridden landscape of Japan. His poetry is in the Symbolist tradition, the fruit of other men's long years of translation. He rejected neo-classicism and the classical language, but equally the coarse realism which many poets assumed was the alternative to formalism. In the twenties, when the proletarian movement in literature was in full swing, Hagiwara insisted on the absolute values of poetry, and scorned what he termed third-rate versifying. His arbitrary judgments won him enemies, but also devoted followers who created the main stream of poetry in the 1930's. Miyoshi Tatsuji (1900–63), after Hagiwara the foremost Japanese poet, wrote a poem entitled "Hagiwara Sakutarō—Teacher!" that begins:

Dark mass of melancholy—
That character I loved,
Doubter and pessimist, philosopher and wanderer,
Crystallized, unchanged and incorruptible,
Like still-warm lava, of strange music.

Miyoshi was the guiding spirit of the magazine *Shiki* (*Four Seasons*), the leading poetry journal of the thirties, which published most of the poets of the period still esteemed today. They included the eccentric, short-lived Nakahara Chūya (1907–37), whose poetry has gained full recognition only in recent years. Nakahara, after a most erratic scholastic career, graduated at the age of twenty-six from the French Department of the Tokyo School of Foreign Languages, and later translated Rimbaud. In his own day he was famed as the arch example of a Bohemian, a dissolute incorrigible who consciously posed as a Japanese Rimbaud, but his best poems speak unaffectedly of the weariness and despair which occasioned his riotous living.

To a Dragonfly

In an autumn sky too perfectly clear
A red dragonfly is winging.
In the empty field I stand,
Bathed in pale sunset.

The smokestack of a distant factory
Meets my eye, blurred in evening light.
Breathing a great sigh,
I kneel and pick up a stone.

When I feel the pebble's coldness
Warm at last within my hand,
I let it go, and now over grass
Bathed in sunset glow it skims.

The skimmed-over grass
Droops earthwards, just perceptibly.
The smokestack of the factory in the distance
Meets my eye, dim in evening light.

Another poet of the Four Seasons school, even shorter lived than Nakahara, was Tachihara Michizō (1914–39). His poetry is exceptionally lyrical, and some critics believe that it raised the modern Japanese language to its highest peak of expressive possibilities.

For Future Remembrance

The dream always returns to that lonely village at the foot of the mountain
—Winds stir in the nettle leaves
And crickets endlessly pipe—
Along a road through a wood silent with early afternoon.

A brilliant sun shines in the blue sky, the volcano sleeps
—And I,

Though I know no one listens, go on talking
Of things I have seen: islands, waves, headlands, sunlight and the moon.

The dream never goes beyond that point.
I will try to forget everything, utterly.
When I have forgotten even that I have completely forgotten,

The dream will freeze amid recollections of midwinter,
Then open a door and leave in solitude
On that road lighted by scraps of stars.

One unusual writer who stood apart both from the poets of the Four Seasons school and their opposite numbers, the poets of social consciousness, was Kusano Shimpei (born 1902), the master of onomatopoeia. Of all languages of highly civilized peoples, Japanese probably has the richest variety of sound effects to represent every conceivable noise, as well as some phenomena (like the twinkling of a star) which only suggest sound. Kusano exploited this feature of the Japanese language and even invented a language of frogs, delighting readers with the curious, meaningless music. His fondness for frogs, he said, stemmed from his belief that they were the true proletarians—a harking back apparently to his early anarchist days. His use of onomatopoeia (to depict the sound of waves) is evident in this poem:

The Sea at Night

From the distant, deep, heavy bottom,
From the dark, invisible, limitless past
    zuzuzuzu zuwaaru
    zuzuzuzu zuwaaru
     gun un uwaaru
The black sea continues its roar,
In the black the lead-colored waves are born.
Splashing their lead-colored manes, the waves break,
And crawl on their bellies up the sopping strand.

Leaden waves are born out there,
And out that way too,
Then swallowed in the black of India ink,
But once again appear and press to shore.
    zuzuzuzu zuwaaru
    zuzuzuzu zuwaaru
     gun un uwaaru . . .

Poetry, like all forms of literary activity, fell increasingly under governmental supervision in the thirties with the start of the wars in China. Not surprisingly, the same period saw a marked development in surrealist or dadaist poetry. The escape from reality into fantasy or a pure poetry, which created meanings of itself instead of expressing existing ideas, characterized such avant-garde poets as Kitasono Katsue (born 1902) and his VOU group, celebrated by Ezra Pound. It is tempting to discover in the great vogue which surrealist poetry has enjoyed in Japan since the thirties something of the long tradition of extremely complicated poetry, often filled with irrational verbal associations, encountered in the Japanese drama. Overtones and associations, rather than ideas, absorbed the surrealists, and thereby saved them from possible ideological sins. The Four Seasons poets too, being uninterested in political matters, escaped trouble from the authorities, and by the time of the outbreak of the Pacific War in 1941 had come to be recognized as the most serious group of modern poets. During the war the poets behaved much like the rest of the population, rejoicing over victories and lamenting the deaths of soldiers, on occasion falling into hysterical outbursts of bellicosity.

The immediate postwar generation grew up in a bleak atmosphere. Hunger, the black market, and the collapse of the old moral values induced despair or a blank craving for pleasure. The most important group of new poets gathered round a journal aptly called *The Wasteland* (*Arechi*). The Wasteland poets wrote of their sense of hollowness and futility, taking comfort (if at all) in a desperate search for human values. Tamura Ryūichi (born 1923), a leader of the Wasteland poets, wrote in a typical vein:

"Why do little birds sing?"
At the Press Club bar
My friend Hoshino introduced me to an American's poem.
"Why do people walk? That's the next line."
We drank our beer
And ate our cheeseburgers.
At a corner table
A middle-aged Englishman lit his pipe;
His wife was lost in a novel about God and the devil.
After the twentieth of September
The nights in this age without faith become autumnal.
We walked slowly along the narrow asphalt streets
And separated at Tokyo Station.
"Why do little birds sing?"
I woke from my dream in profound darkness
Moved
By something falling from extremely high,

Then once again I plunged
Into the dream, towards "the next line."

The wasteland mood appears frequently in the postwar poetry, though
sometimes altered by surrealist or even traditional *haiku* techniques, as in
this poem by Andō Tsuguo (born 1919) entitled "Tubers" and found in a
collection divided in *haiku* fashion by the seasons of year.

> Worms, mole-crickets, slugs
>
> When eyeless things
> Go searching for the eyes
> Of dead things which
> Address them amiably
>
> The smell of their breath
> From a whole year back
> Crowds before them
>
> The corpses of small birds,
> Like forgotten tubers,
> Lie fallen this month.
>
> Wakeful children
> Wander a sky
> Which could not be inhumed
>
> Tomorrow,
> Peaches. Grasshoppers. Cumulus clouds.

The tubers of this poem suggest *The Wasteland*, though the season is
June here, and the roots are not being stirred into activity by the rain so
much as rotted away. Only the sky escapes the seasonal decay and offers
a promise of the summer of childhood.

A still later generation of Japanese poets, raised in more cheerful times,
seems to have escaped from the wasteland and to be intent on creating
poetry explosive in its intensity but curiously unconcerned with the moral
and political issues that torment older Japanese. Poetic production since
the war has remained largely under the domination of the older generation, notably Miyoshi Tatsuji and Nishiwaki Junzaburō, a professor of
English literature whose translations of T. S. Eliot have been seminal.
Nishiwaki has favored surrealism in his own poetry, and influenced
younger poets with his intuitive, flashing style. Contemporary Japanese
poetry is generally difficult, both in syntax and imagery, and even when not
written under any direct influence from the West is likely to reveal kinship with the works of Eliot, Yeats, Rilke, or the French modernists.

My discussion has thus far been restricted to poems written in the new form—irregular in length and composed directly or indirectly under Western influence. This does not mean that the more traditional Japanese verse forms, the *tanka* and the *haiku*, were abandoned. Far from it. After an initial period of about twenty years of relative inactivity following the Meiji Restoration, a time when the existing schools of *tanka* and *haiku* failed to reflect the changes in the new society, a revolution occurred in the *haiku* with Masaoka Shiki (1867–1902), and then in the *tanka* with Yosano Tekkan (1873–1935). It would be tedious and repetitious to chronicle the successive shifts of taste within these two types of poetry. In both cases revolution meant first of all a rejection of prevailing modes of composition. In the *haiku*, Shiki attacked Bashō, long venerated as a god, and advocated instead the pictorial techniques of the eighteenth-century master Buson. Shiki also concerned himself with the *tanka*, rejecting the *Kokinshū*, the ideal of nineteenth-century *tanka* poets, in favor of the ancient collection, the *Manyōshū*. Yosano Tekkan and his wife Yosano Akiko began in 1900 the publication of the magazine *Myōjō*, which served as the organ of the new *tanka*. The pages of *Myōjō* were soon splattered with such untraditional words as "passion," "blood," "purple," "flesh" and so on, suggesting the wildly romantic strain characteristic of the new poetry. Yosano Akiko's collection *Tangled Hair* (*Midaregami*), published in 1901, stirred women readers in particular, not only because of the lyrical beauty, but because her poetry seemed to proclaim a new age of romantic love. Using the familiar classical language of the old poets, Yosano Akiko moved readers with her self-proclaimed emancipation:

> kazu shiranu   Of the numberless steps
> ware no kokoro no   Up to my heart,
> kizahashi wo   He climbed perhaps
> hata futatsu mitsu   Only two or three.[5]
> kare ya noborishi

Myōjō served as a focal point for activities by *tanka* poets in the early 1900's. One frequenter of the Yosano salon was Ishikawa Takuboku (1885–1912), who emerged in the course of his short life as probably the most popular *tanka* poet in all Japanese history. Takuboku also wrote poems in the modern style (one is quoted in part above), but he owed his fame to his *tanka*, and remains today a literary idol thanks to the dozen or more verses that everyone knows and to the romances spun around his tragic life. The interest he showed in anarchism and socialism has especially endeared him today with "progressive" critics. His most famous *tanka* runs:

Tōkai no	On the white sand
kojima no iso no	Of the beach of a small isle
shirasuna ni	In the Eastern Sea,
ware nakinurete	I, my face streaked with tears,
kani to tawamuru	Am playing with a crab.

Many of Takuboku's poems might be dismissed as sentimental, but Japanese find their melancholy charm peculiarly attractive. The lonely boy, weeping as he plays with a crab on the empty shore, certainly struck a warmer chord of sympathy than the poetry of the new style, expressing loneliness in terms of dark and confusing symbols. The simple lyrical impulse of the *tanka* enabled it to survive even after the successes of the new poetry movement had opened to Japanese poets channels of expression far more varied and flexible than the rigid thirty-one syllables of the classical form. The form itself sustained what in a freer verse might be little more than an inarticulate cry of emotion. The poet needed not devise an elaborate structure for his *tanka*; the structure was already there, waiting for its delicate burden. For a poet like Hagiwara Sakutarō the limits of the *tanka* would have constituted an intolerable impediment to his poetic expression, but for innumerable other Japanese, the poetic impulse consisted of a single perception or reflection which could only be vitiated if expanded to greater lengths.

Both the *tanka* and *haiku* were inevitably influenced by developments in the modern poetry. European influence, the adoption of words of foreign origin, the use of the colloquial in place of the classical language, the acceptance of irregular lines in place of the traditional fives and sevens—all aroused the passions and bitterly divided the *tanka* and *haiku* poets, to an even more pronounced degree than the modern poets, if only because it was possible to invoke tradition more effectively. Unlike the case of modern poetry, moreover, the conservative forces proved victorious in the end. Most *tanka* and *haiku* are written today in the classical language, and despite English or French words that may be introduced to lend an exotic note, the themes are often reminiscent of the past. Modern themes, even when employed by good poets, tend to seem contrived or precious when presented in the traditional form and language.

teiden no	Tonight a breakdown
yoru no rōka ni	Of electric current: my dog
inu nemuri	Snoozes in the hall;
inu no shizukeki	I can hear the murmur of
ibiki kikoyuru	His tranquil canine snoring.

Miya Shūji (born 1912)

ichō ochiba	Fallen gingko leaves
yogoreshi minato no	Have dirtied the harbor streets;
machi no tsuji	At the road crossing
niguro no hei ni	A negro soldier stopped me
michi wo kikarenu	And politely asked the way.

Kimata Osamu (born 1906)

dokubō ni	I can only think
aku e no shikō wo	My friend who has forgotten
wasurekoshi	His taste for evil
tomo wa nukegara to	In solitary confinement
shika omowarezu	Is but the husk of himself.

Kasugai Ken (born 1940)

The *tanka* and *haiku* of today are distinct from modern poetry in one important respect: they are not considered to be exclusively the business of trained poets. Literally hundreds, perhaps thousands of *tanka* and *haiku* groups publish journals devoted to works by members, who are drawn from all levels of society. The daily newspapers carry *tanka* and *haiku* columns in which verses by readers are appraised by leading professionals. Labor union magazines and businessmen's journals alike feature *tanka* and *haiku* columns; the *haiku*, being shorter, is generally more popular.

It is easy for a Japanese, even of modest education, to write a poem in seventeen or thirty-one syllables. An ability to dash off a *haiku* at a drinking party is prized as a social asset. Naturally enough, the quality of most amateur *haiku* is deplorable. However, the most influential article written about the *haiku* since the war (in 1946), "On Second Class Art" ("*Daini Geijutsu-ron*") by Kuwabara Takeo, a professor of French literature at Kyoto University, asserted that the difference between a *haiku* composed by an acknowledged master and one by a bank clerk or a railway engineer was hardly perceptible. Taking a hint from the method used by I. A. Richards in *Practical Criticism*, he asked a group of colleagues to evaluate various *haiku*, some by masters and some by dubs, first removing the names of the poets. The results were so chaotic that Kuwabara felt justified in his claim that most people judge *haiku* by the poet's reputation and not by the works themselves. He asked if it were likely that a short story or a long poem by a master would be confused with one by an amateur, and concluded that the *haiku* must be a second class art, not objectionable as a mildly artistic diversion for amateurs, but certainly not to be considered a serious vehicle of literature.

Kuwabara's article aroused enormous controversy, as was to be expected, and diverted many budding young *haiku* poets to other fields. It is difficult to say that an art with the enormous following of *haiku* is not flourishing, but Kuwabara's article certainly shook the foundations of the art in a manner from which it has not recovered. The *tanka*, though not specifically a target of Kuwabara's, was susceptible to much the same criticism. It moreover has suffered from its intimate association, as the oldest and therefore "purest" Japanese verse form, with the ultranationalistic activities during the war. The *tanka* poets were vociferous in the adulation they offered to the mystique of the Imperial Family and the Japanese civilizing mission. The student who today writes *tanka* is therefore regarded with suspicion as a possible embryonic fascist, no matter what subjects he may choose. The seventeen-year-old boy who assassinated the leader of the Socialist Party wrote a *tanka* in his prison cell before committing suicide.

On the whole, the future of the *tanka* and *haiku* does not seem promising, despite the many magazines and newspaper columns. The two poetic forms will undoubtedly survive, as almost every traditional art has survived in Japan, practiced by retired old gentlemen and smaller numbers of active young men. The future of poetry in Japan would seem to lie, as in other countries, with the professional poets of the modern school. We may regret the diminishing of purely Japanese poetic arts, and fear that the new poetry will be little more than a reflection of Western writing. But modern Japanese poetry has by now achieved its identity. Though part of the larger stream of world poetry and no longer an entirely distinct flow, it is as Japanese as Japan in the middle twentieth century can be. Here is what Takamura Kōtarō (1883–1956) wrote about his poetry, and in a sense of all modern Japanese poetry:

My Poetry

My poetry is not part of Western poetry;
The two touch, circumference against circumference,
But never quite coincide . . .
I have a passion for the world of Western poetry,
But I do not deny that my poetry is formed differently.
The air of Athens and the subterranean fountain of Christianity
Have fostered the pattern of thought and diction of Western poetry;

It strikes through to my heart with its infinite beauty and strength—
But its physiology, of wheat-meal and cheese and entrecôtes,
Runs counter to the necessities of my language.
My poetry derives from my bowels—
Born at the farthest limits of the far east,
Bred on rice and malt and soya-beans and the flesh of fish . . .
Western poetry is my dear neighbour,
But the traffic of my poetry moves on a different path.

(translation by Ninomiya and Enright)

NOTES

1. George B. Sansom, *The Western World and Japan*, p. 428
2. Translation by T. Ninomiya and D. J. Enright in *The Poetry of Living Japan*.
3. The tree *karamatsu* (or *rakuyōshō*) is the larch, but I have taken the literal meaning of "Chinese pine" for reasons of rhythm.
4. Poem by Ishikawa Takuboku. "V NAROD" means "to the people" in Russian.
5. Translation by Shio Sakanishi in Keene, *Modern Japanese Literature*.

Shiki and Takuboku

THE MEIJI period was a time when all traditional Japanese institutions, including the art of poetry, were subjected to violent attacks and changes; it was also a time when these institutions not only managed to survive but even to increase in vigor despite temporary, occasionally drastic modifications. The revolution in modern Japanese literature created new forms of literature, mainly derived from the West (like the *shintaishi*, or "poems in new style"), and filled the existing forms with new ideas and vocabulary, preserving them from the annihilation that seemed to threaten. Who could have guessed, looking at the etiolated *tanka* and *haiku* composed during the 1860's and 1870's, that a hundred years later poets would still be employing these forms for serious purposes?

It is possible to exaggerate the abysmal level of the traditional poetry in the early Meiji era, but little in the *tanka* of the Keien school, the predominant one, suggests a living literature. By the middle of the nineteenth century the *tanka* seemed to have exhausted its usefulness.

The revolution in Japanese poetry of the Meiji period began with a distinctively modern poet, Masaoka Shiki (1867-1902), who nevertheless belonged squarely within the old traditions. His fresh outlook, as a man of the new era, inspired his contemptuous attacks on advocates of the conventions, but deep roots in Japanese poetry kept him ever from questioning the validity of the *tanka* or *haiku*. He experimented with the new-style poems, and on occasion expressed his belief that the future of Japanese literature lay with the novel rather than with poetry, but *tanka* and *haiku* came as naturally to him as breathing. An amusing passage in his journal *A Drop of Ink* described how, when Shiki should have been studying for entrance examinations, he spent his time writing *haiku*:

> Towards the end of the year (1891) I rented a house in Komagome where I lived by myself. The place was extremely quiet and ideal for studying, but somehow I could not bring myself to study the subjects of my examinations. The only thing I read was *haiku* and novels. Two days before the examinations I finally began my preparations. I stowed away everything that was near my desk—*haiku* books and anything else. Then I placed on the desk only the notebooks needed for my examinations. As I sat there quietly before my desk, transformed from a chaotic mess into neatness

itself, it gave me a pleasant feeling, so pleasant, so buoyant in fact, that *haiku* kept bubbling up inside me. I opened a notebook, but before I could read a page a poem had already formed in my mind. I wondered what I could write it on, since I had carefully removed every blank notebook or sheet of paper from the desk. So I wrote the poem on the lampshade. Then another one came to me. And another. It was so much fun I gave up all pretense of studying for the exams, and before long I had covered the lampshade with *haiku*.

These *haiku* apparently have not been preserved; but judging from others written by Shiki about the same period, they were probably not of great literary value. Indeed, we cannot help but be struck by the discrepancy between the keen appreciation Shiki evinced for the beauty of other men's poetry and his own curiously unpoetic spirit. He lacked poetic imagination, and his verses rarely display any overt emotion. He is perceptive and intelligent, and though these are admirable qualities in themselves, they clash with the lyric intuitiveness of the traditional *tanka* and *haiku*. The *haiku* attracted Shiki more than the *tanka*, and among *haiku* the descriptive verses of Buson rather than the intuitive manner of Bashō. In place of beauty of tone, suggestion, ingenuity of expression and other traditional values of the *tanka*, he attempted to make clarity and strength the marks of excellence. His personal emotions figure little in his poetry. Instead, he proclaimed the importance of *shasei* ("depiction of life") in poetry. This poetic stance, an insistence on objectivity and precision of language, may have been the only one Shiki's severe, unemotional character could permit.

Shiki's personality seems to have been formed largely by his studies as a boy of the Confucian classics, a training that may have inspired his rational outlook on the world and also his indifference to such Buddhist themes, beloved by earlier poets, as the transience of earthly life and so on. Most people who had this Confucian education expressed themselves most naturally in *kanshi*, poems in Chinese, but Shiki chose the *tanka* with its quite different attitudes. He studied *tanka* with the local poets in Matsuyama, his hometown, and learned to compose the bloodless verses typical of the Keien school. One written in 1885, when Shiki was on vacation in Matsuyama from his school in Tokyo, has been preserved:

miwataseba	When I look round me
yomo no keshiki mo	The scene in all directions
yoshino yama	Is lovely: at Yoshino
ima wa sakura no	Now the cherry blossoms
sakari naruran	Must be in their full glory.

It is hard to imagine any poem more antithetical to the mature Shiki than this hopeless pastiche of *Kokinshū* imagery built around a deadly pun on *yoshi* ("lovely") and Yoshino, the name of a mountain. The meaning of the poem is close to zero, but the very fact it was preserved suggests it was probably considered superior by his teacher. The poem indicates also the long road Shiki had to travel before he could reform the *tanka*.

Shiki's intelligence, fostered by his Confucian training, was one of two dominant factors in his life, the other being his illness. In 1888 Shiki, then a student in Tokyo, visited Kamakura. He was caught in a heavy rain and twice coughed blood, the first signs of the illness that would confine him to a sickbed and eventually take his life when he was 35. In 1889 he again coughed blood, and on this occasion wrote a series of poems about the *hototogisu*, a kind of cuckoo, a bird described in Chinese legends as having coughed blood. His pen name Shiki was the Chinese name for the *hototogisu*.

The unmistakable signs of an illness that at the time usually proved fatal did not seem to have depressed Shiki greatly. Until he was absolutely immobilized by his illness he led an active, even excessively active life. He volunteered in 1895 for service as a war reporter in China during the Sino-Japanese War, and endured not only the discomforts of military life but the harsh treatment of the officers. He should have realized that his health would be unequal to the strain, but he was convinced that life would not be worth living unless he could see service at the front. He returned from China so seriously ill that he was at once carried to a hospital, seemingly on the point of death. His family was summoned from Tokyo, to witness his last moments, but Shiki miraculously recovered. This experience should have chastened him, but once again he embarked on a frantically active life until he coughed blood again, this time (in 1900) at the start of the illness that finally killed him.

Even when confined to his bed, Shiki remained surprisingly active, demonstrating a fortitude that may have owed something to his Confucian training. But, given Shiki's dependence on close observation as the source of poetic statement, being confined to a sickroom was peculiarly frustrating. A philosopher like Pascal might write his thoughts almost unhindered by his being bedridden, but Shiki's commitment to the "depiction of nature" restricted him to the world of immediate experience, and forced him to compose poems about the flowers in his sickroom or the corner of the garden he could see, as in this *haiku* written shortly before his death:

kubi agete	Lifting my head
ori ori miru ya	I look again and again—
niwa no hagi	Clover in the garden.

Sickness did not impair Shiki's critical faculties. Even in his pain he could deliver a resounding manifesto or analyze poetry with precision. He continued to read astonishing quantities of *haiku* submitted for his opinions, discussed poetry with visitors, sketched flowers, and wrote daily columns for the newspapers. His chief creative activity was the composition of three journals: *A Drop of Ink* (January to June, 1901), *Stray Notes from a Supine Posture* (September, 1901, to July, 1902), and *My Six-Foot Sickbed* (May to September, 1902). *Stray Notes*, which was not intended for publication, is the closest of the three to a diary, describing in detail what Shiki ate and drank, when his bandages were changed, and the times of his bowel movements. Some admirers of Shiki praise this work most highly because of the unadorned truth of its descriptions, but one needs a morbid curiosity to appreciate it all. *Stray Notes* contains some moving passages, but Shiki's despondency and self-pity, his intemperate criticism of all around him, even the sister who waited so selflessly on him, are the other face of the Confucian stoicism he showed the world. The two other journals, intended for the public, may be less sincere, but they give us a more attractive picture of the man, and their literary value is matched in modern Japanese literature only by the diaries of Ishikawa Takuboku. The long traditions of the literary diary in Japan, going back to the ninth century, had a last flowering in their hands. Shiki's intelligence and enormous appetite for life, even in his sickness, give his journals an endearing vitality. Here is a typical passage:

> Six or seven years have gone by since first I took to my sickbed, and I have been completely unable to leave it these past two years, even to be taken for a ride in a car two or three times a year as I used to. All I know about the rapidly changing appearance of Tokyo are the bare facts I read in the newspapers, or what my visitors tell me. No matter how badly I might like to see something, it is quite beyond my strength. But let me list the things I would most like to see for the first time:
>
> moving pictures
> bicycle races and stunts
> lions and ostriches in the zoo ...
> automatic telephones and red letter boxes
> a beer hall
> women fencers and Western-style theatre
>
> But I haven't time to list them all.

There is something peculiarly appealing not only about Shiki himself but about the brave new world of Meiji Japan which he glimpsed from his sickroom. Shiki's compulsion to work may have saved him from despair, but occasionally his suffering was too much for him, as we know from this passage from *Stray Notes*:

> The house was silent now and I was alone. Lying on my left side I stared at the writing set before my eyes. Four or five worn-out brushes and a thermometer, and on top of them, lying quite exposed, a blunt little knife a couple of inches long and an awl—an eyeleteer for punching papers. The suicidal impulse that sometimes comes over me even without such a stimulus suddenly surged through me. The thought, as a matter of fact, had flashed through my mind when I was writing the telegram. But I could hardly kill myself with that blunt little knife or the awl. If I could get to the next room, I knew there was a razor there. Once I had the razor, cutting my throat would be simple, but unfortunately, I am unable even to crawl now. There was no choice. It was not impossible to sever my throat with even this little knife. Or I could pierce a hole in my heart with the awl. I could certainly kill myself that way, but it would be protracted and painful. The best thing would be to drill three or four holes into myself and die quickly. I tried to think over everything logically, but in the end fear won out, and I could not make up my mind. I wasn't afraid of death but of the pain. I thought that if I found the pains of my illness unbearable, how much more horrible it would be if I failed in my suicide attempt and lived on. I became afraid. But that was not all. When I looked at the knife I felt something like a current of fear welling up inside me . . . .

The unexpectedly prompt return of his mother ended this anguished indecision. The passage gives us a frightening glimpse into Shiki's heart, but it is perhaps no truer than the passages from his other writings of the time, filled with curiosity about the world and a love of life. He eagerly scanned the newspapers each morning, and an article about a filial son who had loaded his aged mother in a wheelbarrow and trundled her to Tokyo so that she might see the sights intrigued him so much that he wrote ten *tanka* on the subject. Newly imported inventions excited him, and he devoted pages of his journals to minute descriptions of baseball.

Shiki was strongly attracted by the West. On the wall of his sickroom hung a framed photograph of the letter sent in the sixteenth century by Date Masamune to the Pope in Rome. Of all Western writers he found Benjamin Franklin most congenial, and although he repeatedly insisted on the inadequacy of his English, he derived pleasure from reading Franklin's *Autobiography* in his sickbed. Shiki must have identified himself with the poor boy who, by virtue of hard work, established himself as a great man. This was typical of the Meiji period, when an American educator achieved immortality by urging Japanese boys to be ambitious, and when *Self-Help* by Samuel Smiles was a major source of inspiration. Shiki's absorption with the West was balanced by his nostalgic awareness of what was uniquely Japanese:

> Japan being an island nation, everything is small, but it has a compensating delicacy of flavor. In poetry and prose it is the short works that have developed, and in painting, the rough sketch and the impressionistic rendering. But when, as today, the whole world is one, a country devoted exclusively to uneconomical smallness will lose out in the struggle for existence. So we import everything—cows, horses, strawberries, cherries— and try to make small things big so that they will be economical. I am in favor of this, but I hope it will not as a result destroy the special Japanese flavor.
>
> This reminds me of the subject of improvement of the race that was so much discussed a few years ago. If human beings could be improved like oxen, I suppose it would be possible after some years for the Japanese to boast physiques as powerful as the Westerners', to be strong, free from illness, and economical human beings, any one of whom can do the work of three men of today. But I wonder if in that case the qualities of the special inborn character of the Japanese people would still exist. I doubt it somehow.

Shiki's preference for the traditional Japanese verse forms may have been in accordance with his belief that smallness was typically Japanese. But he was determined that poetry of the Meiji era not be a new rehashing of the themes and language of the *Kokinshū*. He insisted that people who continued to write their *tanka* in pure Japanese would destroy Japanese literature, and denied the concept of a special poetic diction: "Any words capable of conveying an aesthetic meaning should be termed the language of poetry." He felt too that one could write *tanka* about trains and other modern inventions, even if they were unpoetic in themselves, providing the poet avoided an impression of bleakness by introducing some poetic insight to the poem:

kisha no oto no	Smoke whirls
hashiri sugitaru	In the budding branches
kaki no to no	Outside the fence
moyuru kozue ni	After the train has passed
kemuri uzumaku	With a roar.

The roar of the train was certainly modern, but Shiki softened the effect by the almost conventionally pretty detail of smoke curling in the budding branches. Shiki favored borrowing Western words and concepts, as the one way of achieving immediacy and relevance in poetry, but he was still bound to the necessity of making a poem "poetic."

Shiki was ready in his *haiku* or *tanka* to mention a foreign importation:

harukaze ni	Spilling over
koborete akashi	In the spring breeze, how red—
hamigakiko	My tooth powder!

Some verses also use foreign words:

rampu keshite	Turning out the oil-lamp
andon tamosu ya	I light the paper lantern—
tōgaeru	Distant cries of frogs.

But even though the things or words were new, the conception was not; we may share Shiki's feelings when, on hearing the distant cries of frogs, a typically Japanese sound, he turns out the foreign lamp and lights a Japanese lantern, but we are hardly startled. Most of his best poems are derived straight from the *haiku* traditions of the past, despite his advocacy of modernity.

kogarashi ya	Cold winter wind:
negi kaeriyuku	Into the forest, returning,
mori no naka	Goes a Shinto priest.

Other poems are so direct that only their unexpressed circumstances give them validity. Who would guess that the following has been acclaimed as Shiki's best tanka:

bin ni sasu	Because the cluster
fuji no hanabusa	Of wisteria thrust in the vase
mijikakereba	Is so short,
tatami no ue ni	It does not reach
todokazarikeri	As far as the tatami.

The point of this *tanka* is that Shiki is lying in bed on the tatami, unable to rise and touch the wisteria: the beauty of the flowers does not extend to the world of his sickness. The excellence of this tanka does not derive from its success as graphic description of nature; we are not interested in the wisteria for its own sake but for what the poem tells us about Shiki's psychological state. This might equally be said of the poems in the *Kokinshū* on the cherry blossoms; they are an expression of the poet's feelings on the passage of time or on growing old, and not an observation of nature. Despite his professed belief in "depiction of nature" as the touchstone of excellence in poetry, his best *haiku* and *tanka* were not bound by this doctrine.

Shiki became the leading force in the revival of both *haiku* and *tanka*. His rediscoveries of classical works and authors also exercised great influence, and his condemnation of *renga*, or "linked-verse," effectively finished this genre as a serious literary form. The *haiku* magazine and the *tanka* magazine he founded even today dominate composition in both fields. His own poetry has lost some of its popularity, but his journals, the products of his long suffering, mark an important stage in the development of a specifically modern Japanese literature.

The life of Ishikawa Takuboku (1886-1912), on the surface at least, much resembles Shiki's. Both were young men from the country who made their way to Tokyo and established themselves as outstanding poets in the four or five years before their deaths. In character, however, they differed entirely. Takuboku utterly lacked the Confucian discipline of Shiki. It is precisely because of this difference that we may say that if Shiki is modern, Takuboku is contemporary. But it is hard, when one examines the childish features of Takuboku's photographs, to realize that this was the author of the stinging, unsentimental judgments that lace his diaries and letters. Shiki wrote unkindly about Ki no Tsurayuki, a poet of a thousand years before, and occasionally expressed disappointment in his contemporaries, but he was more interested in ideas than in personalities. Takuboku is intensely personal. His poetry is almost entirely about himself or people he knew, rarely about nature. Living a decade after Shiki he finds himself in a world as different as the Japan after the Sino-Japanese War was from the Japan after the Russo-Japanese War of 1904-5, which marked the emergence of Japan as a world power. Takuboku lived in a world of incomparably greater sophistication, and the European books he read were not the *Autobiography* of Benjamin Franklin or Samuel Smiles but Ibsen and Gorki. In literary tastes a century, not ten years, separates the two men.

Takuboku's *tanka* are superior to Shiki's because they made no concessions to being poetic. They are colloquial in manner and sharply responsive to Takuboku's passing moods. Shiki's *tanka* on the wisteria hints at his suffering, but Takuboku's *tanka* strike us with both fists.

Sometimes he drops into sentimentality, repeating such words as *kanashiki* ("sad") or *namida* ("tears") in a manner incongruous in so tough-minded a poet, but his successful *tanka* make a powerful assault on the reader's mind. Takuboku was familiar with the traditions of the *tanka*, but unlike Shiki, he disregarded them. Shiki once stated that a poem about the wind blowing over streetcar tracks lacked elegance, but Takuboku never concerned himself about elegance. Takuboku was certainly less profound than Shiki. None of his *tanka* would stand up to the detailed and extended treatment that has been given to Shiki's best *haiku*. But the impact of his poetry is overpowering, especially his *tanka*, where his sudden perceptions and emotional reactions are captured in molten state. Nothing in earlier Japanese poetry really prepares us for such a tanka as:

kagiri naki	My sister pitied
chishiki no yoku ni	My eyes that were burning with
moyuru me wo	Immeasurable
ane wa itamiki	Craving for knowledge:
hito kouru ka to	She thought I must be in love.

The words "craving for knowledge" especially suggest an area of experience never treated in the *tanka* before Takuboku.

Takuboku's life is often portrayed as a tragic instance of the indifference of society to the poet. The disasters that struck him in the last year of his life were certainly unspeakably tragic, and his early death was a great loss to the world of letters. But, compared with Shiki, Takuboku must be termed fortunate. Even compared to most poets today, Takuboku was fortunate in his friendships, in the recognition he received, and also in the support society gave him.

Takuboku grew up in a lonely village of northern Japan, the son of a poor Zen priest. His education was surprisingly good; it may be doubted that a young man growing up in such a small village anywhere else in the world could have obtained as good an education. Takuboku learned to read English fluently and acquired a surprising knowledge of Western culture. In 1902, when he was seventeen, he made his first trip to Tokyo, where he met Tekkan and Akiko Yosano, the reigning powers in the world of *tanka*. He was at once accepted into their circle, and took this recognition as his due. He profited by his stay in Tokyo to buy books in English, and began making his translation of *John Gabriel Borkman* of Ibsen.

After returning to his village he continued his studies of English poetry and Western music. Unlike Shiki, who found Western music incomprehensible, Takuboku enjoyed playing the violin and attended church for the pleasure of hearing music on the harmonium. Shiki roared with laughter when someone played him on the phonograph a record of Italian opera, but Takuboku wrote eulogies of Richard Wagner.

Takuboku became a teacher in the local elementary school, but lost his job in 1907 after leading a student strike against the principal. He moved to Hokkaido, where he worked for various newspapers, and eventually, in 1908, made his way to Tokyo. He left his wife and daughter in Hokkaido, promising he would send for them as soon as he had the money. But we know from his diaries, marvels of outspoken honesty, how restive the thought of family obligations always made him. From 1908 to 1910 he devoted himself to writing both poetry and prose, especially the diaries.

Takuboku had good friends in Tokyo, notably the philologist Kindaichi Kyōsuke, who lived in the same lodging-house, and the Yosanos. He knew almost every literary figure of consequence well enough to borrow money. His friends generally responded to his appeals, and found him employment. Somehow he seems to have impressed everyone as a genius: even when he was utterly unknown as a novelist he was commissioned by a newspaper to write a serial novel, an honor inconceivable today for an unknown. In 1909, at the age of 24, he became the editor and publisher of *Subaru*, the best literary magazine of the day. Undoubtedly his talents earned such recognition, but the confidence of so many people is not often accorded the young.

Takuboku did little to repay this confidence. His diaries reveal his contempt for almost all his acquaintances. At one point he declared his intention of sacrificing even his closest friend, Kindaichi, to his writing:

> Shackles! Shackles of affection! Why have I never really ever been able to write until now?
> I have made up my mind. I must break the shackles. Three people have showed me the deepest affection—Miyazaki and the Yosanos—and then Kindaichi. It's difficult to say who is the closest, but Kindaichi is hardest to write about if only because he lives in the same place. I have made up my mind. I must throw off the shackles of affection and start on my manuscript. As the first step, as the preface to the novel of my life, I must destroy what I find hardest to destroy. I shall write a story called "Shackles" describing as coldly and sharply as possible the exact nature of the relations between Kindaichi and myself.

This entry for January 10, 1909, in his diary is concluded by a note in the remarks column: "My first night as a writer, an unforgettable night." Takuboku's readiness to destroy his friendship with Kindaichi in the interests of his development as a writer suggests a devotion to his craft of unusual proportions, but he was incredibly sloppy with the writing of his serialized novel. His diary tells us: "I wrote and sent off the first episode of Chapter IX while talking to my friends." But he was furious when an editor refused to publish the completed novel.

Takuboku complained incessantly of how short he was of money, but whenever he obtained any, he spent it recklessly. When he was sent a money order for 20 yen by a long-suffering friend, he at once spent 3 1/2 yen on a book by Oscar Wilde. (He sold the book two days later, probably unread, for 1 yen 30 sen, having by then run out of money.) Reading Takuboku's diaries we cannot help being surprised at the readiness of people to supply him with funds, and even that he managed to keep his job at the newspaper despite his repeated failures to appear for work.

Takuboku's failings are inescapable, but we forget them when we read his poetry and the devastating account he gives of himself in his diaries and letters. His *Romaji Diary* in particular is a masterpiece. Near the beginning he explains why he chose to write this diary in Roman letters:

> Why did I decide to keep this diary in Romaji? Why? I love my wife, and it's precisely because I love her that I don't want her to read this diary. No, that's a lie! It's true that I love her, and it's true that I don't want her to read this, but the two facts are not necessarily related.

Takuboku's frankness of expression would be striking even today. For 1909 it was incredible. Takuboku in this diary is at once more powerful and more artistic than in any of his consciously literary works. His letters are almost equally vivid. Sometimes it is hard to tell what precisely Takuboku is attacking. His thoughts were often confused, and within a short space of time he might undergo a complete change of belief. He was exhilarated by the news of the outbreak of the Russo-Japanese War: "Today's newspaper reports that the tense situation between Japan and Russia has suddenly become extreme. I hear that reservists in the village have been called. The gauntlet has been thrown. A Heaven-sent chance has been given. What wonderful news!" But at the first news of Japanese casualties, his enthusiasm for the war quickly subsided. At one period, like so many other young men of the time, he was attracted by Christianity, and he writes of moments spent in silent prayer, but his *tanka* speak of his later clashes with his sister, a practicing Christian. Politically he was also unstable. In 1906 he wrote, "I respect the rights of the individual too much for me ever to become a socialist," but four years later, mainly as a result of the alleged assassination attempt on the Emperor Meiji and the trial of the supposed culprits, who were socialists, Takuboku's views underwent "a great change." "From now on," he wrote in his diary, "I shall build up a collection of books and periodicals on socialism." Unfortunately, his diaries for the last two years of his life are disappointingly terse, and it is difficult to estimate how deeply he was affected by his new political views. No doubt it comforted and inspired him to have a cause with which to associate himself. In a letter of July, 1908, he had written to a friend, "My stories, in a broad sense, are my confessions; at the same time, they are the only weapon I have with which to rip apart the falseness of people. They are the only weapon I have with which to destroy present conditions and to build a new world." It may be that Takuboku's failure with his stories induced him to turn elsewhere for support.

Takuboku's stories are failures because they lack novelistic skill. They are either thinly disguised recountings of his experiences in his village or in Tokyo, or else almost plotless conversations irrelevantly tied to hastily sketched characters. Takuboku was constantly starting new stories, often taking the trouble to invent names for all the characters only to abandon the piece after a page or two. His long serialized novel *Chōei* (Shadow of a Bird) is at once conventional and badly organized, though it has brilliant flashes. The short stories are interesting mainly as records of what Takuboku was thinking at a particular time, not for their characterizations, insights or style. The best of Takuboku's prose is in his diaries and letters, suggesting that he was most effective at impromptu expression. When he revised his old diaries for publication he invariably lessened their literary value by larding them with conventional emotions, rather like a painter who turns his watercolor sketch into a large oil painting by inflating or diluting his original inspiration. Takuboku is starkly direct in his diaries and letters, but his more polished prose is often vitiated by preconceptions of what made for fine writing.

Takuboku's letters are also marked by humor, though it is sometimes unintentional. Unlike the severely Confucian Shiki, Takuboku brimmed over with romantic ardor, and a letter from a lady poet invariably induced erotic fantasies. He carried on a long and passionate correspondence with a woman in Kyushu whom he had never seen:

> Darling. My beloved one. Why is it not possible for us to meet? . . . .
> Why, when I love you so, can I not see you and tell you what is in my heart?

He begged the woman for a photograph, but she was strangely reluctant. At last one came. Takuboku noted in his diary: "A letter and a picture from Kyushu. Slanting eyes and a rather big mouth—she's certainly not a beauty." His ardor was immediately cooled. Another correspondent, Hirayama Yoshiko, excited equal passion until Takuboku learned that she was actually a man named Hirayama Yoshitarō.

Takuboku died so young that it is foolish to tax him for a lack of maturity. Nevertheless, it is hard to escape the feeling that he remained to the end a brilliant, headstrong child, capable of strong passions but not always of understanding them. Again and again Takuboku struck out in rage, though it is not always clear at what. He wrote to a friend, "I don't know how to express it. I feel it's either everybody else die or I die, one or the other.'' He seemed loath to accept any responsibilities, whether as a writer, a friend or a husband. He envied Ilya, a character in Gorki's story, "The Three of Them," and wrote in his *Romaji Diary*, "Ilya was a bachelor. I always think: how lucky Ilya was to have been a bachelor! There's the difference between the unhappy Ilya and myself." He added, "Ilya's plan was the greatest plan any human being could conceive. He tried to escape from life, no, he did escape, and then with all his strength he rushed from life—from this life of ours—into a limitless path of darkness. He dashed out his brains against a stone wall."

Takuboku attributed his unhappiness to marriage and to his lack of money. Probably the real cause was frustration over his inability to write fiction. He frequently reported in sick to the newspaper office so that he could spend the day writing a story, but more often than not he never got beyond the first two pages.

> I wrote three pages and couldn't think of another line. I tried to correct some poems, but just spreading out the paper was enough to make me sick. I thought of writing a story about a man who is arrested by a policeman for sleeping in a vacant house, but couldn't find the energy to lift my pen. I said to myself, 'I positively will give up my literary career.' 'If I give up literature, what shall I do?' *Death*! That's the only answer. Either I must have money or else be released from all responsibilities.

If Takuboku had lived longer he might have developed into a first-class novelist or poet of the modern-style verse (*shintaishi*), but I doubt that he would have written better *tanka*. The traditional form proved a perfect medium for Takuboku's flashes of irritation, nostalgia or affection, but it was obviously incapable of sustained expression. Takuboku's *tanka* today enjoy greater popularity than any written in the thousand year history of the form. When the Meiji period began it seemed likely that both *tanka* and *haiku* would wither away as literary forms because they were inadequate to describe the complex emotions of the new Japanese. Shiki and Takuboku proved this was untrue, and gave new life to the classical forms, but both men in their journals and essays pointed to a new kind of Japanese literature in which the place of *tanka* and *haiku* would of necessity be modest because it shared more with the rest of the world than it did with traditional Japan.

IV. THREE MODERN NOVELISTS

Tanizaki Junichirō

THE WRITINGS of Tanizaki Junichirō are apt to surprise equally by their exceptional diversity of subject and manner, and by their equally exceptional consistency of themes. The diversity is likely to attract our attention first. Tanizaki derived materials for his novels from the distant past of the Heian and Muromachi periods, from the war chronicles of the sixteenth century and the popular fiction of the early nineteenth century. Still other works were closely based on personal experience. His inspiration was usually Japanese, but at the outset of his career he was influenced especially by Baudelaire and Poe, as he later recalled with some shame: "It is not my intention to debate here whether having been influenced by the West was beneficial or harmful to my writings, but no one knows as well as I—to my great embarrassment—in what extremely superficial, indeed mindless ways this influence revealed itself." Apart from European influence, two journeys to China, his only travels abroad, added an exotic touch to some of his writings and provided the basis for harshly objective comments on Japan. Tanizaki used his materials freely, whether Japanese or foreign, sometimes producing carefully documented historical tales, sometimes works that, despite their factual appearance, are almost entirely of his invention.

Tanizaki's methods of narration embrace almost every variety of technique, including the normal third-person account; the first-person confession; the mixed contemporary and historical style in which the narrator (often Tanizaki himself) intrudes at times into the telling of a story from the distant past; and the novel composed of letters or diaries. The diversity of Tanizaki's work is suggested moreover by the remarkably contrasting shapes and appearances of the first editions of his books, each intended to produce a distinct impression by its format, type, binding and even paper as well as the content.

So great is the variety of works Tanizaki wrote in the half-century between 1910 (the year of his début with *The Tattooer*) and 1962 (the year of *Diary of a Mad Old Man*) that it is only on reflection that we perceive the striking consistency of themes throughout the works composed over this long period. Most conspicuous was his utter preoccupation with women. His novels are filled with superbly evoked portraits of women, but with rare exceptions he seemed uninterested in depicting male characters. This is true, of course, of much modern literature in Japan; the men, in fiction at least, tend to be weak-willed and negative, no match for the women. Tanizaki created some characters that might be described as alter egos of himself—Sadanosuke in *The Makioka Sisters* comes most quickly to mind—but he failed to impart to them his own immense masculine energy and purpose. It seems improbable that Tanizaki was incapable of drawing such a character; rather, his absorption with women was so great as to make him see in men only the mirrors or slaves of his female characters.

The characteristic male in a Tanizaki novel is an abject figure whose greatest pleasure is to be tortured by the woman he adores. This is true whether the hero is a figure of the distant past or a contemporary. This masochistic worship of women, this glorification of demonical women who reduce men to grovelling slaves, is certainly not a heritage of the traditional Japanese literature. We cannot imagine Prince Genji craving to be trodden on by Murasaki or finding his greatest pleasure in waiting on her like a servant, but this is precisely true of Seribashi in *Ashikari* or Sasuke in *A Portrait of Shunkin*. Of course, women are frequently depicted in the old literature as monsters of jealousy or deceit, and Saikaku's heroines (like Tanizaki's) sometimes exhaust their partners by excessive sexual demands; but although the worship of cruel women may have in fact existed in traditional Japan, Tanizaki was undoubtedly indebted to Western influence for literary expression of this phenomenon.

Tanizaki's first important story, *The Tattooer* (1910), concludes with the tattooer Seikichi becoming the victim of the work of art he has created. The girl into whose back he has etched a monstrous spider flashes a smile of triumph as she realizes she now is capable of trapping men within her terrible web. One theme, first given expression in the same story, was to persist through all of Tanizaki's later writings: Seikichi is first attracted to the girl by catching a glimpse of her naked foot. We are told: "To his sharp eyes a human foot was as expressive as a face. . . . This, indeed, was a foot to be nourished by men's blood, a foot to trample on their bodies."[1]

An extreme expression of Tanizaki's foot-fetishism, as he himself called it, was *Fumiko's Feet* (1919). In this story an old man, infatuated with the beautiful feet of his young mistress, asks a young painter to draw her portrait in a pose that best reveals her feet. When he himself is bed-ridden and too feeble to play with the girl's feet in his accustomed manner, he asks the willing painter to roll like a dog at Fumiko's feet and allow himself to be trampled by her. The old man dies blissfully happy because during his last moments Fumiko's foot has been pressed against his forehead.

Almost every work of Tanizaki's has passages revealing his fascination with women's feet. In the play *The Man with the Mandoline* the hero, a blind man, drugs his wife so that he can fondle her feet while she sleeps. Sometimes, as in *A Portrait of Shunkin*, it is the woman who insists on warming her feet against a man's face or chest, sometimes it is the man who longs desperately to feel the weight of a cruel woman's feet. In Tanizaki's last major work *Diary of a Mad Old Man* (1962), the tottering old man gets down on his hands and knees in the shower-room for the privilege of cramming his daughter-in-law's toes into his mouth. In the same work the foot-fetishism that runs through Tanizaki's entire career is given its grand finale in the description of the tombstone that the old man erects almost at the cost of his life: it is a reproduction of his daughter-in-law's footprint, enlarged to heroic size, and meant to stand in triumph forever over the abject old man.

A related aspect of foot-fetishism and the craven masculine surrender to the female, the desire to abase himself before her, is the man's fascination with her excreta. I can hardly recall a Western novel that even mentions the heroine's going to stool, but this is a frequent, almost obsessive theme in Tanizaki's works. *The Makioka Sisters* (1942-47) alone contains more detailed and graphic references to bowel movements than one would find in a whole library of Western novels, and the last sentence of the work is the unforgettable: "Her diarrhoea never did stop that day, and even after she boarded the train it still continued." In *A Portrait of Shunkin* the attentions of Sasuke to his mistress Shunkin in the lavatory are lovingly described. In *Secret Tales of the Lord of Musashi* (1935) the hero manages to find his way to the beautiful princess by creeping up through the hole in her toilet. In *The Mother of Captain Shigemoto* (1950) the ninth-century courtier and lover Heijū falls madly in love with a palace lady who refuses him. Determined to cure himself of his passion, he decides to obtain possession of her chamber pot, supposing that when he sees that the contents are exactly like those of a quite ordinary person's chamber pot he will be disillusioned. He snatches away the pot from a lady-in-waiting and carries it home. But he cannot bring himself to open the covered leather box, not because he is afraid of being disgusted, but because he wants to savor the pleasure. "He took it in his hands again, lifted it up and looked at it, put it down and looked at it, turned it around, tried calculating the weight of the contents. At last, with great hesitation, he removed the lid, only for a balmy fragrance like that of cloves to strike his nostrils." He probes the contents, more and more astonished by the exquisite fragrance. Instead of being disillusioned he is now frantically determined to become intimate with so extraordinary a woman. Carried away by his delight, "he drew the box to him and sipped a little of the liquid in the contents."

Tanizaki's absorption with the excretory processes was not confined to his fiction. In his essay *In Praise of Shadows*, for example, he devotes pages to describing the traditional Japanese toilets, which he finds infinitely more agreeable than the gleaming Western vessels. He declares, "It may well be said that the most elegantly constructed works of Japanese architecture are the toilets." In another essay, *All About Toilets* (1935), he writes, "A certain nostalgic sweet remembrance accompanies the smell of a toilet. For example, when someone who has been away from home for a long time returns after an absence of years, when he goes into the toilet and smells the odor he knew long ago, it brings back better than anything else memories of his younger days, and he really feels the warmth of 'I'm home!' " But in excreta as in feet Tanizaki insists that they belong to a beautiful woman. The steam from another man's urine on a cold day definitely does not please him.

Even a superficial acquaintance with the literature of psychoanalysis reveals how intimately connected fetishism is with the reiterated mentions of the excretory processes. Here is Freud on the subject: "Psychoanalysis has cleared up one of the remaining gaps in our understanding of fetishism. It has shown the importance, as regards the choice of a fetish, of a coprophilic pleasure in smelling which has disappeared owing to repression. Both the feet and the hair are objects with a strong smell which have been exalted into fetishes after the olfactory sensation has become unpleasurable and been abandoned." Various of the followers of Freud have pointed out that fetishism is associated with a clinging to the mother and the strong desire to identify with her, and with a castration anxiety. Case after case is reported of foot-fetishists whose memories of their mothers are lovingly entwined with fecal smells. But it is not within my powers to psychoanalyze Tanizaki; suffice it to say that Tanizaki's fetishism and coprophilia both seem to be associated with the longing for the mother, which is a powerful though intermittent theme in his works.

The heroines of Tanizaki's novels generally suggest in appearance what he wrote of his mother, who was small (less than five feet tall), delicate of features, well-proportioned rather than frail. On the whole Tanizaki had less to say about the faces of his women than their feet. The features are classical, we are told, but they are deliberately blurred, as in the description of Oyu-san in *Ashikari*: "There was something hazy about Oyu-sama's face, as if one saw it through smoke. The lines of her features —the eyes, the nose, the mouth—were blurred as if a thin veil lay over them. There was not one sharp, clear line." The narrator in *A Portrait of Shunkin* tells us, "There is a photograph of her at thirty-six which shows a face of classic oval outline and features so delicately modeled they seem almost ethereal. However, since it dates from the eighteen-sixties, the picture is speckled with age and as faded as an old memory.... In that misty photograph I can detect nothing more than the usual refinement of a lady from a well-to-do Osaka merchant family—beautiful, to be sure, but without any real individuality."[2] In a late work *The Bridge of Dreams* (1959), again, we are told, "I cannot recall my first mother's features distinctly... all I can summon to my mind's eye is the vague image of a full, round face.... All I could tell from the picture was that she wore her hair in an old-fashioned style."[3] The clearest identification of this dimly perceived beauty with his own mother was given by Tanizaki in the story *Yearning for My Mother*, written in 1918, the year after his mother's death. When he finds her in his dream she is insubstantial, hardly more than a beautiful shadow.

The function of the male in Tanizaki's stories is to worship this unearthly creature. In *Ashikari* Seribashi's slavish devotion to Oyu-san not only keeps him from presuming to have physical relations with her, though sometimes they share the same bed, but even from having relations with his own wife. In *The Bridge of Dreams* the narrator's attachment to his stepmother, who has blended completely in his mind with the mother he lost when a small child, is so great that even after he is married he "was always careful to take precautions against having a child—that was the one thing I never neglected." The young man in this story still suckles at his stepmother's breast at the age of eighteen, and there is more than one hint that he has sexual relations with her. He marries only to provide the stepmother—whom he always refers to as Mother—with a devoted servant, and when the stepmother dies he immediately gets rid of his wife, preferring to live in his memories.

But if this mother figure is gentle and dimly perceived even when in her presence, she is often cruel. The fear that the mother may refuse the child her love apparently belongs to the same complex of phenomena associated with foot-fetishism I have already mentioned, but in Tanizaki's stories the cruelty of the beloved woman becomes a source of allure. For his male characters it is not enough to grovel before a beautiful woman, to kiss her feet and even to crave her excreta; he must feel she is cruel. The old man in *Diary of a Mad Old Man* describes his ideal of a beautiful woman: "Above all, it's essential for her to have white, slender legs and delicate feet. Assuming that these and all the other points of beauty are equal, I would be more susceptible to the woman with bad character. Occasionally there are women whose faces reveal a streak of cruelty—they are the ones I like best. When I see a woman with a face like that, I feel her innermost nature may be cruel, indeed I hope it is."[4] The fascination Naomi, the heroine of *A Fool's Love*, exerts over the hapless hero lies as much in her cruelty as in her exotic beauty. Shunkin is conspicuously cruel to Sasuke, referring to him contemptuously as a servant. Even a seemingly compliant and inarticulate Kyoto lady, Ikuko in *The Key* (1956), will betray and destroy her husband. Indeed, the cruelty of a woman, her delight in observing pain, is often what first attracts a man to her. The hero of *Secret Stories about the Lord of Musashi* is captivated as a boy when he sees a beautiful young woman smile as she carefully cleans and dresses a severed head. He is in particular driven to an ecstasy of delight when he sees her tending a head from which the nose has been cut, a *mekubi*, or "female head," an obvious reference to castration. The whole life of the future Lord of Musashi is determined by that sight, and he desires nothing more than to recreate the scene, if possible becoming the severed head over which the smiling young woman bends. Oyu-san in *Ashikari* is certainly not a monster, but she demands not only obedience but utter sacrifice from her slaves. At the end of *Manji* (1930) Mitsuko destroys the health of her two worshippers by insisting that they drink heavy sedatives each night before going to bed, to insure that they will not be unfaithful to her. Such examples of cruelty only serve to inflame the men who wait on these beautiful women. Even if cruelty destroys a man's body it can only foster his passion.

Men sometimes figure in the novels in the role of consort to the queen bee, destined to be discarded once they have fertilized the women they worship. But in *Manji* the males are contemptible and even unnecessary. Sonoko is satisfied with her homosexual love for Mitsuko and has no use for her husband; Mitsuko, for her part, though tied to the feckless young man Watanuki, derives her greatest pleasure from the adoration of Sonoko, another woman. In other stories, however, the male is necessary, if only to provide the woman with a suitable object for her sadistic impulses. Kikkyō in *Secret Stories of the Lord of Musashi* is drawn to Terukatsu because he alone can enable her to wreak vengeance on her husband, Norishige. Terukatsu supposes that once he has performed the service demanded of him—cutting off Norishige's nose and destroying his castle—Kikkyō will surrender herself to him, but he discovers that the queen bee, her object attained, has no further interest in her abettor.

The woman usually express no particular preference in men, as if their features made no difference. It is true that Itsuko in *The Key* is attracted by Kimura's young body, but there is never any suggestion that she loves him or values him as anything more than the instrument of her lust. For that matter, though Itsuko is repelled by her husband's body, she is not averse to intercourse with him, providing he is sufficiently active. Tanizaki, reflecting the sentiments of his female characters, seldom describes the faces of the males. One of his rare descriptions of a man's face, Watanuki's in *Manji*, is not so much a portrait as a forewarning of his treacherous character. Sonoko, though at first she finds Watanuki attractive, is quickly disenchanted.

But if handsome male features do not seem to interest women, ugliness is no obstacle. Kikkyō is more devoted to Norishige after his nose is cut off (his mouth has already been made into a hare-lip, and one ear has been shot off) than when he was whole. In *Diary of a Mad Old Man* the old man does not wish his daughter-in-law to see him when he removes his false teeth and looks, in his own words, exactly like a monkey, but she insists that it does not make any difference. Indeed, the indifference of Tanizaki's women to men suggests the indifference of a cat to human beings. Perhaps it was no accident that Tanizaki throughout his life was fascinated by cats.

I have so far described themes that remained astonishingly constant in Tanizaki's writings for over fifty years. My examples have been chosen from every period of his career, and many others might be adduced. I think that these are the basic themes of his books, but the last impression I would like to give is that his writings are monotonous or that he failed to respond in any way to the enormous changes that occurred in Japanese society. At one level at least Tanizaki's writings present an evolving set of ideas about traditional Japan and the West. This is express-ed even in the preferences in women of his different heroes. For example, Jōji, the hero of *A Fool's Love* (1925), seems to embody Tanizaki's own feelings of about 1915. Jōji is enslaved by the European-looking beauty of Naomi (whose very name sounds foreign), so much so that he feels ashamed of his own typically Japanese features. At the end of the novel they are living in the foreign section of Yokohama, and he has accepted her demand that she have the right to entertain foreign male friends without interference from him. The implied condemnation of this surrender to the cult of Western beauty suggests that Tanizaki himself was no longer so susceptible. This is developed in *Some Prefer Nettles* (1929) into a rediscovery of traditional Japanese beauty. Kaname, the hero, is attracted by the West, particularly by the worship of women as goddesses, but in the end he finds himself succumbing to the quiet charms of an old-fashioned Kyoto woman. Tanizaki's former adulation of Western things is replaced by a new appreciation of traditional Japanese culture. In the decade after *Some Prefer Nettles* he gives us a collection of portraits of typically Japanese women, each composed and classical of face but harboring the ferocity of a tigress. The period was brought to an appropriate close with Tanizaki's translation into modern Japanese of *The Tale of Genji*, bringing new life to its great gallery of beautiful women.

It may have been the anxieties of war, perhaps even a fear that as the result of the war that began in 1941 Japan would be changed beyond all recognition, that drew Tanizaki back from the past to modern Japan, the Japan of the 1930's. With something of the elegiac spirit of a chronicler recording (lest people forget) the last days of Rome before the barbarian invasions, he recreated in *The Makioka Sisters* the city of Osaka in days of peace and luxury. The military authorities were right when they decided in 1943 that *The Makioka Sisters* was subversive, for in this novel Tanizaki indicates that Western elements had become precious parts of the lives of cultivated Japanese and were no longer merely affectations or passing crazes as in the days of Tanizaki's youth. The youngest sister, Taeko, is condemned for her waywardness, an excess of Western freedom, it is true, but the inarticulate Yukiko, a typically old-fashioned Japanese beauty, shows to best advantage in Western clothes.

The conflict between East and West in the minds and lives of the Japanese has now become the most hackneyed of all themes, the first one that leaps in pristine freshness into the mind of every maker of documentary films or television producer. But for Tanizaki this subject, which had absorbed him in the 1920's, lost all appeal and interest after the war. In the last novels the so-called conflict completely melts away. Tanizaki is no longer obsessed by his preference for the past. Utsugi, the old man of *Diary of a Mad Old Man*, has nostalgic remembrances of his mother, but he delights in the up-to-the-minute costumes of his daughter-in-law, Satsuko. Quite unlike the Tanizaki of *In Praise of Shadows*, Utsugi is eager to tear down the old, Edo-style house he grew up in and to erect instead a bright new Western-style house where he can live more independently of his wife. In the end he builds a swimming pool in the garden big enough for Satsuko to practice synchronized swimming. Old man Utsugi has accepted Western things as inevitable and even attractive elements in Japanese life. Like all the heroines of Tanizaki novels, Satsuko has a dazzlingly white complexion—in *In Praise of Shadows* Tanizaki had lovingly dwelt on his fascination for white skin, not the matter-of-fact white of a European woman's, but the mysterious, glowing ivory of a Japanese face—but she shows to advantage when sunburned. Satsuko's feet, of course, are important, but their shape is rather unlike that of Tanizaki's earlier heroines, for she has always worn shoes. Satsuko bathes in a tiled shower, rather than in the scented wooden tub Tanizaki lovingly described in *Some Prefer Nettles*, but this does not make her less desirable to her eager father-in-law.

Tanizaki's early period as a writer was certainly marked by infatuation with the West. About 1918, he tells us, "I had come to detest Japan, even though I was obviously a Japanese." He dreamed especially of the kind of women he saw in foreign films. "What I sought were lively eyes, a cheerful expression and a clear voice, a body that was healthy and well-proportioned, and above all, long straight legs and adorable feet with pointed toenails cased in snugly fitting high-heeled shoes—in short, a woman with the physique and clothes of a foreign star." Tanizaki was in the mountains at Hakone at the time of the Great Earthquake of 1923. He was deeply worried about his family, but "almost at the same instant joy welled up inside me and the thought, 'How marvellous! Tokyo will become a decent place now.'" He had visions of a new Tokyo: "Orderly thoroughfares, shining, newly-paved streets, a flood of cars, blocks of flats rising floor on floor, level on level in geometrical beauty, and threading through the city elevated lines, subways, street cars. And the excitement at night of a great city, a city with all the amusements of Paris or New York, a city where the night life never ends. Then, and then indeed, the citizens of Tokyo will come to adopt a purely European-American style of life, and the young people, men and women alike, will all wear Western clothes. This is the inevitable trend of the times, and whether one likes it or not, this is what will happen."

Tanizaki could hardly have been a better prophet of what in fact did take place in Tokyo. However, after the earthquake he decided to move to the Kansai, and gradually his attitudes began to change. He discovered that "I loved the old Japan as a form of exoticism, in precisely the sense that a foreigner treasures the prints of Hiroshige." He visited Nara and Kyoto, again just like a foreign tourist. Gradually he shifted to a more positive appreciation of Japanese culture as it survived in the Kansai, and to an increasing distaste for Tokyo, which he considered a shoddy imitation of the West. Yokohama, where Tanizaki had in earlier days enjoyed dancing with foreign women, became in *A Fool's Love* the symbol of the unhealthy Japanese mania for the West. In contrast, the world described in *In Praise of Shadows*, is essentially that of Osaka, a city where the merchant class created a solid and substantial culture capable of resisting Westernization better than Tokyo, a city where the descendants of the old inhabitants had been pushed aside by latecomers, peasants attracted to the big city.

Manji, the first novel of Tanizaki's Osaka period, began to appear serially in 1928. The curious title is intended to suggest by the shape of the character *man*, rather than its meaning, the peculiarly twisted relations of the four characters who form the four arms of a swastika: Sonoko, Mitsuko, Watanuki and Sonoko's husband. The manner of narration curiously anticipates that of Durrell's *Alexandria Quartet*. We keep returning to the same incidents as seen from different points of view, with results as bent and devious as the swastika itself. The novel is set in motion when the principal of the art school Sonoko attends remarks that the face she has drawn of the goddess Kannon does not resemble the model's. Sonoko at once imagines that she has unconsciously drawn the features of a fellow student, Mitsuko, whose beauty she had noticed, though they have never spoken. Later, when she and Mitsuko become friendly, Mitsuko informs her that the principal had been bribed to make this remark, which implied some kind of homosexual relationship between Sonoko and Mitsuko, in order to discredit Mitsuko and remove her as a rival in a prospective marriage. To make matters more complicated, we later learn from Watanuki that Mitsuko herself first sent an anonymous postcard to the principal suggesting a relationship between Sonoko and herself in order to free herself of an unwanted suitor. Other scenes are sometimes repeated several times, each time with a quite different interpretation.

The novel is masterfully contrived, but the contours of the mechanism are softened by the use of the monologue style—Sonoko relates her experiences to the author, occasionally answering a question—and especially by use of the Osaka dialect. When Tanizaki began serial publication of the novel he wrote in standard Tokyo speech. Only after six months did he shift to Osaka dialect, but before publishing the work as a book he unified the style throughout. The Osaka dialect in this and sub-sequent novels gave a quality impossible to achieve in standard speech. It served not merely to establish the scene as Osaka, a kind of local color, but to make an involved story more plausible by rooting it in the indolent, affluent upper class of Osaka, quite a different breed of people from those in Tokyo, and making the characters grow from that milieu. It was not simply a matter of having characters say *areshimasen* instead of *arimasen*, but of expressing the personality that goes with the dialect. *Manji* in standard speech not only would lose its charm, but its character would be altered; it would be like reading it in a foreign translation, though paradoxically this was the language Tanizaki originally used in writing the first half of the book.

Tanizaki used assistants to render his own Tokyo speech into Osaka dialect. This gave rise to gossip that the novel, certainly without ante-cedents in Japan, was a translation or adaptation from the French. In the preface to the first edition Tanizaki scotched such talk: "The rumors are all groundless. This work is entirely the product of the writer's mind and there was neither a model nor a source." Perhaps Tanizaki was in fact influenced to some degree by the English novel about Lesbian love, *The Well of Loneliness*, which he read in the original, but he transformed whatever influences may have existed by the unique structure of *Manji* and by the special atmosphere evoked by the Osaka dialect.

Ashikari (1932), also a story of the Kansai, is a narration within a narra-tion. Tanizaki, the antiquarian, visits Minase, the site of the palace of the thirteenth-century Emperor Gotoba. In a manner reminiscent of Mérimée describing Roman ruins in Spain as a prelude to his story of Carmen, but more subtly, Tanizaki passes from the present-day loneliness of Minase to the Minase evoked by the poets, and then to the Minase of fifty years ago as Seribashi, the man he accidentally encounters, relates the story of Oyu-san. The use in this story of Kansai dialect would have been a mistake, for it would have called attention to the narrator, and it is essential that he be the transparent medium for the story who vanishes at the end. Tanizaki's intent in this story is quite the opposite of the usual kind of historical fiction. He wrote: "My wish has been to avoid impart-ing any modern interpretations to the psychology of Japanese women of the feudal period, but instead to describe them in such a way that I will recreate what those long-ago women actually felt, in a manner that appeals to the emotions and understanding of modern people." By preserving a distance between himself and his characters he kept intact the understated reserve that he felt to be an essential element especially in the women of the Kansai region. Some critics at the time evidently objected to this remoteness, but Tanizaki defended himself in a postscript written to *A Portrait of Shunkin* (1934): "In response to those who say that I have failed to describe what Shunkin or Sasuke are really thinking, I would like to counter with the question: 'Why is it necessary to describe what they are thinking? Don't you understand their thoughts anyway from what I have written?'"

Even at the height of Tanizaki's absorption with the Kansai, the last preserve of traditional Japan, he returned at times to more overt descriptions of his abiding, perverse inclinations. *Secret Stories of the Lord of Musashi*, as the title indicates, belongs to an entirely different world. It deals with a man, rather unusually for Tanizaki, and is set in the Kantō during the sixteenth century. The theme, suitably announced in a preface written in stiff, formal Chinese, is the distorted sexual passion of the hero. Terukatsu, unlike the passive males of *Manji*, *Ashikari* or *A Portrait of Shunkin*, is a martial leader, and his exploits are worthy of his heroic age. But, as Tanizaki reminds us in the preface, the sexual lives of heroes are often surprising. Terukatsu, for all his martial prowess, is a masochist who craves the cruelty of a beautiful woman. In this respect he shows his kinship with Seribashi, Sasuke and old man Utsugi.

Tanizaki employed a favorite technique in this work: he describes finding various old accounts of Terukatsu, and attempts to piece them together into a biography, emphasizing the aspects of his life that normally do not appear in typical accounts of the lives of great generals. The novel opens superbly. Terukatsu, a boy of thirteen, is initiated into the world of manhood by being led to a room in a besieged castle where women are washing, arranging and fastening name-tags to the heads of enemy dead. The scene, filled with a morbid, glowing quality, ranks with Tanizaki's finest achievements, and indeed with anything written in this century. Tanizaki may have derived inspiration from *Oan Monogatari*, an account of her experiences in Ogaki Castle at the time of the Battle of Sekigahara in 1600 by a young woman of the warrior class. But all that *Oan Monogatari* contains that is relevant is this single passage: "I remember that the heads which had been taken by our side were collected in the keep of the castle, each one with a tag attached to it.... There is nothing to be afraid of in a head. I sometimes went to sleep among all the heads with their carnal smell." Tanizaki may have been less influenced by the text than by the contemporary illustration that shows women in elaborate kimonos preparing the severed heads.

Terukatsu in later life not only enjoyed witnessing the spontaneous, indefinable cruelty of women, he even sought to provoke it, especially in women of the mildest dispositions. His wife O-etsu, an innocent girl of fifteen, is given to such girlish pleasures as hunting fireflies. In later life she takes orders as a nun and is known for her piety and saintliness. But in an unforgettable scene of the novel Terukatsu compels the priest Dōami (one of his biographers) to go down into a hole in the floor, leaving only his head exposed above the floor level, and to pretend that he is a severed head. Terukatsu, having made O-etsu drunk, tests her courage by asking if she will cut off Dōami's nose. She professes her willingness, though he eventually requires her only to drill a hole in Dōami's ear. She performs this service gladly, laughing all the while. When O-etsu recovers from her inebriation she recalls with mortification her wanton behavior. Terukatsu for his part is satisfied at having thus converted his angelic wife into a monster of cruelty, but this achieved, he loses interest in her.

Tanizaki intended to continue *Secret Tales of the Lord of Musashi* beyond its present conclusion, and even prepared a rough outline of subsequent developments. Although this project was never realized, he referred to it even in his late years, sometimes promising to return to this novel after he had completed his revised translation of *The Tale of Genji*. It is a pity he did not; even so, it ranks as one of his masterpieces.

The three complete translations of *The Tale of Genji*, the first of which appeared in 1938, and the third in 1965, the year of his death, unquestionably brought this great novel within the reach of the Japanese reading public—earlier critics had complained that it was easier to read in English translation than in the original—but we must regret the novels Tanizaki might have composed had he not chosen to devote years of his life to this task. Surely there can be no question of his having run out of things to write. After the first version of *The Tale of Genji*, in fact, Tanizaki wrote *The Makioka Sisters*, by far his longest novel and perhaps his best (though atypical because of the peculiar wartime circumstances of composition). Between the first and second Genji translations Tanizaki also wrote such important works as *The Mother of Captain Shigemoto*, and between the second and third translations he wrote two of his most popular works, *The Key* and *Diary of a Mad Old Man*.

The Key was a sensation from the moment the first episode appeared in the magazine *Chūō Kōron*. The magazine totally disappeared from the newsstands as clamoring customers demanded not *Chūō Kōron*, but *The Key*. The attraction of the novel, needless to say, lay in the outspoken descriptions of the sexual activities of a fifty-five-year-old professor and his forty-four-year-old wife. The maniacal single-mindedness of the professor, determined to have his fill of sex before impotence overtakes him, and who directs his cravings not at a stranger but his own wife, leads to disastrous consequences for his health, but he persists in his experiments. His ladylike Kyoto wife is by no means unresponsive, but because she is too proper to admit such errant behavior in her normal life, he must ply her with brandy to overcome her qualms. Moreover, in order to arouse her own sexual interests he makes use of a young man, a student of his, who is supposedly interested in the professor's daughter. In the end the professor dies, exhausted by his sexual overexertions, but the three survivors, apparently undisturbed by this event, plan a ménage à trois. The young man will marry the girl but devote his energies to the mother.

Tanizaki's method of narration in *The Key* consists of two diaries, one kept by the husband, the other by the wife. The device is brilliantly handled in a male-female interplay, and given an ironic twist by the knowledge of each that the other is reading his diary. But it is a question whether the book is more than a tour de force. The characters are hardly more than puppets, and Tanizaki excluded from his novel anything unrelated to the central theme of sex in middle age. This may have been the best way to treat the subject, but the lack of shadings and depth is suggested by the absence of references to the foot-fetishism or coprophilia that consciously or unconsciously runs through his more deeply felt works.

It is fitting that Tanizaki's last novel, *Diary of a Mad Old Man*, like the last works of many other great artists, should have been comic. This does not mean that his earlier works are unrelievedly serious. *Secret Stories of the Lord of Musashi,* despite its macabre themes, is humorous in its description of the relentless pursuit of Norishige's nose, and some short works, like *The Cat, Shōzō and the Two Women* (1936), are amusing throughout. But *Diary of a Mad Old Man* is in its self-satire a wonderfully comic work, and at the same time true to Tanizaki's deepest feelings as *The Key* is not. It is as if Tanizaki, still intrigued by the old themes of his writings, is now able also to see them at such a distance that they appear comic. It is a captivating book, marred only by the weak ending. Probably this was because the logical ending, the death of the old man, was the one subject Tanizaki at this stage of his life could not treat with humor.

In 1934 Tanizaki wrote of himself, "I am basically uninterested in politics, so I have concerned myself exclusively with the ways people live, eat and dress, the standards of feminine beauty, and the progress of recreational facilities." No doubt this is how he chose to see himself, sometimes at least. But the more complex side of his writing, expressed in countless variations, surely imparted a distinctive quality, sombre, grotesque or comic, that contributed much to the greatness of the man I consider to have been the finest modern Japanese novelist.

NOTES

1. Translation by Howard Hibbett in *Seven Japanese Tales*, p. 163.
2. *Ibid.*, p. 8.
3. *Ibid.*, p. 108.
4. Translation by Howard Hibbett, p. 27.

Dazai Osamu

IT WOULD probably surprise most Japanese to learn how differently the translated works of Dazai Osamu (1909-48) have been evaluated abroad, as compared to their reputation in Japan. Of course, the difference comes in part from the process of translation itself, which inevitably alters the flavor of the originals, flattening or (more rarely) enhancing the qualities considered most characteristic of the author; in part too it results from the circumstance that only two novels and a few short stories have been translated, not enough to permit the Western critic to form an accurate impression of the entire work of Dazai. The most striking aspect of Dazai's reputation abroad, however, is that (unlike most Japanese writers who have appeared in translation) he has not been treated as an exotic or obscure oriental. One American reviewer wrote, "Almost alone among recent Japanese literary imports, *No Longer Human* is strikingly free of cherry-blossom reveries and puzzling Oriental character motivations." Other reviewers have compared Dazai to Camus or Kafka, and the ancestry of his novels has been traced to the European masters of the nineteenth century. The *Times Literary Supplement*, a notoriously severe journal, said of *No Longer Human* that "it achieves in a high degree the ironical poignancy of Dazai's model, Dostoevsky. It is, in fact, a consummate work of art."

I cannot recall ever having read a Japanese criticism of Dazai which either likened him to Dostoevsky or claimed that one of his novels was a "consummate work of art." Perhaps the English reviewer was foolishly enthusiastic, but I think it likely that the Japanese reluctance to employ such superlatives stems not only from oriental modesty but from the different meaning Dazai's work possesses when read in the original language. It is impossible when confronted with Dazai in Japanese not to be aware of his profound connections with the autobiographical fiction which has such a long history in Japan. The tendency among Japanese, then, has been to consider Dazai's fiction as one might consider his letters or diary, as somehow supplying evidence about the personality or beliefs of the author, or demonstrating the relationship of the author to his themes. The artistry of the writer has consequently tended to be overlooked or subordinated to other considerations. It gives the Japanese reader pleasure when he feels he can detect Dazai Osamu's deepest emotions emerging through the characters in the novels; this, of course, is not the manner in which one appreciates, say, characters in a Dostoevsky novel who possess a life quite apart from the author's. The Japanese reader may even feel a sense of betrayal if he discovers that the "I" of a Dazai novel is actually quite unlike the author. It is rather like discovering that a man has lied in his diary. One remembers the consternation when new evidence revealed that *The Narrow Road of Oku* by the revered "saint of poetry" Bashō departed at times from the truth in the interests of artistic excellence.

Dazai complicated the distinctions between autobiography and fiction by including in most of his writings an important character who *might* be considered the author himself. In the case of *The Setting Sun* (*Shayō*, 1947) we may even obtain the impression that all three main characters—the girl Kazuko, her dissolute brother Naoji, and the novelist Uehara—represent no more than different aspects of the author; the reader who can identify himself with any one of the three may therefore feel a special affinity for Dazai himself. The extraordinary popularity of Dazai among young people during the past fifteen or more years certainly owes much to this sense of identification. The critics have fostered the tendency to equate Dazai with his works; even stories seemingly unrelated to Dazai's life, such as those directly derived from European prototypes, have been interpreted in terms of autobiographical elements. It is easy, of course, to discover details of Dazai's life recorded almost unaltered in the chain of autobiographical stories beginning with *Omoide* ("Remembrances," 1933): his family circumstances, the political position of his father, his schooling, his relations with his brothers, and so on. The list could be prolonged indefinitely, and there are even photographs to confirm some descriptions in the fiction. Many elements found in the early autobiographical stories were to reappear again and again in later works, culminating with *No Longer Human* (*Ningen Shikkaku*, 1948). The recurrence of such material may suggest that Dazai could not escape from his own life, but for most Japanese readers this is not a failing; for them the essential interest in Dazai's writings is the portrait of the author.

The Western reader receives a different impression from, say, *No Longer Human* because, not knowing as much about Dazai's life as a Japanese, he may imagine that the work is entirely fictional, though he will surely sense that Dazai is personally involved. But even if all the facts were known, the tendency among Western critics would probably be to evaluate Dazai's writings in terms of his success in making his personal experiences meaningful to all readers, and not in terms of his success in revealing himself. A reviewer in India, comparing the character Yōzō in *No Longer Human* with the salesman Gregor Samsa in Kafka's *Metamorphosis*, found that Yōzō's discovery that he had lost his human qualifications resembled the metamorphosis of Gregor Samsa into a cockroach. He continued, "But as in the case of Kafka's eerie tales, there is far more in Dazai's story than can be summed up in a neat moral. It brings us face to face with the formless, nameless, terror of life. Dazai gives it a form and a name. We cannot expect more from any writer." This comparison between Dazai and Kafka certainly seems to me more rewarding than attempts to contrast the actual details of Dazai's childhood with their fictional versions.

It is obvious, of course, that some aspect of Dazai himself is present in all works from the earliest. This fact can be interpreted unfavorably, as meaning that he failed to create a fictional, objective world in the manner of the great nineteenth-century novelists, but Dazai shares this failing with many of the best twentieth-century authors, and it is absurd to insist that all writers conform to a single standard. Even if Dazai had not invented one incident in his novels—of course, this is not the case—his method of treating existing material and, above all, his literary style would have made him a creative artist.

Dazai had a remarkably precocious awareness of his particular domain as a writer, as we can tell from one of his first stories, *Gyofukuki* (1933). The untranslatable title was borrowed from a Chinese story known to Dazai only by name, but the direct inspiration came from the adaptation of this story by the eighteenth-century Japanese novelist Ueda Akinari, a tale called *Muō no Rigyo* ("The Dream Carp," 1768). Akinari's story is about a priest living by Lake Biwa who loves to paint pictures of carp. He dreams that, being very ill, he wanders in delirium to the edge of the lake and plunges in. He swims about happily as a carp, only to be caught by a fisherman. Just at the moment when he is about to be cut up into *sashimi*, he awakens from the dream, only to discover that all the events have actually occurred, leaving the reader to wonder where to draw the line between fantasy and reality. In Dazai's story an unhappy girl, living with her brutish father in a remote place, is driven by wretched circumstances to commit suicide by throwing herself into a deep pool. Transformed after death into a fish, for a while she enjoys the sensation of swimming about freely, but at the conclusion of the story the fish, still under the spell of the terrible gloom which had afflicted the girl, swims deliberately into a whirlpool, there to commit a second suicide. In this story Dazai not only twists the original material in a highly original manner, but gives expression to his own morbid fascination for suicide. Suicide was to figure so prominently as a theme of Dazai's writings that we may find it strange that he managed to stay alive so long. But despite the persistent darkness of mood in his stories, one is led in the end to the judgment that the personality of the author was not interchangeable with that of the characters in his fiction. Dazai, knowing in which moods he was most effective, generally clung to them, but this was a deliberate posture; he did not merely pour out his thoughts as they welled up. He was, above all, an artist.

Dazai's concern for style is revealed in the almost obsessive interest he displayed in words and their implications:

> "To fall for," "to be fallen for,"—I feel in these words something unspeakably vulgar, farcical, and at the same time extraordinarily complacent. Once these expressions put in an appearance, no matter how solemn the place, the silent cathedrals of melancholy crumble, leaving nothing but an impression of fatuousness. It is curious, but the cathedrals of melancholy are not necessarily demolished if one can replace the vulgar "What a messy business it is to be fallen for" by the more literary "What uneasiness lies in being loved."

The most extreme example of Dazai's preoccupation with language is found in the scene in *No Longer Human* where Yōzō and Horiki play their game of tragic and comic nouns, followed by a game of antonyms. A novelist with so hypersensitive an interest in words suggests a poet, and indeed, much of Dazai's writing is close to poetry. In his first collection, *Bannen (Declining Years,* 1936), this quality is most pronounced. Sentences with no apparent logical connection to those surrounding them are impressionistically inserted, sometimes creating unforgettable vignettes. The style itself is deliberately non-realistic and intuitive, moving us strangely even when we do not understand exactly what is meant. The "Moonflower Diary" section of *The Setting Sun* is a late example of this poetic spirit, conveying in its incoherence a sense of tremendous emotion:

> They say the wisteria of Ushijima are a thousand years old, and the wisteria of Kumano date from centuries ago. I have heard that wisteria clusters at Ushijima attain a maximum length of nine feet, and those at Kumano of over five feet. My heart dances only in those clusters of wisteria blossom.
> *That too is somebody's child. It is alive.*

Logic, inevitably, is the love of logic. It is not the love for human beings.

This otherwise realistic novel is given its particular appeal not only by the poetic passages of Naoji's diary, but by the presence of the mysterious snakes that appear first at the time of the death of Naoji's father, later when the mother's illness becomes apparent, and finally when the mother dies. The incidents concerning the snakes are related by Kazuko, who assures us that she has seen them with her own eyes. Short of deciding that she is insane, we have no choice but to believe her, yet with another part of our mind we know that the snakes have a symbolic, poetic meaning, and without them the novel would lose its artistic overtones.

The conscious artistry of Dazai reveals itself also in the construction of his writings. Surely no modern Japanese novel has a superior beginning and ending to *No Longer Human*. The device he employs in the prologue, the three photographs of the subject at different stages of his life, has since been imitated by other writers, but still has overpowering impact. It does not matter whether or not the photographs described are related to actual photographs of Dazai; the prologue sets the mood of the novel flawlessly with a poetic economy of words. And there is something peculiarly appropriate in a novel about Japan, the country of photographers, that the hero be introduced in this manner. The photographs are the sad proof of the existence of a person who, in his own words, was never a human being.

The epilogue to the same novel is perhaps even more remarkable. Many Japanese novelists seem to encounter difficulty in ending their works, leaving the reader to feel that the book is still incomplete, or that it might have ended earlier, but *No Longer Human* acquires its full intensity only with the last words. Dazai employs the frequently used convention of the writer who has been entrusted with the notebooks of a deceased person, and in the epilogue, where we leave the notebooks for the world of the objective outsider, we are suddenly made to see that the picture Yōzō has painted of himself in the notebooks, for all its unspeakable honesty, is grossly inaccurate. The madam of the Kyōbashi bar tells us, "The Yōzō we knew was so easy-going and amusing, and if only he hadn't drunk—no, even though he did drink—he was a good boy, an angel." This would hardly occur to the reader as the proper description of the Yōzō *we* have known, but with these words we sense the turning of a kaleidoscope: just as most people, incapable of perceiving their own faults, tend to justify their every action, so Yōzō has only been able to interpret his actions, however welcome to others, in the most distorted terms. What he has reported may be factually correct, but it is essentially wrong. The reversal of our ideas comes as a shock. Yōzō has insisted that he is not even a human being, but the final judgment is that he is superior to other human beings—"an angel"—and we suddenly realize that, paradoxically, this is true. Yōzō, despite his self-proclaimed loss of human character, has acted throughout in an almost excessively human manner, if to be human means to be aware of oneself and one's condition. The author with this final touch has transformed the novel from a confession into a complex work of art.

Dazai's most perfect artistic creation may be *Otogi Zōshi* (*Bedtime Stories*). He managed in his adaptation of these fairy tales, known in general outline to every Japanese child, to impart the characteristic Dazai flavor, normally associated with an extremely dark outlook on the world, without violating in any way the lighthearted spirit of the originals. Dazai's mordant humor was a well-established part of his style from *Dōke no Hana* ("Flowers of Buffoonery," 1935) onwards, and numerous anecdotes in his autobiographical writings indicate how often Dazai was given to clowning, even as a child. Even in his last bitter works there always remains a thread of humor: at the end of *No Longer Human*, Yōzō, afflicted by depression and illness, takes a large dose of sleeping pills, only to discover that he has been provided with the wrong medicine, and has actually taken a powerful laxative instead. There is nothing appealing about Dazai's portrayal of himself as a clown: "I was fascinated by my own face. Whenever I got tired of reading I would take out a mirror and practice smiling, frowning, or meditating chin in hand, and stare without tiring at my reflected expression. I mastered a whole repertory of expressions guaranteed to make people laugh." (*Omoide*) The kind of humor found in such late works as "Cherries" (*Ōtō*, 1948) is harrowing. But in *Otogi Zōshi* the humor is real and brings genuine laughter. One of the delights of the collection, moreover, is to find here familiar figures from other Dazai stories—the heartless man who passes for a saint, the impractical artist, the scheming woman, and so on—drawn with even greater perception than in the stories involving Dazai more personally. The deceitfulness of society, a fact which never ceased to trouble Dazai, is perfectly evoked in the tale of *Urashima-san*, more effectively even than in *No Longer Human*. Freed of the self-imposed necessity of writing about his own experiences, Dazai could express his views easily and gracefully within the framework of an existing story. His humor here was the more brilliant because untouched by self-pity or self-hatred. The stories of *Otogi Zōshi* are virtuoso examples of Dazai's style divorced from the mood which it generally served to create.

Another purely literary feature of Dazai's writings that strikes anyone reading the collected works is his genius for the short, effective scene. This ability is undoubtedly related to the poetic talents I have already mentioned. Even an unimportant, dull story will suddenly come alive briefly with a superb passage which stamps the work as a lesser piece by a master, rather than as merely a failure. *Chiyojo* (1941), for example, is the inconsequential account of a girl forced by her uncle to become a child literary prodigy. We read along, hardly able to recognize this story even as a minor work by Dazai, until suddenly a new character, a teacher sent for to improve the girl's style, appears, and for a few splendid pages we have pure Dazai:

> He would come out with the most obvious things, after carefully consulting his little notebook. "Description is the most important part of style. If your descriptions are unsuccessful, nobody will know what you're driving at." Then, returning the notebook to his breast pocket, he might say, "Take this snow, for example. How would you describe it?" With a sharp glance through the window at the powdery snow falling in torrents outside, like something out of a play, he would continue, " 'The snow is pouring down.' No, that won't do. It doesn't suggest the feeling of snow. 'The snow is streaming down.' No, that's no good either. Well, then, how about 'The snow is fluttering down?' Still not quite strong enough. 'Rustling down?' Now we're getting there. Gradually we've come closer to the feeling of snow. Yes, this is becoming interesting." He would fold his arms, shaking his head in admiration at his own discovery. " 'Drizzling down?' How about that? No, that sounds more like rain. Well, then, shall we settle on 'rustling down'? Or maybe a combination, 'rustling and fluttering'? That's an idea."

Sometimes it is not the appearance of a new character but a brief incident or even a single line which captures us. One of the earliest stories *Ha* ("Leaves," 1934) contains this short passage of dialogue:

> My brother said, "I don't think novels are worthless. They just seem to me a little long-winded. They build up an atmosphere for a hundred pages simply so they can say one line of truth."
> I answered very hesitantly, as if it were hard to pronounce the words, "That's right. The fewer the words the better. Providing you can convince the reader with nothing else."

This seems to have been Dazai's attitude throughout his career. *Ha* itself, though not a successful work as a whole, contains many brilliant flashes, including the unforgettable vignette of the little Russian girl who sells flowers at Nihonbashi, or such statements as: "He spent three full years of his life educating his wife. By the time her education was more or less completed, he began to wish he were dead." We can imagine this single line of print being developed by another author into hundreds of pages. Dazai's genius for the short scene was to contribute also to the success of his mature works. One can never forget the scene in *The Setting Sun* in which Kazuko, working as a conscripted laborer during the war, exchanges a moment of sympathy and understanding with an officer who lends her a book of poetry, nor the heartrending scene in *No Longer Human* when Yōzō, entering a pharmacy for some medicine, notices that the proprietress is propped up on crutches. Such moments of silent recognition are perfect examples of Dazai's artistry.

Dazai is able in the same manner to evoke a place or person with a remarkable economy of language. His recollections of scenes known from childhood in Tsugaru, or of the views of Mount Fuji, or of different corners of Tokyo where he has known misery, are generally achieved with a few telling details. One never has the impression that Dazai has carefully filled notebooks with observations so that he will be able to provide local color when needed. Instead, the reader senses that each scene has been distilled through Dazai's poetic imagination into its essential ingredients. The reader is often surprised on returning to a favorite passage to discover how short it is; it has grown within our imagination because the essentials were all present. The same is true of Dazai's characters. He rarely mentions details of physical appearance except when absolutely necessary to our understanding of the character. We can never forget, say, Horiki in *No Longer Human*, with his hair pomaded and parted in the center, or the description of Uehara in *The Setting Sun*, as seen after long absence by Kazuko, who has been dreaming of him:

> Was he my rainbow, M.C., my reason for living? Six years. His hair was as unkempt as before, but it had now become sadly lusterless and thin. His face was bloated and sallow, and the rims of his eyes, a harsh red. Some of his front teeth were missing, and his mouth was continually mumbling. He gave me the feeling of an old monkey squatting with its back hunched over in the corner of a room.

But Dazai never tells us, where the information is not vital, that a character had a round face or broad shoulders or any other conventional descriptive matter. His characters tend to be fixed in our minds as the result of one utterance or gesture, rather than through exhaustive description. "Flatfish" in *No Longer Human* is forever epitomized in one paragraph:

> I can never forget the indescribably crafty shadow that passed over Flatfish's face as he laughed at me, his neck drawn in. It resembled contempt, yet it was different: if the world, like the sea, had depths of a thousand fathoms, this was the kind of weird shadow which might be found hovering here and there at the bottom.

The pathetic Yoshiko in the same novel, who has suffered agonies because of her feckless husband, still innocently trusts him, as we learn from one line:

> Yoshiko silently offered from her handbag the hypodermic needle and the remaining morphine. Is it possible she actually believed after all that it was just an energy-building medicine?

The terrifying irony of the situation—the narrator is being sent to a hospital to be cured of drug addiction, but his wife presents him with his hypodermic needle and morphine to take with him—is surely a touch of Dazai's genius.

I have thus far been discussing Dazai in terms of his purely literary skills. This approach may seem almost paradoxical in view of the intensely personal nature of his writings, the subject of so much criticism by Japanese, but I have been anxious to insist on his excellence as a craftsman because it tends to be obscured by his reputation as a writer of autobiographical fiction. But of course it is impossible to deny the unmistakably autobiographical impulse which charges Dazai's work, and a comparison between the early *Omoide* and *No Longer Human* affords absorbing insights into Dazai both as a chronicler of his own life and as an artist. The personality of the speaker is clearly the same in both works, and certain incidents recur almost unchanged in the later book. The chief difference is that the "I" of *Omoide* is still a human being with recognizable bursts of affection for his family and other people. Although he dislikes his elder brother, he by no means considers him a total stranger:

> My brother knew I had been collecting unusual insects. The paper bag he offered me rustled with the clawing of insect-legs inside. That faint sound told me of a brother's love.

What a contrast with the cold, utterly unsympathetic elder brother described in *No Longer Human*! Dazai's affection for his younger brother is another endearing element in *Omoide*, but had to be suppressed in *No Longer Human*, where no suggestion of human ties would be possible for the non-human Yōzō. At the end of *Omoide* the younger brother shows the narrator the picture of a servant-girl with whom he imagined himself to be in love, a scene possessing a warmth that is not merely the product of artistic skill. But if our impressions of Dazai as a person are more favorable in *Omoide* than in *No Longer Human*, we cannot help noticing the superior literary quality of the latter. The author has stripped away everything not essential to his theme, and at the same time given maximum importance to each incident. Undoubtedly *Omoide* depicts the boy Dazai much more faithfully, and this autobiographical quality has its own interest, but the way in which the mature artist has transformed the material is a tribute to Dazai the artist.

Gyakkō ("Against the Stream," 1935) carries forward the story, at once more impressionistically and more urgently. The first of its four episodes opens in a manner suggesting *No Longer Human*:

> He was not an old man. He had barely passed his twenty-fifth birthday. Yet "old man" might be the best designation for him, after all. He had lived each year that an ordinary man lives, three or four times over. Twice he had unsuccessfully attempted suicide.

Here, obviously, we have a description of Dazai during the period of *Bannen*. The next episode, "The Thief," tells of Dazai's actual experiences at Tokyo University, where he pretended for years to be studying French literature without attending a class or learning anything of the French language. This period in his life, marked by attempts at suicide, addiction to liquor and drugs, an abortive interest in Communism, and his unsuccessful love-suicide, would later be chronicled in *No Longer Human* with greater mastery than Dazai was capable of when so close to the events, but the reader cannot help share emotions so intensely stated:

> I am a thief. A notorious subversive. Artists never used to kill people. Artists never used to steal. Swine! You and your paltry, smart-alecky friends.

The unsuccessful love-suicide was the most traumatic of his experiences and marked the depth of his depression. He refers to this event again and again in his writings, sometimes, as in *Dōke no Hana*, with brutal realism; sometimes as in "Of Women" (*Mesu ni tsuite*, 1936), in analytical terms; sometimes, as in *Obasute* (1938) with an awareness of the almost farcical aspects; sometimes, as in *Tokyo Hakkei* ("Eight Sights of Tokyo," 1941) with terrible bitterness; and finally in *No Longer Human*, in the final development of the theme, as an expression of the essential nature of the character Yōzō.

In his revelations of the love-suicide and other sordid episodes of his youth Dazai does not hesitate to disclose the worst about himself. He is so ready to impute to himself the basest motives that we may feel in reading the chain of autobiographical stories something akin to masochism. At the same time, however, we must bear in mind that the story is incomplete in one fundamental respect: during this period of violent emotion and despair Dazai was desperately intent on becoming an author. Already in *Omoide* he had expressed this determination:

> In the end I discovered a safety valve, a miserable little safety valve—writing. In this, there were many like me, I could sense, all concentrating like myself on their crazy lamentations. I prayed secretly again and again, "May I become a writer! May I become a writer!"

There is little, however, in the autobiographical stories to suggest the seriousness with which Dazai applied himself to his self-appointed task, or that creative efforts gave him any satisfaction. When Yōzō tells Flatfish that he would like to become a painter (Dazai sometimes disguised his writers as painters), Flatfish merely laughs. Yōzō himself admits that except for a few terrifyingly self-revealing portraits painted as a boy, he never painted anything of consequence. In the novel, art occupies Yōzō very little, and his work quickly degenerates into foolish cartoons or pornography; in reality, Dazai was deeply committed to his work, as we can gather from what he wrote about *Bannen*:

> I sacrificed ten years of my life to this one volume of short stories. For ten full years I didn't know what it was to eat the cheerful breakfast of the good citizen. For the sake of this one book I lost sight of my place in life, was constantly wounded in my self-esteem and buffeted by the cold winds of the world, and I wandered around in a daze. I squandered tens of thousands of yen. I could not lift my head before my brother, knowing the hardship I had caused him. I burnt my tongue, wore out my heart, and deliberately harmed my body beyond any possibility of recovery. I tore up and discarded over a hundred stories. I ran through 50,000 sheets of manuscript paper. And all that remained, barely, was this one volume. Nothing else. The manuscript came to almost 600 pages, but the fee was a little more than sixty yen. Yet I believe in it. I believe that *Bannen* will take on deeper colors as time goes on, that it will surely penetrate deeper and deeper into your eyes, your heart. I was born only to write this one book.

Surely this statement should dispose of any impression that Dazai was merely a diarist, scribbling down whatever gloomy thoughts happened to come to mind. But in his *Bannen* period, though clearly he was highly absorbed with his writing, he deliberately excluded any suggestion that the creation of works of literature could alleviate the heartaches of his life.

Not until *Fugaku Hyakkei* ("The Hundred Views of Fuji," 1939) did Dazai choose to portray himself as an author who had won recognition (particularly among young people). This story is conspicuously more cheerful than those in which the "I" is a person without fixed occupation, and at the same time is the closest to autobiographical writing of anything in Dazai's works. Instead of the self-destroying monster who normally frequented Dazai's pages, we have a recognizable human being, friendly to the young people who gather around him, appreciative of the kindness of the maid at his inn, sensitive to the beauty of Fuji, and capable too of a marriage quite dissimilar to the acts of desperation described in the other stories. This relatively happy period, which includes the delightful short *Mangan* ("A Vow Fulfilled," 1938), shows Dazai at his most attractive, but he must have sensed that his forte lay elsewhere. The character of the devoted, attentive husband and father would not suit the Dazai of fiction.

It is true that at the end of "Villon's Wife" (*Buiyon no Tsuma*, 1947) the dissolute poet (often assumed by readers to represent Dazai himself) discloses that he stole in order to provide his wife and child with money for New Year, but we remember this less than the indifference he most often displayed. The hero of most Dazai stories is dissolute; he even suggests in *The Setting Sun* that this is desirable, when Kazuko writes to Uehara: "For all I know, you may earn the gratitude of people in years to come by recklessly pursuing your life of vice rather than by your 'splendid career.' " In *Kirigirisu* ("Grasshoppers," 1940) the paradox is even greater: the wife, who has loved her husband as long as he was dissolute and irresponsible, abandons him when he turns respectable and achieves social prestige. In *Katei no Kōfuku* ("The Happiness of the Family," 1948) the leading character is a model husband and father, but a heartless monster in the office where he works; the conclusion is that "The happiness of the family is the root of all evil."

Dazai thus not only portrayed himself in terms of dissolution and despair, but often approved of these qualities, at least in his fiction. He decided that having once established the dark atmosphere of *Bannen*, this would be his characteristic milieu, as a painter might choose a palette of sombre colors. The small group of cheerful stories clustered around *Fugaku*

Hyakkei is so winning that we may regret Dazai's decision, but it was justified when viewed in terms of the artistic successes of later years. At the same time, Dazai may thereby have prevented himself from developing into a novelist of even greater range and power.

One way in which Dazai attempted to enlarge his scope was by adapting stories derived from Western sources, including *Kakekomi Uttae* ("Direct Appeal," 1940) on the betrayal of Christ by Judas, *Hashire Merosu* ("Run, Melos!" 1940) about a young Greek who proves to a wicked king his loyalty to a friend, and *Onna no Kettō* ("Duel of Women," 1940), based on a German story originally translated by Mori Ōgai. These works were followed in 1941 by his long novel in the form of a play, *Shin Hamuretto*, or the new Hamlet. These are the most difficult of Dazai's works for a Western reader to appreciate. Dazai's characteristic skill is evident in the breathless narration of *Kakekomi Uttae*, and the reader welcomes the sunny tale of Melos, after so many cynical accounts of human nature, but I for one find something peculiarly unconvincing in Dazai's handling of foreign themes. He could transform with brilliance the characters in the original *Otogi Zōshi* or in Saikaku's *Tales from the Provinces* (*Shokoku-banashi*, 1685) into lively, modern Japanese, but his foreign characters seem uneasily poised between two worlds, as if Dazai were unwilling to make them completely Japanese and yet incapable of creating believable non-Japanese. My opinion, I must state, is not shared by most Japanese readers. *Hashire Merosu* is not only frequently acclaimed as one of Dazai's best short stories, but it has been widely adopted for use in school textbooks. But just as a novel written about Japanese people by a non-Japanese novelist would undoubtedly seem false to a Japanese audience, so these new versions of European stories are likely to puzzle a European reader. Perhaps the best is *Kakekomi Uttae*, if only for its vivid narration and powerful ending, and for its indication of one aspect of Dazai's interest in Christianity.

The innumerable references to Christianity in Dazai's works are another source of difficulty for a Western reader. Christianity seems at times to have filled a spiritual vacuum in Dazai's life, and some think that at the end he genuinely considered himself to be a Christian. But the mentions of Christianity are hardly more convincing than an American beatnik's references to Zen. In *The Setting Sun* especially there is such excessive quotation of the Bible that this was the one place where I felt it necessary to abridge in making a translation. The quotations and frequent references to Christianity at no point suggest sincere belief or even the desire to believe. Dazai is intrigued by Christianity, and he is delighted to discover appropriate passages to insert in his books, but whatever degree of faith he may have attained in private life, in his writings Christianity is a disconcerting and not very important factor. It failed to give his works the additional depth he sought.

The basic lack of depth in the writers of the time, Dazai among them, may be attributed to the times. *Bannen* was written as the militarists were taking control of Japanese life; the works of Dazai's middle period were all subjected to wartime censorship; and the works of his last period were published amidst the confusion of post-war days. If Dazai had been writing ten years earlier or later his works might, under more favorable conditions, have acquired the broadness of scope they lack. But this is mere conjecture. The reader must be grateful that Dazai was able to grasp the nature of the society in which he lived and to describe it magnificently. During the war Dazai alone continued to publish works of indisputable literary merit, and thereby encouraged young writers bored and disappointed by the propagandistic works—or else the silence—of other authors. Dazai's uncompromising devotion to his art, especially amidst the general paralysis of literature during the war, earned the admiration of the reading public.

It is true that even Dazai on occasion seems to have followed the tide of militarism during the war. His short story *Jūnigatsu Yōka* ("December Eighth," 1942), describing the outbreak of the war, has been cited by some critics to prove that Dazai acquiesced before the trend of the times, but the same story has also been included in collections of "resistance literature." Whichever view is correct, the lighthearted, objective tone of the story distinguishes it from the mass of works composed under the emotional impact of the declaration of war. A few of Dazai's wartime stories were banned in entirety by the government and could be printed only after the end of the war, but his chief works of the wartime period— *Udaijin Sanetomo* ("The Minister of the Right Sanetomo," 1943), *Shokoku-banashi* ("Tales of the Provinces," 1944), *Tsugaru* (1944), and *Otogi Zōshi* (1945)—appeared like shining stars over the sunken horizon of literature. As the titles of the works indicate, Dazai, in common with most other writers during the war, avoided insofar as possible treating contemporary subjects in his fiction.

The life of the thirteenth-century ruler and poet Sanetomo was a particularly popular subject during the war. Probably this was because Sanetomo's dual career suggested the proper path for all writers in wartime Japan. Dazai was provided in *Udaijin Sanetomo* with the opportunity to relate in a highly moving fashion his conceptions of aristocratic truth;

he appears to have found in Sanetomo the embodiment of all he most respected in human beings.

Shokoku-banashi is a collection of short stories derived from Saikaku's work. Nothing is harder in Japanese than successfully rewriting in the modern language a work of the classical tongue, but Dazai, thanks to his fluent style, was triumphant. *Tsugaru* tells in curiously moving terms of Dazai's journey during the war to his birthplace in northern Japan, a work of non-fiction which contains some of his finest pages.

Otogi Zōshi, mentioned above, is one of the masterpieces of Dazai's art. These tales, originally related to his daughter during the fierce wartime bombings of Tokyo, form a central part of Dazai's literary patrimony.

One peculiar work, dating from the end of the war though not published until September, 1945, was *Sekibetsu* ("Regretful Parting"), an account of the life in Sendai as a medical student of the celebrated Chinese novelist Lu Hsün. Dazai's novel was commissioned by the Information Office of the Japanese Cabinet and the Literature Patriotic Association (*Bungaku Hōkoku-kai*) as part of a program intended to encourage novels embodying the ideals of the Greater East Asia War. It was incredible that Dazai, a writer lacking in political reliability or even citizenly virtues, should have been chosen to fulfill this patriotic task, and even more incredible that a work on Lu Hsün, a man associated with the resistance movement against Japan, should have been his subject. To prepare himself for the novel Dazai devoted considerable time to research in Sendai, and he attempted conscientiously to evoke an authentic atmosphere of 1904. Despite—or perhaps because of—these scholarly touches, *Sekibetsu* was a failure. Dazai's extensive revisions to the novel in 1947, when it was reprinted, indicate that he was dissatisfied not only with the wartime sentiments he sometimes had put in the mouths of his characters, but with the construction of the story itself. The only way Dazai could have succeeded with *Sekibetsu* was to make Lu Hsün his *alter ego*; the devastating irony shared by the two men might have made this possible. But despite the touches of Dazai in the portrait of the youthful Lu Hsün, the positive, affirmative utterances ring hollow. Dazai may have felt impelled to write about Lu Hsün, but 1945 was not the right moment.

The immediate postwar days were chronicled by Dazai in many short stories including the wryly humorous "A Visitor" (*Shinyū Kōkan*, 1946) with its savage portrait of a boorish acquaintance in the country. The atmosphere of Tokyo at the time is best suggested by "Villon's Wife," though *The Setting Sun* seemed to its first readers the literary embodiment of the changing society. Ten years earlier Dazai had written that Japan was in a transitional phase, but only with the wholesale destruction of the old culture and ideals did his opinion gain full force. Kazuko says of herself and Uehara, a man belonging to an entirely different class, "Victims. Victims of a transitional period of morality. That is what we both certainly are." The decline of the aristocracy, the major theme of the novel, is related to attitudes expressed by Dazai in *Udaijin Sanetomo*, but here he seems to be associating himself almost equally with the aristocrat who has deliberately rejected his birth and breeding (Naoji), the dissolute writer who drinks out of despair over a future which holds no promise (Uehara), and the aristocrat who hopes that by bringing a bastard into the world she will push back the old morality (Kazuko). *The Setting Sun*, because of this division of Dazai's personality, creates an impression of objectivity that contributes to the success of the novel, but the author is as immediately present as in any of the more obviously autobiographical works. The relatively optimistic ending, suggesting that the illegitimate child Kazuko will bear is likely to live in a better world than the one against which she struggles, certainly accounted for the greater popularity of *The Setting Sun* with foreign readers than the uncompromisingly grim *No Longer Human*.

No Longer Human is set in the Japan of the 1930's, and conveys fairly accurately the general mood of the times, but Dazai was not especially interested in creating a period piece. It was the one book he had to write, his final attempt to elucidate himself and his unhappiness. For Japanese readers, especially of the younger generation, it is a compelling expression of the malaise and disillusionment shared by those who cannot accept the ideals of their elders. It is not so much an attack on the habits and traditions of Japanese society as a record of alienation from them. Yōzō, by his own testimony, is constantly performing for the benefit of others in the hope of ingratiating himself and concealing his true nature. But the others are all acting too and with much greater hypocrisy. The difference is that their performances are in accord with the unspoken conventions of society, and seem so natural that no one dares to say, "You did it on purpose," as the half-wit Takeichi told Yōzō. Aware of his peculiar role, Yōzō dreads that he will be discovered. The young man of today who resents the necessity of conforming to Japanese society will find spiritual kinship with Yōzō, and when he eventually realizes the impossibility of continuing the struggle, he may like Yōzō contemplate suicide. Yōzō's weakness (and that of many young Japanese who resemble him) is not his lack of human qualifications, but his lack of the non-human powers of resistance which enable the rest of society to survive.

It is inevitable that people who experience less trouble than Dazai in accommodating themselves to the world and its ways should feel impatience or even active dislike for his writings. The note of self-pity which is sounded often, though generally with ironic overtones, offends those who either have never been afflicted by Dazai's doubts or else have overcome them. But it is meaningless to reproach Dazai for having revealed himself so brutally. He *had* to write *No Longer Human* in order to purge himself for once and for all of the devils which had long beset him. The book is not literally true, as we have seen, but it is sometimes embarrassingly close to what we suppose is the truth about Dazai. The language is occasionally exaggerated, and we may be revolted when Yōzō admits that he cannot even recall the name of the woman with whom he attempted to commit suicide. Such a self-centered attitude is so repelling that we may decide that Yōzō's problem was simply that he never loved anyone more than himself. The surprising statement at the end of the book, "It was his father's fault," seems to suggest that if Yōzō's father had been more understanding the boy would never have grown up to be such a failure. But the novel itself offers little evidence to support this belief. Yōzō was disqualified as a human being because, unlike his brothers, he was sensitive to insincerity, to the conflicting motives of others, to the insipidity of the world. This awareness made for Yōzō's unhappiness, but it was a virtue and not a vice. The terrible strength of the awareness inevitably drove him to excesses of self-pity and even to cruelty. Yōzō, far from being non-human, carries certain human virtues to such excess that we may agree with the madam of the Kyōbashi bar who tells us at the end, "When human beings get that way, they're no good for anything."

What was Dazai to write after *No Longer Human*? Having at last spewed out the poison which had accumulated within his system from childhood, he could not write still further versions of the same autobiographical data. He would have to start anew. It was possible now even for him to write a book without bitter, sardonic overtones. *Goodbye*, left unfinished at the time of his death in June, 1948, might have developed into a genuinely comic novel. It approaches farce in its account of how the hero ingeniously rids himself of a series of women in his life, and the brilliance of its colloquial dialogue is remarkable even for Dazai. It is impossible to tell, of course, how the novel would have developed.

Perhaps Dazai, fearing that he could not complete *Goodbye* or any other book, now that *No Longer Human* was written, was driven closer to suicide, but *Goodbye* seems to me rather the work of a man who has made a fresh start. I should prefer to believe the theory that his suicide was not premeditated. Probably we shall never know, but the last tantalizing fragment of Dazai's writing indicates that a new writer was emerging.

Criticism of Dazai's writings in recent years has often been unfriendly, and his faults have been given more attention than his merits. Such attention offers at least negative evidence to his continuing popularity, and the unkindness of the criticism may be no more than a reaction to the extreme admiration his works still excite among a large class of readers. Whatever the criticism, it seems safe to assume that Dazai's writings will remain as powerful evidence not only of the author's artistic excellence but of the Japanese acquisition of a modern literary sensibility.

Mishima Yukio

MISHIMA YUKIO was not only an extraordinarily prolific novelist, playwright and essayist, but he wrote so precisely and copiously about his work that he seemed to have left few questions for the critic to answer. He analyzed influences on his novels, traced successive changes in his style, described the functions of characters in his novels and plays. In essays on literature, politics and aesthetics he provided the kind of background to his fiction that critics normally must piece together from scattered clues in an author's work. Mishima moreover displayed such unusual self-awareness that one easily obtains the impression that not a word in his writings, not a gesture in his much-advertised public life was accidental. It would have been hard to catch him unaware and point out truths of which he himself was ignorant. But although few writers have been more articulate about themselves and their activities, the ultimate question to be asked about any author—what makes his works good?—can only be answered by others. This perhaps is the area Mishima left for his critics to explore.

Mishima wrote various openly autobiographical essays including *Watakushi no Henreki Jidai* ("My Age of Travels," 1964) and *Sun and Steel* (1968); other works, though cast in the form of novels, stories or plays, bear such close resemblance to what we know of his private life that they provide material for the biographer, as well as for the critic who wishes to analyze how Mishima transformed his experiences into art. But Mishima clearly stands at the opposite pole to the typical writers of modern Japanese fiction, those authors (like Dazai Osamu) who, whatever the guise they adopt, write autobiographical fiction, as if they themselves were the only subjects they can honestly describe in an age of fragmentation and isolation. A major difficulty when discussing Dazai is to keep from identifying the heroes of his novels and stories so closely with him that we read the works for what they tell us about the author, rather than as literary products. The difficulty in discussing Mishima is to penetrate the dazzling variety of works to find a single author. Mishima's intense dislike for the self-indulgent manner characteristic of the "I novels" (*watakushi shōsetsu*) may account for his preference for heroes who could not conceivably be mistaken for himself—a stammering

Buddhist priest, the proprietress of a successful restaurant or the owner of a spinning mill. Even if we can find traits in these characters resembling those of their creator, this is still quite a different matter from being able to see through the thin camouflage to the sensitive, suffering face of the author of the "I novel." Mishima's dislike of the writings of Dazai in particular led him to adopt a totally dissimilar literary stance.

The reasons for this dislike can be inferred even from Mishima's early, atypically autobiographical novel *Confessions of a Mask* (1949). Like Dazai's *No Longer Human* this is the story of a boy's gradual discovery that because he is not like his fellows, he must wear a mask to protect himself from their attacks. The two novels even have some similar scenes, such as the one where the boy prances around in a strange costume to amuse or dismay his family. In Dazai's novel the boy deliberately acts the part of the clown, hoping that this "service" will keep people from discovering the truth about him, how unlike the others of his family he is; this is the mask he felt obliged to wear for the rest of his life in the presence of "human beings." The mask becomes his defense against their insistence that he play their game of deceit. No matter how desperately he sometimes longs to remove this mask and bare his true face, he dares not, for fear of the wounds that surely would be inflicted. The mask to the end conceals a face that is totally different in expression, or at least the "I" supposes so. The boy in *Confessions of a Mask* does not parade in female attire as an act of service to the grown-ups; in fact, he knows it will annoy them, but his masquerading gives him a pleasure he cannot resist. Only later does he feel compelled to put on his mask, but once he does he convinces himself that it has become an integral part of his nature: his greatest desire is to make the mask his real face. Dazai described his agony at having to wear a mask and pretend to conform to the way of "adults;" as a result, his books continue to exert an enormous appeal over young people who share his sense of alienation. The suffering of the artist is his badge of distinction, and the mask his only armor against an unsympathetic world. With Mishima, however, the mask enables the novelist to become whatever man he chooses to be. Mishima's "pranks"— his cult of physical prowess, his appearance in gangster or samurai films, his whole repertory of martial activities—were often decried as needless stunts intended merely to attract attention, but they were in fact a means of subduing the sensitivity, timidity and self-pity that Dazai carefully preserved behind his mask; they were Mishima's efforts to make his mask a living part of his flesh.

If anyone had attempted in 1941, when Mishima, at the age of sixteen, wrote his first published work, *Hanazakari no Mori* ("The Forest in Full Bloom"), to predict his appearance at forty-five, a reasonable guess would have been precisely the kind of harried-looking, middle-aged intellectual Mishima at that age would most detest. By an amazing effort of will and intelligence Mishima was to make of himself a totally different man and author. His early works are gifted but precious, employing an exceptionally rich vocabulary and displaying an almost morbid sensitivity. Mishima's effective and seemingly effortless use of an archaic style was, of course, a tribute to his precocious mastery of language. It would be hard to imagine an English-speaking boy of sixteen writing a story in seventeenth- or eighteenth-century idiom except as a feat of sophomoric virtuosity. But Mishima's story *Chūsei* ("The Middle Ages," 1946), to take one example, employs the language of the Nō plays to relate movingly the death of the youthful shogun Yoshihisa and the grief of his father, Yoshimasa. The story is saved from being a pastiche by the author's evident identification of himself with Yoshihisa. The pathos and beauty of early death would run through most of Mishima's writings from these early works to his most recent masterpieces.

Confessions of a Mask traces Mishima's life from his earliest recollections through his childhood in an upper middle-class family, his education at the Peers' School and Tokyo University, his wartime experiences, and finally, his decision, for unstated reasons, to give up his job at a ministry. The facts and incidents in the book, insofar as they can be checked with avowedly autobiographical information, are all true, if incomplete. The author's intent, however, was obviously not to write reminiscences of childhood in the conventional manner—the usual mixture of happy excursions to the old fishing hole and tearful hours after the death of a pet rabbit—but, as the title indicates, to give his confessions. He was attempting, as he himself testified, to vanquish the monsters in his inner heart. In literary terms *Confessions of a Mask* was a grand, if precocious, summation of all that he had learned as a writer, a mixture of styles and moods. But above all, it was a confession, and like any other confession it had to be public in order for it to be valid. But just as the priest in the confessional box is often unable to make sense of the fragmentary, if painfully truthful, phrases that pour from the confessant's lips, the meaning of Mishima's confessions was probably not understood by most of his readers, even those who enjoyed the book as the story of a sensitive boy turning into an adult. Some critics, the most sophisticated, termed it a "parody" of the confessional novel in which the author allegorically described the impotence of the times by describing an impotent hero.

A few, of a more down-to-earth turn of mind, even imagined that the impotence had been caused by the malnutrition common in postwar Japan! Most readers, however, probably read *Confessions of a Mask* as an "I novel," much in the vein of Dazai, about a boy whose inward-turned sensitivity prevented him from leading a normal sexual life. It did not matter to Mishima that the book was misunderstood. The purpose of a confession is not to elicit sympathy or understanding but to purge oneself of poison. Mishima describes a young man who is not only incapable of sexual relations with a prostitute—this might be ascribed to fastidiousness—but of feeling physical desire for the girl he supposes he loves. He is drawn instead to Ōmi, an older classmate of a rough and unintellectual disposition, and at the end of the book his sexual desire is further aroused by a sweating workman he sees in a café. The narrator gives as the background for his seemingly inexplicable attraction to coarse but superbly muscled men, rather than to a beautiful girl, and his even more inexplicable compulsion to wound and kill the objects of his desire, the pictures that had fascinated him as a small child—youthful knights killed in battle, samurai committing *seppuku* and, above all, St. Sebastian dying in the pride of his youthful beauty.

St. Sebastian became an obsessive theme in Mishima's writings, intimately linked with the beauty and pathos of early death. Mishima quoted in *Confessions of a Mask* several of his youthful compositions; the longest, describing St. Sebastian, was inspired by the Guido Reni painting that had brought on the narrator's first ejaculation. This vision of Adonis, the young god whose blood must be shed, runs through such different works as *Patriotism* (1960), *The Sailor who Fell from Grace with the Sea* (1963), *Eirei no Koe* ("The Voices of the Heroic Dead," 1966). Mishima does not mention in *Confessions of a Mask* how often as a child he was taken to see Kabuki performances, but surely this theatre, with its traditions of bloodletting, whether in the form of *seppuku* or scenes of general mayhem, must have nurtured the boy's fascination with blood and the tragic death of young heroes.

The narrator of *Confessions of a Mask* exults in the thought of an early death, imagining that his frail, unattractive body will somehow, miraculously, attain the glory of a St. Sebastian. The war seems to assure precisely such a death, but when it ends with the narrator unharmed, far from experiencing the relief and sense of liberation of most of his contemporaries, he feels frustrated and cheated. He had hoped, like the hero of *The Temple of the Golden Pavilion* (1956) who dreamt of perishing together with the building he adored, to die in a final holocaust that would destroy

Japan. But the thought of suicide did not occur to him; on the contrary, he was delighted when he failed his army physical examination. Only later would Mishima come to associate early death and suicide, the necessary link being the belief in some ideal that transcended fear of pain or other sources of irresolution. The hero of *Homba* ("The Runaway Horse," 1969) is not merely willing to die for the cause he believes in, but insists on death, and eventually kills himself, to the sorrow of those who struggled to save him.

The necessity for beautiful people to die young is, of course, understood by every author. Murasaki Shikibu could allow Genji to live only so long as he remained beautiful. Romeo and Juliet must both die before they become ugly or their love cools. This perception developed in Mishima into an article of faith. The young army officers who participated in the February 26, 1936, assassinations and revolt, or the *kamikaze* pilots who plunged with their airplanes into American ships, were beautiful because of their ideals, their youth and their deaths. In 1966 Mishima wrote, "Among my incurable convictions is the belief that the old are eternally ugly, the young eternally beautiful. The wisdom of the old is eternally murky, the actions of the young eternally transparent. The longer people live, the worse they become. Human life, in other words, is an upside-down process of decline and fall."[1]

Mishima's attention in *Confessions of a Mask* is so taken up by the account of his emotional development that he scarcely alludes to his intellectual or literary activities as a young man.[2] At the Peers' School he enjoyed the encouragement of teachers who recognized his gifts. He was influenced by the attitudes of a literary group called *Nihon Roman-ha* (Japanese Romanticists), led by the critic Yasuda Yojūrō (b. 1910). The members of this group, unlike most of the rest of the Japanese literary world, were deeply interested in Japanese classical literature, and their influence over Mishima would distinguish him from other writers of his generation; again and again he turned to this literature for inspiration, ultimately in his monumental *Hōjō no Umi* ("The Sea of Fertility," 1969–71) based on a Heian romance. During the war the members of the *Nihon Roman-ha* group became increasingly political in their emphasis on "Japanese spirit," and after the war their writings were rejected by most intellectuals as part of the discredited nationalism of the militarists. Mishima, however, never rejected these ideals, and in the 1960's especially his commitment to the traditional Japanese virtues and political conceptions grew, as we can tell both from his novels and public pronouncements.

In November 1944, in the midst of a losing war and an acute paper shortage, Mishima's collection of stories *Hanazakari no Mori* was published. This recognition of the talents of a nineteen-year-old boy was all the more extraordinary because the stories were not glorifications of the war effort but works of purely literary content. His devotion to literary excellence, at a time when most published writings were at a deplorably low level, undoubtedly reflected the influence of the *Nihon Roman-ha*; in the postface the young author thanked his teachers at the Peers' School for the love of the Japanese classics they had instilled in him, and also expressed his conviction that in the post-war world it would be impossible for critics in any country to discuss poetry without reference to the *Kokinshū*.

In the last stages of the war, however, when distrust of effete foreign ideas had become extreme among the militarists, Mishima's love of literature was no longer to be excused because of its nationalistic overtones. His fondness for such writers as Raymond Radiguet and Oscar Wilde was particularly suspect. Nevertheless, as he later recalled, "During the war there was some faint degree of individual preference permitted, but the post-war society at once reopened the free market of crude ideas and artistic conceptions; the times were such that society discarded without a second thought whatever did not suit its predispositions. The boy who, in a small group, had given himself the airs of a genius, became after the war no more than a helpless student whom nobody could take seriously."[3]

Mishima had entered the Law Faculty of Tokyo Univeristy in 1944. In the following year he was mobilized for work at a naval dockyard, where he saw the end of the war. He then returned to Tokyo University, and after his graduation in 1948 entered the Ministry of Finance. Six months later, when his short stories were beginning to be accepted regularly by the leading literary magazines, he resigned his post to devote himself entirely to writing. This was the background to *Confessions of a Mask*, the work that established his reputation.

Confessions of a Mask is still an absorbing book, not only for what it reveals about the youth of a man who became a great novelist, but because of the intensity of the writing and the penetrating honesty of the confession. It retains its popularity today; but if it possesses in abundance the virtues of a first novel, it also has some of the usual faults. The characters in the book other than the "I" are sketchily drawn; they exist only as objects that momentarily occupy the attention of the narrator. The book ends with the implication that the narrator will throw off his mask of compliance to society and accept his perverse desires.

It might have been anticipated that his next novel would continue the confessional mood, in the tradition of the "I novel." But Mishima made the critical decision to become a novelist and not a self-chronicler. He would, of course, use materials directly derived from personal experience,[4] but never again did he "confess." His next major work, *Thirst for Love* (1950), at first glance appears totally unrelated to Mishima himself. It is set near Osaka, a part of Japan Mishima had hardly visited, and the central character is a woman, Etsuko, a widow who becomes her father-in-law's mistress. Etsuko lives on a suburban farm in a house full of relatives and servants, each one sharply drawn, in contrast to the shadowy figures of *Confessions of a Mask*. Mishima has said that this novel was written under the influence of François Mauriac. It is not difficult to find in the neurotic Etsuko traces of Mauriac's Thérèse Desqueyroux, and the tight dramatic structure of *Thirst for Love* also owes much to Mauriac. This influence helped Mishima to develop into a novelist capable of transcending his personal experiences.

Mishima had begun his readings in European literature while at the Peers' School. He was especially attracted to the novels and personality of Raymond Radiguet, who died at the age of twenty. Mishima has never lost this enthusiasm for this young, classical genius, and it may have been through Radiguet that he first approached the equally classical Mauriac; from Mauriac he went beyond to Racine. German literature also impressed Mishima, but though he read widely in English and American literature, being especially taken with Wilde and Yeats, it seems not to have exercised any direct influence. Mishima once expressed the view that "surely there can be no foreign author as much to Japanese tastes as Mauriac." He explained this in terms of a Japanese fascination for details— the expression on a woman's face when, on the point of weeping, she holds back the tears; just how far back one can see in a woman's mouth when she smiles; the pattern the wrinkles make in her dress when a woman turns around. Mauriac is a master of such details but, according to Mishima, American novels afford little pleasure of this nature and therefore have never had much appeal for the Japanese.[5] *Thirst for Love* abounds in details; they suggest not only Mishima's indebtedness to Mauriac but his place in the tradition of Japanese literature.

But there is also something so unique to Mishima in this work that one is tempted to describe it as a kind of sequel to *Confessions of a Mask*. The climactic scenes are one in which Etsuko gashes the back of Saburō, the farmer-boy she loves, and the final one, when she kills him. Saburō is the strong, sunburned young man, devoid of any intellectual preoccupations, who would reappear in many subsequent novels, a healthy young animal who cannot fathom Etsuko's complex desires. Etsuko's "thirst for love" is, of course, intelligible in terms of the surface meaning, but it is given added poignancy if seen as the extension of the hopeless attachments of the narrator of *Confessions of a Mask* to Ōmi and the other young men.

Yet whatever personal elements are involved in *Thirst for Love* it is clearly a rejection of the "I novel." Mishima's decision was confirmed by the publication, also in 1950, of *Ao no Jidai* ("The Blue Period"), the first of his novels modelled on actual events. This is the story of a Tokyo University student who lends money at usurious rates of interest, is caught, and finally commits suicide. In dealing with the objective reality of a newspaper account Mishima could sometimes, as in the case of *After the Banquet* (1960), follow the facts so closely as to expose himself to a suit for invasion of privacy, or he could depart so far from the facts, as in *The Temple of the Golden Pavilion*, as to retain only the bare outlines of the events. In either case Mishima used these materials to expand his range as a writer far beyond the limited canvas of the "I novel."

At the same time that Mishima was writing these major novels he began to produce a steady stream of short stories and novellas that displayed his exceptional richness of imagination. They are most interesting when they treat the lives of quite ordinary people, the office workers and shopkeepers who figure only marginally in his novels. The short story *Nichiyōbi* ("Sunday," 1950) tells of the excursion of a boy and a girl who work in the same office. There is something indescribably appealing about these young Japanese who cheerfully brave the Sunday crowds on the train, are completely enchanted by the artificial lake they visit, even though it is foul and turbid, and start for home with the conviction that they have spent a most wonderful day together. The ending, like that of various other short stories by Mishima, comes as distinctly too much of a surprise for what has gone before, and suggests the baleful influence of Maupassant. Other short stories seem like the scenarios for longer works. The novellas, clearly superior to the short stories, rank with the novels and plays among Mishima's finest achievements. *Death in Midsummer* (1952), *Patriotism*, and *Eirei no Koe* are examples of the varied uses he made of the novella form.

Mishima's search for an objective world of literature took another form in the plays he wrote, beginning in 1948. They are cast in every idiom, including the traditional, metrical language of the puppet stage; their subjects range from contemporary events back to themes inspired by the Nō dramas or by the plays of Euripides and Racine.

Some Japanese critics rank Mishima higher as a playwright than as a novelist. This view seems extreme, but it suggests his success in creating a world quite independent of the introspective novel.

Mishima made his first trip abroad in 1952, visiting the United States, Brazil, France, England, Italy and Greece. His travel accounts record the powerful impressions evoked by this journey, and his literary works written years afterwards still contain echoes. Above all, Greece was to affect his writing most deeply. Greece had attracted Mishima ever since his childhood, as we know from *Confessions of a Mask*. The statues of the Greek gods (but certainly not the statues of Buddhist divinities!) had formed his ideals of beauty, and Greece itself had appeared to him a country where the sun and the sea had combined to produce beautiful gods. Mishima may have feared that the realities of twentieth-century Greece would disillusion him, but in fact his visit gave him the intensest pleasure, and awakened a new world within him. After publishing in 1952 the two parts of his long novel *Forbidden Colors*, a powerful but gloomy evocation of the sodomite underground in Tokyo, Mishima decided to write *The Sound of Waves*, the result of his realization in the Greek sunlight that the darker side of human nature, the side that had absorbed him hitherto, was not the entire truth.

Mishima turned for inspiration (as Raymond Radiguet had turned when writing *Le Diable au Corps*) to the Greek romance *Daphnis and Chloë*. He gave the story a wholly Japanese atmosphere by transforming the shepherd and shepherdess of the original to a fisherboy and fishergirl on a small island. No characters could be more remote from Mishima himself and the world he had previously described than Shinji and Hatsue, the hero and heroine of this novel, but Mishima manipulated the familiar old tale brilliantly, giving it new life by his skilful use of telling details. Perhaps he thought of *The Sound of Waves* as essentially an exercise in stylistics for the connoisseur's enjoyment; certainly the enormous popular success of the novel came as a great surprise.

Greece meant to Mishima not only sunlit strength but the rejection of its opposite, the dark, self-absorbed look of the intellectual. One day in 1955 he was examining an exhibition of photographs taken of the mummies at the Chūsonji Temple, when he happened to notice the face of a man near him. Suddenly, he relates, "his ugliness infuriated me. I thought, 'What an ugly thing an intellectual face is! What an unseemly spectacle an intellectual human being makes!' "[6] This revelation, which had long been germinating, made him hate the sensitivity in himself, the sensitivity that so easily expressed itself in the martyred look of the intellectual. He decided he must do something drastic about his appearance, and shortly afterwards began to practice weight lifting, with such vigor and persistence that eventually he was able to create, from the most unpromising material, the muscular torso of the Greek statue.

Mishima's absorption with Greek ideals was reflected also in his increasing classicism. His interest in the classical literature of both Japan and Europe had already provided him with material for his own work. His short story *Shishi* ("The Lion," 1948) is a reworking of the Medea story, and the "modern Nō play" *Kantan* (1950), the first of a series, showed he could freely and imaginatively employ classical Japanese themes and forms to create new works of literature. But Mishima's classicism had a wider meaning, involving a shift of emphasis in his works to structure, themes and intellectual content, as opposed to the baroque lushness of, say, *Forbidden Colors*. His style had already shifted from the archaisms of his early period and the heavy influence of translated literature, particularly the works of Radiguet and Stendhal, in his first novels, to the leanness of style of Mori Ōgai (1862-1922). Ōgai's masculine, intellectual diction often suggests a translation from the Chinese; the favored tense is the historical present, and there is a rigorous insistence on purity of language. Mishima decided about 1950 to imitate Ōgai, as a means of checking any tendency towards a poetic, sensitive style. This does not mean that Mishima's writings were at once marked by laconic simplicity; on the contrary, he followed Ōgai in the unhesitant use of rare characters and words when they corresponded exactly with the desired nuance of meaning, and his thoughts and perceptions are often exceedingly complex. The use of the Japanese language for intellectual, rather than emotional, expression is an aspect of his classicism.

Mishima's classicism is apparent also in the construction of his novels, whether *After the Banquet*, describing middle-aged love, or *Kemono no Tawamure* ("The Sport of Beasts," 1961), about an abortive murder, but it is given its most extreme expression in the play *Madame de Sade* (1965). Here he adopted most of the conventions of the Racinian stage—a single setting, a reliance on the *tirade* for the relation of events and emotions, a limited number of characters each of whom represents a specific kind of woman, and an absence of overt action on the stage. He managed these conventions brilliantly, removing everything superfluous to his theme, the quest of the absolute. A later play, *Suzaku-ke no Metsubō* ("The Fall of the House of Suzaku," 1967), is based on the *Heracles* of Euripides; the ancient story had for him a universality of theme that permitted transference to the Japan of the 1940's.

Perhaps the finest example of Mishima's classicism is *The Temple of the Golden Pavilion*. Although the central incident—the burning of the famous temple by a young priest—was not a classical legend from the distant past but an event that occurred in 1950, it surely was as familiar to every reader as the Atreus story to the Greeks, and the interest of the novel lies not in discovering how it ends—this is known from the start—but in the relentless march of circumstances that make the final act inevitable. The priest who burned the temple in 1950 was apparently insane, and his act, if described faithfully, could never become the subject of tragedy; but Mishima sees the symbolic truth of the act, and in the novel Mizoguchi emerges as a character worthy of Dostoevsky. As a boy Mizoguchi was told by his father of the incomparable beauty of the temple, and when he comes to live nearby as an acolyte its beauty so dominates him that he is incapable even of making love to a woman of less absolute beauty. In the end he realizes that he must destroy the temple if he himself is to live. Mishima has so constructed the novel that we agree, not out of sympathy with the priest's act but because we cannot see any other solution.

The novel is written with the greatest economy, despite its length. The characters are relatively few, but strongly delineated, and a rhythm is given the whole by the recurrence of a Zen *kōan*, or riddle, about Nansen killing a kitten. The priest Nansen decides a dispute between two temples about ownership of the kitten by killing it. Later, his chief disciple, Chōshū, returns and when he is told what happened, he removes his muddy shoes and places them on his head. Nansen says, "If only you had been here, the kitten could have been saved."

The riddle is read to the priests of the temple by the Superior on the day of Japan's surrender in 1945. The priests are mystified by its meaning and by the Superior's failure to refer to the defeat. No explanation is ever offered, though it may be that Chōshū, accepting the humiliation of filth on his head, represents Japan in defeat; if Japan had shown such humility earlier the tragedy of the war might have been averted. The same riddle is given another meaning by Kashiwagi, a bitter, club-footed priest. For him the kitten is beauty, killed by Nansen because it causes disharmony; but Chōshū, putting his shoes on his head, satirizes so easy a solution. In still another interpretation, Kashiwagi suggests that Mizoguchi wishes to play Chōshū in protecting beauty with knowledge. But Mizoguchi, wondering if his feelings about beauty are not the cause of his great affliction, his stuttering, answers, "Beauty, beautiful things, those are now my most deadly enemies."

If Mizoguchi becomes Nansen, the destroyer and liberator, his Chōshū is the Superior, a man who accepts evil as calmly as he accepts the cartons of cigarettes given to Mizoguchi by an American soldier as a reward for trampling on a prostitute and causing a miscarriage. Mizoguchi later sees the Superior squandering temple funds on a geisha, and when he taunts him with it, the Superior accepts the humiliation as of no importance. The last Mizoguchi sees of the Superior is when he is praying in a posture of abject humility.

Mizoguchi, though totally unlike the narrator of *Confessions of a Mask* in most ways, may remind us of him, especially in his desire to perish in the war together with the temple. And although he is a badly educated country boy and has difficulty speaking because of his stammer, he is as articulate as the precocious "I" of Mishima's earlier novel. The conversations between Mizoguchi and his friend Kashiwagi are not believable as utterances that could have come from the lips of students at a third-rate university, but Mishima, in an essay written two years after publishing *The Temple of the Golden Pavilion*, stated, "With respect to the conversations in my novels, I believe I have already freed myself to a considerable extent from Japanese fastidiousness. Japanese writers enjoy displaying their delicate skill at revealing in an indirect manner, by means of conversations, the personalities, temperaments and outlook on life of their characters; but conversations that are unrelated to the personalities and temperaments of the characters, converastions that are read for their content alone and, finally, long conversations that fuse into the same tempo with the descriptive passages, are the special quality of the novels of Goethe, and of the German novel in general."[7] Mishima remarked that Thomas Mann in particular had inherited from Goethe the "epic flow of conversation."[8] It is noteworthy that he characterized the style of *The Temple of the Golden Pavilion* as "Ōgai plus Thomas Mann."[9]

The exceptional popular success of this novel, despite its difficulties of content and style, was a tribute to Mishima's novelistic genius. Perhaps also readers sensed some personal identification between the author and the priest who burnt the temple.

It would not have been surprising if Mishima, having achieved a style that was at once highly artistic and popular, had decided to explore its possibilities further, and perhaps establish it definitively as his own, much as a certain style is associated with such novelists as Nagai Kafū or Kawabata Yasunari. Instead, he chose totally different techniques for his next major novel, *Kyōko no Ie* ("Kyōko's House," 1959). The journal he kept while writing this long work, which occupied him for a year and a half, provides precise information on what he was attempting to do.

"When I am developing a single character in one of my novels, I sometimes feel him quite close to my own thinking, but sometimes I drive the same character away from myself and let him wander into independent action. The attitudes of the hero change convulsively, as the course of composition dictates.

"In *Kyōko no Ie*, in order to resolve this contradiction which has always appeared in my novels (and was most extreme in *Forbidden Colors*), I have avoided having a single hero, but have represented various aspects through four different heroes. The painter represents sensitivity, the boxer action, the actor self-awareness, and the businessman knowing how to get along in the world. It is naturally to be expected that the personalities of these characters will become abstract and purified. I think I can say, strictly speaking, that I have for the time being given up any attempt to create characters as single, coordinated, organic entities."[10]

Mishima might have said that Mizoguchi was himself, different though the two men are, just as Flaubert said Madame Bovary was himself. In order to prevent this from happening in *Kyōko no Ie* he deliberately created four heroes who have extremely little in common, who have almost nothing to say to one another when they occasionally meet, and whose stories are related almost independently. Mishima was attempting to portray not a single person but a whole generation, but one cannot escape the feeling that Mishima identified each of his characters with himself. Seiichirō, the successful businessman, is convinced that the world is heading for a crack-up; this prospect gives him great pleasure, though it can hardly be true of many other successful Japanese businessmen! Mishima's experiences with body-building occasioned much in his descriptions of the actor Osamu, and his boxing practice must have helped when writing about Shunkichi, the champion boxer. His work as an author is behind his descriptions of the painter Natsuo. But beyond such surface resemblances to their creator, the four men seem curiously uniform in their outlook, in no way suggesting the diversity of a generation. Mishima explained his intent:

"The characters in the book run about in one direction or another as their individual personalities, their professions and their sexual tendencies command them, but in the end all roads, no matter how round-about, flow back into nihilism, and each man helps to complete the sketch-map of nihilism that Seiichirō first proposed. This was my plan as I first conceived it."[11]

Mishima termed *Kyōko no Ie* his "Study of Nihilism," justifying his presentation of such a study in the form of a novel on the grounds that the "spiritual state known as nihilism is essentially emotional in content, and it is therefore more appropriate for a study to be made in the novel of a novelist than in the theoretical researches of the scholar." Mishima's ambitious plan puts this novel in a class of its own, quite distinct from the entertainments and confessions that make up the bulk of Japanese literary production, but it is a failure. Mishima attempted to develop philosophical convictions in a novelistic manner, but the book is extraordinarily static, unconvincing and even boring. The reasons for its failure will certainly preoccupy Japanese critics for many years to come,[12] but it is surely worthy of admiration that a writer who could easily have succeeded with a more conventional novel chose a new and risky course.

The failure of Kyōko no Ie came as a great blow to Mishima. He had originally decided to write this long novel in imitation of Western authors, taking many months to complete it, and not serializing it first in a magazine, in the usual Japanese manner. But the pressures of journalism, infinitely greater in Japan than in the United States or Europe, made it extremely difficult for Mishima to persist with his work, and time and time again, as we know from his journal, he felt great weariness and even dejection. At one point he noted, "Of late I no longer feel any envy with respect to other people's lives, but on the other hand I keep thinking of impossible things. For example, I think how amusing it would be if I were eighteen again and were a jazz singer or something like that."[13] After the shock of the cold reception given to Kyōko no Ie, the novel that had cost him the greatest effort, Mishima turned to precisely such "impossible" things. He took the part of a gangster in a film, recorded jazz songs, appeared before the public in costumes that did indeed suggest he was eighteen once again.

But Mishima's depression did not last long. In 1960 he published one of his most perfectly constructed and executed works, After the Banquet. Though less ambitious than Kyōko no Ie, it is in every way more successful. The characters are not abstractions but believable human beings whose actions and utterances create three-dimensional personalities. Perhaps Mishima himself felt that a novel of this kind represented a step backwards from the highly conceptual fiction that had absorbed him for some years, but the gifts of a novelist—the knack of telling a good story, and the ability to create memorable characters—were not to be disprized.

Kazu, the heroine, is the best of Mishima's many brilliant portrayals of middle-aged women. At the beginning of the novel she appears as a self-satisfied, rather vulgar woman, sure of her hard-earned position in society as the proprietress of a fashionable restaurant. She is attracted to one guest, Noguchi, a former Conservative Party prime minister who has shifted his political affiliations and now, perhaps as a proof he has not fallen behind the times, professes socialism. Little that Noguchi says or does in his awkward, aristocratic manner is intended to please Kazu, but as they become more intimate the prospect of marrying him, becoming a member of his distinguished family, and eventually sharing the same dignified grave, comes to dominate Kazu and persuades her that she is really in love with a desiccated old man.

The romance of a fifty-year-old woman and a sixty-year-old man could hardly be farther removed from Mishima's usual preoccupation with youth, but it is beautifully handled. Kazu's attraction to Noguchi's gentlemanly authority, and Noguchi's attraction to Kazu's volatile energy make convincing even so tardy a love affair. The action of the book is centered around a campaign for the election of the Governor of Tokyo. Noguchi, eager for power but unwilling to unbend and abase himself so as to obtain it, conducts his campaign with the same haughty dignity and awareness of his personal incorruptibility that he displays in his relations with Kazu. He models his conduct on what he supposes to be the ways of an English aristocrat, preferring a shabby, worn suit to the vulgarity of new clothes. But he nevertheless wants political power. In the end it is Noguchi's aloofness that seems a snobbish pose and Kazu's reckless enthusiasm a manifestation of genuine incorruptibility.

The incidents in *After the Banquet* were modelled very closely on the marriage of the well-known statesman Arita Hachirō and the proprietress of Hannya-en, a Tokyo restaurant known for its magnificent garden. Arita sued Mishima for invasion of privacy and eventually won the case. But the novel is definitely not a *roman à clef* the interest of which depends on our recognition of the real identities of the characters. Mishima used the facts freely, and his success may be judged by the high reputation the novel achieved abroad, where none of the reviewers was aware that it was based on actual events. Angus Wilson wrote that Mishima had created in Kazu "a woman of Balzacian dimensions and Flaubertian truth."

After the Banquet has much to say about politics—it presents the best account in fiction of a Japanese election—but it is not a political novel in the usual sense. If one had to guess Mishima's political views from the contents, one could only conclude that he was sympathetic to the socialists and dismayed by the tactics and policies of the conservatives. In fact, Mishima's political views, as they evolved about this time, were at once more radical and more conservative than those of either Noguchi or his opponent. He had become increasingly concerned with Japanese tradition, especially the martial aspects—the sword of the "chrysanthemum and the sword"—perhaps as the result of his own study of the traditional martial sports. He published in the same year as *After the Banquet* the novella *Patriotism*, an expression of his admiration for the spotless purity of the young officers who chose to die in the February 26 incident because of their love for the emperor. The hero of this story, Lieutenant Takeyama, is not included in the coup because his friends are reluctant to involve a newly married man in a suicidal endeavor. He resents having been excluded, and decides he must kill himself, to prove he was no less ready than they to die for the emperor. His bride, aware of what it means to be the wife of a military man, does not attempt to dissuade him, and after he has committed *seppuku* she plunges a dagger into her throat.

Mishima did not intend the scenes of their suicides to be either pathetic or horrifying; he felt, on the contrary, that Lieutenant Takeyama and his wife had achieved the greatest joy in life. They die still young and beautiful, still deeply in love, and secure in their belief in an ideal. The emperor-worship that emerges as a theme in this work would appear frequently in Mishima's subsequent writings, both the fiction and critical essays, and was reflected also in his public life, notably in his creation of the Shield Society, a small private army designed to "shield" the emperor from any attack. The heroes of *Eirei no Koe* or Isao in *Homba* die for this cause, and they die happy.

Mishima's emperor-worship was not, however, a worship of the present emperor. Indeed, in *Eirei no Koe* the ghosts of the heroes of the February 26 incident and the *kamikaze* pilots of 1945 reproach the emperor bitterly for having betrayed them by declaring he was not a god. The men know, of course, that the emperor is an ordinary human being with ordinary human weaknesses, but in his capacity as emperor he must be a god. If the emperor had understood the significance of the February 26 incident and supported the young officers who so disinterestedly killed for his sake, even if (or especially if) he ordered them to commit suicide, he would have performed like a god, and not like a mere ruler, surrounded by old politicians. And, when the emperor declared he was not a god, less than a year after the *kamikaze* pilots had joyfully died with his name on their lips, he made their sacrifice a pitiable, meaningless gesture.

Mishima once declared that he believed in the infallibility of the emperor.[14] This of course did not refer to the present emperor in his human capacities, any more than a belief in papal infallibility implies unconditional acceptance of the pope's views on modern art. The emperor, in his capacity as a god, is the incarnation of Japanese tradition, the unique repository of the experience of the Japanese people. To protect the emperor was thus for Mishima to protect Japan itself. It would be a mistake to identify these political views with the Japanese right wing. In his novel *Homba* especially Mishima demonstrated his awareness of the corruption of professional supporters of the imperial cause. He was sure that only the purity of the young, the readiness of the young to die for their beliefs (unlike rightwing politicians whose declarations of absolute loyalty become more and more suspect as they age), could save Japanese culture from disintegration under the double threats of greed and westernization.

It is not necessary to accept Mishima's political beliefs to admire his writings. Even the non-Japanese who finds them—and the persistent xenophobic strain—a source of irritation must in the end admit at least the skill with which he presented them. The officers who took part in the assassinations of the 1930's behaved, by normal western standards, in a frightening and even demented manner; but Mishima insisted that these normal western standards do not apply to Japan, and that Japanese traditions must be considered in their own terms.

During the seven or eight years after the appearance of *After the Banquet* Mishima continued to write prolifically, both serious novels and others intended for serialization in the popular magazines; the latter, though they took up precious time, brought in the income he deemed necessary to sustain his style of life.

Utsukushii Hoshi ("Beautiful Star," 1962) was Mishima's most conspicuously *avant-garde* novel. He borrowed the familiar features of science fiction —flying saucers and interplanetary travel—to expound in a long, often brilliant dialogue his views on the present condition of man. This novel, though not wholly successful, was further evidence of Mishima's continued interest in experimentations in the craft of fiction. *The Sailor who Fell from Grace with the Sea*, a smaller-scaled work, is about a man who at the age of twenty must have been much like Saburō or Shinji and who, under different circumstances, might have turned into a Lieutenant Takeyama; but now he is thirty-three and faced with the prospect of settling down to bourgeois respectability. A group of precocious boys, resenting his betrayal of his freedom, decide that the sailor must die, and they carry out the murder with the utmost self-possession. The sailor, who has long dreamed of glory descending on him from the heavens, achieves at last a kind of glory he never anticipated.

In the 1960's, even as he wrote these other works, Mishima was again planning a large-scale work that would have the same significance for the forty-year-old Mishima as *Confessions of a Mask* for his twenties and *Kyōko no Ie* for his thirties. The novel gradually took form as a work in four parts. It would cover a period of sixty or seventy years, and in each part would have a young hero who is linked by ties of reincarnation with the other three. One character, an observer of the action, would appear through all four volumes, and he alone would know the secret of the reincarnations. The theme of reincarnation, together with that of dream prophecies, was borrowed from the Heian period novel *Hamamatsu Chūnagon Monogatari*, and certain elements in the plot of the old classic reappear in much altered form in Mishima's novel. The work was given the overall title *Hōjō no Umi*, "The Sea of Fertility," the name of a region of the moon, but each of the four volumes had a title of its own.

The first volume, *Haru no Yuki* ("Spring Snow," 1969), describes the world of the Japanese aristocracy about 1912, just after the Meiji era had ended. Mishima's long association with the aristocracy, ever since his childhood days at the Peers' School, had led him repeatedly to choose for his characters members of this tiny fraction of Japanese society, and he wrote with a unique knowledge of their speech and attitudes. His account in *Haru no Yuki* of the aristocrats who built the Victorian mansions still standing here and there in Tokyo is curiously affecting, even to readers totally unfamiliar with their life. The billiard room, the well-stocked wine cellar, the racks of suits tailored in London, the cut-glass chandeliers and the freshly starched tablecloths obviously attracted Mishima himself, but he did not neglect to describe the Japanese aspects of their lives as well—the spacious garden with its pond and artificial hill, the servants in kimonos eternally dusting and, above all, the elaborate etiquette that revealed itself most conspicuously in the distinctive language.

The hero of *Haru no Yuki*, Kiyoaki, is a flawlessly beautiful boy but, like others of Mishima's handsome heroes, he does not respond easily to the affection shown him by others. He knows that the girl Satoko loves him, but he is incapable of responding until, as the result of her formal engagement to a member of the imperial family, it becomes difficult and even dangerous for them to meet. Then his love and hers develop into an uncontrollable passion, and they take ever greater risks to be together. Satoko becomes pregnant shortly before her marriage, and takes refuge in a convent. Kiyoaki follows her there, begging permission again and again to see her, but he is refused. The delicate youth, exhausted by these hardships, falls ill and dies, leaving behind a book recording his dreams and a prophecy to his friend Honda that they will meet again. *Haru no Yuki* is the supreme product of the skill Mishima had acquired as a novelist. It contains a most moving evocation of romantic love, that seems his ultimate expression of what he himself termed *tawayameburi*, the way of the graceful young maiden, an archaic term referring to the traditional beauty and charm of the Japanese girl. The work is colored by a strong feminine sensibility, no less than the Heian novel from which it is ultimately derived. As Japanese prose it is remarkably beautiful; one feels as if the lyrical style of Mishima's early works, so long held rigorously in check, had suddenly burst into full flower.

The second volume, *Homba*, by contrast, is an example of *masuraoburi*, the way of the warrior, an ideal associated less with the Heian period than with the age of the *Manyōshū* (or, if the time sequence is to be observed, the Kamakura period.) The hero, the boy Isao, is not beautiful, but he is a superb swordsman, and the strength of his ideals gives his face a striking purity of expression. His father, a former servant of Kiyoaki's, runs a school of right-wing activists, and the boy's mind has been filled, ever since he was a small child, with the emperor-worship so common among the young officers of the 1930's. But unlike his father, who is venal, despite his professions of absolute devotion to the emperor, Isao is ready to die in order to purify Japan of the corruption of the politicians and businessmen. He gathers around him a small band of students who plan to assassinate their chief enemies and blow up the Bank of Japan as the prelude to a "restoration" of the emperor to full sovereignty. Isao is inspired especially by writings about the patriots who in the 1870's fought the pollution of the country by the newly introduced Western objects and beliefs. These men were so fanatically pure that they refused to use guns, even when fighting a modern army, and they perished, swords in hands. Their resistance was futile but beautiful; and Isao, moved by their example, is resolved to carry through his coup, even when, having been betrayed, he knows he cannot succeed.

Isao is brought to trial. He is defended by Honda who met the boy after a fencing tournament and accidentally discovered, when he saw Isao bathe under a waterfall, the birthmark that revealed he was a reincarnation of Kiyoaki. Honda up until this point has been portrayed as an eminently dispassionate, prudent man, but he is so moved by Isao's consecration that he resigns his judgeship to defend the boy. Isao, after he is released from prison (thanks to Honda), kills a banker who has profaned the Ise Shrine, then commits *seppuku* facing the rising sun.

In *Homba* Mishima treated themes that had occupied him since *Patriotism*, and succeeded in giving them their most powerful expression. *Homba* is less appealing as a novel than *Haru no Yuki*, but the task was more difficult, to evoke the masculine ideals of Japan that have sometimes in the past resulted in terrible acts of slaughter, but have indelibly imprinted all of Japanese civilization.

The third volume of the tetralogy, *Akatsuki no Tera* ("The Temple of the Dawn," 1970), is prevailingly religious in tone. The theme of reincarnation, so muted in the second volume it might appear almost unnecessary, is here given full statement, and the first half of the book is dominated by religious experiences. The climax of *Akatsuki no Tera*, and perhaps of the entire four volumes, is the descriptions of the ritual slaughter of a goat at a festival in Calcutta, and of the burial ghats in Benares where the life-giving river and the pyres on the banks evoke the endless cycle of birth, death and rebirth. The single most effective moment of the book occurs in a cave at Ajanta when Honda sees the trickle of a waterfall and suddenly, instinctively, is aware of Kiyoaki's presence.

Honda is still the observer, but in this volume it is he, rather than Kiyoaki's reincarnation, the Thai princess Jinjan, who is the central figure. His role as the eternal observer is electrifyingly altered when we discover that he has built a peephole in the wall of his guest room so that he may observe what goes on at night.

Honda first met Jinjan in Bangkok before the war, when she was a child of seven, treated as a half-wit because she kept insisting that she was really Japanese and could remember her former lives. Honda asked her the dates when Kiyoaki and Isao died, and she answered without hesitation. But when, after the war, Jinjan comes to Japan as a student, she tells Honda that she remembers nothing of the past. He was attracted to the girl initially because he realized she must be a reincarnation of Kiyoaki, but when he sees her again as a young woman she arouses in the middle-aged man a desire to attain through her young vitality a participation in life he has always denied himself.

The post-war scene becomes degenerate and corrupt as the ideals that sustained the old society, whether the beauty of Kiyoaki or the dedication of Isao, are sacrificed to vulgar materialism. The aristocracy in particular shows itself in a contemptible light, serving as whores and pimps to the American military, selling stolen goods to make a living, or professing superficially "progressive" political views, to keep in step with the times. The cynicism and self-destructiveness of the upper classes make the Thai princess, who seems to embody the unaffected grace and strength of some wonderful young animal, seem all the more desirable. But Honda's hopes of becoming Jinjan's lover and possessing her vitality are destroyed when, peeping through the hole into the room where the Thai princess and a

Japanese countess are to spend the night, he sees them locked in a passionate embrace. At the end of the book we learn that Jinjan, like her two previous incarnations, has died young, bitten by a cobra in her garden.

The last volume bears the title *Tennin Gosui* ("The Five Marks of Decline of the Heavenly Being," 1971). This is a Buddhist term referring to the marks of decay that indicate the impending extinction of a deva inhabiting the world of desire, and refers in this instance to the heavenly being we have known as Kiyoaki, Isao and Jinjan. The story begins in 1970, when Honda is seventy-six. The bearer of the telltale birthmark that reveals a new reincarnation of Kiyoaki is a boy of seventeen named Tōru. Though Tōru is no less beautiful than Kiyoaki his body shows one of the five marks of deline of the heavenly being, copious perspiration under the arms. Tōru, far from being an aristocrat, works at a harbor signal station, but his mysterious birthmark convinces him he is no ordinary human being. Honda happens to visit the station and notices the telltale birthmark. He decides to adopt Tōru, convinced that he has once again witnessed transmigration, and determined this time to link himself to the mysterious being he has seen in different guises. Honda gives Tōru the education of a young gentleman, but he shows no gratitude; indeed, he takes special pleasure in betraying those whose confidence he has gained and in humiliating Honda. A close friend of Honda's decides to put Tōru in his place. She tells him that he is a fake reincarnation and will no doubt lead a long and uneventful life. Tōru takes poison. It does not kill him, but he is blinded. Our last view of Tōru shows a man whose flowers have withered; perspiring freely, his unwashed body gives off a foul odor, his clothes are dirty, and he has lost his place in the world. Perhaps Mishima meant us to realize that the semi-divine being we have seen for the fourth time has lost its magic and will dissolve into common clay.

The last chapter of the novel depicts the convent in Nara where Satoko, now very old but still beautiful, receives the aged Honda. Satoko insists that she has never heard of Kiyoaki and suggests that he was no more than a figment of Honda's imagination. Honda wonders if perhaps he too has never existed. Satoko replies, "That too is as it is in each heart." Unreality is now acceptable to Honda as the ultimate truth about the world. But it may not be so for all readers; the tetralogy is so solidly anchored in facts and things that it takes more than a word from the abbess to make everything disappear.

The importance of this last book to Mishima can hardly be exaggerated. Again and again in his conversations and letters he stated that he had poured all of his skill and experience into the work, and that when it was completed he would have nothing left to say, and nothing left to do except kill himself. Nobody took him seriously, not even after he published in September 1970 an article glorifying action, even action doomed to failure. He cited the philosophy of Wang Yang-ming (1472–1528) and the Japanese exemplars of this philosophy, notably Ōshio Heihachirō who killed himself after a revolt in 1837. The only question in Mishima's mind seems to have been how he would die. The manner he finally chose accorded not only with his philosophy of action—"active nihilism" he termed it—but with the particular traditions he had exalted since writing *Patriotism* in 1960. His decision to commit *seppuku* might be traced back even farther, to the pictures of samurai he admired as a child, and even to St. Sebastian.

Mishima chose to die while his mental and physical strengths were at their peak. The political gesture he made, attempting to arouse the Japanese armed forces (and indirectly the whole country) to the arid banality of material prosperity, was probably his way of imparting to his suicide a dignity that would make it more than an act of self-indulgence. He could have had little hope of success in changing the course of Japanese politics, but he died as he wished, wearing the mask he first put on many years before.

NOTES

1. *Ninīroku Jiken to Watakushi* in *Eirei no Koe*, pp. 221–22.
2. His story *Shi wo kaku Shōnen* ("The Boy who wrote Poetry," 1954) is a thinly disguised account of these activities.
3. *Watakushi no Henreki Jidai*, pp. 20–21.
4. The critic might profitably compare the account of New York found in Mishima's travel book *Tabi no Ehon* (1958) with that in his novel *Kyōko no Ie* (1959).
5. *Ratai to Ishō* (in *Mishima Yukio Bungakuron Shū*), p. 183.
6. *Watakushi no Henreki Jidai*, pp. 53–54.
7. *Ibid.*
8. *Ibid.*, p. 215.
9. See the article by Hasegawa Izumi, "Mineruba to Marusu" in his *Mishima Yukio Kenkyū*, p. 9.
10. *Ratai to Ishō*, p. 204.
11. *Ibid.*, p. 267.
12. See the interesting article by Etō Jun, "Mishima Yukio no Ie," in Hasegawa, *op. cit.*
13. *Ratai to Ishō*, p. 181.
14. Hayashi Fusao and Mishima Yukio, *Taiwa Nihonjin Ron*, p. 177.

V. SOME JAPANESE ECCENTRICS

The Portrait of Ikkyū

THE ART OF portraiture, though practiced and developed in the Far East over the centuries, has seldom been esteemed as highly as landscape, religious or other types of painting. Only rarely have the great artists been drawn to portraiture in the manner of a Titian, Velazquez or Rembrandt, attracted by a handsome face or fee. European studies of Chinese and Japanese art, accepting the indigenous judgment that portraiture is of less importance than other varieties of painting, have generally skirted the subject or devoted to it not more than a page or two in an extended study. The relative scarcity of surviving Chinese portraiture of artistic value may account for the neglect of this genre in China, but it is harder to understand in Japan, where portraits, particularly of the Zen masters, abound. A Japanese critic, writing in 1949, complained that some portraits had never been photographed even though they had been designated as national treasures forty years earlier. This failure of Japanese portraiture to arouse enthusiasm at home or abroad probably reflects more on the sitters than on the artists. I hope in this essay to suggest how one great portrait, that of the Zen priest Ikkyū, came to possess its unique place in Japanese art.

In principle, I think it is fair to say that we need know nothing about the subject of a portrait to be moved by it. This certainly would be true, for example, of Rembrandt's *Man with the Golden Helmet*. But can we say the same of the famous portrait of Prince Shōtoku, the great lawgiver and patron of Buddhism of the seventh century? Payne found that the prince in this earliest of Japanese portraits looked "earnest, keen-eyed, and vigorous." These surely are admirable qualities, but the features hardly show individuality, or suggest that the prince differed conspicuously from other noblemen of his day. And what may we say of the two boys accompanying Shōtoku, sometimes identified as his son and younger brother? They share more than a family resemblance; the angles of the eyebrows and the feet are perhaps their most distinguishing features. It has been claimed that the purpose of portraiture in the Far East is to read the sitter's soul and not merely to transcribe his features. If such had been the intent of the painter here, we could only conclude that the subjects had exceptionally bland, undifferentiated souls. Obviously, however, the painter, working a century after Prince Shōtoku's death, was attempting to create a dignified image for public worship, rather than a portrait of one or more souls. His style, known to the Japanese as "the Chinese manner" (kara-yō), belongs to the tradition of such early examples of Chinese portraiture as the Yen Li-pên scroll in Boston.

The lack of individuality noticeable in Prince Shōtoku's portrait is common to many varieties of Japanese depiction of the human face. The superb Tale of Genji scroll does not suffer from the fact that the various personages are virtually indistinguishable one from the other. Even in such professed examples of portraiture as the paintings of the thirty-six immortals of Japanese poetry the most we can say is that the men and women can be told apart by their costumes and by the presence or absence of a beard. In many woodcuts by Harunobu and other ukiyoe artists not even this is possible. All the figures in Harunobu prints tend to have the same face, not because he held the conviction that basically the people he depicted had identical souls, but because any display of individuality in a face would destroy the childlike loveliness of the scene as surely as in a Fragonard pastorale.

Harunobu's prints are not portraits, of course, but their uniformity of expression and features does not differ greatly from what we find in works which are officially styled likenesses of famous men. In the portrait of Fujiwara Mitsuyoshi attributed to Takanobu, a master of the early thirteenth century, the face is dignified and the bearing aristocratic, but can we say much more? If it had been identified instead as the portrait of Taira no Shigemori, would it not be possible to find in it the "gentleness and grace" frequently noted in Takanobu's portrait of Shigemori? Or, if identified as Ashikaga Yoshimasa, could we not find the peculiar combination of elegance and insensitivity typical of that man? The famous portrait by Takanobu of Minamoto Yoritomo has more distinctive features, it is true, but whereas Yashiro found that he had a handsome head "of compelling energy and masculinity," Rowland was struck by the "lean, severe character of the sitter" and the "cruelly determined face." These descriptions may not be mutually exclusive, but would anyone be struck by the "lean, severe character" of the sculptured figure of Yoritomo?

Both the painting and the sculpture have been described as realistic, but a mere difference in the age of the sitter could not alone account for the startling discrepancies in the portraits.

It is true of the Japanese state portrait, as Marianna Jenkins noted of the European state portrait, that its "primary purpose is not the portrayal of an individual as such, but the evocation through his image of those abstract principles for which he stands. . . The symbolic character of the work should exact a note of abstraction and impassivity in the rendering of the face of the sitter. Unless he be endowed with unusual beauty, a detailed study of his features might necessitate the recording of physical defects that detract from the purity desirable in a symbol, and the evocation of individual moods would tend to reveal just those marks of personal feeling that stress the humanity of a man rather than the remoteness of a superior being."[1] The Takanobu portraits are splendidly executed, but they are neither endearing nor possessed of true individuality. The principles the men were believed to personify—resolute leadership in the case of Yoritomo, prudence and reliability in the case of Shigemori—may have guided the painter in his depiction of the features, but principles are not necessarily interchangeable with the personality of the subject. Portraiture in Japan, like biography, has tended to deal with a man's achievements and opinions, not with his inner life. Contrary to the oft-reiterated insistence that the portraitist must dip below the surface to paint the real man, we feel that Takanobu tells us nothing about Yoritomo or Mitsuyoshi except as a public figure. If we consult the biographies of such men we find little more. There were severe and mild rulers, rulers known for martial prowess and others for their devotion to letters, but we search in vain for descriptions of the inner conflicts, wasting emotions, or humor that might make the biographies or state portraits more than effigies on the coin of the realm.

But probably it is a mistake to look for personality in these figures. Friedländer remarked that "from the fifteenth century the awakening of personality tended, in Italy, in the direction of the portrait."[2] Individuality first showed itself in Japanese portraiture about the same time, particularly in depictions of the Buddhist clergy. The emergence to the surface of strongly individual traits may be linked to the rise of Zen Buddhism, which insisted on the realization of the Buddha-nature within the self and tended to encourage individuality to the point of eccentricity. The techniques of portraiture at the time derived much from the realism favored in the Kamakura period even when depicting demons and other imaginary beings, as well as to Chinese prototypes. These portraits not only suggest actual men, as opposed to stylized images, but their features tend to be repeated from portrait to portrait rather than varying according to the artist's concept.

The earliest religious portraits known in Japan were apparently the paintings of the Shingon patriarchs brought back from China by Kūkai in 806. These works are badly preserved, but they seem to be idealistic representations, much in the manner of the eleventh-century portrait of Zemmui (Fig. 5), an Indian monk who travelled to China in the eighth century. No attempt is made to suggest Indian features nor, indeed, those of any person in particular, but the picture moves us by its overwhelming expression of religious devotion. The use of portraits in religious worship, found in both Shingon and Tendai rituals, became even more important in Jōdo Buddhism, a development of the twelfth century. Images of the founders of the main sects, like the fourteenth-century portrait of Shinran, were offered homage in special halls (miedō) erected for the purpose. In this and other works of the period, even those outside the Zen traditions, the subject is given features which suggest individuality as well as piety.

The most significant religious portraits, however, are associated with Zen Buddhism. The critical importance of the relationship between master and disciple in Zen occasioned the production of proofs that the master recognized a pupil. When a disciple gave evidence of having attained satori, for example, the master wrote for him a certificate (inka) which established his credentials as a full-fledged Zen adept. The teacher at the same time often presented the disciple with a portrait bearing an inscription in his hand. Naturally, this chinzō, as it was called, was of the highest importance to the pupil, not only as a memento of his teacher but as evidence that he followed the authentic traditions. Worship of the chinzō also became a part of the funeral observances for Zen priests. Many surviving chinzō were executed during the forty-nine days of mourning after the subject's death, though modelled when possible on portraits made during his lifetime. In form the Japanese chinzō followed, initially at least, Chinese examples. The portrait of the Zen master Wu-chun (Fig. 4), now in the Tōfukuji in Kyoto, was painted in 1238 as a farewell present for the Japanese priest Ikkoku. Cahill has described this work as "perhaps the finest extant Chinese portrait." For Ikkoku, however, the beauty of the portrait probably counted for less than the mark of esteem it represented. Almost all the Japanese priests who studied Zen in China during the early thirteenth century were pupils of Wu-chun, but presumably only a favored few received a portrait.

The *chinzō* of Wu-chun did not itself create the style in Japan. Older examples survive, such as the portrait of the priest Shunjō, dated 1227. Shunjō was a priest of the Ritsu sect, a small sect which like Zen insisted on discipline. On his return to Japan from study in China he brought with him a Chinese artist who painted his portrait. Shunjō is shown seated cross-legged in a draped chair, his shoes on a low platform before him, a whisk in his right hand—all features of the Zen *chinzō*. This portrait and a few other examples suggest that the *chinzō* may have originated with the Ritsu sect though it achieved its full development with Zen.

Portraits in the *chinzō* style were made not only of recently deceased priests but of historical figures. In this case the features traditionally associated with the person would be retained—big, staring eyes for Daruma, a mouth opened in a shout of *katsu* for Rinzai. The *chinzō* were hung in a fixed order. In one instance, which seems to be typical, six *chinzō* were hung side by side, the two central places being occupied by Daruma and Eka (Hui-kuo). The adoption of an order of precedence in hanging the pictures tended to determine the direction in which the portraits faced, those to Daruma's right facing left towards him, those to the left facing right towards him. Daruma himself often looks directly into the eyes of the worshipper. The almost invariable use of the three-quarter face in the *chinzō* probably owes much to the manner of hanging in facing groups. In the *chinzō* portraits of the Muromachi shoguns, most of whom became Zen priests in their later years, the order of display was so carefully prescribed that it is sometimes possible to identify portraits whose features are otherwise indistinguishable by the direction they face. Facing pairs of figures are found also in the portraits of the thirty-six immortal poets. Possibly the pairing originated in the familiar Amida triptychs showing Amida in full face and the attendant bodhisattvas in three-quarters view turned towards him. The profile, though known, is relatively rare in Japanese portraiture.

The groups of portraits hung at different temples naturally varied, according to the founder and the important abbots. The same man might face left in one temple and right in another. We have mirror images of the great priest Musō Kokushi, presumably made for different sets of *chinzō*. Certain priests like Musō or Ikkyū were so popular that temples even casually related were eager to claim association and hang their portraits. About twenty portraits of Ikkyū survive, all facing to his left.

The most famous portrait of Ikkyū, the sketch made by his disciple Bokusai (Fig. 3), served as the basis of his *chinzō*. Artists customarily made six or seven sketches from life and then submitted them to the sitter for his approval. If none pleased the sitter, he would ask for another selection, and if still not satisfied he might change the artist. The only grounds for rejecting sketches ever mentioned in contemporary accounts are insufficient resemblance to the subject. We may assume, then, that this sketch pleased Ikkyū and closely resembled him. Bokusai was not only a proficient painter but Ikkyū's appointed successor and the compiler of the official chronology of Ikkyū's life. The intimacy of this relationship may account for the effectiveness of the portrait in capturing at once the external features of the man and an unmistakably individual quality underneath. It is impossible to sum up this face in a few adjectives, as the portraits of Yoritomo or Shigemori have been characterized; this is a full human being, indefinable and completely alive.

At first glance the portrait looks like a mere sketch from life. In comparison with the more finished *chinzō* its nervous vitality suggests the captured moment of a snapshot. In the absence of documentation we cannot be sure how the picture was painted, but its composition seems to stem from Zen traditions rather than the frozen moment. The first thing to strike us in this portrait is the eyes, turned towards us though the head faces left. The pose is unusual for a *chinzō*, but not unique. Precisely the same angle of the head and eyes may be found in the celebrated portrait executed in 1334 of Daitō (Fig. 6), the founder of the Daitokuji. The effect produced by the two portraits is, needless to say, quite different. It has been said of Daitō's that "of all the innumerable *chinzō*, this displays the greatest dignity of appearance." Ikkyū's, on the other hand, has a growth of beard and unshaven skull, unseemly in a Zen priest, and the look is penetrating rather than dignified. But we know from Ikkyū's poetry of his special veneration for Daitō; one poem begins, "Kyōun is truly Daitō's heir." Painting Ikkyū with his eyes directed towards us may have served, then, to confirm his affinity with Daitō. The growth of beard and hair, however, points beyond Daitō to Rinzai, usually depicted unshaven, and eventually to Daruma himself. Daruma in the portrait by Kei Shōki is not only hirsute but his eyes are turned towards us like Daitō's and Ikkyū's. This pose, as Friedländer pointed out, creates an "illusion of movement, of action, of life... particularly when a look at variance with the position of the head meets our eyes."[3]

The inscription written by Bokusai above his sketch of Ikkyū was apparently joined to it at a later date, perhaps after Ikkyū's death, to make a hanging scroll. The poem on the *chinzō* in Shūon-an is in Ikkyū's hand, confirmation that this was the official *chinzō*. The poem on the sketch reads:

The posterity of Kasō do not know Zen,
Who before Kyōun's face dares expound Zen?
For thirty years the weight on my shoulders has been heavy;
Alone I have borne the burden of Sung-yüan's Zen.

The poem on the Shūon-an *chinzō* is identical, except that it mentions the posterity of Rinzai rather than of Kasō. The meaning of the poem in either case is the same: Ikkyū considers that he alone maintains the true traditions of Zen masters in Japan (like Kasō, his own teacher) and in China (Sung-yüan). This bold declaration is typical of the man, and his eccentricity was the product of a certainty that he was following the path of orthodoxy, unlike those Zen monks who bowed to the conventions of the world. Ikkyū's individuality was not mere eccentricity; his complexity, as shown in this paradox, was genuine. We may feel that this remarkable portrait tells us everything about the man, as a great European portrait would, but the more we learn of his life, the deeper the impression created by the painting.

Ikkyū was born on New Year's Day of 1394, the son of the Emperor Go-Komatsu, the hundredth sovereign of Japan. For reasons which escape us now, Ikkyū's mother was forced to leave the palace before he was born, and he was never openly acknowledged as an imperial prince. Nevertheless, he frequently visited the palace, and when Go-Komatsu was dying in 1433 Ikkyū was summoned to his bedside. We know little about Ikkyū's mother save for a letter she wrote him shortly before her death. In this remarkable document she urged him to become so outstanding a priest that he might consider Shaka and Daruma to be his servants. She added in a postscript, "The man who is concerned only with expedients is no better than a dung fly. Even if you know by heart the 80,000 holy teachings, unless you open to the full the eyes of your Buddhist nature, you will never be able to understand even what I have written in this letter."

Ikkyū's mother had sent him at the age of five to a temple to become an acolyte. He showed unusual aptitude in his studies. By eleven he had progressed to the Vimalikirti Sutra, and in the following year began to compose Chinese poetry, soon establishing a reputation. His exceptional piety and devotion to monastic rules provide a marked contrast with the notoriety he later acquired as a profligate. After four years spent in unremitting study under a hermit monk known for his especial purity of character, Ikkyū was cut adrift at the age of twenty when his master died. He spent a week in meditation at the Ishiyama Temple by the shores of Lake Biwa, but failing to obtain consolation, decided to commit suicide by throwing himself into the lake. He was saved at the last moment by a man sent by his mother who, knowing of his despondency, had feared he might turn to self-destruction.

Ikkyū decided to study under Kasō Sōdon (1352–1428), a Zen master known for the severity of his discipline. Kasō, following the tradition begun by Daruma, who accepted Eka as his pupil only when he had demonstrated the strength of his resolve by cutting off his arm, at first barred the gate to the temple and refused to let Ikkyū in. Ikkyū persisted, sleeping in the alleyway before the temple or in fishing boats tied up along the lake shore, never going far from the gate. One day Kasō left the temple to perform a religious service in the nearby village. Noticing that Ikkyū was still waiting by the gate, he ordered an attendant to throw water on him. Ikkyū was still waiting when Kasō returned. This time Kasō admitted him inside. He questioned the young man and, becoming aware of his unusual ability, relented and accepted him as a pupil.

For three years Ikkyū led a life of extreme austerity under Kasō's guidance, eking out a bare existence from the alms given by the local fishermen and from the money he obtained by making perfume sachets and dolls' clothing. In 1418, when he was twenty-four, Kasō bestowed on him the name Ikkyū—literally, "a rest," or "a pause." The meaning of this name, ultimately derived from the Buddhist scriptures, is suggested by a poem in Japanese composed by Ikkyū:

uroji yori	From the world of passions
muroji e kaeru	I return to the world beyond passions,
hito yasumi	A moment of pause.
ame furaba fure	If the rain is to fall, let it fall;
kaze fukaba fuke	If the wind is to blow, let it blow.

The poem derives from the Zen concept that the two worlds, the material and the non-material, are both essential. To be involved exclusively in the material world, the lot of most men, is to be torn by constant passions. The path of enlightenment leads away from the material world to the negation of self and the ties to worldly passions. This is the "return" Ikkyū mentions in his poem. But if a man gives himself exclusively to the non-material world he cannot continue his daily existence in this world; it becomes necessary then to return to the material world. In between the two worlds, in the pause that refreshes, is perfect freedom, and an indifference to rain, wind or any other external. This was Ikkyū's chosen position.

Two years later, in 1420, when Ikkyū was twenty-six, he experienced enlightenment. Late on a summer night, when rain clouds hung low over the lake, Ikkyū was sitting in Zen meditation in a small boat when, hearing the cawing of crows, he suddenly cried out in wonder. He felt that at that instant all uncertainties had melted away. Returning to the temple, he waited impatiently for the dawn, when he might tell Kasō what had happened. Kasō, when informed, said merely, "You have reached the realm of the *rakan*. You still are not a *sakka*." Ikkyū replied, "If that is the case, I am delighted to be a *rakan* and have no desire to be a *sakka*." Kasō answered, "You are truly a *sakka*." It was customary for a teacher after his pupil had experienced enlightenment to present him with a certificate, as I have mentioned. Such certificates were highly desired by priests as proof of their standing in the authentic line of Zen masters. As may easily be imagined, there were numerous forgeries and abuses in the issuance of the certificates. When Kasō presented Ikkyū with a suitably inscribed certificate, Ikkyū threw it to the ground and walked away. Certainly Ikkyū intended no disrespect by the gesture. We know how deeply he venerated Kasō: in the following year, when Kasō was suffering from dysentery, his other disciples used brushes and pans to clean up the mess, but Ikkyū insisted on using his hands. His devotion to Kasō and to the ascending line of Japanese and Chinese masters of Zen was absolute, but his contempt for the worldly ambitions and vanity of the priesthood, symbolized by the certificates of enlightenment, made him spurn any token of recognition.

In 1422 a ceremony marking the thirty-third anniversary of the death of the seventh abbot of the Daitokuji was celebrated. Kasō, despite his persistent illness, attended. The other priests came in resplendent brocades, but Ikkyū wore a rusty black priest's robe and battered straw sandals. Kasō asked why he had chosen so undignified a costume. Ikkyū replied, "I alone ornament this assembly. I do not intend to ape the ways of false priests." After the ceremony someone asked Kasō who would be his successor. He answered, "Ikkyū, though he acts like a madman."

Ikkyū's madness was the expression of unending rage at the stupidity and corruption of the Zen priesthood. He took for his sobriquet the name Kyōun—"crazy cloud"—and the character *kyō* for madness sprinkles his poetry. From his early days in the priesthood he had sought the most difficult, demanding masters. He could be satisfied with no less, and he poured bitter vituperation on the ordinary, complacent priests busy with ceremonies, fund-raising, parish clubs and the like. In his revolt against the conventionality of other priests he went to the opposite extreme. Once he left Kasō's temple, a few years before Kasō's death in 1428, Ikkyū openly gave himself to sensual pleasures. In 1440, when the thirteenth-anniversary services for Kasō were held at the Daitokuji, a number of parishioners had assembled from the prosperous port city of Sakai, bearing lavish presents for the occasion. Soon they were gossiping about mundane matters with the priests. Ikkyū, annoyed at such unseemly behavior on the occasion of memorial services for his late master, dashed off two poems, pasting one on the wall and sending the other to Yōsō, a senior disciple of Kasō who was presiding over the ceremonies. The first poem, for the benefit of the noisy gift-givers, ran:

> I've left in the temple the things I've always used,
> My wooden spoon and bamboo plate, hung up east of the wall.
> I don't want your useless furniture around me;
> For years a peasant's hat and cloak have been enough.

The detachment from the world expressed in the poem is not surprising in a Zen priest, though Ikkyū's point is that he will not join his fellow-priests in accepting presents. His poem addressed to Yōsō, however, was anything but conventional:

> For ten days in this temple my mind's been in turmoil,
> My feet are entangled in endless red tape.
> If some day you get around to looking for me,
> Try the fish-shop, the wine parlor or the brothel.

The last line was not mere swagger on Ikkyū's part, an expression of contempt for the traditional prohibitions on eating fish, drinking liquor or indulging in sexual intercourse. His collection of poetry *Kyōunshū* is filled with extraordinary admissions of his indulgences in fleshly pleasures. He wrote of one attempt to free himself of this addiction:

> Ten years in the gay quarters, and still I couldn't exhaust the pleasures;
> But I broke away and am living here in empty mountains and dark valleys.
> In these favorable surroundings clouds blot out the world,
> But those winds over the roof from the tall pines grate on my ears.

No doubt the music of the brothels was more to Ikkyū's taste than the lonely wind through the pines, the traditional delight of the hermit. Ikkyū sometimes wrote as if he had no doubts about his manner of life:

> To sleep with a beautiful woman—what a deep river of love!

> Upstairs in a tall building the old Zen priest is singing.
> I've had all the pleasure of embraces and kisses
> With never a thought of sacrificing myself for others.

Or again:

> Kyōun is truly Daitō's heir—
> Why do they call *zazen* sessions so holy?
> I remember long ago nights of song and fornication,
> Even as a novice in pleasure I knew how to tip the saké cask.

Undoubtedly these frank avowals of indiscretions were intended to point up the hypocrisy of other priests, who secretly indulged their flesh though they mouthed the usual pious words about continence. Ikkyū was convinced that the lip service of such priests, rather than overt transgressions, would destroy Zen:

> Who of the disciples of Rinzai transmits his teachings?
> His school will perish through the blind donkeys.
> My friends have worn-out sandals and bamboo staffs;
> Chairs and platforms beget a Zen of fame and greed.

An unkempt priest, perhaps an open frequenter of the licensed quarters like Ikkyū, was more likely to transmit Rinzai's teachings than the high priest ensconced in his episcopal chair. Ikkyū was supremely confident of his abilities as a priest, however flagrantly he disobeyed the Buddhist precepts:

> Who realizes that Kyōun belongs to the wild wind?
> Mornings he is in the hills, at dusk in the city;
> If in teaching I used the stick or shouted *katsu*,
> Tokuzan and Rinzai would blush in envy.

Mornings in the hills and dusk in the city suggest the two aspects of Ikkyū's life—his unflagging devotion to the purity of Zen and his seemingly contradictory indulgence in the city night life. But, he insisted, if he chose to act the part of the Zen master, with rebuking stick and shouts of *katsu*, like the teachers of the past, he could perform well enough to make Rinzai and Tokuzan themselves blush before him. Ikkyū had little use for the formal precepts:

> Those who keep the precepts become donkeys, those who break them, men.

Precepts, numerous as Ganges' sands, play havoc with the spirit:
The new-born babe is already bound with marriage ties,
But flowers blossom and fall unfettered spring after spring.

Here the naturalness of the flower is contrasted with the artificial, constricting ties imposed by men. One can imagine what Ikkyū's behavior must have been like during his relatively brief stays at the Daitokuji. He was an iconoclast, upsetting the pat formulas of prayer adopted by the other priests, ever resorting to new eccentricities in the hope of jogging them from their complacency:

Kyōun is the demon of the Daitokuji;
The students rage at contests with his wild spirit.
What use are the old examples and the *kōan*?
After how much bitterness must I still think up new stunts?

Sometimes, however, Ikkyū had qualms about the effect of his harsh words. One poem is entitled "Confession of a Malicious Tongue."

With spears of words how many men I have murdered!
With odes and quatrains my pen has reviled my fellows.
In hell I'll be torn to pieces for the sins of my tongue;
In the world of the dead I won't escape the flaming carriage.

Of all those Ikkyū subjected to his merciless criticism, none fared worse than Yōsō Sōi (1376–1458), a distinguished priest, the twenty-sixth abbot of the Daitokuji, whom Ikkyū reviled as a poisonous snake, a seducer and a leper. Little we know about Yōsō confirms these charges. His portrait (Fig. 7) suggests instead that he was a mild-mannered, inoffensive, and probably devout priest who was content to go along with the world. Ikkyū was especially enraged over Yōsō's translation of the Zen precepts into simple Japanese; he was sure that this was a device for corrupting nuns and extorting money from merchants, by promising enlightenment in return for their favors. Ikkyū's hatred of Yōsō was acerbated by the latter's appointment as *zenji* in 1457, the first time an abbot of the Daitokuji had been honored with this title by an emperor during his lifetime. Ikkyū viewed this honor to Yōsō as excrement thrown in the face of Kasō, his revered master, who had never received this honor. Yōsō died in 1458 under circumstances not revealed by official biographies, but Ikkyū gave in his work *Jikaishū* a most graphic account of how Yōsō died of leprosy. The work, though entitled "Self Admonitions," is devoted mainly to savage attacks on Yōsō. Over a hundred poems in

Chinese reiterate Ikkyū's belief that Yōsō was "a villain unparalleled in the history of the Daitokuji" who had prostituted Zen for money. One poem begins:

> A merchant ship arrived the other day at Sakai Port;
> It has no fish for sale, its only wares are Zen.

Ikkyū's conviction that Yōsō was trafficking in Zen may have had some foundation. The seventeenth-century Zen priest Chōon declared in his memoirs that Yōsō has started the practice of *kazoemairi*—the selling of certificates to ignorant laymen attesting they had gained enlightenment. If true, Ikkyū's wrath is more easily comprehended.

Ikkyū's hatred of the certificates, first evidenced when he refused his own from Kasō, was aroused anew in 1461 when a disciple asked him for one. Ikkyū, unable to tolerate this in a pupil, left the Zen sect. He wrote, "On the sixteenth day of the sixth moon of the second year of Kanshō I returned the *chinzō* of the National Teacher Daitō to the main temple and joined the *nembutsu* sect." We do not know how long he remained within the Pure Land faith, but his last years definitely were spent as a Zen priest. Probably it did not take Ikkyū long to become disillusioned with the Pure Land sect, and to become aware that Zen best suited him.

The collection "Self Admonitions" shows little contrition, but Ikkyū's poetry at times reveals doubts beneath his confidence. One poem begins,

> Ikkyū's sins fill the wide heavens,
> Though the world recognizes me as leader of my sect.

Two poems were directed specifically against his own writings:

> Man is stupid as a horse or ox, the dumbest of beasts;
> Poetry and prose are basically the instruments of hell.
> Arrogance, false pride, the pain of mental and emotional ties—
> What a pity men tempt demons to follow in their tracks!

> Masterpieces of poetry and prose, a voice of gold and jade!
> Words, words, phrases, phrases, everybody is impressed.
> But do you suppose Yama will admit the charm of an elegant verse?
> Beware the iron bar and the demons' glaring eyes!

Ikkyū's poetry is not highly ranked today. We are told it lacks lyricism and the restraint of true poetry. The critics base these views on the more traditional poetry by Zen priests, the evocations of nature or intimations of beauty found in such a poem as "Looking at Blossoms in the Rain" by Gidō:

> For three years I have not paid a visit to the capital,
> How often has the east wind aroused nostalgic thoughts!
> Today, under twilit eaves in the spring rain,
> Looking at the blossoms I remembered old delights.

Ikkyū's verse clearly lacks Gidō's elegance, but it speaks to us with great strength in a voice that does not merely echo some Chinese master. His passions are genuine and not the simulation of other men's griefs:

> In my heart a hell grows—
> Mental and emotional ties from ages past.
> Prairie fires cannot burn it away;
> With spring winds the grass grows again.

The passions in his heart, aroused again and again like grass by the spring wind, continued to burn until old age. At seventy-three he fell in love with a blind woman named Mori:

> The most elegant beauty of her generation,
> Her love songs and charming party tunes are the newest.
> When she sings it breaks my heart, that dimple in her lovely face:
> It is spring in the long-ago forest of apricot trees.
>
> Blind Mori every night accompanies my songs;
> Deep under the covers mandarin ducks whisper anew.
> Her mouth promises Miroku's dawn of deliverance,
> Her dwelling is the full spring of the ancient Buddhas.
>
> After the tree withered and the leaves fell, spring returned;
> The old trunk has flowered, old promises are renewed.
> Mori—if ever I should forget how much I owe you,
> May I be a brute beast through all eternity!

A painting survives showing Ikkyū at seventy-eight and Mori. Ikkyū is seen above in a round *chinzō* image; Mori, a plump woman of about forty, sits below, a small drum before her. His poem, in Chinese, ends with the lines, "Blind Mori sings love songs upstairs; A song from her before the flowers brings ten thousand years of spring." Her poem, in Japanese, runs, "I float or sink in uncertain, troubled sleep; without tears there can be no consolation."

Other poems describing Ikkyū's amours are more overt, but there is no trace of unpleasant prurience. Karaki Junzō, the distinguished literary historian, explained Ikkyū's behavior as a kind of nihilism, a conviction that the world was emptiness. Certainly the old authority and order had crumbled in the Japan of the late fifteenth century. The capital was utterly destroyed in the warfare of the 1460's and 1470's, and effective government was not restored. Karaki wrote, "Men discarded their external ornaments or had them torn away. Rank, class, scholarly attainments became of secondary or tertiary importance, and men emerged as individuals with their own particularity. Men had become skeletons. The recognition that only the skin of the floating world covered these skeletons marked the birth of man in his naked form." The skeleton was a favorite image with Ikkyū. His curious work *Gaikotsu*, written in 1457, describes under the guise of a dream about skeletons his belief that the world is an illusion. "What man can help but be a skeleton? Men and women fall in love because the bones are hidden beneath the outer skin, but when the breath stops and the body disintegrates, such externals disappear. You cannot tell then who once was mighty and who was base. Remember that under the skin you fondle lie the bones, waiting to reveal themselves." *Gaikotsu* is illustrated with drawings reminiscent of the European representations of the Dance of Death. In one, skeletons, pallbearers, carry a third skeleton over whom an elaborate priestly robe has been thrown. The poem states, "Why should you decorate this temporary outer form? Didn't you know in advance it would come to this?" For Ikkyū, seeing meaningless pretense everywhere, the external trappings of religion were but skin covering the bones. A famous anecdote tells how Ikkyū once appeared in his usual shabby costume to offer a service for a rich man. The man, annoyed at Ikkyū's informality, sent him away. Ikkyū reappeared, this time in splendid attire, and was welcomed in. Ikkyū thereupon removed his outer robe and offered it homage.

Stories about Ikkyū's wit are so numerous as to fill a thick volume, and even today every Japanese child knows about one Buddhist priest, Ikkyū-san. Most of the stories are apocryphal and some downright silly, but they suggest the effect on the public of the wit of this man. He is credited also, though dubiously, with authorship of two famous Nō plays, *Eguchi* and *Yamamba*, and is known also as a founder of the tea ceremony, a mentor to *renga* and *haikai* poets, the teacher of the Nō dramatist Zenchiku, a master calligrapher and painter, and as an innovator in vegetarian cuisine. His portraits were highly popular; of the surviving twenty, some have inscriptions written in China, indicating Ikkyū's fame reached abroad.

Bokusai's portrait of Ikkyū holds us from the first glimpse. It is, above

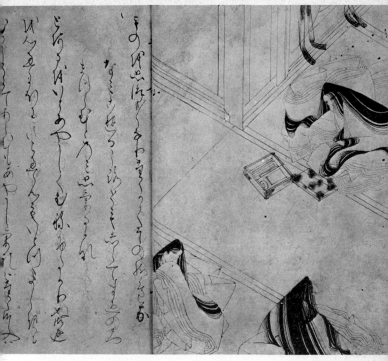

1. Album leaf of *The Tale of Genji*. Artist unknown. Late seventeenth century. Ink on paper. Yamato Bunka-kan, Nara Pref.

2. *Bashō Departing for Northern Japan*. By the haiku poet Yosa Buson (1716–83). Ink and color on paper. Itsuō Museum, Ikeda, Hyōgo Pref.

筆峰百練不知禪
㑳空畫寄誰説謗
三十年来肩上重
一人荷擔松源禪
前住大德一休わる
頂相自賛誤誤謹拜畫

3. *Portrait of the Priest Ikkyū*. By Bokusai (d. 1492). Ink and color on paper.
Tokyo National Museum, Tokyo.

4. *Portrait of Wu-chun.* Dated 1238. Ink and color on silk. Tōfuku-ji, Kyoto.

5. *Portrait of Zemmui* (Subhākara-simha). Mid-eleventh century. Ink and color on silk. Ichijō-ji, Hyōgo Pref.

6. *Portrait of Daitō Kokushi.* Dated 1334. Color on silk. Daitoku-ji, Kyoto.

7. *Portrait of Yōsō Sōi.* By Bunsei. Dated 1452. Ink and color on paper. Daitoku-ji, Kyoto.

8. *Head of Hanako.* By A. Rodin (1840–1917). Dated 1908. Bronze. National Museum of Western Art, Tokyo.

9. *The Surrender of the Chinese Admiral Ting Ju-ch'ang after the Battle of Wei-hai-wei.* By Migita Toshihide (1862–1925). See p. 270. Collection of the author.

all, the face of an individual, as striking, strange and unorthodox as Ikkyū's life and poetry. There are better Chinese poems than Ikkyū's and better executed portraits than this one, but the poems and the portrait burn into the mind. From the life, from the poems and from this portrait we know that this is what it means to be a man.

NOTES

1. Marianna Jenkins, *The State Portrait*, p. 7.
2. Max J. Friedländer, *Landscape, Portrait, Still-life*, p. 231.
3. *Ibid.*, p. 236.

Fujimoto Kizan and *The Great Mirror of Love*

FEW MEN have been more devoted to their chosen profession than Fujimoto Kizan (1626–1704). From the time when he made his first precocious visit as a boy of twelve to a house of prostitution until, some forty years later, he completed his massive study, *The Great Mirror of the Art of Love* (*Shikidō Ōkagami*), he never swerved in his single-minded investigation. Scarcely a fact survives concerning how Kizan made a living or how, indeed, he spent the rare hours when he was not in a brothel, actively engaged in his researches. Some *haikai* poetry of a nondescript nature made its way into contemporary anthologies, but Kizan wrote no poetry after he was thirty-two, seemingly begrudging even the few minutes away from his subject that the composition of a poem in seventeen syllables might have entailed. But if he preferred to draw a veil over his mundane activities, he unstintingly described his life in the haunts of pleasure.

Kizan's huge masterpiece, *The Great Mirror*, was known by reputation and in excerpts during the centuries after his death (at a surprisingly ripe old age, considering the arduous nature of his studies), but the complete manuscript was not rediscovered until 1941. The text was published by Professor Noma Kōshin of Kyoto University in 1961, and within a few years of publication the price had shot up many times.

Having said this much, in the hopes of whetting the reader's appetites, I must duly record that I have not found one line in the 581 closely printed pages of *The Great Mirror* that seems less than perfectly decorous, a model of good taste. I may have skipped something, or perhaps there are *double entendres* that escaped me, but certainly the prevailing impression is of a work of great elegance that owes more to the aesthetic ideals of *The Tale of Genji* than to the rich traditions of pornography dating back to Kizan's day. The brothels of the licensed quarters and the surrounding theatres and restaurants were the inspiration of Japanese popular culture in the seventeenth century, and a visit, far from being considered a sordid gratification of the flesh, represented an act of participation in the most refined artistic activities of the day. Moreover, in a society otherwise hemmed in by regulations restricting personal liberties, the licensed quarters were islands of freedom, where the merchants, thanks to their money, could insist on equal treatment with the haughty samurai. The prostitutes sometimes took their professional names from characters in *The Tale of Genji*, to give the merchants the illusion they had bought the favors of some exquisite court lady. Rowdiness or a hearty vulgarity had no place in this world.

The growth of the licensed quarters in the principal cities of Japan was, paradoxically, a result of the adoption of Confucianism as the official state philosophy. In the attempt to construct a society that would be stable and permanent, the Confucian philosophers prescribed a rigid order governed by codes of behavior that emphasized loyalty to the ruler and filial piety toward the father. Each household was considered a microcosm of the state, and the respect due its head was as absolute and unconditional as the loyalty due the sovereign. The head of a household, it is true, was expected to support his family, but any display of affection toward his wife or children was considered unseemly.

The Confucianists condemned love as an irrelevant and possibly disruptive element in family relations, but they tacitly recognized the necessity of permitting men to amuse themselves on occasion. The government in fact deliberately established "bad places" as a means of dissipating the energies of the unruly warrior class. No disgrace surrounded a visit; indeed, a man who refused to go, preferring the sedate pleasures of his own household, would have seemed unattractively virtuous, possibly a miser, and certainly without taste. But the prohibition on love was even stronger there than within a household: a man was free to divert himself to the degree that his finances permitted, but if by mischance he fell in love with a prostitute it threatened the stability of his household and often led to disaster.

Kizan wrote his grand study of the art of love without a glance at emotional attachment. The love he described of course included physical pleasure—he was sure that a prostitute afforded infinitely greater pleasure than any amateur—but also the entire ambiance of the licensed quarters. He became fascinated with the usages of the world of prostitutes and at an early age decided to devote his energies to learning and glorifying them, establishing a Way, in the manner of the Confucianists. Sometimes Kizan even spoke of himself in the self-laudatory tones of the founder of a new religion, reciting how he had turned his back on the humdrum lives led by the ruck of men so that he might consecrate himself to the difficult and time-consuming task of mastering the old traditions. His first book, a series of evaluations of prostitutes in Osaka written in 1657, has a preface that includes these lines:

I have been a devotee of this Way ever since that long-ago autumn of my thirteenth year when I first squeezed a hand under a trailing sleeve. I served an apprenticeship in winks and like gestures, then at the end of the following year investigated for myself the truth about tête-à-tête of love. During the thirty years that have passed since I came into this world and the eighteen since first I awakened to the Way, I have cultivated the art unremittingly, day and night, forgetting food and sleep, and I have mastered its supreme doctrines. I claim moreover that it was I who first established it as a true Way, and gave it the name of the Art of Love. When I have died who will succeed me as the patriarch of this Art of Love and point out to the young their follies? Deeply concerned that future generations may wander off on false paths, to their eternal confusion, if I myself do not establish the ultimate principles of this art, I made a great vow to save the world. In the spring of last year I resolved to compile a work in twenty volumes describing the secrets of the art. However, what with illness and being dragged off to parties, the manuscript still languishes at the bottom of a drawer, unfinished. If I am able in the years of life left me to bring this work to fulfillment, it will surely be a treasure for future generations. . . . Some people consider me no better than a madman for having abandoned society to take up this Way. But is this not like a bird or a fish that never tires of its wood or water—though it takes a bird or a fish to understand why? If a man has a wife and family and thinks of nothing but amassing worldly goods, how can he escape the usages of the vulgar world? I am all alone, a cloud drifting with the wind, uncertain as the dew on a blade of grass. Having been born with a not overly generous portion of talent and brains, in what other field could I have established myself as the world's leading authority? When I consider this fact, what have I to regret in my decision to follow this Way and give my insignificant person entirely to it? Praise from the vulgar will not gratify me, nor will their slander make me unhappy. What a feeling of confidence fills me when I think that, thanks to this Way, I hold the world in the palm of my hand!

Obviously Kizan was not entirely serious: his rather ponderous phraseology suggests he was parodying the conventional Confucian or Buddhist proclamations of consecration to the faith. But despite the undeniably agreeable aspects of Kizan's vocation, he was quite in earnest when he insisted that his endless visits to the brothels had a scholarly purpose. It took him over twenty years to complete the work he first planned in 1656, and *The Great Mirror* (1678), leaving its subject matter aside, is a model of learning. Quotations from the Chinese and Japanese classics sprinkle the pages, giving a dignified and even erudite tone to his account. In one section, divided into twenty-eight subsections in the manner of the twenty-eight subsections of the Lotus Sutra, Kizan recorded the progress of a rake, suitably embellished with quotations; however, Kizan's rake ends not in the gutter but as an adept attaining the Great

Ultimate, symbolized by the drawing on the last page of the recitation, a perfect circle.

Kizan devoted minute attention to every aspect of a courtesan's appearance and behavior. Each article she wore, each gesture she made had to be governed by tradition, no less surely than the performance of a Nō play. Kizan wrote, for example:

> Laughter. It is most delightful when, something amusing having happened, a courtesan smiles, showing her dimples. . . . But for her to open her mouth and bare her teeth or to laugh in a loud voice is to deprive her instantly of all elegance and make her seem crude. When something is so extremely funny that she *must* laugh, she should either cover her mouth with her sleeve or else avert her head behind the customer's shoulder.

Again, we are told: "A courtesan should be careful never to mention foodstuffs by name, regardless of the variety. This is true of course of fish or fowl, but even with respect to vegetables it is not advisable to name them." This proscription may account for the invention of elaborate euphemisms for every kind of food, some still used by geishas ("flower of the waves" for salt, or "the purple" for soy sauce), and suggests also a general embarrassment over the business of eating; even today a geisha never eats in the presence of a customer, and gracious dining at a Japanese restaurant implies being in a private room where one can eat unseen by strangers. The etiquette of the licensed quarters tended to spread to polite society, and the innumerable circumlocutions about food used by housewives today may have originated in this manner.

Kizan meticulously enumerated the social graces expected of courtesans:

> For a courtesan an ability to drink is second in importance only to an ability to play the samisen. A woman who is a complete teetotaler commits one of the three cardinal faults of a courtesan, and is the object of particular dislike. A courtesan who drinks will naturally go well with a drinking customer; if, on the other hand, the customer does not drink, she herself has merely to refrain from drinking. A courtesan who does not drink will have difficulty keeping a conversation going with a drinking man. . . .
> The most important things for a courtesan are the first impressions she makes on a guest and the atmosphere in her room. For this reason there is no courtesan who does not smoke. . . . A courtesan does not keep smoking until the tobacco has turned completely to ashes. She should smoke a little, then turn her pipe over on an ashtray while half of the tobacco has still to burn.

The exact color of a courtesan's G-string and the way she should scratch herself if stung by a mosquito are given equally careful attention.

The prostitutes of the time were divided into classes, ranging from the great courtesans at the top, who demanded exorbitant fees from customers and even then might not sleep with them, down to unfortunate women who expected no more than a small coin for their favors. Kizan devoted scant attention to the lower ranks. His interests, clearly, lay in the upper reaches of the hierarchy, and the accomplishments he prescribed were for elegant women reigning over apartments in a lavishly appointed brothel.

> A courtesan should be able to write poetry. She should at least be familiar with the old language so that she can recite poems describing the changing of the seasons. It is a mistake to assume that only crude, ignorant men buy prostitutes. If a woman can converse adequately with a cultivated customer, why should he ever look elsewhere?

Again,

> It is unfortunate for *anyone* not to be able to write, but for a courtesan it is a disaster. They say that playing the samisen is the most important of the artistic accomplishments of a courtesan, but in fact writing comes first, and the samisen only afterwards. As long as a courtesan writes well it does not matter if she is incompetent at the samisen, but even for a samisen virtuoso it would be unfortunate if people said she wrote a bad hand or that her grammar was shaky.

The exchange of letters with customers formed an important part of the ritual of the licensed quarters. Kizan warned, "A man should never write a prostitute unless he has heard from her first." But for the women, as a matter of business, it was essential to retain desirable customers by writing protestations of love. It was frequently stated in Kizan's day (and later) that a man could not trust a courtesan when she assured him of her love, but every man wanted to believe that he was the first ever to have stirred genuine feelings in a courtesan's heart. A most interesting section of *The Great Mirror* deals with pledges of love (*shinjū*) offered by courtesans to their customers.

> Question. Does it ever happen that a courtesan gives pledges of love even though she has no genuine feelings for a man?
> Answer. Pledges can be either genuine or non-genuine. Only one out of ten women sends a pledge because her heart has genuinely been moved by some man. Eight or nine women out of ten send them not out of true intimacy but as a means of assuring their future, once they have become acquainted with a man.

A letter professing love might suffice for some men, but others demanded more convincing proof. Kizan, probably exaggerating, related that "there are boxes for pledges in the houses of men about town in which they collect the fingers, nails, hair, and oaths that have been sent them." Kizan devoted much space to discussing the different varieties of pledges a courtesan sent a man to persuade him that her love was genuine.

> Pulling out a fingernail is extremely painful, but since the act is performed without having been solicited by the man, it is listed as a first pledge of love. Oaths, by comparison, are easy to write down and need not be shown to any outsider, but since they are never written unless they have been agreed to by both man and woman, they represent a higher level of pledge. Pulling out the fingernail is never requested by the man, or if requested is not performed. The nail is pulled out when the man, having become a courtesan's regular customer, a visitor who appears even without invitation, shows interest in some other prostitute and seems likely to shift his affections. Or it may be that he has left after a squabble and not visited her again even after some days have elapsed, or has refused to accept her written apologies and relations seem about to break.

Kizan went on to discuss not only the exact circumstances when it is appropriate to pull out a fingernail and send it to a vacillating customer, but also the ways an accomplished courtesan can conceal the missing nail and get a new one to grow back quickly, so that other customers will not be repelled.

Oaths of love were most impressive when sealed or written in blood. Here too the requirements of decorum were exact. Blood was not to be smeared directly onto the paper from whatever source the signer chose— that would be crude. A man should draw blood from a finger on the left hand, a woman from the middle or ring finger of the right hand. A needle is inserted into the skin between the base of the nail and the first joint of the finger. Blood is squeezed out, and the signer holds his hand over his name on the written oath; then, tilting the hand to the right, he lets a drop of blood fall on the name. For making the incision a fine needle was to be avoided and a coarse needle preferred. Whole documents written in blood naturally required more than a single drop. "If there is not enough blood available for the purpose, the document can be finished up in ink."

The next higher stage involved the woman's cutting off her hair and sending it to her lover. (One is reminded of Mathilde de la Mole in *Le Rouge et le Noir*!) Unlike fingernails, however, this gesture was practiced also by non-professional women; if, for example, a wife had asked her husband for a divorce and been refused, she might cut off her hair to disfigure herself. But a courtesan generally sent only a lock of hair, suitably wrapped in paper. Kizan distinguished the circumstances under which a knife, scissors, or a dagger would be most appropriate for severing the lock.

The next level of pledges was tattooing. The man wrote the inscription to be tattooed, and his writing was then transferred to the place of his choice on the courtesan's body. Tattooing could be performed either with a razor or a needle, but when a razor was used the lettering tended to blur, so a needle was preferred. The inscription generally took the form of an abbreviated version of the customer's name, together with the word *inochi* (life), meaning either that the courtesan would love the man as long as she lived, or else that she would not renounce her love, even if it cost her her life. Some men apparently insisted on including not only their names but lines of verse, but Kizan felt that this was extremely childish.

The supreme pledge was cutting off a finger. Kizan commented:

> The other four varieties of pledges—fingernails, oaths, locks of hair, and tattooing—can be carried out, as part of a calculated scheme, even if the woman is insincere. But unless she really loves the man, it is hard to go through with cutting off a finger. . . . Nails grow back in days, a head of hair in months, oaths can be hidden away, and tattooing can be erased when a woman no longer sees a man. But giving up a finger makes a woman a cripple for life, and she can never restore things to what they were. The act should therefore be performed only after grave deliberaton.

But although Kizan urged caution, he also asked, "If a man says he will forgive a prostitute her misdeeds, providing she clears up his doubts by cutting off her finger, what prostitute would refuse?"

Kizan, in his usual systematic manner, discussed the etiquette and procedure involved. The room in which the operation takes place should be locked and bolted to keep out curiosity-seekers. Smelling salts and drinking water should be kept ready, since nine out of ten women faint after the finger is severed. The finger should be laid on a wooden pillow for the operation as the safest place. (He gives a horrendous story of a woman who used a balcony railing for the purpose, lost the finger in the garden below, and had to cut off a second finger to satisfy her implacable lover.) Kizan distinguished two ways of cutting off the finger, and recommended cutting off only the first joint, sparing the base of the nail; this was likely to promote the growth of a new nail and minimize disfigurement.

The courtesan sent a severed fingertip as proof positive to a man that she loved him, despite her inconstant calling and the familiar scepticism directed at courtesans' assurances. The man, impressed by her sacrifice, would normally resume his relations with the woman, but these relations, in the nature of things, could only be temporary. It is true that men sometimes bought a prostitute's contract, at a great expenditure of money, and he would then be free to establish her outside the quarter as his mistress and even as his wife. This was the subject of many novels and plays, but seems to have happened relatively seldom. A grimmer possibility, the double suicides of customer and prostitute, when they despaired of being able to live together in this world, inspired especially the dramatist Chikamatsu. But most men seem to have been satisfied with the relaxed atmosphere of the brothels, the companionship more amusing than that of a wife, and the pleasures of drink and sex. Some became connoisseurs, in the manner of Kizan. On the whole the Confucian scheme worked, though it condemned women to servitude, whether in the brothel or the home. In Japan, no less than in the France of Alexandre Dumas *fils*, it might have been said, "Marriage is a chain so heavy that it takes two, and generally three, to support it." Trouble arose only when two of the three tried to bear the chain alone.

Kizan's *Great Mirror* is of intrinsic interest because it so absorbingly describes the ceremonies and traditions of the licensed quarters at the time of their most brilliant flowering. It provides also the background for the great Japanese literature written at the end of the seventeenth century, notably the novels of Saikaku and the plays of Chikamatsu. It stands as a worthy monument to Kizan's long years of research.

Hanako

OCTOBER 8, 1907, the celebrated Hanako, the toast of a dozen European capitals, landed in New York. A newspaper headline proclaimed:

> Tiny Jap Actress
>   Now in America
>   Hanako San, Just 70 Pounds of Ability,
>   Arrives on the Potsdam.

"She is 26 years old," the article inaccurately reported, "weighs seventy pounds to the ounce, and is not quite four feet tall . . . . She rose from the position of geisha girl in a Yokohama music hall to her present station as the Bernhardt of the Flowery Empire." When asked which she preferred, Paris or New York, Hanako unhesitantly replied in her broken English, "Broadway—much better."

Four days after her arrival Hanako was taken to Weber's Music Hall by her American hosts, but, as the *New York Herald* disapprovingly noted, "Never once in the course of the evening did she move a muscle. . . . Perhaps also her ignorance of the English language—assuming that she is not familiar with our tongue—was a handicap with which Weber's abdominal pad and thirty-six pairs of the shapeliest legs on Broadway could not successfully cope."

Hanako's appearance in New York followed triumphs in Europe, but in Japan she had been virtually unknown. In 1901 the adventurous Hanako, then aged thirty-three and an entertainer in the provincial city of Gifu, responded to the call of an impressario who planned to stage a Japanese show in Copenhagen, and with scarcely a word of good-bye to her family, sailed for Europe. At the time many troupes of Japanese entertainers—dancers, acrobats, jugglers and the like—regularly toured the European circuits in half-hour variety turns, lending the evening's show a suitably exotic flavor. Hanako's dances apparently created no unusual stir, and she would probably have returned to Japan like the other performers after a few years of playing in the smaller cities of Europe had she not been discovered by Loie Fuller, the American dancer.

Miss Fuller had earlier been the backer of the European tour of the great Japanese actress Sada Yacco and her company of thirty. "These thirty," Miss Fuller recalled, "cost me more than ninety of another nationality would have done; for apart from everything I was obliged to do to entertain them, I had constantly to go down on my knees to secure permission to attach to each train that carried them an enormous car laden with Japanese delicacies, rice, salted fish, mushrooms and preserved turnips."

Loie Fuller eventually wearied of paying the expenses of Sada Yacco's company, and found in Denmark another group of Japanese actors. She was particularly impressed by one actress who played minor parts. "She was pretty withal, refined, graceful, queer, and so individual as to stand out, even among those of her own race. When the rehearsal was over I gathered the actors together and said to them, 'If you are going to remain with me you will have to obey me. And if you do not take this little woman as your star you will have no success.' And as she had a name that could not be translated, and which was longer than the moral law, I christened her on the spot Hanako."

Hanako's real name, Ōta Hisa, was somewhat shorter than the moral law. But whether by intent or accident, Loie Fuller and subsequent biographers of Hanako invariably got almost every fact wrong. The 1922 edition of *Who's Who in the Theatre*, for example, states that Hanako was born in 1882 (fourteen years late), and that she "made her first appearance on the stage, as a child, in Tokyo ... and subsequently performed in a number of roles at the Imperial Theatre, Tokyo, where she eventually became 'leading lady.' " But Hanako in fact had had no stage experience in Japan, and her career as an actress was almost entirely thanks to Loie Fuller's intervention and guidance. Not only did Miss Fuller decree that Hanako would be the star of the company, but (apparently undaunted by her total ignorance of the Japanese language or of Japanese drama) she rewrote all the plays of the repertory in order that each might terminate with a death scene for Hanako.

René Chéruy, a former secretary of Rodin, once told Loie Fuller how much he had been impressed by one of Hanako's death scenes—"kneeling before a mirror and applying her makeup while chatting rapidly, until her jealous lover stepped from behind and strangled her with a scarf. I remarked to Loie that I really had no need to know the Japanese language to comprehend and enjoy the gist of the short play. It is then that Loie Fuller told me that all that scene of acting had been taught by *her*, Loie, to the diminutive Hanako."

Miss Fuller, Pygmalion-like, was fascinated by the actress she had created. She described one of Hanako's death scenes: "With little movements like those of a frightened child, with sighs, with cries as of a wounded bird, she rolled herself into a ball, seeming to reduce her thin body to a mere nothing so that it was lost in the folds of her heavy embroidered Japanese robe. Her face became immovable, as if petrified, but her eyes continued to reveal intense animation. . . . Finally with great wide-open eyes she surveyed death, which had just overtaken her. It was thrilling."

Hanako was a great success in Copenhagen, and the troupe embarked on a nine months' tour of Europe. "Her success in Finland bordered upon popular delirium," Loie Fuller declared. Hanako played in all the royal theatres of Europe and finally came to Paris. Her triumph in that city was chronicled by an American reporter: "A young Japanese actress, Hanako, who is performing in a little theatre at the end of a narrow passage off the boulevard, is all the rage of Paris today. The room in which her performances are given holds a hundred people at most, and every night and matinee it is packed with society people in magnificent gowns, who flock hither to gratify their craving for morbid sensationalism."

Miss Fuller and the Japanese troupe remained together for about a year. The other Japanese then sailed back to Japan from Marseilles, but Hanako was lured to Antwerp by "a low-lived compatriot" and worked in a "cheap concert hall" where she sang and danced for the amusement of sailors, patrons of the place. (M. Chéruy, hearing of this from Loie Fuller in later years, was astonished. "I had no idea that the Japanese merchant marine had enough business connections with Antwerp to justify the presence of 'geishas' for the entertainment of their crews.") Hanako, in despair over her predicament, appealed to Loie Fuller to save her from this fate worse than death, and her benefactress sent money and clothes. Hanako escaped from the brothel (if that is what it was; Miss Fuller is not clear) and made her way to Paris.

A theatre manager in Paris offered to present Hanako and three other Japanese actors in a play, providing that Miss Fuller could guarantee that it was a good one, easily intelligible even to people who knew no Japanese. She thereupon wrote a Japanese play, "The Martyr," which met with so favorable a reception that she followed it with "A Drama at Yoshiwara." These two works were to become the mainstays of Hanako's repertory while in America.

The reviews of Hanako's New York performances were generally laudatory. "A good-sized audience was held silent for thirty-two minutes by the remarkably clever mimicry of the Japanese actors, headed by Mme. Hanako. . . . 'The Jashiwara' is intensely interesting in spite of the Japanese dialogue, which to our uncivilized ears resembles nothing so much as a dog fight." (The critic of the *Atlanta Journal* was later to report that, "The Jap lingo, as spoken rapidly by these players, sounds like the inarticulate gibbering of apes; there is no cadence, inflection or emphasis to aid a surmise to its meaning; but the grimaces and gestures are so graphic that the eyes, if not the ears, easily followed the story of 'The Jashiwara.' "

After a successful tour of New England, the Japanese actors headed for the less appreciative American hinterland. The *Des Moines Register* for November 3, 1907, bears a headline: "THE MARTYR", A GHASTLY THING. The critic found the faces of the Japanese actors much like those of gorillas. "I have seen such faces on oriental fans, vases and screens, and I recall some like them in nightmares; but never hitherto have I seen them alive. Hanako, the starred tragedienne of the company, enacts a belle supposed to be irresistibly charming; yet she could be no unsightlier woman unless her pigmy size were increased to ordinary size. . . . She dances awkwardly on stilts, and is clumsily blithesome in antics that make her and the three others look like decrepit, yet still tricky monkeys in a cage." Hanako's famous "hari-kari" scene is described: "The actress uses a trick knife, the blade of which recedes into the handle, and at the same time releases a red fluid so that the illusion of a blade slowly piercing her body to a depth of six inches and of blood spreading from the wound over her white robe is a grisly sight."

Such intemperate and crude comments would be inconceivable today, when every critic is resolutely determined to prove that he "understands" the culture of distant countries, and all phases of Japanese civilization are treated with extreme deference. In a sense, however, the critic of the *Des Moines Register* was more acute than the enthusiastic critics in New York and the European capitals: Hanako's plays were fake; she herself was an actress who could not have appeared on the Japanese stage; and every means legitimate or otherwise was exploited in the hope of intriguing foreign audiences. (In one play Hanako wore a costume sewn with small electric bulbs; suddenly the onstage illumination was extinguished, and Hanako's figure outlined in lights was seen moving in the steps of a Japanese dance.) Judged by any objective standards, the performances could scarcely have merited the extravagant praise they received. But almost everyone who saw Hanako, even critics accustomed to the greatest actresses of the day, felt something indefinable and magical underneath the sensational and sometimes tawdry surface of her performances, a flame which illuminated her from within. It was to take two artists—a French sculptor and a Japanese novelist—to define the allure that the audiences felt.

Hanako's American tour was profitable, and when she sailed from New York in December 1907 she left behind many admirers. A leading poet of the day, Edwin Markham, paid tribute to the art of "the agile actress whom some call the 'Japanese Duse,'" and proclaimed that "even her back is eloquent." But those who waited for Hanako's return were disappointed. She crossed the Atlantic again in January 1909, but after only one performance in Brooklyn her show was closed for lack of suitable scenery or costumes.

Hanako's greatest triumphs occurred in Europe after her first American tour. In the Mid-West the critics had been severe, but in Berlin and Vienna Hanako was a sensation. The *Morning Telegraph* reported in a despatch from Vienna dated April 2, 1908, "Mme. Hanako Has Won Over Vienna. Japanese Actress Repeats Her Berlin Success. . . . Madame Hanako is now appearing at Ronacher's Variete and judging by the reception she received and the unanimously favorable press criticisms, she is likely to outdo her Berlin triumphs, which is saying a good deal, considering that she was the talk of the artistic and literary circles of the German capital for a month." Hanako gave a special performance attended by "nearly all the prominent actors and actresses in Vienna," including Eleanora Duse. Long styled "the Japanese Duse," this time Hanako appeared before the Italian Duse.

Hanako had performed in London as early as October 1905, before her Paris success, when Arayama's Company of Japanese Artistes had presented "The Hara-Kiri" as a curtain raiser to the major work of the evening, "What the Butler Saw." The troupe apparently enjoyed only moderate success, but Hanako's return to London in July 1908 excited general acclaim. The *Sketch* printed a photograph of Hanako captioned, "A Brilliant Japanese Actress Repeats her Continental Success at the Hippodrome." Her play on this occasion was "Otake," the Loie Fuller version of a work often presented in London in English under the title of "A Little Japanese Girl."

From 1908 to 1914 Hanako toured Europe with her company. The general mobilization found her in Germany. Alarmed by the prospect of war, she hurried to Paris, and eventually went on to London, appearing in November 1914 in her familiar vehicle "Otake." In December she "quaintly represented" the part of Lady Isabel, the weeping mother, in a burlesque of "East Lynne," a performance that boasted of one person from each of the Allies in the cast. In May 1915 Hanako appeared in a comedy entitled "Oya, Oya" in which she sang, danced and played the samisen.

Hanako's star seemed to be on the wane. Her next role was designated in the cast of characters merely as "Part of His Luggage." A more rewarding assignment followed in November 1915, when Hanako appeared in the part of Jack, "a dear little British tar," in the burlesque melodrama "They All Love Jack." Photographs show her in a sailor suit and a fringed beard, a pipe clenched between her teeth. The plot was summarized, "The fun consists in M. Léon Morton's fascinating way of planning the murder of a dainty Japanese, played by Mlle. Delysia, who is rescued by a little British tar in the person of Hanako. Tragedy, however, is not thereby averted, for all the characters end by committing hara-kiri."

Hanako's last role on the English stage was in one of her earlier successes, "Ki-Musume" (A Japanese Virgin), in which she appeared in January, 1916. Though by now forty-eight, Hanako was still convincing in the part of a nineteen-year-old girl. One reviewer commented, "The strangeness of Mme. Hanako's methods did not prevent her from expressing and arousing more poignant emotion than our stage has dreamed of for years, so entirely has it ignored the natural human feelings."

Hanako returned to Japan in 1916, intending to recruit a new troupe of Japanese dancers for Europe. The gravity of the war seems not to have made much impression on her until the following year, when the ship ahead of hers in the Europe-bound convoy was torpedoed. The increasing stringencies of the war made it harder for her troupe to find engagements, and Hanako finally gave up the stage to open a Japanese restaurant called Kogetsu in Dorset Square, London. The restaurant boasted the only rooms in purely Japanese style in Europe, and was honored by the patronage of the present emperor, when as Crown Prince he visited England. In 1922 Hanako returned to Japan, and lived in retirement in Gifu with her sister until her death in 1945. In later years she emerged only rarely from obscurity. In 1940, for example, an enterprising reporter requested her opinion (as an expert in European affairs) on the German invasion of France. Hanako replied, "Those Germans are certainly strong!"

Hanako's extraordinary success on the European stage was a curious by-product of the rage for great actresses that swept Europe and America during the early years of the century. Bernhardt, Duse, Réjane and others drew impassioned audiences not only at home but in countries where their languages were not readily understood. Sada Yacco's performances, though in Japanese, so impressed Max Beerbohm that he declared that if, like Paris, he were forced to choose among the goddesses Bernhardt, Duse and Sada Yacco, he would award the golden apple to Sada Yacco. Hanako's talents were no match for Sada Yacco's, but she was wildly acclaimed, if only because she afforded audiences the chance to indulge in the sensational realism of her hara-kiri scenes while congratulating themselves on their appreciation of the mysteries of oriental drama.

Whatever her limitations as an actress, Hanako's stage presence must have been exceptionally striking. We know what a spell she cast over Auguste Rodin, her devoted admirer for over ten years. Rodin first met Hanako at the Marseilles International Exposition of 1906, and invited her to visit him in Paris. M. Chéruy remembered a lunch at Rodin's house attended by Hanako, a male Japanese companion, and Loie Fuller. "The conversation was nil, neither she nor the companion having any comprehension of French or English." Another of Rodin's secretaries, Judith Cladel, saw Hanako modelling for one of the masks Rodin made of her. "Hanako did not pose like other people. Her features were contracted in an expression of cold, terrible rage. She had the look of a tiger, an expression thoroughly foreign to our Occidental countenances. With the force of will which the Japanese display in the face of death, Hanako was enabled to hold this look for hours." (Hanako later told her family in Gifu what a terrible strain it had been to hold this pose, which was quite foreign to her normally cheerful countenance. "I felt funny for days afterwards," she said.)

Mlle. Cladel described the finished mask, "I cannot say that it resembles death; on the contrary, it is so lifelike that it is almost supernatural. One might call it a condemned person, a being so terrified by the approach of death that all the blood had rushed to the heart." She sensed under the outward, alien expression "a poor creature that has loved and suffered. It is a pitiable face that has been molded by life."

Rodin sculpted several masks of Hanako. In addition to the one described above, showing Hanako in the throes of one of her death scenes, there are calmer ones, no less intense for their composure. A biographer of Rodin wrote, "Rodin pushed to the furthest limits of expression the mystery, the anguish, the unhappy sensuality of this face. He imbued it with such harmony and musicality that some have mistakenly imagined that they stood before a mask of Beethoven. The mistake is understandable if you examine the bust of Hanako at Meudon, charged with tragic grief and a mute ferocity." Another biographer reported that Rodin in fact had considered using these studies of Hanako for his intended bust of Beethoven.

Hanako in later years often reminisced with her family about Rodin's kindnesses—how he would send his carriage to the stage door after her performances, how warmly he received her in 1914 when she fled from Germany to his house in Meudon. Rodin insisted that Hanako live in his house as one of the family, and declared his intention of making a new mask that would immortalize her. But the approach of the fighting induced Rodin himself to take refuge in England. When he left France his wife divided his fortune, in gold coins, between Rodin and Hanako. Shortly before his death in 1917 he directed that Hanako be given two masks of her he had sculpted. She took the masks to Japan in 1922, and they remained in her house in Gifu, the object of pilgrimages by numerous Japanese artists. Hanako's house was destroyed in 1945 during the bombing of Gifu, but the masks were safe because they had previously been sold to a private collection in Tokyo.

Hanako's meeting with Rodin inspired not only works of sculpture but a short story written in 1910 by the celebrated novelist Mori Ōgai. The story relates how a Japanese medical student in Paris accompanies Hanako as her interpreter to Rodin's studio. The student is ashamed to present such a poor example of Japanese womanhood to the great sculptor; Hanako, though only sixteen (here the author departs radically from the facts!), looks more like a servant than an actress. Rodin, however, seems pleased by the girl and her answers to his questions about her life in Japan, and presently he requests permission to sketch her in the nude. Hanako consents, and the student is asked to withdraw to an adjoining room.

To pass the time until the sitting is completed, the student examines Rodin's books, and opens one by chance to an essay by Baudelaire on the metaphysics of toys. Baudelaire claims that a child's interest in his toys is aroused by a curiosity to discover what makes them run, and in the end he breaks the toys to find the secret within them. Just as the student is finishing the essay, Rodin summons him back to the studio. Learning that the student has been reading Baudelaire's essay, Rodin remarks, "The human body as a form in itself is of no interest, but it is a mirror of the soul. What concerns me is the flame visible through the outward form." The story concludes with Mori Ōgai's quotation of a description of Hanako's beauty taken from Rodin's printed conversations, "She has not a particle of fat on her. Her muscles stand out boldly, like a fox-terrier's; her tendons are so developed that the joints to which they are attached have a thickness equal to the limbs themselves. She is so strong that she can rest as long as she pleases on one leg, the other raised at right angles in front of her. She seems to be rooted in the earth, like a tree. Her anatomy is quite unlike that of a European woman, but no less beautiful in its unique strength."

The story *Hanako* is related in such simple, matter-of-fact terms that at first reading it seems more like reportage than fiction. But Mori Ōgai was no mere reporter; he used the framework of the incident to make the point that Rodin, as an artist, was able to detect a beauty in the Japanese girl to which her own compatriot was insensitive. Rodin did not consider Hanako simply as an exotic object, a toy which ran about making strange noises; he sought the vital spark within her. His intuitive appreciation of Hanako made the Japanese student's commonsense attitude seem superficial and even contemptible. Mori Ōgai suggests that understanding requires more than familiarity.

But was Rodin's reason for asking Hanako to pose in the nude in fact his desire to search out the flame within her? M. Chéruy suggested that the request for a short nude sitting "came perhaps from a 'faunesque' curiosity of the aging sculptor rather than from a strictly artistic motive." This interpretation may be right, but Mori Ōgai with an artist's perception saw the importance of Rodin's request, and perhaps even the ultimate source of the fascination that Hanako exercised for a decade over the audiences in Europe and America. Beneath the trumpery of her death scenes and the false exoticism designed for foreign tastes, there surely burned a flame to which audiences, no less than a child with his toy, instinctively responded. Hanako must have been a great woman.

NOTE

A detailed study of the background of Ōgai's story *Hanako* was published in Japanese after the appearance of the above article. I have corrected several mistakes of fact thanks to this study, which is called "Mori Ōgai no Hanako" by Hirakawa Sukehiro, included in *Hikaku Bungaku Kenkyū*, No. 13, 1967.

VI. THE JAPANESE AND
THE LANDSCAPES OF WAR

The Sino-Japanese War of 1894-95
and Japanese Culture

THE SINO-JAPANESE War of 1894-95 is as remote and uncontroversial to most Japanese today as the Spanish-American War is to us. The leaders of Japanese thought are little interested in a half-forgotten conflict which, insofar as it is discussed, is usually dismissed as a stage in the development of Japanese capitalism. The grim volumes of the official history of the war certainly do not invite perusal except by a specialist in military campaigns, but the now forgotten deeds of bravery and violence inspired works of literature and art that may still intrigue us. I shall not deal here with the causes of the Sino-Japanese War, nor its battles, nor its effects on Japanese industrialization; instead, I shall attempt to show in what ways the war affected Japanese culture.

1. JAPAN AND CHINA IN THE EARLY MEIJI PERIOD

The distinctive cultural feature of the war was provided by the enemy—China, the model or object of emulation of Japan throughout most of its history. From the eighteenth century, it is true, scholars of national learning had denigrated China, insisting on the mystical supremacy of the Land of the Gods; and the scholars of Dutch learning, in their enthusiasm for European civilization, frequently criticized the lack of a scientific spirit in China, contrasting the accuracy of Dutch medical books with the fantasies recorded by the Chinese anatomists, or the "spiritually" evoked scenes of the Chinese painters with the realism of European depictions. Nevertheless, Chinese cultural influences remained exceedingly strong in nineteenth-century Japan. The Meiji Restoration, though ushering in an era of uncritical imitation of Western things, did not funda-

259

mentally alter the prestige of Chinese culture. The visits of the Emperor Meiji to Shintō shrines were recorded in classical Chinese on stone monuments, and the Confucian philosophy of the Tokugawa rulers, though modified, was not displaced by either a "pure" Japanese or a Western system of thought.

Japanese feelings towards the country China, as contrasted with Chinese culture, were more ambivalent. As early as the eighteenth century Hayashi Shihei had depicted China as a potential menace to Japanese security, and some advocates of national defence took this view seriously. The defeat of China in the Opium War naturally revealed to the Japanese how much weaker militarily China was than a European power like England, but the tradition of respect for China was not easily shattered. Most Japanese of 1890 believed China was a powerful country. The inconclusive war with France of 1883–85, carefully reported in Japan and even depicted in woodblock prints, had considerably restored Chinese prestige, and the reinforcement of the Chinese Navy with warships far superior to any possessed by the Japanese had even aroused consternation. The visit of the Chinese fleet in July of 1890 inspired the caption writer for the newspaper *Kokumin Shimbun* to an ironic poem: "The Chinese have been showing off, and all the cowards are scared."[1] Toyama Masakazu (1848–1900), a leading educator and writer, at one time President of Tokyo University, described his impressions on visiting the Chinese flagship *Ting-yüan*:

> Not long ago, as a member of the House of Peers, I was invited by His Excellency Ting Ju-ch'ang, Commodore of the Chinese North Pacific Fleet [to inspect his flagship]. . . . The *Ting-yüan* is truly a splendid warship, reputed to be virtually without peer within the various navies of the East. When I examined the guns I was struck by their large calibre and by the remarkable ease with which they could be maneuvred. The ship moreover is armored throughout with thick steel. The officers, from the captain down, all appear exceedingly well trained. They are very polite to visitors, and most of them understand English. . . . I thought how truly fortunate it was that the East now boasts a fleet with a warship of this quality, manned by officers of such distinction. I did however regret somewhat that many sailors seemed rather listless, pale and undernourished. Otherwise, I was enormously impressed.

At the suggestion of a Japanese naval officer, Toyama also visited that day the Japanese flagship, *Takachiho*. He was assured that the smaller Japanese guns were more maneuverable than the heavier rifles of the *Ting-yüan*, but was not entirely convinced. What struck Toyama most aboard the *Takachiho* was the sailors: "Although the ship was to sail the following day and had already raised its sails and was getting up steam, the sailors were gathered in their quarters. Some were sewing their trousers, some writing letters back home, some reading. Our warships are manned by sailors who long for home, their families, their wives and children. Is it not sad that we force such sailors, such officers, to worry about winning a war with a foreign country? If war breaks out, our first line of defence against the enemy is our warships. Our officers and men, ceaselessly pondering day and night how to win naval engagements, are gentle men of Yamato who think of their parents, their families. It is our duty as citizens to see to it that they do not die like dogs. . . . Such were the feelings I had on visiting the Chinese warship and the *Takachiho*. Some people are given to comparing the Chinese and Japanese, but I dislike such comparisons. The Chinese and ourselves are like elder and younger brothers. We should definitely not make the Chinese our enemies."[2]

Even amidst their fears aroused by the visit of Admiral Ting's fleet, seemingly a show of strength to impress the Japanese, Toyama and others expressed their respect for Chinese culture. Admiral Ting and the other Chinese officers were honored at a banquet given at the Kōyōkan in Tokyo by the Asia Society (Ajia Kyōkai). The poems exchanged by guests and and hosts, in Chinese of course, consist mainly of graceful compliments paid by the Chinese to the local scenery and to the entertainment they had been offered. This typically undistinguished poem is by Ch'en En-shou, second in command of the *Ting-yüan*:

> Japan has lovely scenery that delights on repeated viewing;
> In Kōyō Hall we listen to drums and strings.
> The three countries join in the pleasure of opening the feast:
> Assembled dignitaries bear witness to their common feelings.
> Although our costumes today are different,
> The Chinese characters are still the same as in olden days;
> We write short poems, we record past events,
> I regret only I have no fine verses worthy of such friendship.[3]

Katsu Kaishū, the noted statesman, offered this verse to Admiral Ting:

> The iron-clad ship is several hundred feet long;
> It chases whales on the Great Eastern Sea.
> We shake hands amidst mountain and river scenes
> And anticipate the pleasures of good friendship.[4]

One can hardly escape the feeling that the members of the Asia Society, no less than Japanese of a millennium earlier, were desperately anxious to impress the Chinese. The various Chinese emissaries who resided in Japan prior to the Sino-Japanese War were entertained with a cordiality not apparent in the more lavish entertainments provided for European or American dignitaries. Japanese visitors to China were not always favored with such hospitality; despite Japanese material progress, which by this time had outstripped the Chinese, they remained "eastern barbarians" in the eyes of many Chinese, who saw no need to win Japanese approbation.[5] The Chinese literati in Japan, however, were feted wherever they went, and they clearly fitted into the Japanese scene in a way impossible for Europeans. The pleasure that Japanese scholars and literary men experienced in exchanging poems with the scholar Wang T'ao or with the diplomat Huang Tsun-hsien was possible in the world of *kanji*, the Chinese characters which transcended national boundaries; this was the world of gentlemen-scholars, an ideal common to China and Japan.

For most Japanese, "the image of China imprinted on our minds before the Sino-Japanese War was of a splendid, romantic and heroic country." The Chinese classics were a basic part of education, and these studies had the effect of glorifying China. Treasured objects of art often depicted Chinese personages in surroundings at once romanticized and easy for a Japanese to appreciate, in contrast to many works of Western art. Japanese cultural dependence was so great that "nobody in Japan was sufficiently confident to claim that Japanese were better than Chinese. They undoubtedly would have been quite content not to be inferior."[6] On another level, the Chinese traders in Yokohama were "extremely well-liked," though some Japanese feared that if the Chinese were permitted to live outside the concessions their superior business skills might overwhelm the Japanese merchants.[7] The Chinese in the concessions, it is true, on occasion showed themselves as arrogant as the Westerners,[8] but such instances were exceptional; China of all countries was closest to Japan. It is a melancholy fact that it took but a few months to destroy the tradition of respect built up over the centuries and turn the Japanese from friendship to contempt.[9]

2. OUTBREAK OF WAR

The Japanese were prepared for the formal declaration of war with China on August 1, 1894, by a series of events in Korea which had steadily embroiled the Japanese forces ever deeper. News of the outbreak of war was greeted everywhere with enthusiasm, and if the initial pitch of enthusiasm could not be maintained indefinitely, there was virtually no trace of anti-war feeling at any later stage. The only resistance to the war, if we may speak of such, came from the writers who chose not to concern themselves with the war in their writings. Among the works published during the war years the most famous—*Takekurabe* by Higuchi Ichiyō, *Kiri Hitoha* by Tsubouchi Shōyō, and *Takiguchi Nyūdō* by Takayama Chogyū—were unrelated to the war. But those whose authors chose the war for their theme expressed themselves with unbounded enthusiasm. Yosano Hiroshi (Tekkan: 1873–1935), on hearing of the declaration of war against China, wrote eight *tanka*, the last being:

inishie ni	What need we yield
nani ka yuzuran	To ancient glories?
mimizuka wo	The time is near
futatabi tsuku mo	When again we shall build
hodo chikaku shite	A mound of ears.[10]

Fukuzawa Yukichi (1835–1901), after warning against overconfidence, urged everyone to devote each word, action, and material good to the promotion of a Japanese victory. Fukuzawa saw a war with China as necessary in order that China might benefit by the enlightenment kept out by her obstinate Manchu rulers. He considered China's interference in Korea an intolerable attempt to prevent the spread of enlightenment, and the war itself not merely a struggle between two countries but a "battle for the sake of world culture."[11] Fukuzawa retained his fervor throughout the war, convinced not only of its necessity but its desirability.

Uchimura Kanzō (1861–1930) was initially no less convinced than Fukuzawa of Japan's mission in the war. He published in August 1894 an article in English entitled "Justification of the Corean War." Though Uchimura was later known for a pacifism largely induced by disillusion with the Sino-Japanese War, in 1894 he was certain that the "Corean War now opened between Japan and China" was a "righteous war."[12] After citing numerous examples from classical, Biblical and European history to prove this contention, he went on, "But leaving all legalities aside, (and we by no means disregard them,) is not a decisive conflict between Japan and China an unavoidability,—we might almost say, a historical necessity? A smaller nation representing a newer civilization lying near a larger nation representing an older civilization,—was there ever such a situation in History without the two coming to life-and-death struggle with each other at last? . . . The Corean War is to decide whether Progress shall be the law in the East, as it has long been in the West, or whether Retrogression, fostered once by the Persian Empire, then by Carthage, and again by Spain, and now at last (last in world's history, we hope,) by the Manchurian Empire of China, shall possess the Orient forever. Japan's victory shall mean free government, free religion, free education, and free commerce for 600,000,000 souls that live on this side of the globe." He issued a call to the nations of the world "to see and understand the cause we fight for. . . . Japan is the champion of Progress in the East, and who except her deadly foe,—China the incorrigible hater of Progress,—wishes not victory to Japan!"[13]

Mori Ōgai (1862–1922), as a professional soldier, was naturally first among the writers to go to Korea, arriving in Pusan on September 4, 1894. His extensive war diary,[14] though a model of his incisive style, is utterly devoid of interest, consisting mainly of dispatches on the deployment of medical personnel. Other writers and artists eagerly volunteered for duty as correspondents at the front. Kunikida Doppo (1871–1908) had some moments of fear and regret after he decided to serve as a naval correspondent,[15] but his articles for the *Kokumin Shimbun* were filled with delight over his experiences. These articles, collected in the posthumously published *Aitei Tsūshin* ("Letters to My Beloved Brother," 1908), overflow with a childish enthusiasm and patriotism, as exemplified by an impromptu address given by Kunikida to the officers of the warship *Chiyoda*: "People of our great Japanese Empire are proud that they have military men brave and loyal as you! You too should always remember this. Above your heads is His Majesty, an Emperor endowed with supreme literary and military virtues. Behind you are your forty million compatriots, all but burning with emotion. You are fortunate. Where else in the entire world are there military men who can compare with you in the good fortune of having above you this Emperor and behind you this people? You are fortunate." Following this oration, there was a shout of *wan̄tsū surii* and all present burst into song.[16]

Masaoka Shiki (1867–1902) was another eager volunteer. He later recalled that "I felt that unless I could see service with the troops somehow, there would be no point in having been born a man."[17] He did not actually arrive in China until April 1895 and his one-month stay produced little writing. The sight of Chinese corpses strewn around gun emplacements at Chin-chou sickened him into writing one of the few negative works inspired by the war:

nakihito no	Hide from sight
mukuro wo kakuse	The corpses of the dead,
haru no kusa	Grasses of spring.[18]

Aboard ship, returning to Japan, Shiki coughed blood, the first sign of the illness which would take his life. The bad treatment he received aboard ship at the hands of the military also colored his later remembrances of his wartime service.

The newspapers were filled with accounts from the front, illustrated by artists like Kubota Beisen (1852–1906), whose prints depicting fearless Japanese troops routing terrified Chinese set the tone for the descriptions. They also carried serialized novels or short stories about the war, some directly describing the conflict, others pretending (in the traditional manner) to treat historical events but spicing their accounts with obviously contemporary references. Tokutomi Roka began publishing *Nisshin Sensō Yumemonogatari* ("Dream Tale of the Sino-Japanese War") in September 1894. In the following month Izumi Kyōka began serial publication of *Yobihei* ("A Reserve Soldier") in the *Yomiuri Shimbun*. At the end of this story the hero, a medical lieutenant named Nogawa Kiyozumi, collapses of sunstroke during maneuvers after a forced march with full military gear under the broiling summer sun. As he lies on the ground his sweetheart Madoka, who has followed the troops disguised as a laborer in order to be close to Kiyozumi, rushes up and identifies herself. A medical corpsman, leaning over Kiyozumi, urges him to release his grip on his sword so that treatment may be administered, but Kiyozumi refuses: "My duty as a military man will not permit me to yield my sword and lose my combat effectiveness. Please let me die as I am. This is my heart's desire." Madoka wails aloud, and the sergeant, clenching his fists, lets fall tears like hail. "*Appare da. Appare da. Yo, yo, yoku osshatta! Rippa da. Ri, ri, rippa na mono da!*" The story ends as a general descends from his horse to kneel before Kiyozumi's body, assuring him (in classical Japanese) that his gallant action will inspire the entire army.[19]

The novelist to profit most by the war was Emi Suiin (1869–1934), whose stories, published in *Chūō Shimbun*, enjoyed such great popularity that he earned spectacular increases of salary. Suiin later recalled that he had desired to serve as a war correspondent, but so huge was the popularity of his stories that the owner of the newspaper refused to let him go. "To tell the truth," Suiin added, "I felt that I was giving my all for the nation, with a pen instead of a sword."[20] *Chūō Shimbun*, thanks in part to Emi Suiin's stories, came to be called "the war newspaper" (*sensō shimbun*).[21]

News of the war was even more exciting to readers than fictionalized accounts. The editors curtailed such normally popular newspaper features as the scandals and murders traditionally found on the third page to devote more space to the war. The poetry columns were taken over by works describing in Chinese or Japanese the poet's exultation. One poem beginning, "*Kai naru kana. Kai naru kana. Aa, kai naru kana*" concluded "*aa kai naru kana. Kai naru kana.*"[22]

The book publishers were quick to take advantage of the aroused interest of the readers. Summer was normally a poor season for books because the Tokyo university students left the city, but after the outbreak of war in August 1894, books sold well, especially non-fiction about China and Korea. The firm of Hakubunkan began publication of the tri-monthly *Nisshin Sensō Jikki* ("True Account of the Sino-Japanese War") in September, followed by the rival *Nisshin Kōsenroku*, ("Record of the War Between Japan and China") published by Shunyōdō. The latter company, long known as the bastion of the novel, postponed publication of fiction indefinitely.[23] The enormous popularity of *Nisshin Sensō Jikki* later occasioned the publication of *Taiyō*, a general magazine aimed at mass readership.

The newspapers, magazines and fiction published at the opening of the war are marked by unmistakable exhilaration and confidence. The Sino-Japanese War, the first conflict with a foreign power in three hundred years, naturally aroused patriotic sentiments, but a consideration of the relative strengths of China and Japan should have induced some anxiety about the possible outcome of the war. The foreign press was nearly unanimous in predicting eventual victory for China once Japan's initial advantages of discipline and preparedness had been dissipated. Even after Japan scored a number of victories foreign opinion remained divided. "I have no hesitation in expressing the conviction that China is certain in the end to triumph if both states are left to fight out to the bitter end a long and exhausting struggle," wrote one expert on the Far East.[24] *The Spectator*, insisting that China was "virtually invincible," decried the admiration aroused in England by Japanese successes. "It would be most unfortunate if, because the Japanese make pretty firescreens, and seem to have been impressionists without knowing it... we should give our moral support to Japan. ... China is the one Asiatic Power whose friendship is of supreme importance to us."[25] But all observers agreed that the Japanese people were united behind the war: "The enthusiasm in Japan continues, and the spectacle of this Eastern nation fighting and maneuvering and organizing with a *verve* and intelligence worthy of a first-class European war has sent a thrill of admiring wonder through the military world."[26] The Japanese, as many doubtlessly sensed, were proving by incontrovertible successes in the war, that their modernization, so often belittled abroad, had been genuine. This may be why the outbreak of war was greeted with enthusiasm even by those who could not really understand why Japan, the longtime emulator of China, had now to crush her.

3. THE CREATION OF HOSTILITY

Hardly had the war begun than *Yomiuri Shimbun* announced a prize competition for war songs which "will arouse feelings of hatred against our national enemy." The Sino-Japanese War was to inspire more and better war songs than any other conflict in which the Japanese engaged. Virtually every event of the war was celebrated, often in songs distinguished both for their words and melody. At first the emphasis was on the justice of the Japanese cause:

> Our empire, rich in benevolence and chivalry,
> Has guided our neighboring country, Korea,
> And is devoting every effort to make it
> Worthy of the name of independent country,
> And to maintain peace in East Asia eternally:
> But China, overweening in its immense pride,
> Claims that Korea is a tributary. . . .[27]

The words, even in the original, can hardly be described as lilting or even singable, but these songs tended to be plaintive narrations rather than infectious ditties.

Before long the burden of the songs shifted from idealism to denigration of the Chinese weaklings or cowards. The song about the Chinese vessel *Ts'ao-chiang*, surrendered to the Japanese, was typical:

> Feckless China, behold the *Ts'ao-chiang*'s end . . .
> *Ts'ao-chiang*, warship in name only,
> Knowing not what to do, flounders;
> "Raise the white flag and surrender!"
> We investigate, to see if it is true,
> They strike the Ch'ing naval flag,
> And set fluttering aloft
> Our own. . . .[28]

Other songs were directed specifically against Li Hung-chang:

> ri, ri, Ri Kōshō no   Li, Li, flat-nosed Li Hung-chang,
>   hanabecha,

cha, cha, chanchan bōzu no ikedori ya	Chang, chang, Chinese prisoners of war,
ya, ya, Yamagata taishō ken nuite	War, war, General Yamagata draws his sword,
te, te, teikoku banzai daishōri,	Sword, sword, hurrah for the Empire, victory.
ri, ri, Ri Kōshō...	Li, Li, Li Hung-chang....[29]

Others, like the many variants on the tune *Miya-sama, Miya-sama*, are rather brutal in their war-spirit. One example runs:

mina-san, mina-san	Ladies and gentlemen,
o-uma no mae ni	What is it rolling
korokoro suru no wa	Before the prince's horse?
nan jai na	That is the pumpkin-head
are wa chanchan bōzu no	Of a Chinaman, don't you know?
kabocha atama wo shiranai ka	*Tokoton yare ton yare na.*[30]
tokoton yare ton yare na	

Toyama Masakazu, who proudly claimed to have written the lyrics of the first Japanese war song, *Battōtai* (The Drawn Sword Unit), was pleased that at last the nation had come to recognize the importance of war songs.[31] The Minister of Education directed that students be taught these songs at school. A 149-page book of Army and Navy songs issued in 1897 included pieces by Sasaki Nobutsuna, Ochiai Naobumi, Ōwada Tateki, Yosano Tekkan, Toyama Masakazu, and a German named F. Schroeder. The effectiveness of war songs in preserving morale during the fighting was noted. On October 15, 1894, for example, two companies led by a Colonel Satō were faced by severe enemy fire. Satō ordered his men to sing; by the time they reached the words "trampling over the four hundred and more counties of China" in the long ballad *Rappashi wo tomurau* ("In memoriam of the bugler"), their morale was up a hundred times and they experienced no difficulty in breaking through the enemy defences.[32]

More important even than the war songs in creating feelings of hostility toward the Chinese were the *nishikie*, colored woodblock prints. Lafcadio Hearn reported that "the announcement of each victory resulted in an enormous manufacture and sale of colored prints, rudely and cheaply executed, and mostly depicting the fancy of the artist only, but well fitted to stimulate the popular love of glory."[33] Over three thousand war prints were published during the course of the war, which lasted less than a year.[34] Kobayashi Kiyochika (1847-1915), the finest printmaker of the

Meiji period, alone produced at least eighty triptychs and another hundred or so cartoons. Other artists were even more prolific. The prints were enormously popular, as we know from a great variety of evidence. A report in the November 1894 issue of *Waseda Bungaku* states, "The *nishikie*, formerly devoted chiefly to actor portraits and the depiction of mores, now treat almost nothing but the Sino-Japanese War or related persons and incidents. The actor portraits are derived from war plays, and the usual portraits and scenes are unavailable except at the largest shops. The *nishikie* come in two varieties. The inferior ones, intended for the pleasure of women and children, are drawn in extremely gaudy colors; the superior ones are rather artistic in comparison, both in design and execution. . . . The lithographs are of course more realistic in picturing the war, but are for the most part uninteresting, and seem likely to be overwhelmed by the *nishikie*."[35]

The newspapers printed many pictures of the war. "Newspaper illustrations formerly consisted of portraits of deceased persons or occasionally of topical cartoons, or else of illustrations to the serialized novels published in the tabloids. Since the Sino-Japanese War, however, it has become an almost universal practice to add illustrations to reports of the news. Not a newspaper but has published two or three illustrated war supplements, notably the *Kokumin* which features frontline illustrated reports drawn by Beisen, Kinsen and other artists."[36]

Newspaper illustrations, however, did not satisfy the public demand for pictures of the war, whipped up with each successive victory. The most popular *nishikie* reputedly sold as many as one hundred thousand copies each, and so dense was the press of crowds at the print stores that special warnings about pickpockets were issued. The bright colors of the *nishikie*, particularly the cruder ones, entranced the public. A passage from *Haru*, the novel by Shimazaki Tōson, describes the scene:

> When he reached Fujimi-chō, there was a crowd of men and women before the print shop, each struggling to get a better look at the blood-thirsty war pictures. "On to Peking! On to Peking!" the eyes of the passersby seemed to say.[37]

Tanizaki Junichirō recalled many years later seeing war prints for sale:

> The Shimizu-ya, a print shop at the corner of Ningyō-chō, had laid in a large stock of triptychs depicting the war, and had them hanging in the front of the shop. They were mostly by Mizuno Toshikata, Ogata Gekkō and Kobayashi Kiyochika. There was not one I didn't want, boy that I

was, but I only rarely got to buy any. I would go almost every day and stand before the Shimizu-ya, staring at the pictures, my eyes sparkling. ... I was horribly envious of my uncle who would buy all the new triptychs as fast as they appeared.[38]

The *nishikie* played a major role in shaping the Japanese image of China. The best artists usually attempted to incorporate some artistic effect in their works; Kiyochika sometimes portrayed scenes only casually related to the war because he had been intrigued by their possibilites of artistic composition. But the *nishikie* by the mass of artists appealed to prospective buyers on a far more elementary level. They uniformly portray the Japanese soldiers in poses of heroic determination and show the Chinese as abject cowards, running pell-mell from combat. Unlike the Japanese, invariably attired in sombre blacks and grays, the Chinese are clad in screaming reds, blues, purples and greens. These were the same colors Japanese artists had used fifteen years earlier for Japanese troops at the time of the Satsuma Rebellion, but by 1894 these crude aniline colors had fallen into disfavor, and were used to suggest primitive taste, if not barbarity. The Chinese are distinguishable from the Japanese not only by their costumes and grotesque grimaces of fear, but by their facial features. No two peoples ever seemed more strikingly dissimilar than the Japanese and Chinese of these prints. The Chinese have jutting cheekbones, broad noses, gaping mouths, slanting eyes and, of course, pigtails. The Japanese are dignified of mien and look distinctly European in their military moustaches and carefully trimmed haircuts. A print issued ten years later, at the time of the Russo-Japanese War, depicts the Japanese and Russians as virtually identical, except for the brownish tinge to the Russians' hair. Not only do the Japanese bear strong facial resemblances to the Europeans, but they stand as tall and maintain a similar dignity of demeanor, unlike the Chinese. The famous print by Migita Toshihide (1862–1925) of the surrender of the Chinese admiral Ting Ju-ch'ang after the battle of Wei-hai-wei, shows the Japanese officers in black uniforms towering over three cringing Chinese clad in green, purple and blue. Two European advisers of the Chinese also bow in defeat, but with greater dignity; they also wear black (Fig. 9). This picture is one of the least denigratory to the Chinese; prints by such hacks as Adachi Ginkō portray the Chinese with savage derision. The cartoons even by Kiyochika show hideous, sub-human creatures, quivering with terror.

The Chinese willingness to become prisoners in particular aroused the contempt of the Japanese. Numerous prints show the Chinese abjectly begging for their lives or allowing themselves to be bound by the Japanese troops. The first Chinese prisoners to reach Japan were greeted every-where with derision. A crowd waited for them at Shimbashi Station in October. A reporter noted that the prisoners seemed unconcerned even by the jeers of the surrounding thousands; some even ate as they walked along, making them look all the more undignified. A woman in the crowd shouted at the prisoners, "*Chanchan no heitai wa anna mono ka?*" ("If that's what the Chinese soldiers are like [I could kill a couple of them myself].") The writer commented, "Indeed this is true. They would be no match even for the women of our country."[39]

The words *chanchan*, *chankoro* and the like, said to be derived from *Chung-kuo-jen* ("Chinese"), remained for many years epithets of con-tempt.[40] Another term in favor at the time, though since disappeared, was *tombi*, a literal translation of the English word "pigtail." The word inevitably gave rise to rumors that the Chinese smelled like pigs or acted like them. One reporter suggested that Japanese troops cut off the pig-tails of the Chinese as a proof of the numbers they killed. This would not be cruel, like amputating ears and noses (in the manner of Hideyoshi's forces in Korea), but would dispel the stubborn doubts of foreigners about the magnitude of Japanese victories. The pigtails eventually could be sold to wigmakers, though Japanese woman might, of course, object to wearing wigs made from the hair of *tombikan*, smelling of pigs.[41]

Though the prisoners were subjected to harsh mockery, the Japanese felt it was essential that they distinguish themselves from the barbarous Chinese by their good treatment of prisoners, the mark of an advanced country. By the time the Japanese captured Pyongyang in Korea they had over six hundred Chinese prisoners. "If we had been like the obdurately ignorant Chinese army, these prisoners would have been cruelly tortured before finally being slaughtered. As a matter of fact, before the fall of Pyon-gyang, when soldiers of ours on patrol were captured by the Chinese, they were subjected to all kinds of humiliation, cords were brutally passed through their nostrils, and they were paraded around, before finally the Chinese lopped off their limbs and murdered them. This is intolerable. But we whose warp consists of mercy and justice and whose woof is civilization (*bummei*) could never follow the Chinese in their barbarous practice and return savagery for savagery. That is why our army has given the pris-oners the best possible treatment. The prisoners from the *Ts'ao-chiang* were sent to Sasebo, later transferred to Hiroshima, and are now lodged in temples in Matsuyama. Their daily rations are almost identical with those of our troops."[42] Japan, it was averred, would abide by the Geneva Convention on the treatment of prisoners, no matter how cruelly the

Chinese behaved. Indeed, many prisoners were so pleased with the treatment they had received that they showed not the least desire ever to return to China.[43] An occasional prisoner might suggest that there was "a lone crane among a flock of chickens"; one Chinese being led off into captivity with thirty or forty others, suddenly broke away and bashed out his brains against a stone wall. "Truly there must be a few such among 400 millions," the Japanese commented.[44] Suicide was the most effective way the Chinese had of redeeming themselves in the eyes of the Japanese; Admiral Ting Ju-ch'ang, who killed himself after the defeat at Wei-hai-wei, enjoyed considerable esteem in Japan. Chinese atrocities against European missionaries were prominently reported as well as notices published by the Chinese army offering rewards for heads cut from the Japanese dead. In contrasts to these examples of barbarity, the Japanese prided themselves on their chivalry in action.[45] Almost every print maker and some oil painters depicted Captain Higuchi, a Chinese waif he has rescued under his left arm, brandishing a sword with his right. In some prints the child's grateful father kneels before the captain, in others the mother hovers behind a rock, frightened by the hail of bullets which do not daunt Captain Higuchi.[46]

The anti-Chinese feeling was levelled specifically at Li Hung-chang. This statesman had formerly been highly esteemed in Japan, especially when General Grant reported in 1879 that Li was one of three great statesmen of the world. Li was sometimes even called the Bismarck of the East. But with the outbreak of war he became a figure of fun, fantastically garbed, generally depicted by the *nishikie* artists in attitudes of astonishment or terror. When confronted at the conference table by a Japanese resolutely laying down demands with a thump of the fist, or when presented with the news of a military disaster, Li looks comically incompetent. In a print depicting Li as he learns of the fall of Port Arthur, a wineglass is clenched in his right hand and an enormous peacock feather towers above his hat. Around the table sit advisers outlandishly costumed in greens, purples and reds, all listening with gaping mouths to some frantically gesticulating soldiers who report the defeat. In the background distracted waiting women pass around soup tureens.

Li Hung-chang figured as the villain of the play *Nisshin Sensō* staged by Kawakami Otojirō in Tokyo on the 31st of August, playing before huge crowds for forty days. The dramatic highlight occurred in the first act, when the Japanese reporter Hirata (played by Kawakami himself) is dragged before Li Hung-chang (played by Takada Minoru). Charged with being a spy, he defends himself by expounding the duties of a newspaper

THE SINO-JAPANESE WAR 273

reporter and referring to the principles of international law. He concludes by denouncing the tyrant Li Hung-chang. Takada Minoru in a pigtail and "Confucius beard" made a great hit with the audience.[47]

Li Hung-chang's reputation in Japan would be restored only after the end of the war when, in Shimonoseki for the peace treaty, he was wounded by a superpatriot. Alarmed lest the reputation of Japan, so carefully nurtured during the war, should be damaged abroad by this act of terrorism, the Japanese were more generous than they had intended with the peace terms, and the Empress herself made bandages for the wounded Li. But generous gestures could not alter the new relationship between the Chinese and Japanese: the prints, songs and war plays had convinced the Japanese that the Chinese were backward, cowardly and even contemptible, unworthy heirs of a once-great tradition.

The belief that China, once a great country, now represented a menace to civilization found expression in the war songs, including the famous *Pekin made* ("On to Peking") by Yokoi Tadanao (1857–1928):

Shina mo mukashi wa seiken no	China long ago was the land
oshie aritsuru kuni naredo	Of the teachings of the sages,
yo wo kae toshi wo furu mama ni	But as dynasties changed and the years passed
shidai ni kaika no atojisari	She gradually has fallen behind in progress.
kuchi ni wa Chūka to hokoredomo	She prides herself on being Middle Flowery Land,
kokoro no yaban wa hampirei	In inverse proportion to the barbarity of her heart;
sono mōmai wo yaburazuba	Unless we destroy her ignorance,
wa ga tōyō no yo wa akeji	The night of the East will never dawn.

The lines were rendered by an English clergyman:

China was wise of old
China is wise no more
Back into darkness has rolled
For all her sages and lore.

She may boast as the Kingdom of Heaven,
Her barbarous heart is of hell,
What light to the East shall be given
Till wisdom her darkness dispel?[48]

It became an easy step to assert that Japan, not China, was the true heir to the ancient Chinese glories. Okakura Kakuzō became the most persuasive exponent of this view which may account for the respect still accorded traditional Chinese culture even after China itself had been discredited.

4. THE JAPANESE HEROES

The counterpart to the denigrating of the Chinese was the creation of Japanese war heroes who were the embodiments of traditional virtues. The heroes of the Sino-Japanese War were all from the humblest ranks. The Russo-Japanese War brought world fame to General Nogi, Admiral Tōgō and to Commander Hirose; the Sino-Japanese War was remembered in terms of heroic first-class privates.[49] This emphasis on the achievements of unknown farm recruits, rather than on trained officers, the descendants of samurai, may have been accidental, but it may have been intended to bring home the lesson that universal military conscription had been the basis of Japanese success. The fact that humble soldiers could perform deeds of gallantry normally associated with the samurai proved that their virtues were shared by the entire Japanese people and not the property of professional soldiers. In contrast to the Chinese, cowardly and ready to become prisoners, even the humblest Japanese was courageous and loyal to the death. The successful charge of some unarmed Japanese coolies against a battalion of Chinese troops was cited as proof of the superiority of any Japanese to any Chinese. A short story by Emi Suiin tells of a soldier with a broken arm who insists nevertheless on going to the front. The young man says, "One arm—that's no problem! Even with two broken arms I could take on any number of Chinese soldiers! Stupid Chinese soldiers! They don't amount to anything."[50] Even the most ardent American zealot never spoke of fighting with *both* hands tied behind his back!

The first war hero of the Sino-Japanese War, as it happens, was an officer, Captain Matsuzaki Naoomi, honored as the first Japanese casualty of the war. Struck by a bullet in the leg he went on fighting until another bullet struck his head. "I'm done for!" (*yarareta*) was his last utterance. Matsuzaki was often depicted in *nishikie*. When the Emperor Meiji was presented with a collection of *nishikie*, his first question was, "Which is Matsuzaki?"[51] (*Matsuzaki wa dore ka.*) He also figured in the first war plays. Nakamura Ganjirō, known for his portrayal of the rather effeminate

heroes of the Chikamatsu love-suicide plays, appeared as Captain
Matsuzaki in Osaka. In the great *mie* of the part, he grabbed two Chinese
soldiers by their pigtails and cried, "*Tombikan, yokku kike! Ware koso
wa Dainippon Rikugun Hohei Taii nani no nanigashi nari.*" ("Pigtails!
Listen carefully! I am none other than the infantry captain of the Army
of Great Japan, such-and-such by name.") At the close of the play Ganjirō
charged onstage waving a sword. Hit by a bullet, he fell crying, "*Susume!
susume! susume!*" "Charge!" at the final curtain.[52]

Captain Matsuzaki's fame was soon eclipsed by that of an ordinary
private who fell in action on the same day, July 29, 1894. Early reports
told of a bugler who, though struck by a bullet, went on bugling to his
last breath. When they found his corpse the bugle was still pressed to
his lips. The incident caught the imagination of the Japanese. Before
long a flood of artistic composition had been inspired by the heroic
bugler, identified as Shirakami Genjirō. The print by Toshihide, showing
the bugler lying on his back, trumpeting to the sky, is the most successful
of the *nishikie*.[53] Shirakami's bravery, first celebrated in *Kokumin Shimbun*,
was compared to the ideal bugler described by the German poet Julius
Mosen.[54] The existence of a European prototype may account for the
remarkable attention attracted by the resolute bugler. On August 16,
1894, Yosano Tekkan published *Rappashu*, followed by *Rappasotsu* by
Kisugi Tengai (1865–1952), which contains the immortal lines, "I blow
my bugle with my soul; its voice is the voice of *Yamato damashii*."[55]
Lengthy poems were composed in Chinese, despite the difficulty of fitting the name Shirakami Genjirō into the prescribed tonal patterns. One,
by a certain Koro Gyoin began:

> The lingering moon was about to sink by Asan,
> The sky was full of stars, the woods bright,
> Ten thousands hearths seemed asleep, ten thousand sounds dead;
> Suddenly swords rang with a clang of metal;
> Our troops shouted as they slashed the enemy positions.
> The barbarian soldiers fled in all directions, confused.
> A bugle sundered the clouds with its echoes clear....

The poem ends:

> The bugle at his mouth, his call still unfinished,
> A cry of pain tells he is fatally wounded.
> The imperial forces owe their victory to your strength.
> Your name will pass into history for a thousand years.
> Ah, you are heroic, Shirakami Genjirō!
> Ah, you are mighty, Shirakami Genjirō![56]

Another poem, *Rappa no hibiki*, translated by Lafcadio Hearn, began:

> Easy in other time than this
>   Were Anjo's stream to cross
> But now, beneath the storm of shot,
>   Its waters seethe and toss. . . .
>
> Death-stricken, still the bugler stands!
>   He leans upon his gun,—
> Once more to sound the bugle-call
>   Before his life be done.
>
> What though the shattered body fall?
>   The spirit rushes free
> Through Heaven and Earth to sound anew
>   That call to Victory![57]

The masterpiece among the poems on the bugler was by Sir Edwin Arnold, published in London on November 14, 1894.

> Shirakami Genjiro
>   Bugler in the Line!
> You shall let our Westerns know
>   Why the kiku shine!
> Why the Sun-flag, gleaming,
>   Bright from field to field,
> Drives the Dragon, screaming,
>   Makes the Pig-tails yield.
>
> Shirakami Genjiro
>   (Okayama man)
> Left his ripening rice to go
>   Fighting for Japan;
> Musket on his shoulder,
>   Bugle on his breast,
> Unto each beholder
>   Linesman, like the rest.
>
> Sad for grey-haired husbandman,
>   Fatherly—in years—
> Sad for pretty Yoshi San,
>   Proudly checking tears;
> No one in the village,
>   Only Genjiro,
> Careless of the tillage,
>   Glad to ship and go.
>
> But the Emperor doth proclaim

Soldiers must come forth!
  Is there not despite and shame
    To Nippon, in the North?
Good at target practice
  And bugle-calls to blow,
Duty bids! The fact is
  Genjiro must go.

Ah, poor boy! the home-place
  Never fairer seemed;
Never out of Yoshi's face
  Softer sunshine beamed;
Yet his country calls him;
  Dai-Nippon hath need;
Whatso'er befalls him
  Genjiro will speed.

The last three verses of this immensely long poem run:

He blew the charge so loud
  It blared across the plain,
It rattled, large and proud,
  From mountain unto main:
He blew so clear and soft
  The Pig-tails made to fly,
Before the Sun-flags, borne aloft
  Could reach the enemy.

And, while he blows the boy's blood
  Fell, scarlet drop by drop,
The bugle's mouth—and his—imbued,
  Nor from that wound would stop
The trickling trickling! Stoutly,
  He sounded *Susume*,
The call that bids all soldiers
  Close in the deadly fray.

To tune of that brave clamour
  The Song-hwan wall was won;
The fierce charge sped, the foeman fled,
  The day's great work stood done.
But when they turned, victorious,
  There! on the crimsoned ground,
Clasping his bugle, glorious,
  Young Genjiro was found.[58]

Toyama Masakazu contributed a lengthy poem, *Ware wa rappashu nari* ("I am a bugler"), one of his series on great deeds of the Sino-Japanese

War. Toyama emphasized the lowly rank of Shirakami Genjirō with exquisite subtlety:

> Okayama kenjin Shirakami Genjirō.
> kare wa mata ikko no rappashu narishi nari.
> hito wa ieri. Kare wa tadatada rappafuki nari to.
> kare wa ieri. Ware wa tadatada rappafuki nari to.[59]

> Shirakami Genjirō, Okayama man,
> He too was a bugler.
> People said, "He is just a bugle-blower."
> He said, "I am just a bugle-blower."

and so on. The gallant Shirakami Genjirō was celebrated even in *kyōka*, though a comic verse form would seem inappropriate:

kuni no tame	For the sake of his country
waga mi no ue wo	He ignores his own fate,
shirakami ya	O Shirakami!
fuku ne to tomo ni	Together with the note he blows
kiyuru tama no o	Fades away the thread of life.[60]

Plays (now lost) were performed in memory of the glorious bugler, the action no doubt padded with references to such creations as Genjirō's sweetheart Yoshi (celebrated by Sir Edwin Arnold) and to his fatherly-in-years father.

Shirakami seemingly attained immortality when in November 1894 the official new eight-volume readers for elementary schools were issued. The seventh volume contains the bugler's story and a picture of Shirakami lying on his back, one knee raised, blowing the charge. The selection concluded, "The name of this bugler was Shirakami Genjirō, and he came from Okayama Prefecture."[61] This identification is of more than usual interest because Shirakami Genjirō, for all the immortality promised him, soon disappeared from textbooks, to be replaced by one Kiguchi Kohei, a first-class private of identical attributes. The authors of *Heroic Japan* explained the mystery: "Shirakami Genjirō was, however, quite another man. Not even a trumpeter, but a second-class private of the First Reserves, he was none the less a comrade of Kiguchi, and belonged to the Ninth Company, while Kiguchi was one of the Twelfth Company men. He also lost his life at Sŏnghwan, being similarly killed by a breast wound."[62] It is not clear why the authorities felt it necessary, many months after the incident occurred, to give credit to Kiguchi Kohei for the deed which had made Shirakami Genjirō famous.[63] Kiguchi's name soon replaced Shirakami's and acquired a legendary character; he became the symbol of the virtue of loyalty to duty (*chūgi*) preached in school textbooks. "Kiguchi Kohei died with the bugle pressed to his lips" came to be featured in second-year elementary school books as the perfect example of *chūgi*.[64] At times in the 1920's when liberal Japanese educators objected to the militaristic tendencies in textbooks, Kiguchi Kohei was a special target.[65] Others, however, praised the loyalty of Kiguchi Kohei as sharing with the selections on the emperor the distinction of being the most successful part of Japanese *shūshin* (moral) education. In the *shūshin* textbooks Kiguchi Kohei figured more frequently than any other soldier of modern times, tying with such figures as Columbus and Jimmu Tennō in total number of appearances.[66] Every Japanese over thirty has heard of Kiguchi Kohei, but it is hard to suppress the suspicion that he may have been the most successful fictional creation of the war.

The second most famous hero was Harada Jūkichi, the heroic scaler of the Gembu Gate at Pyongyang who let the Japanese forces into the city. Harada Jūkichi too was a familiar figure in the *nishikie*, and his deed was commemorated in poetry and prose. One song bearing his name was especially famous. It includes the verses:

ame yori shigeki dangan no	Diving under bullets thicker than rain,
shita wo kugurite jōheki no	He scrambles up the castle wall,
mashira no gotoku yojinobori	Like a monkey
hirari to tobikomu sono hito wa	And lightly jumps inside; this man
kore zo Harada no Jūkichi shi	Is none other than Mr. Harada Jūkichi
tsuzuite Mimura shōtaichō	Following him, platoon commander Mimura.[67]

The emphasis is definitely on second-class private Harada rather than on Lieutenant Mimura. Eastlake and Yamada, less interested than the Japanese authorities in celebrating the glories of an anonymous son of Yamato, declared in *Heroic Japan* that "Harada Jūkichi had the distinction of being selected to open the gate because the Lieutenant desired in some measure to reward him for his intrepid obedience."[68] But Harada, not Mimura, received the Order of the Golden Kite, and his house was deluged with presents from well-wishers. Even before Mimura's platoon broke through the Gembu Gate, however, a suicide squad had already scaled the wall. A member of this squad named Matsumura Akitarō, at first supposed dead, survived and returned to Japan. The authorities, fearing that his story if known would lessen Harada's glory, forbade him to disclose it.[69] Matsumura Akitarō spent the rest of his life in the back of an antique shop, gloomily staring at old relics, a man of silence. Harada Jūkichi, for his part, found the role of the hero too demanding. He sold his Order of the Golden Kite and drank the proceeds. For a time he appeared on the stage, reenacting his epic deed; his last recorded performance was in 1900 in Osaka. When Harada's story was presented at the Kabuki-za in *Kairiku Renshō Asahi no Mihata* ("Repeated Victories on Land and Sea; the Glorious Rising-Sun Flag"), his part (called Sawada Jūshichi) was performed by the great Kikugorō. Harada himself in the part struck people by the close resemblance of his poses to Kikugorō's.[70]

The third hero of the war remains anonymous to the end. He was the sailor who gallantly extinguished a fire aboard the *Matsushima* during the naval battle off Wei-hai-wei. Dying, he asked the second-in-command if the enemy flagship *Ting-yüan* still had not sunk. The sailor, assured that the *Ting-yüan* had been knocked out of action and that the *Chen-yüan* was now under fire, said with his dying breath, "Please strike the enemy."[71] His words became the theme of the most haunting song to come out of the war, *Mada shizumazu ya Teien wa* by Sasaki Nobutsuna. It concludes:

mada shizumazu ya Teien wa	"Hasn't the *Ting-yüan* sunk yet?"
kono koto no ha wa mijikaki mo	These words though brief
mikuni ni tsukusu kunitami no	Will long be engraved in the hearts
kokoro ni nagaku kizamaren	Of loyal subjects who strive for Japan.
mada shizumazu ya Teien wa	"Hasn't the *Ting-yüan* sunk yet?"
kono magokoro no kotono ha wa	These words of sincerity
mikuni wo omou kunitami no	Will be recorded in the burning breasts of
moyuru mune ni zo shirusaren	Loyal subjects who love Japan.[72]

The unknown sailor, like the bugler and the wall-climber, emerged as a symbol of the anonymous Japanese masses. The wave of exultation and self-confidence that foreign observers noted owed much to the conviction that it was the Japanese people who had vanquished China. Hearn wrote, "It is a race feeling, which repeated triumphs have served only to strengthen."[73] The combination of denigration of the Chinese and elevation of the Japanese, the implicit object of the war art, had succeeded in its object, though by literary or artistic standards it may seem foolish or even pathetic today. Disappointment in the war was felt only by those who expected it would result in artistic works of the highest aesthetic quality.

5. LITERARY AND ARTISTIC IMPORTANCE OF THE WAR

Shortly after the war began an anonymous correspondent for *Waseda Bungaku* related his hopes for wartime writing:

> What influence will this great event exert on our literary world? Will the results be good or bad? . . . For the information of readers I should like to describe in general the thoughts I have had on this subject.
> 1. The result of the hatred of the enemy felt by our people, imparting to them a clear consciousness of the nation, an awareness of what it means to be a Japanese, and a sense of the fairness and justice of our heroic undertaking in Korea, is likely to be beneficial in raising the cultural level of the thoughts and emotions of authors and readers.
> 2. The glorious victories of our forces, each report stirring the spirits of our people and lifting to the heights its national pride, will stimulate the hot passions of the poets, the most sensitive of men, and should result in poetry and prose of such splendor and eternity as to move the demons and gods.
> 3. The war, by causing writers and readers to pay close attention to present realities and to turn their eyes to the future, will naturally result in lessening the habit of vainly reflecting on the dead past, of depicting dead matters simply because they are dead; it will make people realize the necessity of studying living societies and living people.
> 4. Literature will, in the nature of things, become concerned with this world; poetry will become subjective and depict for the most part emotions felt at a particular time. Novels and plays will also come to reflect more obviously matters of interest to the public. Probably too, novels and plays written to embody the particular views of an individual will be shown greater favor than at present.
> 5. The *shintaishi* (poems in the new style) which at the moment seem moribund should now, if ever, put forth sprouts again and reach their fulfillment.[74]

After the end of the war many critics expressed disappointment over what actually had been produced. Takayama Chogyū complained in June 1897, that "with the exception of a small number of superficial war stories written by authors of the second rank or worse, not a single man celebrated patriotism or righteous courage."[75] Most of the poetry and fiction quickly disappeared from sight, as quickly as the immortal names of the triumphs and heroes were forgotten; the plays were never printed and survive today, if at all, in manuscript; the paintings are forgotten, and the numerous prints, the cheapest of all woodblock prints today, have never been studied and are rarely even collected. Yet, in a curious way, most of the prophecies made in *Waseda Bungaku* were fulfilled: excitement over the war increased the readership of newspapers and magazines markedly, an increase later channelled into magazines of a higher cultural level; no poetry or prose of "splendor and eternity" came out of the war, but this was too much to expect of so short a period— a longer war with a less monotonous string of victories might have produced better literature; the war did shift the attention of writers from the past to the present, though the results were not always what the *Waseda Bungaku* writer anticipated; individuality came to acquire greater importance in Japanese literature; and, finally, the *shintaishi* movement received an impetus which brought new life.

THE DRAMA

The drama perhaps provides the best example of the manner in which the Sino-Japanese War affected artistic production. It provided Shimpa ("the new school") with its first great successes and established the foundations for the modern Japanese theatre, even though the plays themselves were trivial.[76]

Shimpa had been founded late in 1888 in Osaka as a kind of educational arm for the *Jiyū Minken* (Freedom and People's Rights) movement. The plays performed, political in content, appealed to audiences through their lively presentation of recent political events. Once, when an actor playing the part of Itagaki Taisuke, the leader of the popular rights movement, accidentally was stabbed in a scene depicting an attempted assassination, he went on performing, the blood streaming from his face, to the delight of the audience.[77] Kawakami Otojirō, one of the founders of Shimpa, opened his first season in Tokyo in 1892, attracting publicity by galloping on a horse up and down before the theatre, accompanied by young members of the troupe. In his eagerness to attract attention, he was not above employing stage tricks of the crudest nature.

The outbreak of the Sino-Japanese War came as a godsend to the hard-pressed Kawakami. On August 12, not two weeks after the declaration of war, Kawakami announced he would present *Nisshin Sensō*, and on August 31 the play opened at the Asakusa Theatre. As Kawakami promised in his first formal announcement, the naval battle in the sixth act was staged realistically, with electrical machinery and a liberal use of fireworks, in the manner of his earlier ventures. The text, by Fujisawa Asajirō (1866–1917), an actor of the troupe, though devoid of literary pretensions, supplied the actors with suitably patriotic or villainous speeches, as in this passage from the scene where the reporter Hirata first sees Li Hung-chang:

> Hirata: Are you the General Li I have heard about? Ha-hah. I knew all along that the Chinese prided themselves on making mountains out of molehills, but to think that you are the General Li who is so renowned for possessing the learning of Confucius and Mencius, the sages who made China famous! A hundred hearings are not worth one look—it's just as they say. Hearing and seeing are two quite different things! Do the likes of you pass for a great statesman in China? *Uwahahahahaa.*[78]

The musical accompaniment for the play, in keeping with the theme, was supplied by bugles instead of samisens, and war songs were liberally incorporated into the text. The enormous success of *Nisshin Sensō* naturally encouraged the production of similar works elsewhere. In Kyoto, the Fukui Mohei troupe put on *Nisshin Sensō Yamatodamashii* ("The Sino-Japanese War and Japanese Spirit") on September 7, and Sudō Sadanori, another founder of Shimpa, staged *Nisshin Gekisen* in October in Yokohama. Osaka theatres were crowded for performances of such notable works as *Nissei Jiken Uwasa no Kachitoki* ("The Sino-Japanese Incident; the Battle Cries Everyone is Talking About.")

Kawakami did not choose to rest on his laurels after his triumph. He decided to see the front for himself in order to obtain new materials. He left on October 22 for Korea and Manchuria. Prints show him in various heroic poses; in one, he stands with a pistol in his hand menacing a kneeling Chinese who begs for mercy; the legend states in part, "Seeking to arouse still further our people's hostility toward the enemy, he travelled at the risk of his life to the distant Manchu land, and standing amidst clouds of dust and rains of bullets, personally inspected conditions at the front." Kawakami's next play *Senchi Kembun Jikki*, based on his experiences, opened in Tokyo on December 3. It proved another hit. Soon afterwards, on the eleventh, Kawakami and Takada Minoru gave a special private performance for the Crown Prince, the future Emperor Taishō. It had originally been planned to stage the scene from *Nisshin Sensō* in which Hirata denounces Li Hung-chang, but it was feared that the scene, though stirring, might depress the Prince by its gloominess. Instead, livelier scenes from the current success *Senchi Kembun Jikki* were performed. "When it was over His Highness vouchsafed words of praise, saying that the play was unusual and interesting."[79] In May of 1895 Kawakami's troupe performed at the Kabuki Theatre in *Ikaiei Kanraku* ("The Fall of Wei-hai-wei"), a success that ran for thirty-five days. To have been permitted to perform at the Kabuki Theatre was a sign of the magnitude of the triumph of Shimpa in plays of a contemporary nature. It not only signalized the emergence of Shimpa as an important factor in the Japanese theatrical world but defined the future functions of Kabuki.

At the very beginning of the war, when Kawakami first announced his intention of staging a play describing recent events, *Yomiuri Shimbun* declared that Kabuki actors, for the most part uneducated, were incapable of representing the Sino-Japanese War; if they ventured to appear in the roles of officers it would be an affront to the dignity of the Imperial Army. Kawakami's actors, on the other hand, had some degree of education, and would not be objectionable even performing as officers. If the Kabuki actors wished to stay abreast of the times by staging a war play, they should try *Kokusenya Kassen* ("The Battles of Coxinga"), which would foster national pride by showing how Watōnai denounced and slew the pigtails.[80]

This statement on the functions of Kabuki was truly startling. The Kabuki actors were accustomed to appear as generals and nobles, even if under slightly disguised names, and ever since the beginnings of Kabuki current gossip had inspired many plays. Moreover, had not the ninth Ichikawa Danjūrō advocated *katsureki*—plays in which historical personages were called by their real names—in order to enhance the dignity of Kabuki by removing the foolish and fanciful elements? If Kabuki were to be condemned to keep the distance of *Kokusenya Kassen* from the war, the burning issue of the day, its whole character would be changed.

As a matter of fact, however, the Kabuki actors quickly responded to the challenge of the Shimpa war plays. On September 11 *Nippon Dai Shōri* ("The Great Victory of Japan") was staged in Tokyo, and on October 10 the Osaka Kabuki players performed *Waga Teikoku Bambanzai: Kachi uta Yamatodamashii* ("Long Live Our Empire: a Victory Song of Japanese Spirit") in three acts. In November the Tokyo Kabuki troupe made a massive attempt to recapture its lost audiences by presenting *Kairiku Renshō Asahi no Mihata* ("Successive Victories on Land and Sea; the Imperial Flag in the Morning Sun") with a text by Fukuchi Ōchi, the leading playwright of the day. Danjūrō appeared as the heroic sailor who asked about the *Ting-yüan* and Kikugorō as Harada Jūkichi, but the play was a dismal failure. The aged Danjūrō was pronounced "more pathetic than dashing" in a sailor suit, and the attempts to imitate the tricks of Shimpa by setting off live gunpowder onstage did not make up for the inadequate plot and performance.[81] Kawatake sums up the results of this fiasco: "It would seem that at this point Kabuki realized that new works of the *zangiri* style or realism of the *katsureki* variety should be left to the modern drama, and resigned itself to the fact they went beyond the limits of its own possibilities. Of course, new works derived from modern life were presented any number of times in later years, but they represented experiments of a collateral nature or special entertainments, and not new developments in the main stream.... At this juncture Kabuki, though appreciated by the public of the time, seems to have lost its contemporary quality which was capable of closely reflecting the present-day, and to have become an increasingly classical and non-contemporary drama."[82] The success of Danjūrō in the familiar old work *Datekurabe Onna Kabuki* in February 1895 confirmed the belief that the domain of the Kabuki actors was not that of Shimpa.

A similar pattern on a much smaller scale was traced by the Bunraku troupe. As early as August 1894, at the suggestion of the great samisen player Tsurusawa Dampei, the chanter Takemoto Tosadayū inserted in an existing play a scene relating the victories in Korea at Asan and Chemulpo.[83] After a few other attempts, some rather successful, at capturing public favor by up-to-date war plays, the company eventually was convinced that modern works were beyond its capacities, though Bunraku like Kabuki had originally developed as a mirror of contemporary gossip. The Western uniforms worn by the soldiers and sailors must have made manipulation of the puppets extremely difficult, for trousers conceal far less of the figures of the operators than a Japanese kimono. In any case, from this time onward Bunraku rarely presented plays treating contemporary life.

The Nō, of course, had never reflected contemporary life, but the outbreak of the war threatened its existence. Theatres were taken over as soldiers' billets. The public showed no interest in Nō plays about the war, though a few were apparently written.[84] Only by staging benefits for the troops (which also brought income to the actors, of course) did the Nō actors pull through the war.[85]

The effect of the Sino-Japanese War on the theatre, to resume, was to create on the one hand the foundations for a modern drama capable of representing realistically contemporary events, and to define as the particular functions of the traditional theatres the performance of works drawn from a classic repertory.

GRAPHIC ARTS

The popularity of *nishikie* during the war has already been described. Inevitably, the quality of most of these prints, produced in a great hurry by artists whose main concern was with pleasing an ill-educated public rather than with producing works of art, was low. The worst of the Japanese war prints bear a curious resemblence to the Chinese prints produced at the same time,[86] possibly because the cheaper varieties of Japanese print were widely known in China.[87] These prints, brightly colored and lighthearted even when the scene depicted is a massacre, were never meant to be taken seriously as art. A few *nishikie* artists, however, took pains with their work, and even produced masterpieces that mark a fitting conclusion to the whole of the *ukiyoe* art. It is possible to date the end of *ukiyoe* art with some precision: a report in *Yomiuri Shimbun* published in the autumn of 1895 noted that sales of *nishikie* had dropped drastically; war prints, of course, were no longer in demand but even the usual actor prints barely sold two hundred copies.[88] The print never again met with wide public demand. At the time of the Boxer Rebellion in 1900 the publishers hopefully commissioned prints, but they sold few copies. Again, during the Russo-Japanese War of 1904–5 many prints were executed, but sales were far smaller than for the Sino-Japanese War and the prints themselves of slight artistic importance. Cheap war prints continued to be produced on a small scale even during the 1930's, and an entirely different kind of print, expensive and aimed at connoisseurs of art rather than the general public, attracted attention, but the *nishikie* was gone. Its place was taken by the photograph. Already during the Sino-Japanese War photographs became a prominent feature of such magazines as *Nisshin Sensō Jikki* and by the time of the Russo-Japanese War magazines consisting mainly of photographs were more popular than the prints.

Photographs played a behind-the-scenes role even in the *nishikie* of the Sino-Japanese War. A few artists like Kubota Beisen actually visited the front, but the rest had to choose between relying on their imagination or consulting photographs. In some instances one can see how a photograph has been translated directly into a print, sometimes with considerable skill; at other times the borrowings consist of architectural details or items of military equipment. None of the photographs I have seen has the least artistic interest; it is not surprising that the public found the *nishikie* provided a more exciting portrayal of the Sino-Japanese War.

The best artist of the period, Kobayashi Kiyochika, was in the doldrums when the war began. He had first gained fame during the years 1876–81 when he produced a great many prints depicting the Tokyo of his day: rickshaws drawn up before Western style buildings lit by gaslight, figures under Japanese umbrellas passing a lighthouse on a rainy night, a huge fire ravaging a quarter of the city. His works, though clearly in the *ukiyoe* tradition, are influenced by Western perspective and shading. Kiyochika is believed to have been a pupil of the English artist Charles Wirgman (1832–91) who originally came to Japan in the late 1850's as a correspondent for *The Illustrated London News*. In the 1860's Wirgman began to publish *The Japan Punch*, starting a vogue for a kind of cartoon known in Japan as "*ponchi-e*" which Kiyochika himself would draw during the Sino-Japanese War. It is not certain that Kiyochika actually studied under Wirgman, though this has often been asserted; at any rate, it cannot have been for very long. Kiyochika also appears to have studied photography with Shimooka Renjō (1823–1914), a founder of the art in Japan, and *ukiyoe* techniques with Kawanabe Gyōsai (1831–89), a devoted follower of Hokusai. From each teacher Kiyochika acquired elements of his style, but the peculiar poetry of his landscapes of Meiji period Tokyo is his alone.

It has often been wondered why Kiyochika suddenly abandoned the landscapes which account for his fame today. Some have suggested that a nationalistic reaction to the uncritical mania for all things Western of the early Meiji period caused people to turn from Kiyochika's depictions of the Rokumeikan era,[89] but this theory does not square with the evident popularity of other *ukiyoe* artists who portrayed the *bummei kaika*. It has been suggested also that Kiyochika's prints, executed with far greater care and detail than others of the time, made them too expensive for the public,[90] but this fails to explain why Kiyochika did not choose to make simplified versions of his Tokyo scenes rather than the book and magazine illustrations which provided his livelihood in middle years. It seems more likely that Kiyochika suffered some kind of shock that affected his artistic production. We know of one such incident. In 1881 fire broke out in Kiyochika's neighborhood. Rushing outside, he began furiously sketching. His wife, not realizing where her husband had gone, waited in their house with their two small daughters, until finally the spreading fire reached their building and forced her to flee with the children. When Kiyochika returned the next morning, exhausted from the night's sketching, the house was in ashes. The wife, enraged at his seeming callousness, left Kiyochika. He never again painted the landscapes which had made him famous,[91] but the sketches of the fire and the prints made from them rank among Kiyochika's masterpieces.

Kiyochika's fascination with fire was a part of his constant absorption with the problem of rendering light. He delighted in night scenes lit by the moon, gaslight, fireworks or flames, in the reflections of light in puddles, silhouettes against a brilliantly illuminated sky, the glow from a furnace on the ironworkers. It may be that after years of hackwork, performed with little love and not much display of talent, Kiyochika's imagination was stirred again by the thought of depicting the Sino-Japanese War—explosions at night, men huddled around campfires, searchlights directed out to sea, burning villages. Almost all his good prints of the war depend on his employment of the effects of light, a matter of no interest to his predecessors in *ukiyoe* or to any other artists of the Sino-Japanese War (except his own pupils). Many artists depicted fire in terms of colorful patches in the sky or landscape, but Kiyochika used light to evoke mood—loneliness, terror, intimacy. Even his failures generally have one beautiful panel of the three, suggesting that though he may have drawn by some publisher's order Captain Asakawa's patrol, or a similar subject, his interest was not in the self-satisfied figure of the central panel but in the shadowy figures fighting in the misty rain or in the Chinese corpses looming from the fog at the captain's feet. He tried to convey with an impressionistic use of color the dazzling intensity of a shellburst or of a ship exploding at night. Unlike Toshihide, whose figures are often effectively drawn portraits, Kiyochika clearly was uninterested in the faces of the various officers he was required to draw, often with no knowledge of their actual features or of their personalities. In his best works lighting and atmosphere, appropriate to the war but not necessarily associated with a specific event, create much of the poetry of his early landscapes.

The prints of Kiyochika were the finest artistic works to come out of the Sino-Japanese War. Yoshida Susugu, the author of an important study of Kiyochika, wrote, "The works of Kiyochika depicting the Sino-Japanese War are the peak in the short history of the *ukiyoe* and *nishikie* art, and would seem to deserve a considerable place within the history of the Japanese print."[92] This is high praise, especially in view of the general indifference to these works—they are not mentioned in any Western book I know of—but it may be that a general prejudice against Meiji art has obscured judgment of these prints.

Artists of the Western style on the whole were not greatly affected by the war. In 1893, the year before the war began, Kuroda Seiki (1866-1924), the founder of the modern art movement in Japan, returned from France. Kuroda went to the front in Korea and executed some sketches, but his main activities of the period lay in another direction. In 1895 he exhibited a nude painting which caused an immense sensation; it was the first nude by a Japanese (except for those of pornographic intent). Some critics have traced to this event the beginnings of mature painting in the Western style.[93]

The war certainly did not inspire the nude, but the free exhibition of such a work, obviously in a foreign style and deriving from foreign traditions, was notable, and Kuroda's repeated and open insistence that most Japanese paintings in the Western style were worthless because the artists did not understand the Western culture behind the style, tells us much about the nature of the war itself. Although it is frequently stated, with justice, that the Sino-Japanese War ushered in a period of strong nationalism, during the war itself the Japanese enjoyed a freedom of expression which contrasted markedly, say, with the situation prevailing during the Greater East Asia War. If no opposition was voiced to the war, doubtless this was because none was felt: casualties were light, victories unbroken, and rising prices or poor business conditions did not afflict people seriously enough to make them doubt "the great trust of a nation regenerated through war" described by Hearn.[94] But at a time when Japanese were rediscovering the glories of their heritage, and the magazine Taiyō was founded specifically to spread Japanese culture abroad (the reverse of a process of borrowing which had begun when Japan first came in contact with Chinese civilization two thousand years before), it is startling that Kuroda Seiki should have expressed so bluntly his disdain for the prevailing school of painting in Japan. In 1895 he founded the Hakubakai, a society which was to dominate Japanese painting in oils for many years. The critic for Waseda Bungaku who predicted that novels and plays, thanks to the war, "would embody the particular views of an individual" might well have included paintings.

LITERATURE

None of the prose or poetry stemming directly from the war is remembered today, save possibly for a few songs.[95] Even at the time, as we have seen, critical judgements were severe. Most writers refrained from treating the war, and the government exerted no pressure to make them support the war effort. Though Waseda Bungaku carried regular articles

on the war and its literary products, *Bungakkai* hardly mentioned it.
Hirata Tokuboku (1873–1943) in an article entitled "Seeing Off the Year
1894" went so far as to state:

> At the present time, to mention war literature is the very quintessence of
> foolishness. . . . What the litterateurs now call war literature or new-
> style military poetry is, as Rohan has said, nothing but the uninteresting
> husk of poetry, the abortive work of poets with rather dubious goals.
> Though they may, thanks to mass hysteria, be popular for a time, there
> is not one particle of eternal poetic values in their work. For writers to
> divert their writing to war is the same as for the masses to drop excitedly
> all enterprise for war. This time is especially one demanding elevated
> thought.[96]

Hirata concluded, "To speak of a war literature at the present time is
the height of shallowness. These are the words with which I send off
the year 1894." It is hard to imagine a more sweeping condemnation of
literature written in support of the war, but no one ostracized the author
for these views. Individualism was accepted, even if it ran counter to
general public feelings, a rare situation in Japan.

It is possible to trace the development of the novel of ideas and of the
pessimistic novel, two varieties which emerged after 1895, to the greater
concern with current problems of the time, but perhaps more important
was the controversy over the Japanese language which began during the
war and eventually led to the creation of a new medium of expression.
The vicissitudes of the *gembun itchi* (identity of speech and written word)
movement and the triumph of Futabatei Shimei's novel *Ukigumo* have
often been chronicled, but it is significant that not one of the works in
prose or poetry dealing with the war was in the colloquial style. At most,
as in Izumi Kyōka's stories, the conversational passages are in the colloquial. Even in the elementary school textbooks prepared in 1894, almost
every phrase is in the classical language. The first sentence in Book One
which is recognizable as either classical or colloquial is in the classical
language "*Ike ni hasu ari.*" The deeds of Shirakami Genjirō and Harada
Jūkichi, needless to say, were also recounted in the classical language.
Clearly the *gembun itchi* movement had not yet swept all before it.

Far from being in the colloquial, the largest part of the war poetry
was in classical Chinese. Throughout the war compositions in Chinese,
often denouncing the Chinese as barbarians, flowed from the pens—or,
rather, the brushes—of the Japanese scholars. Even in magazines of wide
circulation like *Nisshin Sensō Jikki* it was not felt necessary to punctuate

Chinese poems for Japanese reading, let alone to translate them. But the sentiments of nationalism inevitably aroused by a war could not easily be reconciled with the use of a foreign language, particularly one associated with the enemy, in expressing the thoughts closest to Japanese hearts. The war stirred not only a revival of interest in the Japanese classics (it might be mentioned that *Kokugakuin Zasshi* began publication in January 1895) but in the proper manner of writing the Japanese language. Although some proposals made at this time were never adopted, and others were adopted only after some time had elapsed, the Sino-Japanese War provided the stimulus for a more fruitful consideration of the national language problem than the *gembun itchi* movement of the earlier period.

Certainly the Japanese language at the time of the war was unsuited to the increase in popular education during the period immediately following. The formal style was larded with Chinese allusions, and even when Japanese words were used they often were transcribed in perversely difficult characters, ostensibly to express slight shades of nuance. Letters were written exclusively in the *sorobun* style with its almost facetious use of Chinese characters to render Japanese sounds. At the opposite extreme, the language of speeches and formal addresses was prolix beyond belief. Any page from an address by Toyama Masakazu, for example, will yield such gems as "*hotondo nai to iu yo na raimei ga arimasuru yo de arimasu.*" The pompous *no de aru no de aru* style was especially popular in the Japanese Diet. No form for the copula had been established for the colloquial, and in the effort to avoid abruptness meaningless locutions multiplied.

During the war itself a number of influential writers devoted themselves to problems of language reform. Okada Masayoshi (1871–1923), whose proposals for reform of the Japanese language were accepted by the Japanese Diet in 1900, leading to the formation of the Committee for study of the National Language (Kokugo Chōsa Kai) in 1902, proposed in 1895 that the use of *kanji* be totally abolished. In a long article published in *Teikoku Bungaku* he advocated the exclusive use of a modified form of *kana* for all writing.[97] His later views were less drastic, but the sharp reduction in the number and variety of characters taught in the schools and used by writers after 1900 certainly owed much to Okada's initial rejection of the Chinese characters.

Other proposals made about the same time were even more dramatic. Miyake Setsurei published in *Taiyō* an article advocating that the Japanese adopt the Korean script. He argued that the *kana* was inadequate for

representing Korean or Western words, complicated to form calligraphi-
cally, and unsuited to writing horizontally. The *kana* might be modified,
he agreed, but if modifications were to be made, why not use Western
script? Proposals for the use of Roman letters were by no means new,
but the revival of strong feelings about the national essence made it
unlikely that the Japanese would adopt the script of the Western countries,
for it would suggest that the nation had acknowledged their superiority.
Adopting the Korean alphabet might then be the best solution. It is
unattractive to look at, but capable of rendering sounds more exactly
than the *kana*, and no one would imagine that Japan, in borrowing the
Korean writing, was bowing before a stronger country.[98]

Saionji Kimmochi (1849–1940), who became Minister of Education in
October 1894, proposed in August 1895 that English be made the central
part of education, and that it might eventually be desirable to eliminate
altogether the teaching of the Japanese language and literature in the
schools.[99] This was not an unprecedented opinion. Toyama Masakazu
had advocated as early as 1884 the urgent necessity of abolishing *kanji*
and promoting the study of English, and Mori Arinori (1847–89),
Minister of Education at the time of his death, had suggested as early as
1872 that English be made the language of Japan. What makes Saionji's
proposal both curious and important is that it was made on the heels of
Japanese victory in the war, at a time when nationalistic sentiment was
supposedly at its peak. It reflects both Saionji's intransigence on educational matters and the flux of opinions concerning the Japanese language
at the time.

The need for creating a unified Japanese language was strongly felt
in 1895, both because of the renewed sense of the importance of Japanese
literature and because of the increased conviction that classical Chinese
or a classical Japanese heavily influenced by Chinese was not an appropriate language for poetry and prose by Japanese. Ueda Kazutoshi (1867–
1937), a scholar of Japanese language and sometime advocate of Roman
letters, urged in 1895 after the end of the war the necessity of establishing
a standard language (*hyōjungo*) and of creating an artistic *gembun itchi*
through the cooperation of writers.[100] Ozaki Kōyō published in September
1895 the story *Aobudō* (Green Grapes) in *de aru* style, and in the following
year began to publish serially his long novel *Tajō Takon* ("Many Feelings,
Many Sorrows") in the same style; these works brought a fully effective
modern-language style to fiction.[101] By the end of the century such
writers as Uchimura Kanzō were publishing newspaper articles in the
gembun itchi style, and the Hototogisu group of *haiku* writers led by

Masaoka Shiki used it for their "sketches from nature." Of course, the use of classical Japanese did not cease immediately, but the years 1895–99 marked the turning point in the development of modern Japanese.[102]

At the same time, the period marked the beginning of a marked decline of both Chinese and English studies. Yoshikawa Kōjirō has pointed out how the Confucian training among literary men went as far as Natsume Sōseki and Mori Ōgai, among military men as far as Yamagata Aritomo and Nogi Maresuke, and among politicians as far as Saionji Kimmochi and Hara Kei, all men educated before this time.[103] But though *kambun* remained a part of the curriculum, taught as a part of *kokugo* (national language), the private schools where Confucian scholars had taught Chinese composition gradually disappeared. Inoue Tetsujirō, an ardent nationalist though a student of Chinese philosophy, urged in 1895 that Chinese studies not be abandoned, even though China itself had shown itself to be corrupt. The Chinese, he declared, lacked the scholarly ability to study their own writings of the past; the Japanese must do it.[104] Chinese studies developed henceforth as a special discipline, much as Inoue suggested, rather than as a basic part of education itself. Similarly, the increased emphasis given to the Japanese language meant that all subjects of a modern nature came to be taught in Japanese, though English had formerly been used in geography, science and like subjects. English continued to be stressed as the most important foreign language, but it was nothing more than that; as a result, the kind of English written by such men as Uchimura Kanzō, Okakura Kakuzō and Natsume Sōseki was not to be attained by later men, who may have been better trained in economics, the sciences and so on.

The effects on literature of the war, then, were chiefly in the urgency given to the creation of a true *gembun itchi* style, free of the pedantic Chinese flavor of the earlier writers.

6. JAPANESE CULTURE AND THE WORLD

It was not surprising that the first war of recent times with a foreign country should have aroused Japanese awareness of themselves. We have seen how this awareness expressed itself with respect to the Chinese. Reactions in Europe and America to the war were closely followed, and the increasing admiration for the Japanese aroused by the victories was joyfully recorded.

It was reported in April 1895: "Ever since the Chicago Exposition foreigners have gradually acquired some knowledge of Japanese culture, but it has been limited to the fact that Japan produced beautiful pottery, tea and silk. Since the outbreak of the Sino-Japanese War last year, however, an attitude of respect for Japan may be felt everywhere, and there is talk of nothing but Japan this and Japan that. Resident Japanese have been invited in truly enormous numbers even to dinner parties and coffee gatherings. Most amusing is the craze for Japanese women's costumes. Many American women wear them to parties, though they are most unbecoming, and the praise they lavish on the Japanese victories sounds exactly as if they were boasting about their own country. It is said that women who fail to wear Japanese kimonos to parties are ostracized for not following the current modes. The popularity of the kimono seems also to have induced American women to perform in Japanese plays. At the end of February last a play was performed at one of the leading theatres on Broadway in New York. Everything from the props to the costumes was ordered from Japan, and the text of the play itself was exactly the same as when performed in Japan. Most of the plays have dealt with vengeance. It is rather amusing to see a samurai wear three swords, but the plays, being Japanese, enjoy such great popularity that they are now much in fashion."[105] Other artistic results of the war were reported the following February: "Japanese painting has come in recent years to be widely appreciated in America, but ever since victory in the war the taste for Japanese art has increased all the more. At present there is a great fad for painting Japanese scenes on the walls of studies and so on, and Japanese artists resident in America are reputedly making large profits."[106]

In Europe, too, admiration for the Japanese mounted. In London a large peepshow showing the *Matsushima* sinking the *Chen-yüan* was popular, and a troupe which had been performing a play about the Sino-Japanese War at the Antwerp Exposition moved to London to give performances. The covers of *The Illustrated London News* were given over to scenes of Japanese war correspondents at work in the field. Sir Edwin Arnold, the doughty champion of Japan, declared that "in attacking China in Corea, she is guarding the civilized world." He saw two dangers overhanging the civilized world, the "Mongol" (represented by China) and the "Slav" (represented by Russia). He warned, "Those do well who dread the sullen and sombre weight of China, controlled, as it is, by the social system springing from that arch-opportunist Confucius, the most immoral of all moralists."[107]

The Sino-Japanese War undoubtedly produced a change of opinion about Japan in the West. Few experts predicted that Japan would win the war against the mighty continental power, and when the initial victories proved not to be flashes in the pan, it was grudgingly admitted that the much-decried "superficial modernization" was in fact genuine. Okakura Kakuzō wryly commented that as long as Japan indulged in the gentle arts of peace she had been regarded as barbarous, but victory in war had induced the foreigners to call Japan civilized.[108]

The rising nationalism after the Sino-Japanese War, so often commented on by historians, had the support of the outside world, confirming the Japanese in the peculiar sense of mission. Nationalism and imperialism and also an industrialization promoted by the indemnity received from China, changed Japan in many ways, but some Japanese critics insisted that basically Japanese culture would remain unchanged. Shimamura Hōgetsu, in reviewing Japanese literature after the war, predicted that its future progress would be based on the essential nature of the Japanese people:

> What is the lifeblood of the Japanese people? History replies: it is *bushidō*, it is *Yamatodamashii*. Truly, the spirit of this one Way pervades all of Japanese history unchanged. . . . what is there except for this which makes Japanese literature Japanese literature?[109]

Shimamura concluded his essay, "Will not the future Japanese literature come to be based, directly and indirectly, on the feelings of the Japanese people aroused by the conquest of China? When will our *Minna von Barhelm* be written?" As far as I know, these questions were never answered, but the national awareness evoked by the Sino-Japanese War certainly provided the impetus for most cultural developments in the years to come.

NOTES

1. As reported by Kunikida Doppo, *Aitei Tsūshin*, p. 159 (Iwanami Bunko edition).
2. *Chuzan Sonkō*, II, pp. 401–5. Toyama is so prolix that any translation inevitably involves drastic reduction.
3. *Kaiyo Shōshū* in *Kaiyoroku*, XI, p. 22a.
4. *Ibid.*, p. 22b.
5. See Takeuchi Minoru, "Meiji Kangakusha no Chūkoku Kikō," in *Jimbun Gakuhō*, No. 36, 1963, p. 92. Takeuchi quotes an article by Sanetō Keishū, "Ōtō no Raiyū to Nihon Bunjin," contrasting the reception given to Wang T'ao in Japan with the cold treatment Oka Senjin received at times in China.
6. Tsurumi Shunsuke, *Nihon no Hyakunen*, VII I, p. 149.

7. *Chuzan Sonkō*, II, p. 405.
8. Recollections by Kishimoto Saisei in *Kamigata*, No. 81, p. 64.
9. Some Japanese, especially men like Oka Senjin who actually visited China, had long since been disillusioned, whether because of the Chinese addiction to opium or their hidebound attitude towards Confucian learning. (See Takeuchi, pp. 80–90.) But most Japanese still believed China to be a major power as well as the source of their own civilization.
10. Reference is made to the Mound of Ears (*mimizuka*) raised by Hideyoshi in Kyoto from the ears and noses of Chinese soldiers killed in Korea. The poem is found in *Nisshin Sensō Jikki* (henceforth abbreviated *NSJ*), No. 2, p. 83.
11. *Fukuzawa Yukichi Zenshū*, XIV, p. 500.
12. *Uchimura Kanzō Zenshū*, XVI, p. 27.
13. *Ibid.*, p. 35.
14. *Ōgai Zenshū*, bekkan 1, pp. 185–278.
15. Itō Sei, *Meiji Bundan Shi*, III, p. 234.
16. Kunikida, *Aitei Tsūshin*, pp. 62–63.
17. Oka Yasuo, "Nisshin Sensō to Bundan," in *Kokubungaku*, IX, No. 12, p. 14.
18. *Ibid.*
19. *Kyōka Zenshū*, I, pp. 221–2.
20. Emi Suiin, *Jiko Chūshin Meiji Bundan Shi*, p. 202.
21. Takagi, "Shimbun ni arawareta Sensō Bungaku," in *Hon no Techō*, No. 46, p. 30.
22. "How delightful it is! How delightful! Oh, how delightful!" etc. *Waseda Bungaku* (henceforth abbreviated *WB*), No. 69, p. 250. Pagination of the first series of this periodical is maddening. Anyone who does not find a reference the first time is respectfully urged to persist.
23. *WB*, No. 70, p. 269.
24. Demetrius C. Boulger, "The Corean Crisis," in *Nineteenth Century*, Nov. 1894, pp. 782–3.
25. *The Spectator*, August 4, 1894, pp. 132–3.
26. *The Illustrated London News*, October 20, 1894, p. 491.
27. Soeda Tomomichi, *Enka no Meiji Taishō Shi*, p. 62. It may be wondered what the Koreans thought of the high ideals expressed by the Japanese. One observer declared, "It is remarkable that the Coreans themselves appear to be unanimously on the side of the Chinese, whose wickedness in upholding the present regime is so loudly condemned." (R. S. Gundry, "Corea, China, and Japan," in *The Fortnightly Review*, No. CCCXXXV. New Series. Nov. 1, 1896, p. 635). But Yi In-jik ,whose story *Hyol ui nu* is considered to mark the beginning of modern Korean fiction, was clearly on the side of the Japanese. Undoubtedly, there were supporters of both sides among the Koreans.
28. In *Shōbō Gunka*, n. p.
29. Hiraizumi Toyohiko, "Nisshin Sensō no koro," in *Kamigata*, No. 81, p. 63.
30. *WB*, No. 71, p. 282.
31. *Chuzan Sonkō*, II, p. 271. Toyama's song *Yuke Nihon Danji* contains some of the most sensational anti-Chinese sentiments. He calls the Chinese "evil monsters," "burglars," "wolves," "the enemy of our mothers, the enemy of our wives, the enemy of our sisters and daughters," and urges that "the pure blood of the divine land not be defiled by the beasts of the enemy country." (*Rikkai Gunka Zenshū*, pp. 24–5.) These are rather strong views for a man who four years earlier had considered the Chinese and Japanese to be "elder and younger brothers."
32. *Nisshin Kōsenroku* (henceforth abbreviated *NK*), No. 13, p. 50. The extraordinary importance of the war songs at this time has been likened to the sung narrations of the *Heike Monogatari* or *Taiheiki* in medieval Japan. (Fukuchi Shigetaka, *Gunkoku Nihon no Keisei*, p. 172.) The songs swept the country, fostered perhaps by the advances in printing.
33. Lafcadio Hearn, *Kokoro*, p. 91.

34. *WB*, No. 3, (Second Series), p. 149.

35. *WB*, No. 75, pp. 54-5.

36. *Ibid.*

37. Shimazaki Tōson, *Haru*, (Shinchō Bunko, 1933), p. 233.

38. Tanizaki Junichirō, *Yōshō Jidai*, pp. 97-8.

39. *NK*, No. 13, p. 50.

40. In 1896, when the first group of Chinese students arrived in Japan, the taunts of *chankoro* were so offensive that many cut short their stay. (See Sanetō Keishū, *Chūgokujin Nihon Ryūgaku Shi*.)

41. *NK*, No. 10, p. 50.

42. *NSJ*, No. 6, pp. 50-4.

43. *NK*, No. 15, p. 33. See also *NSJ*, No. 9, p. 79.

44. *NSJ*, No. 9, p. 100.

45. A dismally contradictory report on Japanese chivalry may be found in James Allan, *Under the Dragon Flag*, pp. 79-95, where the massacre of Chinese at Port Arthur is described in gory detail. Allan also writes of "placards, in the sacred imperial yellow, inciting these atrocities" committed by the Chinese. "The bodies of the Japanese soldiers, killed in encounters with the enemy as they closed on the place, were often found minus the head or right hand, sometimes both, besides being ferociously gashed and slashed. Corpses were still hanging on the trees when the fortress fell, and it is not surprising that their former comrades should have been maddened by the sight, though of course the officers are greatly to blame for permitting the fearful retaliation which ensued to be carried to such lengths. The massacre seems to have been allowed to continue unchecked until no more victims could be found." (p. 67)

46. Captain Higuchi was celebrated in song (see Horiuchi Keizō, *Ongaku Gojūnen Shi*, p. 159) and in poetry (see *Bungakkai*, No. 29). Eastlake and Yamada, in *Heroic Japan*, head their account of Higuchi's gallant gesture with the title THAT BABY! (pp. 333-4).

47. *Engeki Hyakka Daijiten*, IV, pp. 314-5.

48. *WB*, No. 89, pp. 278-9.

49. Virtually every hero in *Yōchien Shina Seibatsu Tegarabanashi* ("Stories for Kindergarten of Meritorious Deeds During the Conquest of China") is a private.

50. *NK*, No. 32, pp. 27-8.

51. *Shimbun Shūsei Meiji Hennen Shi* (henceforth abbreviated *MHS*), IX, p. 164.

52. *Kamigata*, No. 81, pp. 40-1.

53. Apparently based on the sketch by Kubota Beisen in *Nisshin Sensō Gahō*, II.

54. Mōzeru in the original apparently refers to Julius Mosen. His poem *Der Trompeter an der Katzbach* describes a wounded buglar.

55. Homma Hisao, *Meiji Bungaku Shi*, II, p. 429.

56. *NSJ*, No. 5, p. 78. I have been unable to identify the poet.

57. Hearn, pp. 92-3. There is a fine description in Horiuchi's *Ongaku Gojūnen Shi* (pp. 155-6) of how Katō, on hearing the story of Shirakami Genjirō's bravery, was immediately inspired to write this poem and the accompanying music. After racing around the practice room three times he went inside, picked up a clarinet and started blowing a tune, but his breath gave out. He next tried a baritone trumpet, but again his breath failed. Finally he scribbled words on a blackboard. Still in a white hot fury of creativity, he persuaded another musician to help him. The music and words were completed in half an hour. The Emperor Meiji was especially fond of this piece, and generally had it played for him by a military band every evening after dinner.

58. Sir Edwin Arnold, *The Tenth Muse*, pp. 151-9. The poem bears the note, "Extract translated from letter of an officer in Marshal Yamagata's Corean Army: 'I send you the enclosed true account of the death of Shirakami Genjirō, a young soldier, who was the first man killed at our battle of Song-hwan.'"

F. Schroeder also wrote a long poem in English on Shirakami Genjirō entitled, "The Bugler of Soeng-hwan." It is dated October 13, 1894. The fifth stanza is typical:

Another rush, as again rings the signal:
Advance, ad—! What is that, out of breath, little Gen?
We look back, he totters, yet his lips to his bugle:
Ad—vance!—Why, your bugle is red, little Gen!

(From Schroeder, *Eastern World*, p. 75.)

59. *Chuzan Sonkō*, II, p. 309.
60. Hirano Sanjirō in *Kamigata*, No. 81, p. 27.
61. *Nihon Kyōkasho Taikei*, Kindai Hen, V, p. 769.
62. F. Warrington Eastlake and Yamada Yoshiaki, *Heroic Japan*, p. 23.
63. Muneta Hiroshi (in *Heitai Hyakunen*, pp. 73-4) describes how, even as the memorial to the gallant Shirakami was being erected in his native village, the news came that Kiguchi and not Shirakami had been the loyal bugler. Muneta offers no explanation of how it was discovered which of two buglers, both from Okayama, and both killed on the same day in the same action, had kept bugling to the death.
64. Karasawa Tomitarō, *Kyōkasho no Rekishi*, p. 259.
65. *Ibid.*, pp. 342, 365.
66. *Ibid.*, p. 673.
67. Soeda, p. 64.
68. Eastlake and Yamada, pp. 54-5.
69. The story of Matsumura Akitarō is told at some length, but with evident embellishments, by Muneta, pp. 109-114. According to Muneta, Matsumura died in 1945 at the age of 78, revealing his story only to his children and grandchildren, with the warning they must never pass it on. See also Soeda, p. 65.
70. *Kamigata*, No. 81, p. 41.
71. *MHS*, IX, p. 149.
72. *Rikkai Gunka Zenshū*, p. 97.
73. Hearn, p. 90.
74. *WB*, No. 69, pp. 249-50.
75. Oka, p. 13.
76. Akiba Tarō, *Nihon Shingeki Shi*, I, p. 303.
77. *Ibid.*, p. 269.
78. Manuscript in Engeki Hakubutsukan at Waseda University.
79. *MHS*, IX, p. 174.
80. *WB*, No. 70, pp. 268-9.
81. Kawatake Shigetoshi, *Nihon Engeki Zenshi*, p. 856.
82. *Ibid.*, pp. 856-7.
83. *Kamigata*, No. 82, p. 22.
84. *WB*, No. 78, p. 257.
85. Yanagisawa Hideki, *Hōshō Kurō Den*, p. 74.
86. James Wheeler Davidson, *The Island of Formosa*, gives some examples. See also *Nisshin Sensō Gahō*, VI.
87. *NK*, No. 36, pp. 65-6. A Japanese officer, describing things which surprised him most in China, mentions the large number of Japanese prints he found.
88. Asakura Haruhiko and Imamura Tetsugen, *Meiji Sesō Hennen Jiten*, p. 373.
89. Yoshida Susugu, *Kiyochika*, pp. 224-5.
90. *Ibid.*, p. 229.
91. *Ibid.*, p. 223. See also Higuchi Hiroshi, *Bakumatsu Meiji no Ukiyoe Shūsei*, p. 63.
92. Yoshida, p. 262.
93. Kumamoto Ken, *Kuroda Seiki Sakuhin Shū*, p. 28.
94. Hearn, p. 89.

95. The war figures in a subordinate role in some more famous works of fiction, such as *Hototogisu* by Tokutomi Kenjirō.

96. Quoted from Kōsaka, *Japanese Thought in the Meiji Era*, translated by Abosch, pp. 266–7. The original may be found in *Bungakkai*, No. 24, Dec. 30, 1894, pp. 35–6. Hirata also states, "We cannot but admire the deed of the brave man who opened the Gembu Gate, and we cannot but think of the hardships encountered by our soldiers on distant expeditions, who tread dangerous ground and brave many difficulties, and there is no reason why literary men cannot turn their thoughts to these heroes and express in writing their poetic emotions. However, a new domain for poetry and literary prose cannot be opened in a day."

97. Summaries of some of the arguments on reform of the Japanese language published at the time may be found in Kikuzawa Sueo, *Kokuji Mondai no Kenkyū*, pp. 78–9. The necessity of language reform as the main task facing writers was the theme of many articles. Tsubouchi Shōyō declared the two urgent questions facing literary men were: (1) what to do about Japanese grammar; and (2) what to do about the writing of Japanese. ("Shin Bundan no Ni Daimondai," in *Shōyō Senshū*, XI, pp. 537–72.) The desirability of using modern language (*kōgo*) was urged by such men as Nakamura Akika ("Shokan Buntai wa kyōsei sezaru bekarazu," in *Taiyō*, I, No. 10, p. 32–7), who objected particularly to *sōrōbun* as being like "using bows and arrows in present-day warfare."

98. *WB*, Jan. 1896, p. 35.

99. *WB*, No. 88, p. 260.

100. *MHS*, IX, p. 287.

101. Hisamatsu Sen'ichi and Yoshida Seiichi, *Kindai Nihon Bungaku Jiten*, p. 287.

102. Ibid.

103. Yoshikawa Kōjirō, *Jusha no Kotoba*, p. 90.

104. *WB*, No. 89, p. 284.

105. *NK*, No. 38, p. 70.

106. *MHS*, IX, p. 369.

107. *The Spectator*, Sept. 1, 1894, p. 263.

108. Okakura Kakuzō, *The Book of Tea*, p. 7.

109. *Hōgetsu Zenshū*, II, pp. 301–2.

Japanese Writers and the Greater East Asia War

JAPANESE literature of the war years (1941–45) has hardly been discussed abroad, and in Japan the tendency, until very recently, was to dismiss the entire production as "sterile," or even to deny that any existed. Obviously more than strictly literary criteria have occasioned this reluctance to consider a most important though painful period in modern Japanese writing. Foreign scholars have hesitated to uncover dirty linen; the Japanese, embarrassed by old remembrances, naturally prefer to allude to the war in terms of its suffering, rather than in terms of the joy which most people had experienced when sharing certain ideals. On occasion, polemicists have attempted to discredit an opponent by quoting his wartime publications, but the sting of their attacks is dulled by the unspoken awareness that almost everybody was involved and, if guilty, equally so.

Contrary to the impression sometimes created by Japanese who are anxious to gloss over the war years, the members of the literary profession were at the outbreak of war almost solidly united behind the militarists. They exulted in the triumphs of the first year, and urged redoubled efforts when the ominous signs of reverses appeared. Only when Japan's defeat became imminent did some writers lose their enthusiasm, though others whipped themselves to an even more frenzied patriotism. There was no resistance to the militarists save for the negative action of a few authors, mainly older men, who refrained from publishing. Some left-wing writers were rounded up by the government immediately after the outbreak of war in December 1941; this fact is well-publicized, though it is less commonly known that, unlike their counterparts in certain European countries, Japanese writers were not executed or left to die of maltreatment in prison. With a few exceptions, those imprisoned in December 1941, were released shortly afterwards on their avowal that they had changed their political views. Most of the released men cooperated with the government during the war in the manner required of all writers.

Some Japanese critics, inspired by accounts of the French resistance, have attempted to prove that the Japanese writers also resisted. At times one cannot be sure. As one critic pointed out in 1958, the vagueness of the Japanese language is such that poems which thirteen years earlier had seemed pro-war could also be interpreted as anti-war.[1] The fact remains that there were no martyrs. Famous liberal or leftist writers confessed their sins, joined the patriotic organizations of writers with desperate eagerness (hoping thereby to escape suspicion),[2] and when the defeat came found few occasions to remember their wartime literary productions. Any parallel with the French resistance is, of course, misleading. Japan was not occupied by a foreign power during the war, nor was there a "free Japan" movement of any consequence. Unlike some Germans and Italians, moreover, no important Japanese writer took refuge abroad rather than live under a hated government; it was obviously much harder for a Japanese to escape to a foreign country than for a German or an Italian, and the Japanese had no tradition of becoming refugees. If we compare wartime literary production in Japan with that in America or England, on the other hand, we find that in the latter countries few first-rate authors engaged in specifically patriotic writing for a domestic audience.[3] In Japan, many excellent writers of prose and poetry were to publish vituperation.

The attack on Pearl Harbor on December 7, 1941, (December 8 by Japanese reckoning) was the climax of many events, and to discuss fully the literature produced at the outbreak of war it would clearly be necessary to go back years earlier. In view of the limited scope of this essay, however, I shall arbitrarily start with the day on which war was declared. The newspapers, predictably, were at once filled with impressions and reflections by literary men, and the monthly magazines followed suit. The tone of these pieces was in every instance that of exhilaration, involving frequent repetition of such expressions as "deep emotion" (*kangeki*), "tears of thanks" (*kanrui*), and "feelings of refreshment" (*harebare shita kimochi*). Nakano Yoshio, who after the war served as editor of the left-wing journal *Heiwa* (Peace), wrote, "The writer, whether he likes it or not, automatically stands at the front lines of ideological warfare."[4]

Most literary men welcomed the opportunity to relate the powerful emotions which had surged within them on hearing that war had been declared. It may be wondered what choice they had. With the exception of a handful of well-established authors who could live on the royalties from reprints of old works (or on the generosity of their publishers), Japanese writers had no alternative but to attempt to make a living by publishing stories or articles, and all publications were controlled by the government. Moreover, the growth in importance of the writers as public figures during the twenties and thirties meant that their opinions were constantly requested, even on non-literary matters. It was considered normal, for example, that a poet and novelist like Satō Haruo should deliver pronouncements on the military situation in the Philippines, though his knowledge of the subject was derived entirely from the press. It would have been difficult for a Japanese author to refuse to comment on an issue on the grounds that he was not sufficiently informed. No doubt some writers who expressed themselves so joyously on December 8 and later feared that unless they appeared enthusiastic they might fall under suspicion of harboring dangerous thoughts, but most of the wartime comments have an unmistakable ring of sincerity. Once the war began, the Japanese writers, with extremely few exceptions, became Japanese first and men of letters second.

The excitement and even relief with which writers greeted the news of Pearl Harbor are easily understandable. After a long period of inconclusive hostilities in China, the total war which most people had expected had at last begun, bringing a sense of relief that the uncertainties were over. For the relatively few writers of pronouncedly right-wing beliefs, the war represented a logical development in the sacred mission of the Japanese people; the more numerous left-wing writers could take comfort in the hope that the war would bring an end to colonialism and the influence of the white man in Asia, and possibly to the capitalist system as it had existed in Japan. Only the writers deeply imbued with European culture had any strong predisposition to oppose the war, though it should be noted that some authors who had lived many years abroad, possibly because of the discrimination they had encountered there, were among the most vociferous of the xenophobes.

The patriotic effusions even of relatively unknown writers continued to be in demand throughout the war—at least the magazines continued to print them, even if the public by the end was weary of the constant exhortations. It would be possible to cite inflammatory writings by almost every recognized author, but the endless cries for the annihilation of America and England are repetitious, and I have therefore made a selection only, intended in part to show how Japanese who originally held many different views came to voice the official, militaristic doctrines. I realize that it is unfair to single out some men by name, for this implies that these writers were more nationalistic than others, though in reality almost every articulate man from the outbreak of the war furiously penned emotional compositions; but unless I mention the actual names it will not be possible to gauge the magnitude of the literary reaction. I earnestly request, however, that it be remembered that *almost everyone was involved*.

Naturally, no hesitancy was expressed about the desirability of the war. Few men, for that matter, chose to be silent. As far as I am aware, no writer was ever punished for his silence, but no one could be sure in advance of this immunity. Many Japanese now excuse their wartime publications by saying, "At the time you had no choice but to write that way." The distinguished novelist and critic Itō Sei, one of those who have thus explained views to which they do not now subscribe, wrote in the newspaper *Miyako Shimbun* soon after the outbreak of war, "This war is an absolute act. It is not merely an extension of politics or the reverse side of politics. It is a struggle which the Yamato people had some day to fight in order to convince themselves from the bottom of their hearts that they are the most excellent people on the face of the globe. We are the 'yellow race' our enemies talk about. We are fighting to determine the superiority or inferiority of the discriminated-against peoples. Our struggle is not the same as Germany's. . . ."[5] Itō described his feelings on first hearing the declaration of war: "I felt as if in one stroke I had become a new man, from the depths of my being." Light with exhilaration, he rushed off to share in the excitement of the city, too overwrought to return home to his family.[6]

Numerous other writers of many shades of political belief echoed Itō's enthusiasm. The novelist and noted champion of liberal causes, Hirotsu Kazuo, related his surprise on discovering how light and cheerful he had become, though he had always imagined that the outbreak of war with America would depress him.[7] Aono Suekichi, long a pillar of "progressive" literary criticism, felt his heart pound with emotion at the news. Before the grand scale of the Japanese military strategy, America and England seemed small. "A people like ours with an Imperial Army which can be trusted absolutely is fortunate indeed. I realized afresh what a great country Japan is."[8] The ex-soldier and chronicler of army life, Hino Ashihei, who was to emerge as the most prominent writer of wartime Japan, reported that he was overcome while listening to the radio by a vision of gods advancing in the skies of Eastern Asia. "I am sure that I was not alone in this emotion. . . . Was there anyone, I wonder, who did not weep with emotion on hearing the Rescript announcing the declaration of war?"[9]

The novelist Nakamura Murao was certain that the Imperial Army, never vanquished in its long history, would smash any enemy. He declared his belief that the Japanese were charged with the duty of carrying out the sacred mission of their holy ruler, the descendant of an unbroken line of ten thousand generations.[10] The conservative Nagayo Yoshio, known for his novel *The Bronze Christ*, wrote, "I never thought that in this lifetime I should ever know such a happy, thrilling, auspicious experience."[11]

He felt as if the dark clouds which had hung over Japan for months, if not years, had been dispersed by the proclamation of war. Many others expressed their delight in the clearing of the air. The doubts of Honda Akira, a noted critic and scholar of English literature, were swept away: "I believe that not only I, but the entire Japanese people, have felt this sense of a clearing. Now the meaning of the words 'holy war' is obvious, and our war goals are pellucidly apparent. A new courage has welled up, and everything has become easier to do."[12] The novelist Mushakōji Saneatsu, known as a Tolstoian Christian and believer in neighborly love, rejoiced at the outbreak of war, seeing in it the opportunity for Asians to wrest back control of Asia from the hands of the Europeans and Americans. He wrote, "What fools Roosevelt, Churchill, and Secretary of State Hull are! It is not to be wondered at that the English and American peoples are unaware of the danger of taking on Japan as an enemy, but for those responsible to be ignorant of it is the height of folly." Mushakōji was to continue until the end of the war decrying the incredible stupidity of Japan's enemies.[13] The eminent novelist Yokomitsu Riichi, who by this time had become reactionary in his political outlook, recorded in his diary, "The war has at last begun, with a great victory. A people which believed that its ancestors are gods has triumphed. I felt something more than mere wonder. What was to happen has happened. That is most natural. When I was in Paris I worshiped the Great Shrine of Ise every night, and at last its power stands revealed."[14]

When we turn to the poetry which celebrated the beginning of the holy war, we move into a domain of even greater emotional intensity. Takamura Kōtarō, who throughout the war kept up a steady outpouring of patriotic poems, often highly xenophobic in content, began his poem "December 8th" in typical terms:

> Remember December eighth!
> On this day the history of the world was changed.
> The Anglo-Saxon powers
> On this day were repulsed on Asian land and sea.
> It was their *Japan* which repulsed them,
> A tiny country in the Eastern Sea,
> Nippon, the Land of the Gods
> Ruled over by a living god.[15]

The *tanka* poets became the most vocal spokesmen of the extreme right. Saitō Ryū, a former general who had participated in the Tsinan Incident and the Army officers' coup of February 26, 1936, published his superpatriotic *tanka* in general as well as literary magazines. His *tanka* on December eighth later served as the theme of a whole volume of poems:

Beiei wo	The time has come
hōmuru toki kite	To slaughter America and England;
ana sugashi	Ah, how refreshing:
shiten ichiji ni	The clouds in the four heavens
kumo harenikeri	Have simultaneously cleared.[16]

Saitō Ryū, together with other *tanka* poets, formed the Dainihon Kajin Kyōkai (Great Japan Tanka Poets Association) which was to attack such varying targets as "art for art's sake," freedom, Communism, and individualism. Not surprisingly in a military man, Saitō sang the glories of war:

katsu to kimete	The cheerfulness
tatakau hei no	Of the soldier who fights
hogarakasa	Certain of victory—
tama ni atarishi	Even when struck by a bullet,
toki mo emitsutsu	He still goes on smiling.[17]

Saitō Mokichi, the doyen of *tanka* poets, contributed his share of verse in celebration of the attack on Pearl Harbor, but his *tanka* are hardly more than slogans versified. His diary entry is more striking. "The Empire yesterday opened war on America and England. My aged blood danced. . . . In the afternoon I worshipped at the Meiji Shrine. I met Prime Minister Tōjō and the Naval Minister."[18] Kawada Jun, another leading *tanka* poet, composed a somewhat bewildering verse:

tsui ni sono	At last, they have
kamen nugisute	Discarded their masks
kiba wo muku	And bared their fangs:
Igirisu yakko	The English villains,
Amerika yakko	The American villains.[19]

During the war the *tanka* was exalted as the purest expression of the Japanese soul. However, the *tanka* of the tenth-century anthology *Kokinshū* or of the thirteenth-century anthology *Shin-Kokinshū* are more concerned with tender passions than with brave deeds, and these collections were therefore not so highly considered as the eighth-century *Manyōshū*, famed for its simple, manly spirit. The career and martial poetry of the thirteenth-century ruler Sanetomo also attracted the attention of a mystifying variety of authors, including not only the *tanka* poets, but the novelist

Dazai Osamu and the critic Kobayashi Hideo. The revival of the *tanka* during the war assumed such proportions that the stigma of ultranationalism has clung to the form ever since.

The victories of early 1942 occasioned innumerable commemorative *tanka* as well as longer poems. The fall of Singapore, marking the apogee of Japanese military glory, was an especially popular subject. Saitō Fumi, the daughter of General Saitō and an important *tanka* poet in her own right, celebrated the event:

hyaku nijū	The flames that burn
yo nen no aku wo	Purging away more than
kiyomuru to	One hundred twenty
moeshi honō ga	Years of wickedness,
yo mo hi mo yamazu	Do not cease, night or day.[20]

The great novelist Shiga Naoya, long associated with Mushakōji Saneatsu in his idealistic, quasi-Christian philosophy, introduced a note of restraint into his jubilant account of the fall of Singapore: "The unquestionable supremacy of the Japanese Army, both spiritually and technically, has astonished even the Japanese ever since the outbreak of war, but we cannot but feel humble when we reflect that a large measure of our victories, reported in such numbers that we cannot fully absorb their magnitude, is due to the blessings of Heaven. The conviction that 'Heaven is with us' makes us feel all the more humble."[21]

Almost all varieties of traditional literary forms shared the wartime boom of the *tanka*, though the *haiku*, possibly because it was considered insufficiently dignified to report the glories of the war, tended to be left out of the limelight. The Nō dramas came in for new attention as works on such themes as the fall of Rangoon were composed. *Yamada Nagamasa* by Kobayashi Shizuo, the distinguished scholar of Nō, tells of the seventeenth-century Japanese adventurer who rose to power in Siam, the scene of the action. Yamada Nagamasa, the protagonist (*shite*), appears in the latter part of the play as a ghost in armor and relates his story to the inevitable priest. "When peace came to Japan I thought that I would have no opportunity to display my talents. I decided to go abroad with my great ambitions and reveal to foreigners the prowess of a Japanese man. I mounted a cloud in the wind and crossed to this country. . . ." Nagamasa's son enters at the end of the play to report that the Imperial Army, advancing with irresistible force, has captured Rangoon. Nagamasa, delighted, resolves to lend his strength to the holy war for the liberation of the Asian peoples. "Now the light of the Land of the Gods, which grows ever more brilliant, will shine to all directions. Ah, how happy this makes me!" But hardly has he pronounced these words than, in the fashion of ghosts in Nō plays, he fades away.[22]

Toki Zemmaro, a well-known poet, wrote a series of Nō plays exalting (or condemning) such famous historical figures as Prince Shōtoku, Dōkyō, the popular Sanetomo, and Kublai Khan, the last in a drama on the *kamikaze*.[23] These works, heavily laden with patriotic and particularly Emperor-worshipping sentiments, were skilfully written but too obviously inspired by non-literary motives. An even more conspicuously propagandistic work, *Miikusabune* ("Imperial Warship") by a submarine officer, Ensign Sako, enjoyed popularity not only on the Nō stage but as a *Sprechchor* in the modern theatre.[24]

Kyōgen, the medieval farces which accompanied the Nō plays, also enjoyed a wartime revival. Among the modern works composed were *Takara no Shima* ("Treasure Island") by Matsuno Sōfū, and *Arawashi* ("The Fierce Eagle") by Miyake Tōkurō.[25] "Treasure Island" tells of two demons, Eiki (English Devil) and Beiki (American Devil), who attempt unsuccessfully to steal some honey, the treasure of the island. Eiki introduces himself, "I am a devil who comes from the distant western end of the world. I grew up on an island, but it became too small for me, and that is why I have seized one island after another ever since, and bloated myself on its treasures. I have gobbled up all the islands in the West, and I intend to go now to the East and swallow up the islands there. I shall take the young devil Beiki along with me. He is another greedy devil and seems to have his eye on the eastern islands. It may prove too difficult if I go alone. . . ." Eiki and Beiki eventually reach the island, but the guardian foils their attempt to steal the honey, and instead sets swarms of bees to sting them.

The name of the other *kyōgen*, *The Fierce Eagle*, was a wartime epithet of Japanese aviators, and the comedy here lies in the contrast between the attitudes of the courageous Japanese aviators and the cowardly Americans. The play takes place in the palace of the Dragon King of the Sea. The king has decided to entertain heroes who have died in the war and sunk to the bottom of the ocean. He receives the protagonist Makewashi (Defeated Eagle), an American aviator shot down by the Japanese, who pretends he is a hero, credited with sinking over fifty enemy ships and seriously damaging seven or eight hundred more. The Dragon King assumes that such a great hero must be Japanese, and Makewashi tries to live up to the role. But when drunk on the Dragon King's saké, he breaks down in tears, saying, "I want to go back home. I miss my girl friend.

I want to dance with her." The Dragon King's suspicions are aroused, and his servant discovers that the so-called Fierce Eagle has American insignia on his *obi*. Makewashi is chased from the palace to the traditional *kyōgen* cries of *yarumai zo* (you won't get away with it!). These *kyōgen* were certainly more enjoyable than most wartime literature, but humor was definitely not a major element in the spirit of the Greater East Asian War, and the function of writers as entertainers or spreaders of cheer during the tense war years was rarely considered.

The most important function of the Japanese writers, it would seem, was to encourage by their manifestations of patriotism the morale of other Japanese. One important obligation was to join the Nihon Bungaku Hō-kokukai (Japanese Literature Patriotic Association). This organization, founded on May 26, 1942, was directly under the Intelligence Agency, and was considered to be a governmental body. Its officers included many outstanding men of letters, and the various sub-sections of *tanka* and *haiku* poets, dramatists, essayists, etc., were headed by leaders in each field.[26] Writers of every political affiliation joined, those of the left (like the poet Nakano Shigeharu and the woman novelist Miyamoto Yuriko) in the hopes that membership in this patriotic organization would shield them from charges that they had not truly renounced their former Communist beliefs. Some of the converts went even further: Kubokawa Tsurujirō, a long-time proletarian critic, related after the first meeting of the Japanese Literature Patriotic Association, "Nazi Germany drove out the Jews. A Jew may be recognized at a glance, but it is not easy to detect an American, Englishman, or other foreigner who wears the skin of a Japanese. . . . We have no choice but to place absolute confidence in the statement made by the Prime Minister in the Diet that our defenses to the north are firm, but I wonder if our ideological defenses in that direction are equally firm?"[27] "Defenses to the north" could refer only to the danger of an attack from the Soviet Union; it was typical of speakers at meetings of the association to be more anti-Communist than Prime Minister Tōjō.

The April 8, 1943 conference of the association was held on the theme "The Creation of a Literature of Annihilation of America and England" (*Beiei Gekimetsu Bungaku no Sōsaku*). Ishikawa Tatsuzō, whose novella on army life had five years earlier been banned because of its critical tone, called for great novels, like those of Tolstoi or Flaubert, in place of the prevalent autobiographical fiction. He declared, "There is no reason why a people which can conceive the grand ideal of the 'eight corners of the world under one roof' cannot create great literature." He urged the importance of a new, major literature which would describe the building of Japan's Co-Prosperity Sphere in Asia. The next speaker, an obscure teacher of Japanese literature, was determined to outdo Ishikawa; he asserted that Tolstoi's writings were no more than tearful confessions, and suggested that if writers insisted on an accompaniment of tears they should follow the example of the Japanese divinity who flooded the world with his weeping, and not satisfy themselves with mere sentimentality. The noted literary figure Kikuchi Kan, the chairman, praised the speaker for this short but deeply moving statement.[28]

The chief literary accomplishment of the Patriotic Association was the publication in May 1943 of *Aikoku Hyakunin Isshu* (Patriotic Poems by One Hundred Poets), edited by Kawada Jun.[29] The nation was canvassed for suggestions of truly inspiring poems; over 120,000 *tanka* were submitted, including duplicates. The poet Satō Haruo, though approving of the new collection, defended the thirteenth-century *Hyakunin Isshu* from charges that it was sentimental: "If one really understands the true intent of the *Ogura Hyakunin Isshu* one will see that it too is a kind of patriotic anthology. . . . It is true that more than forty of the hundred poems included are love poems, but they actually have a patriotic message."[30] The convenient ambiguity of the Japanese language saved many seemingly frivolous works from the disapproval of the wartime censors.

Another important organization to which many writers belonged was the Daitōa Bungakusha Taikai (Greater East Asia Writers Congress).[31] It held three meetings: in November 1942 and August 1943 in Japan, and in November 1944 in Nanking. At the first session, fifty-seven delegates attended from Japan (including Taiwan and Korea), and twenty-six from Manchuria, Mongolia, and China. The prevailing tone of the congress was set even before it officially opened: on November 1, 1942, as soon as the Manchu, Mongol, and Chinese delegates reached Tokyo, they were ushered to the Imperial Palace and the Meiji Shrine to pay their respects. On the following day they worshipped at the Yasukuni Shrine, sacred to the Japanese war dead. The predominance of Japan and Japanese ideals at this congress of supposed equals was unmistakable. Japanese was the only official language at the sessions; speeches made by Chinese delegates in their own language were interpreted into Japanese, but remarks delivered in Japanese were never interpreted into any other language. The central importance of the Japanese language was insisted on even by the foreign delegates. A Manchurian delegate declared, "Japanese has now become the language of East Asia, and East Asian literature, especially Japanese literature, will now shed its light throughout the world." A

Korean delegate chimed in, "I believe that it is exceedingly important that the Japanese language be widely diffused in order that we may annihilate the policy hitherto adopted by the Americans and English in their colonies of keeping the masses ignorant. We must spread culture to the billion people of East Asia, at the same time disseminating among them the spirit of the foundation of Japan—'the eight corners of the world under one roof.'" A delegate from Taiwan resumed, "Only by knowing the Japanese language may one come in contact with the great spirit of 'the eight corners of the world under one roof,' the guiding principle of East Asia." Messages to this effect were prepared for radio broadcast to Chungking, the Axis Powers, and the United States.

The theme of the second congress was "The Annihilation of America and England and the Activities of Writers." A memorable moment at one session was provided by a returned soldier anxious to remind the writers that the military threat to Japan was even more serious than the threat posed by American and English culture. He declared, "We would have nothing to worry about even if a thousand volumes of the collected works of Shakespeare dropped from the sky, but bombs would be quite a different matter." The eminent critic Kobayashi Hideo delivered an address at this congress which, by its lack of frenzy and his total failure to employ the word "annihilation," stood out from more conventional speeches.[32] Fujita Tokutarō, a scholar of Japanese literature, must have dampened somewhat feelings of brotherhood among the delegates when he launched forth into a blistering attack on any Chinese who dared pronounce the characters for his name in some other fashion than *fuji-ta*.[33]

The Japanese attending the Greater East Asia Writers Congress ranged from the fanatical Fujita and the no less violent Togawa Sadao, the chairman, to men genuinely moved by the ideal of seeing Asian writers united. The famous declaration of Okakura Kakuzō—Asia is one—was quoted *ad nauseam*, and to it was joined the frequently expressed hope that all Asian nations would soon be independent. It seems paradoxical now, but it was normal at the time for the extreme right-wing *tanka* poet Ōta Mizuho to publish in September 1942 a series of poems dedicated to Mahatma Gandhi.[34] Other right-wing zealots inveighed tirelessly against the colonialist, imperialist powers. These political sentiments carried overtones of an anti-white bias.

In the only humorous story I know about the outbreak of war, Dazai Osamu related the reactions of a typical housewife to the news:

At breakfast I asked my husband, "Will Japan really be all right?"

"Do you think we'd have gone to war if everything wasn't all right? We'll win, no doubt about it." The tone of the words, for him, was unnaturally stiff. No matter what my husband says, he invariably turns out to be wrong, and his opinions are not to be relied on. All the same, I decided I would try very hard to believe this one serious thing he has come out with. As I was tidying up the kitchen my mind went over all kinds of things. Can a mere difference in the color of their eyes and hair make me hate our enemies so much? Yes, I wanted to pound them mercilessly. It was different when we were fighting with China. Really, I couldn't stand the thought of nerveless, animal-like American soldiers lumpishly ambling over our dear, beautiful Japanese soil. I wanted to shout, "If you take even one step on this holy soil, your feet will rot away! Our pure Japanese soldiers—please get rid of them somehow!"[35]

Dazai is presumably caricaturing often expressed sentiments, but Hino Ashihei was more serious two years later when he wrote a poem with the lines:

At that time
On a coral reef in the Pacific Ocean
Our guardian warriors
Repulsed and smashed the ugly enemy.
When the voices of the gods cried out in anger,
The swarms of hairy, twisted-nosed savages
Sank and rotted idiotically
In the equatorial waters.
Now the brutal, headstrong enemy,
Panting heavily,
Approaches menacingly the Land of the Gods.[36]

A combination of the brotherhood of Asia and a latent aversion to the non-Asian (as expressed in these selections) united many delegates to the Greater East Asia Writers Congress. For others, it was merely a pleasant occasion to meet writers from abroad.

The varying motives of men within a single organization ostensibly dedicated to war propaganda have recently been discussed by Ōkuma Nobuyuki, one of the directors of Dainihon Genron Hōkokukai (Great Japan Press Patriotic Association) from its inception in 1943. He dispels with a few withering sentences the suggestion made by certain progressive writers that the organization actually served "the resistance"; Ōkuma establishes that it was under direct army control and never dared offer the least criticism, let alone resistance. The task of this association was to carry out ideological investigations against civilians, and the chief preoccupation of the members was how to take over the leading magazines, a dream which they finally realized in the closing days of the war. So much for the alleged resistance. But, Ōkuma points out, the members of the association by no means shared uniform motives. Some were right-wing fanatics, but there were also many intellectuals like Ōkuma himself who were socialists, eager for an end to the capitalist system. Such men believed in the truth of G. B. Shaw's dictum that war promotes socialism. The wartime tightening of the economy seemed to them a rationalization of the existing system and a move towards socialism. Ōkuma believes that the reason why the intellectuals in the organization were hoodwinked by Japanese fascism was that it so much resembled socialism at first contact.[37] Certainly many slogans of the extreme right were readily accepted by writers of entirely different views. It was natural that when the war ended, the disparate groups immediately fell apart.

The attitude of the militarists towards the writers is puzzling. How, for example, could they have trusted the changes of heart professed by their former enemies? Or why, after suppressing several stories by Dazai Osamu, did they permit him to continue publishing, and eventually even commission him to write a novel embodying the ideals of the Greater East Asia Joint Declaration? Dazai's novel *Sekibetsu* ("Regretful Parting"), one of the few works actually commissioned by the government, was an outcome of the Greater East Asia Conference of November 5-6, 1943.[38] This conference, attended by such dignitaries from abroad as Wang Ching-wei, José Laurel, Ba Maw, and Wan Waithayakon, was primarily political, but in its wake the various sections of the Greater East Asia Writers Congress drew up plans for cultural cooperation among the nations represented. It was decided to sponsor major novels by Japanese authors which would embody each of the Five Great Principles, including "Co-Existence and Co-Prosperity," "Independence and Amity," "Economic Prosperity," and so on. Not until January 10, 1945, however, was the final selection of authors determined. Dazai Osamu was chosen to write on the principle "Independence and Amity." The subject was the Chinese novelist Lu Hsün's life as a medical student in northern Japan, tracing the development of his feelings towards Japan from the first frustrations to his gradual discovery that the Japanese possess true compassion and understanding. Lu Hsün is described in the novel as realizing that the deep sense of moral propriety of the Japanese goes back to the Emperor Meiji's Imperial Rescripts on education and the army. Inspired by Japanese example, Lu Hsün gives up his studies in Sendai in order to work for Chinese independence.[39] It is incredible that the Japanese military authorities should have sponsored a novel on Lu Hsün, remembered today for his part in the anti-Japanese struggle, in its program for encouraging friendship for Japan. The choice of Dazai Osamu, an author famed more for his dissipation than for his political reliability, is equally bewildering. Yet when the book was finally published in September 1945, Dazai stated that even if he had not been commissioned, sooner or later he would have wished to treat the theme. In his hands, Lu Hsün emerges as a slightly Sinicized version of Dazai himself, rather than as a pillar of independence and amity.

Apart from commissioning Dazai's novel and the play "Onna no Isshō" ("A Woman's Life") by Morimoto Kaoru,[40] the army recognized the importance of literature by mobilizing writers and sending them to the conquered territories abroad. Again, one is struck by the strange choices of overseas reporters. The progressive critic Nakajima Kenzō was sent to Malaya (along with the apolitical novelist Ibuse Masuji, who spent his time lecturing on the ancient Shinto scriptures); the left-wing critic Shimizu Ikutarō and the ex-Communist novelist Takami Jun went to Burma; the progressive Oya Sōichi and the radical Takeda Rintarō to Java; the conservative Kon Hidemi and the Marxist philosopher Miki Kiyoshi (who in 1945 was arrested and died while imprisoned on charges of pacifism) to the Philippines. Their reports, together with illustrations by well-known artists, regularly appeared in the monthly magazines.[41]

The other side of the army's sponsorship of positive literature was the pressure it exerted against works of a negative nature. The most celebrated instance was that of Tanizaki Junichirō's novel Sasameyuki (The Makioka Sisters). The first two episodes appeared in the January and March 1943 issues of the magazine Chūō Kōron. It was planned to have the novel appear serially every other month, but the May 1943 issue had no episode, and the June issue contained the notice: "Having taken into consideration the possibility that this novel might exert an undesirable influence, in view of present exigencies at this decisive stage of the war, we have regretfully decided from the standpoint of self-discipline to discontinue further publication." The editor, Hatanaka Shigeo, has since related how he was summoned before a board of army officers to explain the publication of Tanizaki's offending novel and one other article. It is not clear what the army would have done if publication of the novel had not been broken off; in view of the general instability of army policies, one abject apology might have satisfied the militarists. But the editors, fearing for the life of their magazine, decided not to take chances.[42] The Makioka Sisters is by no stretch of the imagination an anti-war novel, but the leisurely pace of its descriptions of pre-war Japan exasperated the militarists, who insisted on a positive, exhortatory literature to suit the heroic temper of the times. Needless to say, it was precisely the relaxed, gossipy atmosphere of *The Makioka Sisters* which most appealed to readers, who were exhausted by the resolute attitudes expressed in other fiction at the time.

There was criticism of *The Makioka Sisters* among civilians, even before publication was abandoned. The April 1943 issue of the magazine *Kaizō*, for example, contains a roundtable discussion on literature by a high-powered group of authors: Shiga Naoya, Mushakōji Saneatsu, Kawabata Yasunari, Iwata Toyoo and, inevitably, Hino Ashihei. Hino, asked by a reporter if he had read *The Makioka Sisters*, answered:

> Hino: I'm sure people will take offense if anyone like myself dares to criticize a great senior writer too outspokenly ... (*Laughter*) As I read along I found myself growing irritated, and it took some effort to get through to the end. I have always admired Mr. Tanizaki's writings, but I felt something heavy-handed in the tone of the present book. He describes scenes of *miai*[43] and of women putting on their makeup, worries about a spot under someone's eye which becomes faint and then becomes dark again, says this isn't true or something else is also true, sends his characters to see a doctor. I couldn't get the thought out of my head that it might not be a good thing to write in that way. It may be, of course, that I'm not flexible enough ...
>
> Kawabata: I wonder if Mr. Tanizaki while he was writing felt attracted by the syrupy, sticky quality of the life he describes, or if he wasn't portraying the stupidity of the bourgeois. ... A great many ordinary readers have been fascinated by this book.
>
> Reporter: Don't you think that young people, even though they may be fascinated, have doubts about its propriety?
>
> Kawabata: If the novel causes them to have such doubts, doesn't that prove that it rejects the life it describes? I don't suppose that Mr. Tanizaki, even though he portrays that way of life, intends to encourage it. I am sure that he himself is quite concerned over this.
>
> Shiga: That's right.
>
> Hino: Do you think so?[44]

It is impossible to be sure whether Kawabata spoke sincerely or if he was attempting to protect Tanizaki. In either case, his attitude seems more praiseworthy than Hino's indirect slurs on the novel. As for Tanizaki, he abandoned writing for general publication altogether, once publication of his book in *Chūō Kōron* became impossible; this was the only form of resistance possible. He continued, however, to write *The Makioka Sisters*, publishing the first volume privately, with money from *Chūō Kōron*, in July 1944. The government made no trouble for him.

The other writer often praised for his silent protest against the militarists was Nagai Kafū. His wartime diaries are filled with probably the most bitter and pointed criticism of the military recorded by anyone in Japan. Even his diary entry for December 8, 1941, a time when other writers were yielding to paroxysms of emotion, has an appealingly cynical coolness: "While I was eating in a Ginza restaurant there was blackout control, and all the street and shop lights were extinguished. The streetcars and cars kept their lights on. Later, when I boarded the Roppongi streetcar, jammed as usual, there was a patriot in the crowd who delivered an oration in an ear-splitting voice." Kafū noted in his diaries every rumor of disaster, every instance he heard of cruelty or corruption on the part of the military. His dislike of the militarists at times seems no more than annoyance over wartime shortages of imported goods. When Kafū learned, for example, that writing brushes made of imported Chinese bristles were no longer available, he gloomily asserted, "The collapse of Japanese civilization is at hand."[45] Again, when he took stock and discovered that he had only one remaining bottle of wine, five or six cakes of English soap, and a little Lipton's tea, he lamented, "How long will the benighted customs of the days when the country was closed and barbarians expelled (sakoku jōi) persist?"[46] But Kafū's anger went much deeper than such irritation: "The actions of the militarists' government in recent years have been without exception stupid and vulgar, regardless of the greatness or smallness of the issue. They have done almost nothing to maintain the national dignity. Japanese history is not without barbarous governments, but I know of no instance of such base and foolish policies as those in practice in Japan today."[47] At one point Kafū turned to reading the Bible (in French translation), not because he planned to become a Christian, but because of Christianity's advocacy of the victory of the weak over the oppression of the strong. The Christian teachings, he noted, had conquered all Europe without the use of force—quite a different matter from the Japanese invasions of China and the islands of the South Seas.[48] In his last diary entry for 1943, he bitterly complained that the poison of dictatorial government had extended to every section of society; at the end of 1944 he recorded, "The nineteenth year of Shōwa is ending and a bleak new year is about to begin. The present sorry state of affairs is unprecedented in all Japanese history, and we have only the militarists to thank for it. Their guilt must be recorded forever."[49]

Kafū did not write for publication during the war years. He lived on his savings, royalties from earlier works, and the generosity of friends. He engaged in no specifically patriotic activity; he immediately sold the war bonds he was obliged to purchase, and when urged to join the Japan Writers Patriotic Association, he threw away the letter without answering it. He freely entrusted his thoughts to his diary, apparently not worried by the prospect that his house might be searched and his harsh criticisms of the government uncovered.[50] Writing his diary, indeed, became almost his only reason for living during the terrible days of the war; he was thrice bombed out of his lodgings and escaped only with the diary, which he kept in readiness by his pillow. The impression of Kafū one receives from his diary is of a thoroughly civilized man. His absolute integrity is all the more noteworthy because of the rareness of this quality in wartime Japan.

The novelist Takami Jun noted in his diary shortly before the war ended that not one literary man had died for the sake of freedom of speech. He himself had been intimidated by the fear of being silenced by the government, but this had never happened. Instead, he had written "compromise" works, for which he now felt ashamed.[51] As the war entered its last stages and the inevitability of Japan's defeat became apparent, other writers who had compromised with the militarists undoubtedly regretted their choice.

But there were many too who remained fervently patriotic to the end. The magazines month after month were filled with ultranationalist poetry and prose, and with inflammatory denunciations of America and England, or even of all Western culture.[52] Writers associated with the traditional literary arts were especially given to extreme opinions. Many magazines were forced out of business by government regulations in the latter part of the war, but an obscure journal devoted to the puppet theatre (*jōruri*) was allowed to continue, no doubt because the government favored this uniquely Japanese art. The editor of the magazine, gratified, took an unusually hard line: "We have reached a stage of confrontation in a decisive battle where everything is at stake in the bitter struggle for survival. All Imperial subjects, and especially men of the *jōruri*, must therefore, as their first task, drive the English language and English writings from our country, annihilate its sounds and music, and advance wholeheartedly with the pure Yamato sounds."[53] The December 1944 issue of *Araragi*, the principal *tanka* journal, featured a patriotic editorial by Saitō Mokichi including: "The July 20th incident—the attempted assassination of the Reichsfuhrer Adolf Hitler, has caused us all extreme concern. Why should the Germans, whom we have all trusted, have done such a thing? It is really most upsetting. . . . Even supposing Hitler lacks military genius, the assassins *should have realized what would happen to Germany if they succeeded in killing the Führer.*" By comparison, the *haiku* journal *Hototogisu* showed extraordinary restraint.

The last months of the war produced many panegyrics of the kamikaze aviators, violent denunciations of pessimism by Satō Haruo, Mushakōji Saneatsu, and others, and much show of bravado or indifference to American air attacks. The poetry especially reached feverish pitches of hatred. "An Oath" by Tanaka Katsumi, printed in the March 1945 issue of *Bungei Shunjū*, climaxed a series of imprecations against the Americans with the lines:

> Villains who, after the defeat at Pearl Harbor,
> Chopped down the Japanese cherry trees which bloomed in Washington.[54]

In the next issue of *Bungei Shunjū*, published after the end of the war in October 1945, Kikuchi Kan, the editor, sadly recounted his difficulties with the military, who had wielded life-and-death powers over all writers. His conclusion, however, was that the military had been able to exert these arbitrary powers because of the mental laxity of the Japanese and their overeagerness to follow any strong authority. Kikuchi Kan's wartime activities do not suggest that he entertained serious doubts about the imperial mission, nor that he obeyed the military authorities only out of desperate necessity. His swift disillusion was, however, typical of many writers. The poet Takamura Kōtarō, who even after the end of the war had published a dire warning that if the Americans dared lay a finger on the Emperor, the Japanese people would to a man defend him to the death, before long wrote a poem declaring that the Imperial Army and not the wicked enemy had deceived the Japanese.[55] Writers of the left were even quicker to renounce their wartime conversions.

The question remains as to the moral propriety of the course followed during the war by Japanese writers. Granted that, like all Japanese, they had certain duties as citizens, did these extend to highly emotional utterances on the sacred Japanese mission? Could the pressures of war excuse, say, this poem by Noguchi Yonejirō?

Slaughter Them! The Americans and English Are Our Enemies

The town overflows with the cry,
"Slaughter them! The Americans and English are our enemies."
I too shout it. I shout till my voice is hoarse. I shout in tears.
These were the countries which nurtured me for twelve years
    when I was young.
Even an act of ingratitude cannot be reckoned against a nation's fate;

The ties of the past are a dream.
America and England in the old days were for me countries of justice:
America was the country of Whitman,
England the country of Browning;
But now they are dissolute countries fallen into the pit of wealth,
Immoral countries, craving after unpardonable dreams. . . .
Some say that Heaven is punishing lawlessness, that this is no
    slaughter of the real America and England.
I made many friends when I lived in America and England:
Some are already dead and never had to hear my cries of "Slaughter
    them!"
How much their happiness is my happiness I cannot tell.
    Those friends who are still alive will probably say to me,
"This is a war between country and country. Our friendship is too
    sacred to be destroyed."
What foolishness! The united Japanese millions will not accept
    such pious palaver.
This is all-out, all-out:
We'll show you how decisively we slaughter you, friendship and all![56]

This poem leaves a bad taste in the mouth, particularly because it was written by a man who had long lived abroad and even won something of a reputation for his exquisite little lyrics in English. Perhaps it is too much to ask of anyone that he should openly have resisted, when to resist invited death, but the attitudes displayed by Noguchi and many other Japanese writers bring to mind the judgment of Laurens van der Post, writing of Japanese military men he had known in Java: "They thought they were performing their duty nobly, beautifully and justly. Yet they were doing the opposite and doing it because their awareness of themselves, and of life, was inadequate."[57]

I should like in conclusion, however, to emphasize one point: I do not believe that the behavior of writers in Japan during the war necessarily reflects tradition or national psyche. During the Russo-Japanese War writers behaved quite differently; hardly any war literature was produced until afterwards, when disillusion had already set in. The Japanese of 1905–6 were certainly less given to war fever than the Americans of 1917. The vastly inflated importance of the writer in the Japan of 1941, the product of the mass media, had forced him into the position of having to be a leader of patriotic activity, and thereby deprived him of the freedom enjoyed by his predecessors of 1905–6. The writer, by becoming a public figure, was under pressure to act with the uniformity expected of all Japanese, and forfeited his right to the individual conscience of the artist. If this analysis is correct, the Japanese literature composed during the

Greater East Asia War should serve as a warning of the dangers facing writers anywhere in the world when they forget that they have obligations not only to their country but their art.

NOTES

1. Sasaki Motoichi, "Gendai tanka wa dō naru ka" ["What will happen to the modern tanka?"], *Tanka Kenkyū*, XV (Jan. 1958), 112–13.
2. Hirano Ken, "Nihon Bungaku Hōkokukai no seiritsu" ["The Establishment of the Japanese Literature Patriotic Association"], *Bungaku*, XXIX (May 1961), 6.
3. I leafed through wartime issues of three important American literary periodicals, *Harper's*, *Nation*, and *New Yorker* (roughly paralled to *Bungei Shunjū*, *Kaizō*, and *Shinchō*), but found no "patriotic" poetry or prose of the kind which regularly appeared in the best Japanese magazines.
4. Odagiri Susumu, "Zoku jūnigatsu yōka no kiroku" ["A Record of December Eighth, Continued"], *Bungaku*, XXX (April 1962), 104.
5. *Ibid.*, p. 109.
6. Odagiri, "Jūnigatsu yōka no kiroku" ["A Record of December Eighth"], *Bungaku*, XXIX (Dec. 1961), 142.
7. "Zoku jūnigatsu," p. 99.
8. "Jūnigatsu," p. 144.
9. *Ibid.*, pp. 145–6.
10. *Ibid.*, p. 140.
11. *Ibid.*, p. 141.
12. *Ibid.*, p. 133.
13. *Ibid.*, p. 139. See also Mushakōji's article "Shōri e no jikaku" ["An Awakening to Victory"], *Bungei Shunjū*, XXII (Nov. 1944), 10–13.
14. "Jūnigatsu," pp. 148–9.
15. *Takamura Kōtarō Zenshū*, III, 3.
16. Yoneda Toshiaki, "Ichi gunkoku-shugisha to tanka " ["One militarist and the tanka"], *Bungaku*, XXIX (May 1961), 55.
17. *Ibid.*, p. 53.
18. "Jūnigatsu," p. 149.
19. "Zoku jūnigatsu," p. 107.
20. *Bungei Shunjū*, XX (May 1942), 13.
21. *Shiga Naoya Zenshū* (Iwanami Shoten ed.), IX, 104–105.
22. *Kanze*, XIII (April 1942), 46–53.
23. Toki Zemmaro, *Nōgaku Shinraishō*, contains five of his modern Nō plays. *Genkō*, on Kublai Khan, appeared in *Nōgaku*, I (Aug. 1944), 18–22.
24. Text in *Kanze*, XIV (May 1943), 2–6. This short work was commissioned by the Japanese Navy and set to music by Kanze Muneie. It was first publicly performed in May 1943 by a brilliant cast including Umewaka Manzaburō as the *shite* (the God of the Equator), and Kanze Tetsunojō as the chief *tsure* (the captain of the warship). The play is devoid of poetry and even of taste, but the presentation in the traditional Nō style apparently produced a powerful impression. Photographs may be found in *Kanze*, XIV (July 1943). For a description of *Sprechchor* performances, see Senda Koreya, "Shingeki to watakushi" ["The Modern Drama and Myself"], *Bungaku*, XXIX (Aug. 1961) 96.
25. Both plays published in *Nōgaku*, I (Sept. 1944).

26. See Hirano, p. 2, for a detailed listing of personnel.

27. Hirano, p. 5.

28. Kubota Masafumi, "Nihon gakugei shimbun wo yomu," *Bungaku*, XXIX (Aug. 1961), 119.

29. The special features of this collection, according to the compiler, were: pure feelings of loyalty, praise of the national polity, and the "basic spirit of our pious ancestors." (Kawada, *Aikoku Hyakunin Isshu Hyōshaku*, p. 25). Poets represented included such atypical "masters" as Sakuma Shōzan, Hayashi Shihei, Hirata Atsutane, and Tokugawa Nariaki.

30. Satō, "*Aikoku hyakunin isshu shōron*" ["A Short Discussion of the *Aikoku Hyakunin Isshu*"], *Kaizō*, XXV (June 1943), 81.

31. See Ozaki Hideki, "Daitōa bungakusha taikai ni tsuite" ["The Greater East Asia Writers Congress"], *Bungaku*, XXIX (May 1961), 9–27.

32. "Bungakusha no teikei ni tsuite" ["On the Cooperation of Writers"], *Kobayashi Hideo Zenshū*, VI, 207–210.

33. Ozaki, p. 22.

34. *Kaizō*, XXIV (Sept. 1942), 123.

35. *Dazai Osamu Zenshū* (Chikuma Shobō ed.), V, 17–18. First published in the February 1942 issue of *Fujin Kōron*.

36. *Haiku Kenkyū*, I (March 1944), 28.

37. Ōkuma Nobuyuki, "Dai Nihon Genron Hōkokukai no ijō seikaku" ["Peculiar Features of the Great Japan Press Patriotic Association"], *Bungaku*, XXIX (Aug. 1961), 6.

38. Text in *Dazai Osamu Zenshū*, VII, 158–270. For the background, see Ozaki Hideki, "Daitōa Kyōdō Sengen to futatsu no sakuhin" ["The Greater East Asia Mutual Declaration and Two Literary Works"], *Bungaku*, XXIX (Aug. 1961), 20–38.

39. When this novel was reprinted in 1947, Dazai made innumerable changes in the text, toning down the patriotic sentiments considerably. See *Dazai Osamu Zenshū*, VII, 374–376.

40. Discussed in Ozaki, "Daitōa Kyōdō Sengen," pp. 33–37. An English translation may be found in *The Reeds*, Vol. VII and Vol. VIII.

41. See Takami Jun, *Shōwa Seisui Shi*, II, 274–275.

42. Hatanaka Shigeo, "'Ikite iru heitai' to 'Sasameyuki' wo megutte," *Bungaku*, XXIX (Dec. 1961), 98–99.

43. Meetings of prospective couples, arranged by go-betweens.

44. *Kaizō*, XXV (April 1943), 118–9.

45. *Nagai Kafū Nikki*, VI, 148. (Entry for April 7, 1943).

46. *Ibid.*, p. 158. (Entry for June 3, 1943).

47. *Ibid.*, p. 163. (Entry for June 25, 1943).

48. *Ibid.*, p. 180. (Entry for October 12, 1943).

49. *Ibid.*, pp. 195, 262.

50. The Japanese fondness for keeping diaries, a tradition dating back to the Heian period, was so strong that even writers fully aware of the danger that they might be searched continued to record their daily thoughts. "I shall have to be careful with this diary," wrote Takami Jun as he began what was to develop into a 3,000-page diary for 1945 alone! See his "Ankoku jidai no Kamakura bunshi" ["A Kamakura Writer During the Dark Ages"], *Bungei Shunjū*, XXXVI (July 1958), 256–303.

51. Takami, p. 298. This entry was written on August 12, 1945, three days before the surrender.

52. The noted painter Fujita Tsuguharu expressed the belief in "Ōshū gadan e no beibetsu" ["Farewell to the Painting Circles of Europe"] that Japan had become the centre of world culture and no longer needed to look to Europe. (*Kaizō*, XXV, [Feb. 1943].) Mushakōji Saneatsu in "Shōri e no jikaku" decried all American art, except for the etchings of

Whistler, which show the influence of Japanese *ukiyoe*. He stated moreover that he would like to drop bombs on New York and Washington on the day of the presidential inauguration in 1945 together with leaflets asking, "Have you learned your lesson?" (*Bungei Shunjū*, XXII [Nov. 1944], 10–13.)

53. *Jōruri Zasshi*, No. 424 (Oct. 1944), 20.

54. Among the author's other indictments we find:
"Villains who, in place of the independence they promised the Phillippines, forced them to buy electric phonographs, refrigerators and sewing machines."

55. *Tanaka Kōtarō Zenshū*, III, 257–8.

56. Noguchi, *Hakkōshō Ippyakuhen*, pp. 119–21.

57. *Venture to the Interior*, p. 225.

VII. THE TRANSLATION OF JAPANESE CULTURE

On Translation

I HAVE BEEN told that in Egyptian Arabic every word means itself, its opposite, and something to do with a camel. The same might almost be said about theories of translation, although it is not always easy to show their relevance to camels. If we start from the assumption that translations should be accurate, we shall discover at once that many of the finest translations (for example, Fitzgerald's *Rubaiyat*) are wildly inaccurate. If we say that a translation should be integral, neither more nor less than the original author wrote, we are made aware that translations which follow this prescription are often unreadable, while the best translators are constantly adding to or subtracting from the texts of faltering masters. If we say that a translation should read naturally, giving no impression of foreignness, we may be stopped short by the remembrance of, say, how much more memorable Motteux's "Curious Impertinent" makes that episode from *Don Quixote* than "The Man Who Knew Too Much For His Own Good" of a more recent version.

The conclusion we may draw from these enigmas of translation is that rules are not meant for translators of genius. If the reader perusing these lines happens to be such a translator, he may break all the rules with impunity. Ugly ducklings will turn into swans and swans into phoenixes beneath the keys of his feather-touch typewriter. Even for the more humanly endowed translators rules or suggestions can at best help confirm him in his good habits; they will hardly make an admirable translator out of a bad one. The following remarks are no more than reflections based on my own experiences as a translator. I urge anyone who remains unconvinced to consider their opposites, or possibly their dromedarian implications.

The chief requirement of a person who would translate from any foreign tongue into English is, I feel sure, a love for the English language and a sensitivity to its possibilities and limitations. These must be maintained despite his knowledge and love for the foreign language from which he is translating, and despite his painful awareness of how much inevitably is being lost. A phrase of wonderful rightness in the original Finnish or Fijian may sound hopelessly wooden in English. The translator who has before him a text employing the fourteen commonly distinguished levels of politeness in Korean will run up against the deadly democracy of the English language, where we use the same verb and level of politeness for "God is," "water is," and "that dirty dog is." The tender love scene where the lovers almost imperceptibly shift from *vous* to *tu* becomes that much the less tender when both parties say "you" all the way through. The lack of the distinction in English between the verb endings used by men and women makes it necessary to supply all the "he saids" and "she saids" which a Japanese novelist normally omits. The list could easily be prolonged, and each instance is the source of heartache to the conscientious translator.

Indeed, he might well form the impression that real translation is impossible. The despair-making Italian phrase *traduttore, traditore*, invariably quoted in such circumstances, will confirm the translator in his gloom. But, despite our knowledge that much is incommunicable in translation, we should not prefer that despair paralyze the hands of the translators. Let people quarrel, say, with Constance Garnett's Dostoevsky, let them point out the howlers and the falsifications, and all that has perished of the beauty of the original Russian, but who can forget his first reading of *Crime and Punishment* in her translation? Someday, perhaps, we may have a perfect translation of Dostoevsky, but we know in advance that it will not be the same experience as reading it in the original. It will be, for one thing, in English, a language very dissimilar to Russian, and the translator will have had to resign himself to sacrificing what the English language does not permit. Any translator who attempts to "expand" English with the constructions or expressions of another language exposes himself and, more important, his text to ridicule. "Little grandfather," for example, surely does not seem as cute to a Russian as to ourselves, and "Where is the august umbrella of my honorable father?" is no closer to the Japanese original than Gilbert and Sullivan to the Mikado. The English language is not to be improved by these means: "grandpa" and "where is Father's umbrella?" are close enough.

The translator must not, however, belittle the possibilities of the English language. Its richness sometimes makes it feasible for a translator actually to improve on the original. Arthur Waley's translation of the great eleventh-century Japanese novel *The Tale of Genji* is a case in point. The translation is that of a master of English prose, and I for one in going from the translation back to the original miss something. Certain subtle expressions are lost in English, it is true, but it is not altogether surprising that twentieth-century English has a greater variety of nuances of meaning than the Japanese of almost a thousand years ago. Indeed, it is sometimes a challenge to the translator to choose which English equivalent of a given Japanese term best fits a particular context. This is still true today. For example, the Japanese words *kusukusu warau* can be rendered in English by such verbs as "giggle," "chuckle," "titter," and "snicker." The translator who always chose the same equivalent each time *kusukusu warau* appeared would have plenty of precedents on his side, but surely it makes a great difference in English what kind of person performs the mirthful act. One might test the translator with a matching exercise.

1. giggle	( )	Santa Claus
2. chuckle	( )	Joe the Juvenile Delinquent
3. titter	( )	Madame Butterfly
4. snicker	( )	Duchesse de Guermantes

It should be apparent from the cast of characters in the right-hand column that the choice of an inappropriate mode of laughing would be unfortunate. What makes it possible for the translator to hit on precisely the appropriate variety of laughter when translating *kusukusu warau* is, of course, his sensitivity to English. He will know without having to look it up in the dictionary that Santa Claus does not titter and that Madame Butterfly could never emit a chuckle.

A translator's awareness of the overtones of English words must also keep him from setting off the wrong train of associations in the reader's mind. I remember one version of the *Analects* of Confucius which contained the memorable "One day when Confucius was seated at the harpsichord." The musical instrument before which Confucius actually sat was one which has no exact equivalent in the West, and rather than call it by its Chinese name and leave everybody mystified, the translator properly chose a Western instrument. But he chose the wrong one; Confucius at the harpsichord immediately becomes an eighteenth-century gentleman in a powdered wig bouncing up and down on his chair as he performs the Turkish March of Mozart. Call it a lyre, and Confucius this time emerges as Orpheus in a white peplos. Arthur Waley, as usual, came up with a winner: he called it a "zithern," and by using this word, at once immediately intelligible and yet slightly remote, he managed to avoid unfortunate and misleading overtones.

The overtones are not connected only with meaning. Consider this verse:

> Night begins to come
> And the darkness falls at once
> In the groves of plum.

Obviously the word "plum" is a disaster. The poem should portray an orchard of white plum-blossoms standing against a darkening sky, but the use of the rhyme "plum" makes the night fall with a leaden thud. Here not only the overtones of meaning (plumb, plum pudding) but the overtones of sound destroy the translation.

In brief, the translator must have an acute sensitivity to English words. This might sound like a prescription for all writers, not only translators, but the translator's command of English is constantly being threatened by the original with which he is working. A poet who was not translating a foreign language would never have wanted to write a verse concluding with "plum." He would have known instinctively that English usage and sound does not tolerate such an expression. But once a man is obliged to translate, his knowledge of the beauty of the original can often persuade him that the most awkward rendering will somehow come across.

In some ways it is more difficult to make a first-rate translation from a language relatively close to English than from a remote language. The latter presents far fewer (if any) temptations to use cognate words or expressions with meanings almost but not quite the same as in English. I imagine that it is a sound principle when translating from the French or any other Romance language to avoid words of Latin origin in one's English, but when translating from the Germanic to use the maximum possible. In other words, it is a good idea to attempt to keep the original language at a good arm's length away so as to avoid contagion.

In translating from a remote language like Japanese there is less a danger of contracting an infection unwittingly than of the translator deliberately desiring to "capture" something of the feeling of the original. This is particularly true when the translation is a joint effort, with one person translating from Japanese into English and another, more gifted literarily, polishing the English. The polisher generally has a strong idea of what is "truly" Japanese and twists the literal versions to this bed of Procrustes. One recent example I know was of a lady polisher who was convinced, it would seem, that everything Japanese was leafy or mossy, and even poems utterly unconnected with leafiness or mossiness were saddled with these adjectives. Other polishers become intrigued with such traditional props of Japanese fiction as the tear-soaked sleeve and, though the old literature is by no means deficient in these sleeves, the polishers multiply their appearances with gusto.

Collaboration is often suggested as an ideal solution to the problem of translating from obscure languages, but I can scarcely think of a successful example. What usually happens is that a strong-willed polisher imposes herself (or himself) on the gentle Oriental translator, and over his faint little protests sets to work bringing out the exquisite charm of the original which she believes she has instinctively detected. Collaboration need not be such an unequal partnership, of course, but I am convinced that it can never be as good an arrangement as a single translator who himself experiences the original, and who summons up from his store of English words the right equivalents. He will know whether or not the characters in a Persian or Chinese story are really exquisitely charming, or whether their dialogues are not in fact coldly realistic. He will recognize the rare moment when it is appropriate to have the Chinese gentleman say, "My heart is ten parts content" or "I am ashes heart," and when this variety of pidgin English is completely inappropriate.

This would suggest the necessity of finding more people who are literarily gifted and are willing to learn difficult languages. I do not know how many young writers are prepared to devote two or more years of their lives to an exclusive and intensive study of Tamil or Chinese or Japanese, but I believe that those who do will find it to have been an eminently worthwhile expense of their time. To make a good translation from any language is a satisfying experience, but this satisfaction is all the greater when the success of the translation depends heavily on the ability of the translator to make an alien age and civilization seem immediate and important.

To make the past come alive, to bring distant places close—these must be very close to the heart of translation. An archaic or exotic flavor is rarely an asset, though many translators have devoted a great deal of trouble to achieving these effects. This is true even in small details. The use of "thou" for example offends most readers; it is hard for them to believe that anybody who gets called "thou" has much in common with themselves. I remember my first reading of the Iliad in a translation sometimes called a classic. It evoked no sonnet from me, though Chapman's *Homer* might have; on the contrary, I found the battle scenes particularly soothing and sleep producing at the close of a long day. No doubt Homer's Greek was also archaic, and certain passages must have seemed rather remote even in Periclean days, but I refuse to believe that Homer's nods were meant to be contagious.

The translator is entitled to resort to every legitimate means at his disposal in order to keep the work he is translating immediate and alive. What is "legitimate" depends of course a good deal on the audience he has in mind—whether a small body of scholars unlikely to be excited in any case or vibrant young readers waiting to be set vibrating. If the latter, he is entitled to cut a work whenever he feels an author has weakened the effect of the whole by an inept or (for an English-reading public) otherwise inacceptable phrase or paragraph. For example, in a Japanese play I once translated there was a description of a beauteous young maiden. In my translation one sentence goes, "Her face was like an hibiscus flower, and her brows were willow-leaves." Unfortunately, the original had one additional phrase, "Her face was like an hibiscus flower with a nose and mouth attached." The line was not intended to be humorous, and I think therefore that fidelity to the original at this point would actually have been to betray the author. Sometimes the objectionable phrases are much longer; when I translated another play I had to discard a whole scene, which had for its only justification a series of thirty-six puns on the names of the thirty-six Buddhist temples of Osaka. Even if I had attempted to translate these puns, no one could have derived pleasure or amusement from them, and an otherwise engrossing play would have been seriously flawed.

Critics unfamiliar with the originals sometimes chide translators honest enough to note that they have omitted parts of a book. This is the risk the translator must take. The alternatives are either to bore and exasperate the critics or else to expose the whole of the translated work to ridicule by attaching noses, mouths, and whatever else the errant fancy of the alien author devised.

An opposite problem also plagues translators—when to expand a text in order to make for smoother reading. There are people who profess that they feel closer to a text if made aware of every word supplied by the translator. The Biblical example often quoted is, "And they saddled *him* an ass." Specialists in philology who know no foreign languages may indeed be grateful, but people who read for pleasure find it irritating to have their attention called to minor words by italics, brackets, footnotes, and the like. As a matter of fact, readers are far less tolerant of translated works than of those in English. Any obscurity in a work translated from, say, the Chinese is laid to the workings of the mind of the inscrutable Oriental or to the failings of the more scrutable translator; obscurities in

English works are quickly leapt over and taken for granted. If the translator has to deal with a work which is ambiguous in the original and susceptible of varying interpretations, it is probably best, except in the rare instances when the original ambiguity is easily transferred into English, to choose one of the possible meanings and state it plainly.

In simple translation problems where explanations might be needed, such as the name of a plant, item of clothing, comestible, or the like, I think it best to choose whichever course is the least conspicuous. A flower which blossoms close to the ground early in the spring and is of a purplish hue may safely be called a violet, even if it eats small animals—provided, that is, its carnivorous activities are not in question. There is no harm either in a work of prose if a few words of explanation are silently intruded. On the other hand, it is better to say "She ate some *sushi*" and let the reader guess what *sushi* is, rather than to interpolate "She ate a lump of cold rice molded in the fingers to an ovoid shape, coated lightly with horseradish, and topped with a small piece of raw fish." Footnotes can be helpful, but some publishers seem to be convinced that a book marred by even a single footnote is destined to be classed as a scholarly publication.

Another problem faced by the translator seeking vividity is the advisability of using language which is either datable (like slang) or restricted as a dialect to one part of the English-speaking world. I think that most people would agree that to translate into Southern U.S. parts of a novel in which a southern Italian dialect was used, would be ludicrous. At the first "you-all" the reader would be engulfed in a wave of associations which have nothing to do with Napoli. Dialects should be rejected, except in very unusual cases. One is tempted to reject slang for much the same reasons, but what is one to do then when translating a book about French gangsters or about ragamuffins in the streets of Tokyo? Slang is certainly the form of speech used by gangsters and street urchins everywhere, and to translate their conversations by "neutral" words might be almost as bad as to suggest the sidewalks of New York in a Burmese setting. Here again the sensitivity of the translator to the overtones of words is the only guide. There is no great harm if in a story about French students in the thirties one of them says "That's swell!" but if used of a student in 1890 it would certainly strike us as peculiar. If one has to translate the Parisian or Tokyo slang of now or the past, I think that the best plan is to choose a vigorous, racy English which is not specifically slang. If, for example, the tough young man in the original rudely tells someone to leave, "Get the hell out of here!" is better than "Scram!"

The resolution of all problems of acceptability and legitimacy in translation depends finally, as I have suggested, on the English style and the general culture of the translator. This is true not only of the choice of words or of knowing when to make deletions or explanations, but of the even more basic matter of what is to be translated. The translator can expect advice from his publisher or friends before he begins working on a French or German novel, but a person translating from an Asian language generally must decide for himself without any help from others what will be suitable for an American audience. An error of judgment can lead to an immense waste of labor if a man spends months on the translation of a book which nobody will publish. The translator's knowledge of literature and his estimation of what may successfully be translated into English should normally protect him against such a misfortune.

It will probably seem strange that thus far I have failed to mention what is usually considered to be a translator's first qualification—proficiency in the language he translates. This ability may in fact be all that is needed when the translation is not of a literary nature, but it takes only third place after ability in English and general cultural background when the translation is of a work of artistry. Even the best translators make lamentable mistakes, and one need not be a great scholar to find them. The possibilities of making mistakes, particularly when translating from a difficult language, are infinite. A mistake arising from ignorance may often be condoned, but one resulting from the translator's carelessness is unpardonable. The translator, needless to say, should be accurate, and the kind of accuracy expected of him is even more demanding than that expected of a scholar. It does not suffice for him any more than it does for a violinist to hit a close approximation of the right notes. Exactly the right note, at exactly the right intensity of loudness or softness, and exactly matched to the notes before and after: that is what is demanded. Not all translators can attain these lofty standards, but anyone who has tried to live up to them will certainly have experienced the excitement of translation, and his work will probably be good.

I like to think of the translator's profession as a noble one. The slander of the Italian "translators, traducers" has gone too long unchallenged. I suggest instead a Japanese pun of my own invention, *yakusha wa yakusha*, or "translators are actors," a suitably obscure phrase, to be interpreted as meaning that our profession also is a second oldest.

Arthur Waley

My first encounters with Arthur Waley could hardly have been described as auspicious. I learned in January of 1949 that he was to deliver a lecture in Cambridge and wrote inviting him to tea. Waley responded with a postcard explaining that he had another engagement, but suggesting I introduce myself at the lecture. That afternoon I waited impatiently for my meeting with the great scholar, who for me was more of a legend than reality. I had never seen a photograph of Waley, and the one thing I thought I knew about him, apart from his books, proved to be incorrect: people in America had informed me that he worked at the British Museum though, I discovered, this had not been true for many years. I had no introduction to Waley, and I cannot now imagine what gave me the courage to invite him to tea. Perhaps I decided that the rules of decorum could be suspended in the case of an idol. Through several frustrating years as a graduate student the example of Waley's achievements, more than anything else, had sustained me in my resolution to study Chinese and Japanese literature, and when I decided in 1948 to go to England the pleasure of meeting Waley had certainly been in my mind.

And now it was about to happen. No doubt it was to help the time pass that I tuned in on the broadcast from Germany of an opera by Wagner. Hardly had Wotan and Fricka started to scream at one another than there was a knock at the door and, in answer to my shout, a total stranger entered. I jumped up in surprise, wondering who this might be. "I am Dr Waley," the visitor said.

In my confusion I hastily turned off the radio and stammered something about having been studying. Waley with a few words arranged a meeting for the following day. Some time later I learned from a friend that Waley had expressed his amazement that anyone could possibly study Japanese while listening to American jazz played full blast. I had no way to explain that the loud noises had been Wagner, not jazz, and that (despite my hasty improvisation) I had not really been studying. I was despondent, sure that Waley would refuse to take seriously anyone with such coarse and incomprehensible habits of study. Only much later did it occur to me that perhaps my best qualification for being accepted as an acquaintance by this great collector of eccentrics was as the strange American who could not study except to the violent throb of jazz.

The lecture that night was a reading of Waley's translations from the Ainu epic, *Kutune Shirka*. I knew nothing about the Ainu except for their reputation of being exceedingly hairy, and it was a revelation to hear their delicate poetry read in Waley's rather high-pitched but precisely intoned voice. Occasionally he interposed a comment, as after he read the passage:

> The fencing done long ago
> Standing so crooked;
> The new fencing
> So high and straight.
> The old fencing like a black cloud,
> The new fencing like a white cloud.
> They stretched around the castle
> Like a great mass of cloud—
> So pleasant, so lovely!

With a smile Waley said the Ainu had certainly done something for fences. After the lecture, inevitably, there were silly questions, including one from myself, asking Dr Waley if *Kutune Shirka* did not remind him of Maeterlinck. I was desperately eager to make an impression, and as desperately aware of my failure.

The Ainu poetry was the third revelation of a literature I owed to Waley. My first acquaintance with his work occurred when I was sixteen and, mainly out of curiosity, purchased a volume of *More Translations from the Chinese*, then being remaindered by a Times Square bookshop for nineteen cents. I knew not a word of Chinese when I bought the book, but my copy (which I still have) is marked not only with the usual under-linings but with strings of crudely written Chinese characters laboriously copied a year or two later, after I had begun the study of Chinese under Waley's influence.

The second revelation had come with *The Tale of Genji*, purchased under almost identical circumstances. The great sympathy I felt for China during the war with Japan had made me reluctant even to consider that the Japanese might also have a culture, but the inducement of the price at which the book was remaindered overcame my prejudices. Again I was overwhelmed. When I entered the U.S. Navy Language School in 1942 to study Japanese, I would have much preferred to be studying Chinese, but I had at least the consolation that one day I should be able to read *The Tale of Genji* in the original.

Like other devoted readers of Waley's translations, I was convinced, though I had scarcely compared any of them with the originals, that they

were entirely faithful. Acquaintances who knew the Far East had told me that despite Waley's refusal to visit that part of the world he had been uncannily accurate in evoking its atmosphere. But delighted as I was with every word of Waley, I longed to read the originals, feeling somewhat contradictorily that they must be even superior to the best translation. While in Hawaii in 1943 on duty with the Navy I persuaded the professor of Japanese at the University to offer a special seminar on *The Tale of Genji*, and I spent my day off each week preparing for the class. I confess that the original text was so difficult, so far beyond my capacities, that I derived extremely little pleasure from it. I turned back to Waley with increasing wonder.

When I decided in 1946, after leaving the Navy, to pursue my studies of Chinese and Japanese literature at Columbia, my inspiration, of course, was Waley. I hoped that like him I would be able to work in both languages, but gradually I came to realize that I was unequal to this task. It was not merely that I found it difficult to gain an adequate command of two entirely different and equally perplexing languages, but a matter of temperament. I was interested and often deeply moved by most Japanese literature, but for reasons that I cannot analyse remained insensitive (or was even hostile) to much Chinese literature, excepting always the poetry. Reading *The Tale of Genji* was nightmarishly difficult, but eventually I could sense the beauty that had attracted Waley; when it came to *The Dream of the Red Chamber*, however, a reading of the first ten or so chapters in the original left me with a distaste for the book I have never overcome. This, of course, is indicative of my limitations; more important, it demonstrates Waley's incredible catholicity of tastes. Certainly he had his likes and dislikes—in Japanese literature, for example, he seemed never to have cared much for the *haiku* or the later drama— but probably never again will there be an orientalist who undertakes translations of such different works as *The Tale of Genji* and *The Analects*, *The Pillow-Book* and *Travels of an Alchemist*, *The Nō Plays* and *Monkey*. I confess I have never been able to read through *Monkey*, though many people enjoy it most of Waley's works; this inability led me to the reluctant conclusion that I could not fruitfully continue my studies of Chinese. The most I could aspire to was to become half of Waley.

As a scholar of Japanese, I have sometimes persuaded myself that Waley preferred Japanese literature to Chinese. Once he told me that *The Pillow-Book* was his own favourite of his works, and even his taste in Chinese poetry (for Po Chü-i rather than Li Pó or Tu Fu) corresponded with Japanese rather than Chinese preferences. Certainly in his early

reer, as he himself said, he sometimes used Japanese instead of Chinese
eanings for characters in his translations of Chinese poetry. ("They
ought south of the castle" became "They fought south of the ramparts"
in later editions, when Waley realized his mistake.) But it would be false
to suggest that Waley in fact preferred Japanese literature. He was capable
of unlimited enthusiasm for any artistic work of excellence, to such a
egree that he would undertake to learn a new and difficult language like
inu solely for the pleasure of reading the literature and communicating
is pleasure in matchless translations.

For me, as for all others interested in translating either Chinese or
apanese literature, Waley was our only predecessor. It is amusing now
o read correspondence exchanged between him and Herbert Giles in
920, when Giles took the younger man to task with avuncular authority
or his departures from the originals. I cannot imagine anyone reading
iles' translations today except as a curiosity or a horrible example of the
ollies committed in the name of rhyme. Giles was by no means incom-
etent in Chinese, however, and he could sometimes catch Waley in a
istranslation. But this was hardly surprising. When Waley first began
is translation of *The Tale of Genji*, for example, there were no modern
nnotated editions of the kind that now abound. He relied mainly on the
ighteenth-century commentaries of Motoori, generally available only in
udgy woodblock editions. Not until the Fifth Part of the translation
as he able to benefit by the scholarship of Kaneko's edition. Even
eginners today, if they are armed with the products of the modern
apanese editors, which explain in straightforward contemporary Japanese
he meaning of the maddeningly ambiguous originals, can point out
with an air of superiority Waley's lapses from accuracy. Waley was aware
n later years of such mistakes, and sometimes condemned passages of
is own translations for being too free (like Murasaki's celebrated discus-
ion of the novel in the Tamakazura chapter of *The Tale of Genji*). But
hese blemishes, though they have been given more than enough public-
ty, are not only pardonable, but essentially do not affect the value of his
work. Waley brought new life to masterpieces of Chinese and Japanese
literature by transmuting them into an incredibly sensitive and supple
English. The beauty of Waley's language is too well known to need
discussion here, but perhaps his greatest achievement was to establish the
tone most appropriate to each of the works he translated, whether Chinese
songs of the third century BC or Japanese prose of the eleventh century.
The Tale of Genji could have been translated into a style reminiscent of *Le
Morte d'Arthur*, or into the nineteenth-century Gothic favoured by Waley's

predecessors in almost all their translations from classical literature. For that matter, a new translation of *The Tale of Genji* might be attempted today into contemporary English or American idiom emphasizing, for example, the guts and sweat of the characters, or into a neutral mid-Atlantic style that belongs to no time or place. But Waley's choice of tone, whether for Sei Shōnagon or Yüan Mei, was invariably definitive. Whatever new translations scholars may produce in the future, hoping to improve on the accuracy of Waley's versions, they are unlikely to alter his tone. Both in Chinese and Japanese literatures he established such strong traditions that it is only fair to say that we all belong to the School of Waley. This does not necessarily mean that we cannot go beyond his work. Ivan Morris's complete translation of *The Pillow Book of Sei Shōnagon* is unquestionably an advance on Waley's partial version. But the voice that Morris uses is Waley's. Anyone who imagines that an original text can itself dictate the appropriate tone or voice is urged to consult Beaujard's accurate and incredibly boring French translation.

The freedom of Waley's translations has often aroused controversy. From his first exchanges with Giles, Waley defended the free translation as necessary in transmitting the poetic quality of a work, an aspect as important as the surface meaning of the words. He described to me once how he had translated *The Tale of Genji*. He would read a passage over until he understood its meaning; then, without looking back at the passage, he wrote out an English assimilation. He would later consult the original again. If the content of the translation was the same, he would let it pass, even if some words had been added or deleted. Such a method could be extremely irresponsible if adopted by a less gifted translator, but Waley's extraordinary knowledge of every period of Chinese and Japanese made it possible for him to comprehend instinctively even passages of the utmost obscurity. He was capable of writing short scholarly articles on grammatical particles, but they did not absorb him nearly so much as his larger-scaled works, intended for the general public, which by their nature were bound to contain errors. Sometimes Waley revised translations made at an earlier time, but when in 1958 he reconsidered in an essay on translation a section of his *Tale of Genji*, he felt he would not wish to alter it because it still conveyed to him the mood of the original.

Waley's translations always combined intuitive interpretation with his scholarly knowledge of the original works. Again and again this combination enabled him to guess what had gone wrong in a text that was

obviously corrupt. Professor Gustav Haloun, to whom Waley dedicated his *Book of Songs*, was a textual scholar of the most rigorous principles, but he considered Waley's emendations to be those of a genius, not to be measured by normal academic standards. Waley nevertheless sometimes made mistakes not only on the meaning of phrases but of interpretation, as he himself admitted after reading Sam Houston Brock's translation of *Sotoba Komachi*, the Nō play he had translated thirty years before. Waley found that his version was "hopelessly overladen and wordy and that it tried in a quite unwarrantable way to improve on the original."

Waley's attitude towards his successors was always friendly, though sometimes I got the impression he felt we had arrived on the scene a little too late, and he had already gathered all the plums. He once mentioned in conversation that although he had continued to read Nō plays in the decades following the publication of his translations, he never regretted his selection. This was discouraging to a young translator who hoped to find some gem that had escaped Waley's earlier notice. Waley was handicapped when translating the Nō plays by the lack of annotated editions explaining the obscure, cryptic references that stud almost every line. He had no guide even to the plays most esteemed by Japanese audiences over the centuries. This meant, however, that his choices were fresh and entirely personal. We of a later generation of translators, with ready access to editions of the Nō plays copiously annotated by excellent scholars, cannot help being influenced by their preferences. The mistakes Waley made because he was insufficiently aided by modern textual criticism were compensated for by his unorthodox and often brilliantly successful discoveries of works the Japanese themselves had ignored.

I got to know Waley well in the months and years following my initial debacle in Cambridge, and we often spoke together long hours, beginning in the early afternoon and continuing until it was too dark to see each other. (I never experienced any of the difficulty in conversing with him mentioned by some. An eminent publisher once complained to me that although he had known Waley for thirty years he had never had a civil word from him!) Our conversations covered many subjects, but we spoke most often of orientalism. He flattered me by asking my interpretation of characters that meant absolutely nothing to me, or by assuming my knowledge was as diverse as his own. I enjoyed it even when for some reason I was left alone in his room and I could examine his books—the well-worn edition of the *Tripitaka*, the many volumes on art, anthropology and history of parts of the world he never touched on in his writings. I wish I had kept a diary recording the substance of our conversations, but it never occurred to me I could forget a word.

On occasion Waley could be devastating. When I showed him my translation of a Chinese play he returned it with nothing more than the query, "Have you ever written any poetry of your own?" Or again, when, having been thoroughly disappointed by the meagre sales and lack of interest in my first book, I expressed the hope that my second book might be better received, Waley thought for a moment and said, "Of course I don't know how other people will find it, but I liked it rather better than your first." This was hardly the reassurance I needed. But Waley's refusal to indulge in flattery made his praise for my *Anthology of Japanese Literature*, which I dedicated to him, all the more precious.

Waley was always ready to meet younger scholars. His letters are dotted with references to visitors—an American studying the Chinese theatre, a Japanese novelist, a Swiss translator. If Waley did not suffer fools gladly, he was a warm and courteous host to anyone who interested him. His sharpest criticism was reserved not for the mistakes of the young and inexperienced but for the tediousness of the old and distinguished. His letters make frequent mentions of the "gruelling" dinners he had to attend and of his dread of forthcoming occasions: "I am very well, but my spirits weighed down by the approach of the King's annual Feast, which I have cut so often that I felt I must face it this year." At such occasions his neighbours at dinner, accustomed to the banalities that pass for conversation, rarely appreciated having Waley beside them. Once, as he told me, he was seated next to an eminent mathematician and made a remark about the similarity in the use of numbers by the Romans and Chinese. The mathematician, horrified by what he took for shoptalk, turned ostentatiously to his neighbour on the other side and began a more normal conversation, on the drain pipes in the Old Court that needed repairing.

The last letter I had from Waley reached me in Japan in November 1961. It was typed: "Thank you for so many things—your letter, the Hanako article which was just what I wanted some one to write and finally the Chikamatsu book. The latter we are reading aloud and I think you have done them perfectly. My hand is still useless for writing, Beryl is very ill with chorea and in a state painful to suffer and of course also painful to witness. In addition I hear I must turn out of my flat. The landlord is the University of London of which I regard myself as an ornament. But a last appeal for grace was not even answered. Work at present is out of the question. I read a great deal out loud to Beryl, as for example Lord Birkenhead's Life of that monster Lord Cherwell, Isaac Disraeli's *Curiosities of Literature*—a marvellous book, Harold Acton's second volume on the Bourbons at Naples, the autobiography of George Sand, the Life of Tolstoy by his son. Nothing Oriental."

Of course, Waley's praise for my translation gave me great pleasure. No praise could have meant more. But the series of disasters described in the letter dismayed me so much that I felt I must see Waley, to offer what comfort I could. I arrived in England in February 1962 and went directly to Gordon Square. The day was dark and the cold penetrating. I climbed the familiar stairs, marvelling as always that a man of Waley's age could still manage them. He met me with no special display of emotion, but suggested we go at once to see Miss de Zoete. He warned me, "Don't ask her any questions. She understands everything and will try to answer. Just kiss her and say you're glad to see her." But when I sat before Miss de Zoete, who was terribly afflicted, the sight was so heartrending that it was quite impossible for me to kiss her. I sat there stunned, conscious only of her suffering and of the infinite tenderness that had made Waley resolve not to send her to a hospital, where ignorant nurses would surely make her last days even less bearable.

We left and went down into the kitchen, where we sat in gloomy silence. I asked whether it was true that he had given up orientalism, and he said it was, both because of the injury to his hand that made writing impossible and because he felt that the subjects he could write about now no longer interested him. He said he planned to spend his remaining years refreshing his knowledge of European literature. I asked if he would not reconsider, and offered to become his amanuensis, but Waley shook off the suggestion. He got up to prepare lunch and warmed a tin of steak and kidneys. I wanted badly to say something of comfort but could think of nothing.

This was the last time I saw Waley, and although I wrote him several times I had no answers. It was a terrible blow not to have seen him again, and it is sad that my last glimpse of him must have been at his deepest point of depression. But to hear his voice speaking again, always graceful and with infinite shadings and accents, I need only open his books.

Confessions of a Specialist

EVERY NOW and then I recall with a twinge how much of my life has been spent studying Japanese. I began quite casually, that long-ago summer of 1941, not with any premonition that a war with Japan was imminent, nor with any thought that my dabbling in an exotic language would soon be judged vital to the national interests. Later, I studied at the Navy Language School, and after four years as an interpreter and translator in the service, doggedly pursued my studies of Japanese at several universities, even though most of my wartime associates desired nothing more than to forget every word of Japanese they had learned.

I sometimes meet these friends, and they recite to me, as if recalling some particularly touching nursery rhyme, the last scraps of Japanese they retain: "Annihilate the enemy at the water's edge!" or something equally nostalgic. They look on me with a mixture of envy and condescension, as a financier might look on a professional golfer or on an executive of the Boy Scouts of America. Sometimes they express wonder that with my talents I never chose to enter the real world but preserved my childish affection for the squiggles of writing that once they too could decipher.

Their attitude is shared by some Japanese. A visitor once smilingly informed a colleague of mine that only misfits ever studied his country's language. Once too, when I applied for a Japanese visa, the young vice consul complimented me on my choice of profession, adding, "You were clever to have chosen Japanese literature. You'd never have become famous in a more competitive field."

Even the most amicably disposed friends are apt to say, by way of praise I am sure, "You shouldn't confine yourself to Japanese. With your intelligence you could write about English or French literature." Recently an editor asked me for some translations of Spanish or Italian poetry, meaning that it was time to stop piddling with exotic trifles and apply myself to a man's work. People find my refusal to desert my profession incomprehensible, or else a confession of weakness, as if I were an opera singer who, fearing to test his voice in the masterpieces of Verdi or Wagner, contented himself with singing "Gems From 'The Mikado.'"

Quite ordinary social contacts tend to become tests of forbearance, thanks to my specialty. When I am introduced as a professor of Japanese to someone at a party, I brace myself for the question, "What ever made you take that up?" How I have longed to forestall that question by asking the accountant, dentist or ballet dancer before me, with the same mixture of curiosity and dismay I have come to know so well, "What ever made you take that up?" But yonder lies the road to misanthropy if not madness.

If I were to answer the inevitable question honestly, I would have to say that I became a scholar of Japanese literature because no other study seemed so exciting. I remember once, when I was a graduate student at Columbia, standing in the stacks of the Japanese collection, gloomily surveying the rows of unfamiliar books, and thinking that never, no matter how many years I devoted to the language, would I be able to read these books with ease. Then another thought struck me. If I shut my eyes and took a book down from the shelf, I could be almost certain that nobody in the history of the West would have ever read it before. I tried the experiment. My hand fell on a volume from the collected works of a nineteenth-century philosopher. I opened the book and, to my aston-ishment and joy, I discovered I could read it. Suddenly a powerful desire to read all those silent, dusty books swept over me.

Of course, I could never have read them all, and their number has easily doubled in the last twenty years, but the excitement of discovery remains. Sometimes I still despair over the difficulty of understanding a text, and stare with resentment at the wavering scrawl in an old book printed from woodblocks perhaps a century and a half ago. At such times I cynically remind myself how unlikely it is a scholar of European litera-ture would be unable to grasp even the surface meaning of a nineteenth-century book. But such exasperating difficulties make the triumphs the sweeter, and the occasional discovery of a work of literary value neglected even by the industrious Japanese can make of translation an adventure.

Translation from the Japanese is categorically a different process from translating a European language. The old writers excelled at suggestion, rather than explicit statement, and they tended to rely on levels of polite-ness or the choice of final particles to intimate even such essential infor-mation as who said what to whom. An intuitive sense of what is intended is necessary when translating, say, the verb *mesu*, which may mean "to eat," "to wear," "to ride in a carriage," or various other actions performed by a person of quality; and the verb *monosu*, literally meaning "to do a thing" has an even wider variety of uses. But consider the masterpieces translators have recovered from tissues of such elusive words—*The Tale of Genji*, hauntingly rendered into English by Arthur Waley, or Ivan Morris's recent *Pillow Book of Sei Shōnagon*, a perpetual source of delight.

The problems of translating Japanese are not confined to works of the distant past. Some modern short stories cannot be translated effectively because they depend on the instant recognition of the associations of an article of clothing or food or architecture unfamiliar to Western readers. The falling of a camellia blossom, for example, immediately suggests a beheading to a Japanese, but how to convey this eerie quality to a Western reader except by tedious explanations? Or how to make a favorite Japanese dessert seem appetizing in English, when it consists of sweetened bean paste with a lump of glutinous rice at the bottom? The translator who successfully overcomes such obstacles deserves to feel that the Japanese story is in some sense his own. He may also take pleasure from knowing that translations from the Japanese are now included in general anthologies intended for American college students, though twenty years ago this was unimaginable.

But this is still not the best part of being a specialist in Japanese. The best part, as far as I am concerned, is being in touch with the whole of the Japanese literary world. I feel I am not merely an intermediary who makes it possible for certain Japanese writers to become known in the United States but a friend and, in a sense, a collaborator. Even Japanese I have never met send me (and, I am sure, other scholars of Japanese) letters and gifts to express their gratitude for making their country's literature known abroad. The most touching mark of appreciation perhaps has been the sale of my book *Japanese Literature: An Introduction for Western Readers*; twice as many copies have appeared in Japanese translation as in English.

The translation of Japanese fiction has also begun to affect the whole of the Western literary world. Ten years ago a distinguished critic could dismiss modern Japanese literature as "an achievement in imitation," but at last the cliché of the Japanese being a race of imitators seems to have been destroyed. Japanese writers now attract the attention of a wide public, both in the United States and in Europe. Perhaps immodestly, I think I have helped, and I am glad for my moment of *satori* in the library stacks that turned me into a specialist.

Yet it would be an exaggeration to suggest that the successful translations of Japanese literature of the past decade have completely changed the old attitudes towards persons like myself who study Japanese. Probably nobody is as timid these days as the English novelist I used to visit fifteen years ago, who invited an Oriental to every sherry party I attended, so that I would have somebody to talk to. But I am still made aware of my oddity when the telephone rings and I am asked to recommend a Zen master, a school of flower arrangement, or a reliable Japanese butler. Is that the kind of question professors of English are asked?

I must admit also I have had doubts about my abilities. I have wondered if being a specialist in so remote a field has not made things too easy. I sometimes yearn to test my strength in the world of adults, to write on *King Lear* or a paper to be called "Metaphor in the Tragedies of Racine." Or better still, I would like to write a lordly article, "Fiction Today," discussing only writings in English (or, preferably, in American), as if no others existed. How delightful it would be if, with the bold statement "Literature cannot be translated," I could free myself from the drudgery of unraveling Japanese sentences, and concentrate on the higher things of which, according to my friends, I am capable.

Two years ago I thought I had this chance. The *New York Times* asked me to review an Argentinian novel, the brilliant *Hopscotch* by Julio Cortazar. The Monday after the review appeared I went to the university, eagerly anticipating the exclamations of surprise from my colleagues. I saw myself enhanced in the eyes of my students—a teacher who might have specialized in something more relevant than Japanese literature, a Renaissance man able to switch effortlessly from one quarter of the globe to another. But no one said a word until I demanded point-blank what people thought of the review. Gradually I became aware that, far from marvelling at my Renaissance versatility, they had been assured there was a specialist in Argentinian literature with the same name.

The letters from readers were even more discouraging. One man wrote to ask if I remembered him—he claimed I had taught him Portuguese two summers before. Another man reproached me for my doctrinaire adherence to a school of South American criticism of which I had never heard. And an Ecuadorian novelist urged me to find a publisher for his book, a masterpiece of sex and violence. "You'll love it!" he promised.

I see that I am fated to remain a specialist. Twenty-seven years after first beginning the study of Japanese, I must learn to acquire the traditional oriental virtues. In face of discouragement, I will be resigned. In face of others' doubts, I will be inscrutable.

A Short Reading List

For Chapter I

Brower, Robert H. and Earl Miner. *Japanese Court Poetry*. (Stanford, 1961).
Cooper, Michael. *They Came to Japan*. (Berkeley, University of California Press, 1965).
Keene, Donald (ed). *Anthology of Japanese Literature*. (New York, Grove, 1955).
Keene, Donald. *Bunraku, the Puppet Theatre of Japan*. (Tokyo and Palo Alto, Calif., Kodansha International, 1965).
——. *Nō, the Classical Theatre of Japan*. (Tokyo and Palo Alto, Calif., Kodansha International, 1966).
Keene, Donald (tr.) *Essays in Idleness: the Tsurezuregusa of Kenkō*. (New York, Columbia University Press, 1967).
——. *Twenty Plays of the Nō Theatre*. (New York, Columbia University Press, 1970).
Morris, Ivan. *The World of the Shining Prince*. (New York, Knopf, 1964).
Morris, Ivan (tr.) *The Life of an Amorous Woman*. (New York, New Directions, 1963).
——. *The Pillow Book of Sei Shōnagon*. (New York, Columbia University Press, 1967).
Seidensticker, Edward (tr.) *The Gossamer Years*. (Tokyo, Tuttle, 1964).
Waley, Arthur. (tr.) *The Tale of Genji*. (New York, Modern Library, 1960).

For Chapter II

Blyth, R. H. *Haiku*. 4 vols. (Tokyo, Hokuseido, 1949–52).
Corman, Cid and Kamaike Susumu (tr.) *Back Roads to Far Towns: Bashō's Oku-no-Hosomichi*. (New York, Grossman Publishers, 1968).
Henderson, Harold G. *An Introduction to Haiku*. (New York, Doubleday, 1958).
Yuasa Nobuyuki (tr.) *The Narrow Road to the Deep North and Other Travel Sketches*. (Baltimore, Penguin Books, 1966).

For Chapter III

Bownas, Geoffrey and Anthony Thwaite. *The Penguin Book of Japanese Verse*. (Baltimore, Penguin Books, 1964).
Kōno, Ichirō and Fukuda, Rikutarō. *An Anthology of Modern Japanese Poetry*. (Tokyo, Kenkyusha, 1957).
Ninomiya, T. and D. J. Enright. *The Poetry of Living Japan*. (London, John Murray, 1957).
Sesar, Carl (tr.) *Poems to Eat* (by Ishikawa Takuboku). (Tokyo and Palo Alto, Calif., Kodansha International, 1966).

For Chapter IV

Tanizaki, Junichirō. *Diary of a Mad Old Man*, tr. Hibbett. (New York, Knopf, 1965).
——. *Seven Japanese Tales*, tr. Hibbett. (New York, Knopf, 1963).
——. *Some Prefer Nettles*, tr. Seidensticker. (New York, Knopf, 1955).
——. *The Key*, tr. Hibbett. (New York, Knopf, 1961).
——. *The Makioka Sisters*, tr. Seidensticker. (New York, Knopf, 1958).